**Hunter Davies** is the [...]
range from biography t[...]
and include three mo[...]
*Beatles*, and *A Walk Aro*[...]
endlessly reprinted. His first novel, *Here We Go Round the Mulberry Bush*, became a memorable film. His last book was the best-selling biography *Wainwright*.

He is also one of Britain's most distinguished journalists and interviewers. For many years he worked for the *Sunday Times* (where he was editor of the Magazine) and subsequently for *Punch*, the *Independent* and the *Daily Mail*. As a broadcaster, he has presented *Bookshelf* and other series on BBC Radio 4. He is married to the novelist and biographer Margaret Forster, and they divide their time between London and Loweswater. He is president of Cumbria Wildlife Trust and in 1996 was elected Deputy Pro-Chancellor of Lancaster University.

Hunter Davies' Lottery numbers, from week one, have been 1, 9, 11, 24, 25 and 36, a combination of family birthdates and house numbers. So far, he has won £10.

*Also by Hunter Davies*

# LIVING
## ON THE
# LOTTERY

*Hunter Davies*

**WARNER BOOKS**

A *Warner* Book

First published in Great Britain in 1996
by Little, Brown and Company
This edition published in 1997 by Warner Books

PICTURE CREDITS:
Camelot: pp. 22, 27, 161; Ian Dobson: p. 128;
PA: p. 51; Rex Features: pp. 41, 105, 114 and 195.

A CIP catalogue record for this book
is available from the British Library.

ISBN: 0 7515 1915 4

Typeset by Solidus (Bristol) Limited
Printed and bound in Great Britain by Clays Ltd, St Ives plc

Warner Books
A Division of
Little, Brown & Company (UK)
Brettenham House
Lancaster Place
London WC2E 7EN

*For my father-in-law, Arthur Gordon Forster, aged 95,
but not too old to get some fun out of the Lottery*

# CONTENTS

# CONTENTS

## *Part Two*
## LIFE AFTER THE LOTTERY WIN

# ACKNOWLEDGEMENTS

Many thanks to David Rigg and Tim Holley of Camelot, plus the three Winners' Advisers, for all their help and encouragement, despite everything. And to Peter Davis, Richard Branson, Michael Hayes, Philip Platts, Alasdair Buchan and Lenny Lottery. Most of all, thanks to the winners themselves for their interest and for agreeing to speak to me, when there was nothing in it for them except winning a place in this book …

# INTRODUCTION

I bought a ticket for Britain's first National Lottery on Saturday 19 November 1994. I never put money on the football pools or on horses. I refuse all raffles and sweepstakes, avoid coin-tossing and guessing which raindrop will drip first, and have tended to murmur piously that you make your own luck in life. I had no interest in betting on the National Lottery but I knew, as we all did, that 19 November 1994 was an historic day, an historic event. I wanted the ticket as memorabilia. I collect such stuff: first issues of newspapers, first days of stamps, first editions of books. And it was a satisfying thing to do. I have it in front of me now. I am appalled to find I had spent £5, but pleased to see the ticket says 'First Day Issue'.

I never intended to take part again or show much interest in National Lottery stories till three weeks later, when an Asian in Blackburn won almost £18 million in the first roll-over week. It wasn't the amount of money which particularly interested me, but his background. He had requested no publicity, but he was hounded and outed and named as Mukhtar Mohidin. It was reported that he had come to Britain some twenty years earlier from Africa, worked endless hours in a factory and had just bought his own house, a new semi-detached, for £49,000. That's it, I thought. Just when he has succeeded in his new life, his whole life has been turned upside down. Will he think his struggles have been made meaningless? I felt his story *before* his win must be just as interesting and revealing of the times in which we live as his new life to come, whatever that might be.

So I wrote to Camelot, suggesting a book about ten major winners, following their lives before and after. It took many meetings and legal formalities, but they agreed to give me certain help, such as access to their officials, and to pass on my

*Hunter Davies' first lottery ticket, 19 November 1994*

name to some of the winners. But it would be my book, in my words, with my opinions, not in any way an authorised or official book. (Note that I haven't been able to use the National Lottery logo on the cover.) But I am grateful to all their officials and most of all to those winners who agreed to see me and talk, when of course there was and is nothing in it for them. How can there be, when you have just become a multi-millionaire?

Mr Mohidin, who first inspired me, is not in this book, alas. He has changed his name, changed his location. I do have stories of two winners who never 'came out' and have managed to live secret lives, so naturally I have changed their names to protect them, though their feelings and opinions, experiences and emotions are all true. The other eight winners appear as themselves. What I did was make contact with my ten winners, at the time of their win, then keep in touch, returning to see them later, mostly between six months and a year afterwards, to observe the changes.

It was the feelings and experiences which I most wanted to capture. The whole nation, this last year, has had moments of idle fantasy, dreaming about how we would feel, how we would react, if the finger chanced to point at us. I have always been fascinated by money, anybody's money, how they got it, how they spend it. Some years ago, my wife and I each produced a novel which became a film and I wrote a biography which sold around the world. It hasn't happened since and is unlikely to happen again, but the effects on my life and attitudes at the time were interesting. Nothing on the scale of these Lottery millionaires, but it gave me a sliver of insight into what can happen after a sudden increase in wealth.

The book also attempts to chart some of the mechanics of the National Lottery – how it began, how it is run, the new jobs and types of jobs that have been created – but I am concerned only with the first year of its existence, from

November 1994 to November 1995. In the Appendix I give some facts and figures from the year, and a survey of my ten winners, but please don't read that until you have finished the book.

There will be bigger stories, probably bigger winners, to come, but there will only ever be one first year. I always think that is the most interesting period in any new development. It's when we see things clearly, freshly, before it all grows a bit grey and cloudy, or far too complex.

Of all the new arrivals of the nineties, the National Lottery has been one of the most controversial and the most comprehensive, infiltrating almost every family, affecting so many aspects of our national life. There is no doubt it is here to stay. Can you imagine any government, of any sort, in the future, wilfully bringing it to an end, when there are billions of pounds washing around in its slipstream, waiting to be basketed up for even half-good causes? This is the story of its first year. And of some of its first winners.

Hunter Davies
London, April 1996

## PART ONE

# LIFE AT THE TIME OF THE LOTTERY WIN

## STEVE AND HELEN, LANCASHIRE

I set off early, heading north towards the M6, about to meet and greet another freshly minted, instantly created millionaire who was about to enter another life. Winners can come in all shapes and sizes, all ages and classes, for that is the nature of random selection, but on the whole, judging by the first six months of Britain's National Lottery, the main reaction of every big winner is much the same – shock.

Usually it's a dull, deadening, muddling sort of shock, which means everything has to be repeated umpteen times. On the telephone the night before, Steve had sounded fairly sensible for a young lad. The 'young' was purely my guess. From his voice, though, I took Steve to be in his twenties. Very Lancashire, perhaps with rural overtones. That would make a change. So far, the winners I'd seen had been mainly urban.

Camelot's Winners' Adviser had been to see Steve just a few days previously, to start the first stages in the process of caring for and handling someone who has suddenly become very rich. This is a new profession, unheard-of before the advent of our National Lottery. The next stage comes later, when they are offered legal and financial help by a panel drawn from the traditional professions.

Steve, apparently, had said 'No publicity'; he didn't want

any of that press conference stuff nor his name and face in the newspapers, but he had agreed to see me. Nothing had been promised. No arrangements had been made, so it could all come to nothing as far as I was concerned, but at least I might meet my first private winner, whom no one else knew about, and observe at first hand those mixed-up, bottled-up, perhaps even messed-up emotions. I might, of course, not get through the front door. Winners' Advisers themselves cannot always predict possible behaviour when handling Lottery-winners. The mood swings can be frequent, and sometimes alarming among those who win – and sometimes for those who don't. A few weeks earlier, in April, a 51-year-old Liverpool man, a father of two, Roman Catholic, had shot himself when he found he had not renewed the ticket which he thought would have won him £2 million. So it goes.

On the telephone, Steve had mentioned 'the wife', which was interesting. Young lads in their twenties don't always have wives these days. He had given me directions for his local town, one I had not been to before, though it has a minor public school and a smallish stately home, but I was through the centre before I'd realised, past the market place and the public school. The street I was looking for was on the outskirts, so Steve had said. Number 13. I carefully parked two streets away, not wanting to attract undue attention. I even found myself looking round in case I'd been followed. You never know. Lenny Lottery, ace sleuth on that very popular newspaper, the *Sun*, has made a full-time job out of writing about Lottery-winners.

The street was half council houses, with a mixture of semi-detached and a couple of small fields. Pre-war council houses, but mostly in good nick, with grass verges, some healthy-looking trees. No signs of the vandalism or abandoned vehicles you get in urban estates. Number 13 was at the end of a terrace. The right-hand house had a neat hedge and looked immaculate with leaded lights, fancy porch, painted walls, lush lawn, pretty trellis, climbing roses. Obviously a caring owner who had bought the house from the council.

Steve's house was rather different. The front garden had a battered wooden fence and consisted of either dried mud or broken concrete slabs, most of it covered with parts of dead bikes, ancient prams, decaying plastic toys and discarded boxes. Round the back I could see a concrete garage, or what had once been a garage, now leaning at an angle, about to give up and die. It might once have held animals but now contained a decaying car and parts of a motorbike.

The door was opened by Steve. Medium height, stocky and overweight, with a bulging stomach and a podgy face, but clear blue eyes and a steady, open, honest sort of gaze. A bit like Gazza in appearance, or perhaps his five-bellied friend. It looked as though he'd had a Mohican haircut at some time, but it was now growing out, forgotten and forlorn, as fashions or life had moved on. He was wearing a blue striped shirt, almost executive in style, but rather crumpled and baggy. In his right ear was an earring.

The sitting-room was like a junk shop, with battered chairs and sofas lined up against the walls. On the floor, at one end, lay a child of about two, curled up in a ball. It turned and rolled in its sleep, then rolled back again, still asleep. At the other end, also curled up but not quite asleep, was a bull terrier. It got up, growled, and advanced towards my ankles, but Steve shooed the dog away.

'Peg, get back!' Steve yelled. 'I said, Get back, Peg. She's only young, like. She won't harm yer.'

I sat down, smiling, and looked around. 'She's a girl, then?'

'Peggy. Yeh, she's got a pedigree name, but I can never remember it.'

A very thin young woman had drifted silently into the room from the direction of what must be the kitchen and was standing watching. No introductions were made, but I presumed this must be Steve's wife. She had a cigarette in her hand. Bright red hair, presumably dyed, cut very short like a boy's. Thin face, wearing tight-fitting jeans and a clean white blouse. She asked if I would like a cup of tea, then disappeared to get it.

Another plump little boy appeared, aged about four, in bare feet and bare chest. He and the little one asleep on the floor were identikit versions of Steve. Same face, same bellies, same shaven hair, each with an earring. The four-year-old had wet hair and wet trousers and came over to examine me, then he gave his brother on the floor an affectionate kick to wake him up and they started pushing and shoving each other, rolling all over the floor, till Steve told them to 'Bee-have'. Which they did, at once. They then left the room and went out into the back garden to play.

In the middle of the ceiling, a gold-plated fan was slowly whirring. A strange thing to have, in a council house. It was a sunny morning in early May, the beginning of a long and almost tropical summer, but it still wasn't that hot, though there were a few flies around. I hadn't heard the fan at first because of the noise of the TV. That was on, and remained on, very loud, tuned permanently to Sky. I would have liked it turned off or down, but knew that was unlikely, not in these sorts of homes, but of course one must not make judgements. They could be all wrong.

'How many children have you got then, Steve?' I asked.

'Three,' he replied. 'That was Darren and Glen.'

'What is the other one called?'

Steve stood up and proceeded to unbutton his shirt, as if he was about to take it off.

'Yeh, it is a bit hot in here,' I said. 'Do you mind if I take my jacket off?'

Steve now had his shirt fully open, his belly bulging, and

was displaying a rather skimpy, shrunken T-shirt. On the front of it was emblazoned the name Lee-zette, which Steve enunciated slowly, so that I could get the right pronunciation. She was at school, he said. 'I can never spell her name right, that's why I have to look it up.'

Below Lee-zette were the names Darren and Glen.

'Still space for a fourth child, so we hope.' Steve smiled. He pulled his shirt back on, but left the buttons undone, so that when he sat down, the layers of his bellies fell forward as if they too were trying to roll on the floor where the boys had been.

'Well, congratulations,' I said. 'I should have said that straight away...'

'Oh aye,' said Steve blankly. Not much sign of emotion, mixed or otherwise.

'Is it true you've told nobody yet?'

'Just a certain person,' said Steve, smiling to himself.

'Who's that then?'

'Just the wife, Helen.'

'No one else?'

'No.'

'What about the kids? Doesn't – er – Lee-zette watch the Lottery?'

'All of them do,' said Steve. 'Usually, like. But not on Saturday. That was about the first time they didn't see it.'

'So they don't know?'

'No.'

'That's good,' I said. 'Keep that excitement for later.'

'I don't plan to tell them at all.'

'Well, these things are hard to keep quiet.'

'That's what the Winners' Adviser said,' said Steve, 'but we're going to stick to it. I don't want anything to happen to the kids. There are daft people around, you know. They might get funny ideas.'

'Any changes in your lifestyle will be noticed,' I said. 'At least among your own family. Then people you think you can trust to keep it totally secret often spread the news – from the best and nicest of motives, just wanting to share in your pleasure ...'

'I told you. Nobody knows owt. That's how I want it to stay.'

'Literally nobody? What about your parents? Are they still alive, or around, living nearby?'

'Me mam's around. In fact she's upstairs.'

'Upstairs?'

'She lives wid us.'

'And you haven't told her?'

'No.'

'But surely she'll find out?'

'Not unless I tell her, and I'm not going to.'

'But she'll ask about me, my visit, won't she?'

'If she does, I'll just say you've come about the new job I'm going to ...'

'What if she's overheard things I've been saying so far?'

'She won't have done. She has her telly on even louder than us.'

'But you've won £2.8 million! Surely she's going to wonder when your life starts changing, as it's bound to? That sort of money does make a difference.'

'We'll face that when it happens. And we'll face any differences in our life, when that starts happening, as well ...'

# THE STORY OF LOTTERIES – FROM THE BIBLE TO CAMELOT

Lotteries have been with us for a long time. There are several mentions in the Bible of property, land or money being divided up into lots and distributed, notably in the Old Testament when the Lord instructs Moses to take a census of the people of Israel and divide the land among them by lot. This would suggest the land was divided equally, with everyone getting the same slice. That was a lottery in one sense, but it's not quite what we mean by a lottery today. Elsewhere in the Bible there is also the element of lots being distributed unequally, i.e. by chance or random means. When the apostles are deciding what to do with some of Christ's clothes, John suggests they should not be split up. 'Let us cast lots for it.'

The Romans were very keen on lotteries of the random sort. The emperors Nero and Augustus often used them to give away slaves, villas and money as a form of public entertainment or during Saturnalian feasts. They were naturally very popular. People have always liked the idea of getting something for nothing.

The notion of contributing something to be involved in a lottery, instead of simply being a lucky member of the right crowd or a drinking chum of the emperor when things happened to be given away, was not formalised till about the fifteenth century. That's when the idea arose of having to pay to be in the lottery. At the same time, people running such a lottery, whether public or private, began to use a paid-in lottery to raise money, either for specific purposes or to make themselves a profit. The moment this was realised, lotteries as we know them were born.

Those early 'modern' lotteries first appeared in various towns in France, Belgium and Italy, and were used as a means of raising revenue to repair town walls, equip armies, provide for the poor. The most popular and efficient of these early civic lotteries – with tickets having to be bought and money given out as prizes – was Il Lotto de Firenze, which was established in 1530.

In England, Queen Elizabeth I licensed a public lottery in 1566 whose purpose was to provide money to repair the Cinque Ports and other public works. James I in 1612 allowed the Virginia Company to run a lottery to finance their colonisation plans for the New World – which led to the settlement of Jamestown and the creation of the state of Virginia.

Public lotteries on similar lines ran continuously in England for around 250 years, from 1566 to 1826, except for a gap of ten years after 1699, when they were banned. They were enormously popular and enormously successful, part of everyday life, part of the culture. The draws became major national events, usually at the Guildhall in London, and were done in style with bands and displays. Carefully chosen orphans or charity boys from the Blue Coat school were given the task of drawing numbers out of revolving drums. Plays, songs and ballads were written and performed to cash in on lottery mania. Henry Fielding sang in his own play, *The Lottery*, at Drury Lane in 1732. His verses still sound pretty modern:

A Lottery is Taxation,
Upon all Fools in Creation,
And Heaven be Praised,
It is easily Raised.

All political parties knew this and it remained part of government strategy for raising money for specific events, public monuments or certain good works, or just generally when they couldn't think where else to get some money quickly, and in cash. In the main, the money did do good. It was lottery money which raised the equivalent of £30 million in the 1750s to help build Westminster Bridge and create the British Museum.

So why did it come to an end? There had always been those against lotteries on religious grounds, believing that gambling was a sin that should not be encouraged. This was one reason why public lotteries in most states of the USA made little headway until relatively recently. The religious lobby played a part in the campaign that ended British lotteries in the 1820s. William Wilberforce, who had led the battle which ended the slave trade in 1807, was a great opponent of lotteries. There are those, of course, who do see it as a form of slavery.

The religious lobby did help to ban lotteries, but just as important in their demise in Britain was financial abuse. In 1826 there was a massive fraud, and some of the organisers disappeared with the prize money. This had frequently happened in the past, hence the ban in 1699, with frauds and fiddles of some kind always being very hard to eliminate. (France banned them not long afterwards, in 1836. Their most notable scandal concerned Louis XIV and a group of his leading courtiers, who managed to win all the top prizes in one French lottery until they were persuaded to give the money back for redistribution.)

Apart from downright dishonesty, there were countless abuses and scams whereby people made money out of the lottery, without contributing to the government's purse. In Britain, lottery tickets had always been expensive – up to £10 each in the seventeenth century – the theory, quite commendable, being that the poor should not be made poorer. You could of course offer the other theory – only the rich can get richer. (These theories are still around, when people complain either about the lottery or the distribution of its funds.)

Those who could not afford a whole ticket, which meant the vast majority, were helped to enter by middlemen, many of them illegal, who divided up the tickets into smaller, cheaper lots. Naturally they made sure the sum of the smaller lots was greater than the sum they had spent. There were also lotteries within lotteries – people selling lottery tickets on what lottery numbers would come up. The government therefore received little of the proceeds or profits on these ancillary lottery schemes, which often took as much money as the lottery itself. Then in 1826 there was dishonesty on a massive scale in their own lottery, so they decided to ban it, once and for all. It wasn't worth the effort, financially or morally. With an expanding empire, and a booming industrial economy, successive governments felt they did not need to stoop to national lotteries when they were stuck for small change. Britain therefore allowed no new national lotteries from 1826 onwards.

Elsewhere in the world, governments have been very keen to encourage them. Australia, for example, has long had a flourishing lottery industry, thanks to their state lotteries. The New South Wales state lottery, begun in 1849, provided the money for the Sydney Opera House in the 1970s. Even in supposedly strongly religious countries, such as Ireland, Italy, Spain and most countries of Latin America, they have proved hugely successful. In the USA, the power of the Puritan heritage, the fear of gangsterism (which usually manages to infiltrate most sorts of gambling) and the vague feeling that lotteries were a funny foreign habit, managed to keep lotteries out of most states until the early 1970s.

In Britain, the subject frequently came up in Parliament, but was always defeated. It was felt Britons already had enough opportunities for gambling, thanks to the football pools and horse racing, each with very strong lobbies, not to mention bingo, small-scale raffles and little lotteries run by charities. Premium Bonds, established by the government in 1957, were a form of lottery, with random prizes, up to £1 million, given out in lieu of interest. In the 1980s, when the economy was supposedly booming, there seemed no real need for a national lottery. It was said that Mrs Thatcher, brought up a Methodist, was personally against them.

Things changed in the 1990s. John Major, a modest banker by profession, was not averse to a national lottery. Government ministers saw it as an easy way to raise money in hard times. As in the reign of Elizabeth I, it was promoted as a method of funding certain causes and enterprises, without having to levy more taxes or the government having to use its existing resources.

There were few moral worries about upsetting the anti-gambling or religious lobbies any more, as there had been in the past. Public opinion polls indicated that over 70 per cent of the population approved of the idea of a national lottery. The campaigners for the lottery were able to point out all the benefits which would accrue, and also raised the fear that Continental lottery tickets might soon be on sale here. Most Continental countries with lotteries tried to stop this happening, for their own self-interest, but it seemed likely that under new European Union laws, Continental lottery tickets could legally be sold in Britain, thus depriving our government of an enormous possible revenue.

By 1992, Britain was about the only so-called civilised country without a national lottery. In Continental Europe, only Albania didn't have one. In the world as a whole, there were 165 national lotteries producing a total annual income of £54 billion. Social historians in the future will doubtless pin down and explain all the various reasons why Britain decided on a national lottery when it did, but the equally interesting question is, why did it take so long?

For about twenty years it had been clear that it was a painless and uncontentious way of helping the arts, charities and sports – modern equivalents of worthy actions like repairing medieval town walls, which authorities know they should do, but don't like spending the money. In Norway, for example, all sport was being completely funded by lottery money. There was also a specific cause, a one-off object, which was proposed as one of the good uses for lottery money, and that was to establish a fund to celebrate the Millennium. A new government department of National Heritage had recently been established, and it was looking for ways of raising funds without having to go through the Treasury. David Mellor, the so-called Minister for Fun, was an active campaigner for the national lottery, though alas he fell from grace before his ministry could lay their hands on the money.

One of the hidden, unstated elements in the government's decision to allow a national lottery, after a gap of some 170 years, was scientific. In looking round the world, especially at the USA, and admiring their efficiency and success in running massive state lotteries, it was clear that the old problem of fraud and dishonesty, which had caused so many problems in the past, no longer occurred. We were now, hurrah, living in the computer age. For 500 years, lotteries had been prone to fiddles and frauds, assorted scams and defects. Winners had basically been drawn from a hat – where the hat might be tampered with, certain players might have inside information and the organisers were not always able to control or maximise all the proceeds from their own creation.

The marriage of computers and mass lotteries meant that a national lottery, on however large a scale, however frequently drawn, could be run in total security, with no scandals, no frauds. Thanks to the latest technology and the use of modern marketing methods, millions could enter, billions could be raised, the state could make a killing, good causes would benefit, thus assuaging most if not all doubting moralists, and everyone would be happy.

And so in October 1993 Parliament passed the National Lottery [etc.] Act 1993. That's the official title of the copy of the Act sold by HMSO, price £7.70 for fifty-six very close-packed pages. The 'etc.' refers to the fact that the Act also corrected or added to various previous Acts and included some legislation concerning football pools and local lotteries run by charities.

The Act was specific on where the money raised by the National Lottery would go, outlining the five beneficiaries – 'for expenditure on or connected with' the arts, sport, national heritage, charities and the Millennium – and how it would be administered. Who would run the National Lottery itself was left to a new creation – the Office of the National Lottery – and a Director General, yet to be appointed, who would hold his or her position for five years, though it was renewable. The length of the National Lottery operator's licence was at this stage not stated, neither were there many clues as to how Britain's first National Lottery licence-holder would be chosen. The Director General, in his or her wisdom, so it declared under section 5 (4), would simply choose a 'fit and proper body'. But, ah-hah, if this body turned out not to be fit and proper, and never had been, then the Director General, under section 10 (1), could revoke the licence. This was all rather general and unspecific, leaving the Director General with the responsibility of working out the details, but never-theless a great deal of attention was instantly paid in certain commercial quarters, trying to work out what the rules might be and how they might qualify.

In July 1994 the Department of National Heritage pub-lished a very tasteful, beautifully printed little booklet telling the world about its very wonderful aims and objects under the title 'Preserving the past, shaping the future'. A new depart-ment, like any new body, has to keep telling people of its existence, explaining and justifying what it is trying to do. The National Lottery merited only three paragraphs, and it was clear from this booklet that they were still fairly in the dark about when it might begin or how lucrative it could be.

> The National Lottery should be running by the end of 1994 or early 1995 ... It will provide a great deal of extra money, bringing huge benefits for the cultural and sporting life of the UK. Although the turnover is difficult to forecast, it is expected that around an extra £75 million a year will be available for each of the arts, sport, heritage, charities and projects to mark the year 2000.

Richard Branson, Britain's favourite entrepreneur, first became interested in a national lottery in 1987. He was on holiday in Ireland, staying with friends, and kept on coming across arts centres, sports halls, youth clubs, all funded by their national lottery. He enquired about other lotteries and found that they too put the proceeds into similar good causes. When he came home, he wrote to Mrs Thatcher, the Prime Minister. 'I suggested we should have a national lottery, as soon as possible, and offered to find and fund a chief executive.' He didn't hear anything for a while, then he was passed on to Douglas Hurd, the Home Secretary, with whom he had a meeting. 'He was very helpful, and so were his civil servants. My idea was to create something like the Ford

Foundation, as we have nothing in Britain of that size and scale, which would distribute the money directly, not letting the government do it. Unfortunately, Mrs Thatcher was not very helpful . . .'

Yet she had appeared at one time to be his best friend, when he helped her with something called UK 2000 to knock Britain into shape. Mr Branson groaned. 'I only met her twice, both at formal gatherings. It was Downing Street which gave the impression I was actively involved with her. When it came to the Lottery, she was decidedly unhelpful.' Why? 'I think it was the influence of the football pools lobby. They realised they would suffer drastically.'

In 1993 Mr Branson sprang into action again, creating the UK Lottery Foundation, a consortium which, if they won, promised to donate their own profits to charity. 'If only Mrs Thatcher had agreed to our idea six years ago, good causes would already have benefited by billions of pounds.'

When I first talked to Mr Branson about a lottery in February 1994, he appeared confident of victory. He was the only non-profit-making bidder. 'No other country in the world lets a commercial firm run its national lottery. If we don't get it, I hope there will be a public outcry.' He was already negotiating with both the BBC and ITV for the TV rights to a Saturday evening programme, which he predicted would have an audience of 35 million. 'I estimate that in seven years we should be able to distribute £2 billion to charities, the arts and sports.' His only minor worry, the day I met him, was that his bid was not getting much publicity in certain newspapers, such as the *Daily Mail*, because their owners, Associated Newspapers, were involved in a rival bid. But the general public seemed to be for him – and his researches showed him that two out of three people would prefer a non-profit-making company to run the lottery. However, I never got clear in my mind how they were going to distribute their 'profits', except that he'd spent the last few months talking to 200 charities. 'I've explained our plans to them, and naturally they are all for it ...'

The origin of Camelot's history doesn't go back quite as far as Mr Branson's. Tim Holley, who became chief executive of Camelot, remembers first hearing about a national lottery in spring 1993, several months before the Act had been passed. At a board meeting of a firm called Racal, someone suggested they should look at the possibilities a national lottery might present. Did anyone know anything about lotteries?

'I didn't know anything personally, but I said I knew a firm which did – GTECH. Nobody else seemed to have heard of them. I said they were an American firm who handled two-thirds of the world's lottery systems. I was detailed to make contact with them next time I was in the States.'

*Tim Holley*

Tim was fifty-three at the time, the chief executive of Racal's Data Communications division, in charge of around 4,000 staff. Racal is a British firm, a world leader in information technology, and in 1993 it had a revenue of around £1 billion. One of its prime contracts is with the British government, providing in effect its communications systems, linking 150,000 government users in forty different departments.

He was born in Somerset in 1940; both his parents were teachers and keen sporting types – his father represented the county at rugby, his mother at cricket and hockey. Tim only managed to get into the county's second rugby team, but he did win a scholarship to a small public school, King's School, Bruton. He left at eighteen to work for Barclays Bank, then moved into computers with ICT, English Electric and then ICL, for whom he worked for nineteen years, creating programmes at first, then processing through sales and marketing till he was running their computer services group. In 1984 he was head-hunted by Racal.

As a computer-trained management man, he had heard of the success of GTECH: how two computer whizzkids had left IBM to go it alone and in fifteen years had transformed American lotteries by using computers. They supplied the software for the Texas lottery, among others, as well as fifteen in Europe.

Tim eventually made contact with GTECH on his next trip to the States, and found he was a bit late. It had already been approached by another British company – De la Rue – about lottery possibilities.

De la Rue is the world's biggest security printers, supplying banknotes to over 100 governments. In 1993 it made profits of £100 million and employed 7,600 people worldwide. It had been involved in the lottery business for some twenty years, supplying instant scratch cards on the Continent. It was naturally very interested in the printing possibilities of a

British national lottery. Its interests did not in fact clash with Racal's, or its expertise, which was in communications systems. De la Rue and Racal therefore decided to join with GTECH in a lottery project. Having got three, why not a fourth? They then brought in ICL, whose speciality was supplying software and services. This is also a British creation, formed in 1968 through a merger of smaller British computer firms. In 1993 it employed 24,000 people in around eighty countries with a turnover of £2.6 billion. (It is now largely owned by Fujitsu of Japan.)

The four companies were equally successful and modern, strong in computer technology, but all rather technical and specialist, hardly known to the general public, not the sort to mount advertising campaigns or deal direct with the man in the street. Most worrying of all, not one of them had any retail experience. This would obviously be vital if they wanted to attack the nation's High Streets. So they started looking for a fifth partner who would make up for their deficiencies.

One possibility was to approach a big retail chain such as W.H. Smith or Sainsbury's, but it was decided this could antagonise other retailers such as Boots or Marks & Spencer. They then started thinking of people who provided goods to the retail trade. Perhaps one of the big brewery firms? No, that could rebound. They mustn't get mixed up with a company selling alcohol or tobacco, not if they were going for a government licence.

Someone suggested Nestlé, until it was pointed out that it was based in Switzerland. One foreign-owned partner, i.e. GTECH, was more than enough. Their hit-list needed to avoid foreigners, alcohol or tobacco. By a process of elimination, it seemed to point to only one real possibility – Cadbury. So they went round to its HQ in Berkeley Square to make a presentation, and not long afterwards Cadbury Schweppes, one of the world's biggest sweets and drinks companies, with global sales of £3.7 billion in 180 countries, a household name in every High Street shop, became the fifth member of their National Lottery partnership.

They had sealed their friendship pact even before the Act had been passed, spending most of the summer of 1993 ironing out the details. All five were public companies, so in board meetings and legal discussions they had to work out the structure of their new project. What would happen, for example, if one backed out? How much should each put in? And what, of course, might be the possible gains for each of them?

All five partners, in their own ways, were hoping to supply goods or services to the new company, should it win the lottery licence, as well as providing themselves with a good investment. Racal could offer communication and electronic skills. ICL could manufacture and maintain the computer terminals to go in the outlets. De la Rue hoped to organise the security printing. GTECH would provide the systems. Cadbury had the point-of-sale skills and knew about mass-market promotions. Informal soundings were made about costs, asking rivals in the respective fields for possible prices, should they be asked to tender. It's called being competitive – before the competition begins.

In October 1993, as the Act became law, they announced their joint venture, naming Sir Ron Dearing as chairman. The five partners agreed to share equal status, with a board member each, but at the last moment ICL became worried about the possible financial scale of the project. 'Bloody mean, if you ask me!' said a non-ICL member. ICL decided to take only a 10 per cent share. The other four partners took $22\frac{1}{2}$ per cent each.

Tim Holley became Racal's man on the new company, Norman Hawkins came from Cadbury, Mike Pollitt from ICL, Charles Cousins from GTECH and David Rigg from

De la Rue. David had also grown up in Somerset, not far from Tim Holley's home, but went to school at Millfield, where he became head boy. He went to Queen Mary College, London, but left without graduating to work for an estate agent before joining De la Rue. For several years he was an international salesman for its banknotes, spending three weeks in every month abroad, before being made head of its New Development Division. This was how he had become involved in its lottery project, on which he had been working for several years, before Tim Holley appeared.

Saatchi and Saatchi were chosen as their advertising agency to handle the creative campaign. 'We wanted the biggest and the best available at the time,' said David Rigg. 'Someone with massive fire-power. If we won, we'd be the biggest lottery in the world, so we didn't want to take any risks. We wanted a firm which would crack every problem which came up.'

The first problem was a title – what to call the new company? Internally, the working title had been LotCo, which turned out to be the name chosen by one of their rivals. It was Saatchis who thought of Camelot, and it was immediately accepted. 'It suggested Dreams of Romance, which appealed to all of us.' It particularly appealed to Tim and David. They'd both been brought up near Cadbury Castle in Somerset, which is supposed to be associated with King Arthur. Saatchis also helped to create their logo – a smiling hand with fingers crossed – which was meant to indicate that the lottery would be fun. The colours would be red, white and blue, to indicate it was British.

In the autumn of 1993, after endless meetings between the members of the new Camelot board and visits to other lotteries round the world, they began to wonder who should actually head their new consortium. In other words, who was to be the boss? Sir Ron Dearing, as chairman, was basically the figurehead, not involved day to day. Informally, three of the

*David Rigg*

board members had already suggested to Tim Holley that he should be the chief executive, but he had said it wasn't up to him. He was still employed by Racal, working on secondment. It was up to Sir Ernest Harrison, the boss of Racal, to decide. 'Then, funnily enough, Sir Ernest himself suggested it,' said Tim. 'He told me he was putting me forward. So in the end I sort of emerged. I was pleased to accept the job. Even though it might last only nine months, it seemed enormously exciting and challenging.'

They then had to find premises. Three of the partners offered free space and they chose ICL's offer, which was some offices in Old Windsor, formerly part of the RC school, Beaumont College.

'The minute I was shown into the office they were giving me,' said Tim, 'I recognised the sofa. It was exactly the same office I had used ten years ago, when I'd been working with ICL.'

At the end of October 1993, the first Director General of Oflot – as his office became known – was appointed. He was Peter Davis, formerly deputy chairman of the Abbey National. In November he issued a draft 'Invitation to Apply' for the operating licence, inviting comments from all interested parties. The applications had to be handed in no later than 14 February 1994.

'We were already up and running,' said Tim, 'but as soon as our application was in, we immediately started making plans for when we had won, realising there was no time to spare. We engaged specialist advisers, such as Warburgs, as our merchant bankers and the Royal Bank of Scotland as our bankers. We talked to the Post Office about using their retail premises and the BBC and ITV about television coverage. We started regular game design meetings, working out exactly the sort of games we would play, if we won. I think we were ahead of our rivals at first, as far as planning was concerned, but they soon caught us up.'

It emerged that there were eight rival bidders in all. The favourite, as far as the media and the public were concerned, was the UK Lottery Foundation, expected by William Hill to win at 7-2. This was headed by Richard Branson, aided by Lord Young, a former trade minister, and supported by other prominent political figures such as Lord Whitelaw. IBM would provide its equipment and Mars the retail expertise, but its most popular selling point was that it would not run the lottery to make a profit, pointing out that in most other countries lottery organisers were either government-run or non-commercial.

Camelot, however, did not consider Branson to be their most dangerous rival. They were more worried about the Great British Lottery Company, backed by Granada, Vodafone, Hambros and Associated Newspapers, who were said to be spending a great deal of money and expertise in mounting their bid. They were also very aware of LotCo, a strong contender, led by the huge Rank Organisation.

Two other bidders were considered strong, but not such serious threats. Rothschilds and Tattersalls were running a consortium that did not appear to have a zippy name, as yet. Their combination of banking and betting was a strong one, but their campaign was fairly low-key. So was the Enterprise Lottery, led by the Tote with help from GEC and Thorn EMI. Then there was Games for Good Causes, backed by Ladbrokes and headed by the boss of Vernons Pools. Finally there was Rainbow, a neat name, but not considered very substantial, which was headed by Sir Patrick Sheehy of BAT Industries. It was considered an outsider because of its limited expertise in computer technology.

Rumours circulated about all eight contenders, clues were picked up and analysed as each did its best to keep informed about its rivals. No industrial espionage took place, however. Certainly not, said Tim Holley. It was normal commercial rivalry.

By January 1994, Camelot had about fifty people working full time on the project, and Tim decided to split them into teams. The main one, of about thirty, was the Project Team – organising and writing out the details of their bid, which was soon amounting to some 2,000 separate documents, stacked in a pile three feet high. He then set up two smaller teams. A Red Team of six people had to go through the pile, check it for repetitions and contradictions, plus a Blue Team of about the same number, whose job was to criticise – looking for weaknesses, postulating what rivals might be doing. In the Blue Team were John Maples MP, formerly a junior minister, an eminent economist who had done some work for the government, and David Clark, who had run the Quebec

Lottery. The Blue Team and the Red Team were kept constantly at work because the Project Team were endlessly having second thoughts, often working through the night to improve their submission. 'I left at three one Saturday night, leaving some people who were there till six in the morning.'

On the morning of Monday 14 February 1994, St Valentine's Day, when all the bids had to be handed in, Richard Branson had arranged for a horse, Desert Orchid, to accompany his bid – an amusing if rather irrelevant publicity gimmick, somewhat ruined by the fact that thick snow fell that morning in London. Camelot had no gimmicks, but they had to hire three vans to carry copies of their bid to London, in case one of them broke down on the way. Their application consisted of 7,000 pages and weighed half a ton.

Oflot had said the final decision would be announced on 25 May, but in the meantime there would be questions for each of the bidders, to which they would have to respond. They would also have a chance to appear before the Director General of Oflot and would be allowed to make a one-hour presentation in person.

'We decided we had to continue working as if we had already won,' said Tim. 'It wasn't arrogance, but common sense. Time would be so short, if we did win.' So a headquarters at Rickmansworth, near Watford, was earmarked – which turned out, by a remarkable coincidence, to be the same building on which Rank had an option, should they win the bid. Camelot then started advertising for staff, which some of their rivals thought was highly presumptuous, or pure publicity. 'It was neither. We had to do it, but we made it clear it depended on our winning.'

Camelot's presentation before Oflot was scheduled for 25 April. A week before, they held a full dress rehearsal in private, using MPs and people with government experience, such as Colin Moynihan and John Maples, to cross-examine them and put the sorts of questions they might be asked.

On presentation day itself, Sir Ron Dearing headed the team, with Tim Holley and four others. They had a batting order in which they would speak, points they would all make, plus a few slides. Only one of the six did not speak formally – Guy Snowden, of GTECH. A GTECH man had to be there, of course, but since he was American, they thought they'd keep his voice to the minimum.

'We were seen in a long thin room,' said Tim, 'in front of the DG and five of his advisers. Their questions kept on coming, which I felt was a good sign. They seemed genuinely interested in our plans. Afterwards, when we talked about it among ourselves, doing a sort of de-briefing, no one said, "Oh, bloody hell, why didn't I mention that?" Given the chance, none of us would have asked for a second presentation. We all thought we'd done as well as we could have done. During the previous weeks, we'd had lots of written questions from them, which we'd carefully answered. Again, I felt that was a good sign. There wouldn't have been so many if they hadn't been interested. That's how I interpreted it. None of the things they'd asked us had made us change the details of our bid. A week before the announcement, I thought to myself – we've won. No, I didn't say it to anyone else. Then I thought if we haven't won, one of our rivals must be absolutely brilliant . . .'

For the big day, 25 May, the eight bidders were informed that a fax would be sent to each one at 9.55 in the morning. A press conference would then be held at 10.00, to announce the winner, and a photo call at 11.30. 'I presumed that was to make sure we would all be in London that day – whether or not we had won.'

Camelot arranged for their fax to be received in De la Rue's offices, not far from the Department of Heritage office near Trafalgar Square. They gave the number for a fax machine that was hardly ever used, except by outposts of the De la Rue empire in the Far East. Just before ten o'clock, Sir Ron, Tim Holley and around thirty other Camelot officials gathered in the little room where the fax was situated, waiting for it to ring.

'Sir Ron had said to me that if it was bad news, he would read it out,' said Tim. 'If it was good news, I would read it out. A couple of minutes before ten o'clock the fax rang, and we all waited. It was a De la Rue fax from Hong Kong, giving lots of boring figures. It was going on for pages and pages, so we tore it off and stopped the machine. Then we waited. The fax started again, with the same boring figures. We had to let it finish this time. It rang a third time – and this was the Oflot fax at last. For some reason, it came through back to front, with the bottom sheet first. My eyesight is rather better than Sir Ron's, and I was able to make out the words "Camelot is the preferred applicant." When it was finished, I tore it off and gave it to Sir Ron, saying he should read it, which of course was going against his instructions. He read it out – and the cheers could be heard down the corridors and in the De la Rue boardroom. Probably across the road in Charing Cross police station as well . . .'

That night they held a party at the Dorchester for about 100 people, an impromptu party. Despite all their confidence and forward planning, they hadn't quite had the nerve to book a victory celebration in advance.

'When I woke up next day, I thought, Oh my God, what have we done? We had promised Oflot to start operating on 14 November, which was only five and a half months away. By that time we had to find and train 35,000 people, arrange and equip 10,000 outlets, open ten regional offices, set up a warehouse, and so many other things . . .'

Camelot had chosen 14 November in their bid after taking soundings from the retail trade. They had said it was the latest possible date before Christmas when they could cope with the launch of any big new product. Otherwise, it would all have to wait till mid-February. They never found out what dates their rivals had promised. 'But we always felt if we promised the government we would be up and running by November, we would get extra Brownie points, because there would then be more money raised for the good causes.'

Camelot, so Camelot naturally thought, must have struck Oflot as the most organised, the best equipped and the most likely to maximise the possibilities of the National Lottery, but in the official announcement they were not required to give reasons for their choice or reveal any details about why the rival bidders had failed. Richard Branson was very disappointed, convinced that his non-profit-making offer would have been best for everyone, the country as well as the good causes.

Peter Davis, the Director General, did subsequently give a couple of clues for his decision. He pointed out that in his terms of reference, he was not legally able to take into account whether a bidder was going to give its own profits away or not. That was not his concern. He just had to choose the operator which best met the objectives set out in the Act. Conservative Party thinking has always been to favour commercial concerns, to go for private enterprise to do the best job in most circumstances, so it would have been unlikely that a Tory government would ever have weighted the rules in favour of a do-gooding, charitable operator.

The other clue, which was confirmed later in a Commons committee, was that Camelot had in fact made 'the lowest bid' in terms of operating costs. It emerged that Camelot's retention of sales revenue was agreed at an annual average of 5 per cent of turnover. (Slightly higher at first, to compensate them for the huge initial outlay, but that will be the percentage over seven years.) Out of this 5 per cent they have to cover all their costs, and make their profit. It has therefore to be assumed that the rival groups were requiring a higher rate, though one or other of them, presumably, could jointly have been 'the lowest'. It can also be assumed that Branson's group was expecting at least 5 per cent – just for the running of the business. As far as Oflot was concerned, Camelot, as a body, seemed not only fit, but proper.

Camelot began recruitment in earnest on 31 May 1994. Teams of specialist interviewers started hiring staff in sales, finance, retail and the other departments. Next day, Tim Holley doubled the size of each team, fearing they would never cope.

Over 15,000 people applied for the 450 jobs available. ICL, one of the Camelot partners, devised an automatic computer system whereby CVs could be screened and matched against their ideal CV. Thus no-hopers were quickly eliminated. 'The quality was excellent,' said Tim. So it should have been, with over two million out of work in 1994, many of them highly skilled and hugely motivated. Twenty or thirty years earlier, they might not have found it quite so easy.

Regional headquarters were secured and staffed in London – very smart offices, just off Trafalgar Square – and in Liverpool, Cardiff, Sunderland, Exeter, Belfast, Glasgow, Watford, Birmingham, Leeds and Reigate. They found a good warehouse in Birmingham, very central, till asbestos was discovered in the roof and they had to look elsewhere, eventually securing something suitable near Northampton.

Camelot's world HQ was established at Rickmansworth, north-west of London, but it was still a shell, yet to be fitted and equipped. The windows had not even been installed, which turned out to be an advantage, as the massive computers could be swung in by cranes, but it wasn't so fortunate for one workman who fell from a window, breaking his leg.

Arranging the first 10,000 outlets was done fairly smoothly, most of them being newsagents and post offices, and even training the 35,000 assistants to work the systems proved not too great a problem. More worrying was getting British Telecom to install the special circuits needed before the 10,000 outlets could operate. The added complication was that every ten or so outlets had to be connected first to a local 'concentrator', which was about the size of a large fridge. Finding 10,000 outlets was in a way easy, as the shops and post offices already existed, but finding 1,100 sites in which to set up and install the 1,100 concentrators, safely and securely, was a lot more difficult. Rooms and buildings had to be bought or rented, usually in back rooms or outhouses of post offices. Until they had been established, the 10,000 circuits could not be connected and operated.

'This became our top priority. Every Monday morning I sent a fax to the chairman of BT telling him what stage we were at, how many circuits had been completed, any problems we were having. They were terrific. They installed 10,000 circuits, and the 1,100 concentrators, in just three months, in time for us to start testing the system. Inside Camelot, there was enormous enthusiasm. People worked ridiculously long hours. The whole ethos was Can Do. No one was saying or thinking Can't Do. In a way, it was all very un-British, really.'

One element that did rather concentrate Camelot's mind was their promise in their application to start operations on 14 November – if not, they would be liable for a penalty of £1 million a day. Seems a lot, but then Camelot were already hoping and planning, dreaming and dealing, wondering and worrying about sums in many millions of pounds – billions, even. The figures, at the time, appeared enormous. It is interesting to recall now what Camelot and the government were forecasting at the time; what sorts of sums were hoped for and what was at stake.

Camelot had been established with a fund of £50 million contributed by the five partners – Cadbury Schweppes, De la Rue, GTECH UK, ICL and Racal – plus £75 million in loans guaranteed by the Royal Bank of Scotland. There were further guarantees from the five partners of £40 million, as shareholders, and £90 million in their role as suppliers of products and systems when it all started. So, on paper, Camelot had a total of £255 million to draw on, either in cash or as guarantees. Quite a sum, for a firm being established virtually overnight. The total set-up costs, which included staff, renting or buying buildings, creating systems, media advertising and promotion, was calculated by Camelot at about £100 million even before one ticket had been sold.

The official handouts and public pronouncements from Camelot and from the government, before the Lottery had started, made it clear it was going to be a very wonderful thing from which the whole nation would benefit. Over Camelot's seven years, the average split of every £1 ticket bought would be as follows:

Prize money – 50p
Government tax – 12p
Good causes (arts, sports, charities, heritage, Millennium)
   – 28p
Retailer's commission – 5p
Camelot's operating costs and profit – 5p

Camelot's press pack, before the launch, said that the expected turnover for the seven years was £32 billion, of which £9 billion would go to good causes. For the first year, its expectations were more modest, assuming a turnover of only £1.4 billion, out of which £500 million would go to good causes. This was higher than the National Heritage's earlier estimate of £375 million for the five good causes. It made clear that the odds of winning the jackpot, i.e. getting the six correct numbers out of the forty-nine, were 14 million to one, but the chance of getting three right and winning £10 was 57 to one. Its estimate of what a normal jackpot-winner could expect, winning the big prize on their own and not sharing it, was £2 million. Five numbers would win between £1,000 and £2,000, four numbers would get £50 or £60, three numbers would be guaranteed £10.

Camelot and the government and everyone else were working in the dark, not knowing what the response of the great British public to a National Lottery would be, after a gap of some 170 years. Would we react in the way Americans and Australians had done to their state lotteries or would many of us prefer to stick to our traditional flutters on football pools, bingo, horses and dogs? Or would we ignore it altogether, as a vulgar pastime for silly people in some very hard economic times?

A couple of weeks before the launch, Camelot's 450 staff attended a company conference in Birmingham where they were told the final plans and shown the TV advertising. They were allowed to play, for one time only, the Lottery itself. As employees, they would of course be barred from the real thing.

They received a free ticket each, choosing six numbers, using the computer machinery going into the shops, and had a chance to win several prizes, including a holiday for two in Paris. The jackpot prize was a brand-new Rover, wheeled into the conference centre for the occasion. The compère for the evening was the ever lovely, ever sprightly, Anneka Rice. All the prizes were won, except the jackpot. An omen for the millions of punters still to compete? The notion of a roll-over week did not apply, as this was a one-off, closed event. The Rover was then returned to the showroom. Like smart retailers always try to do, Camelot had secured the Rover on sale or return, so lost nothing on its neat bit of internal public relations.

In the week before the grand opening, there were endless tests of the system and all staff. 'Balls-achingly boring, but it had to be done,' said Tim. There were also outside tests and inspections by Oflot's independent accountants, Deloitte Touche, making sure all systems were secure and foolproof.

'During all those eighteen months' preparation, since I'd first started on the project, I'd lost no sleep at all. Problems are there to be solved. I was used to making decisions. And I'm willing to change decisions, if they don't work. I'd even gone off on holiday in August, three months before the opening, which some people thought I shouldn't have done, in case there were problems. I only went to Cornwall, so I could quickly get back. But on the night of 13 November, for the first time, I had a bad night. I woke at four in the morning, thinking about all the things that could go wrong. In the event, nothing did. We had arranged an inaugural breakfast party at the Tower of London, complete with fireworks, which John Major, the Prime Minister, came to.'

There were also inaugural events at Camelot's regional headquarters in Edinburgh, Cardiff and Belfast. On Saturday 19 November 1994, the evening of the first draw, they held a rather grand party at the Natural History Museum in Kensington, inviting their major suppliers, directors, politicians and VIP guests.

The first day's sale of the first week of Britain's National Lottery brought in £7 million. The first week's total was £48.9 million. That was about double what most people had expected. Overnight, Lottery tickets had become the country's single biggest consumer product. Camelot, which had been in existence as a company only little more than a year, was taking in more cash than Sainsbury's or Marks & Spencer, companies in existence for a hundred years. Britain's National Lottery was about to become the world's largest, in terms of money taken

and people playing, thus eclipsing the five previous biggest –
Spain, Japan, France, New York and Florida.

Camelot were very happy. The government was pleased.
And several lucky people were about to be delighted.

## KEN SOUTHWELL, YORK

Ken Southwell was the first big winner. Big in the sense of fame and coverage, in that he was a jackpot-winner who immediately came out, went public and, even more surprisingly, seemed to enjoy being out and being public. At the time, anyway.

He was first in the chronological sense as well, winning with his first line on the day of the first Lottery, 19 November 1994. There were seven jackpot-winners that day, and each received the sum of £839,254. The media treated it as a major event. Ken's win seemed not just big but somehow awesome.

Four winners decided to stay private. Three others, including Ken, allowed their names to be known. That was roughly the proportion of known to unknown winners in the early months, before the hounding of the truly big winners became a national sport.

Ken, aged thirty-four, lived in a village outside York, so that began a pattern of big northern winners, but he has to be called white collar, even managerial class, rather than strictly working class. Winning large sums, of course, does rather make a nonsense of all social classifications.

He was born in York and brought up by his mother, along with his sister Christine. He never knew his father, as his parents had divorced many years earlier. He passed the eleven

*Ken Southwell*

plus and went to Nunthorpe Grammar School, where he got
six O levels, then decided to leave at sixteen. Most of his
friends were leaving, and he didn't fancy the Sixth Form.

His first job was in the police force, starting as a cadet at
a police training college near Durham. 'I had a fabulous time.
It had the equipment of a public school, and I passed another
five O levels.' At eighteen he was a fully-fledged police
constable, ending up on traffic duties, which he didn't find so
fabulous. 'You can only take so much scraping people off the
motorway.'

At the age of twenty-six, after eight years in the police, he
gave it up. 'There wasn't a specific reason – but it's very
indicative of me, wanting to move on. I couldn't face the idea
of doing the same thing for another thirty years or so.' He
went into engineering, after seeing advertisements for people
with decent O levels to be trained in air conditioning. From
there he moved into communications engineering, working

for a firm specialising in installing satellite systems. At the time of his win he had been working indirectly for Camelot, installing some of their sophisticated satellite equipment – a nice coincidence, which, for some reason, was not made much of at the time. Perhaps because it could have looked as if he were a Camelot employee.

Mostly, his work involved installing satellite receivers for Sky television, on the bigger contracts like multi-distribution systems for hotels, or supervising engineers who were doing the domestic jobs. His job title was Senior Communications Engineer. He was earning a basic £15,000, which came to around £20,000 a year, as his job meant a lot of travelling round the north of England and a lot of overtime.

He was living at the time of his win with Julie, a secretary in a York financial services firm, in her house, which she owned, in Copmanthorpe, a village about six miles from York. She had shared a house for some years with another bloke, which they had sold when they'd split up and she'd bought her own smaller house on the proceeds. Ken himself had lived with another partner some years previously, but that had ended rather acrimoniously. In his spare time he had played in a semi-professional pop group; mainly guitar, but he can manage a tune on most instruments. He'd always been a fan of Sting. He looks a bit like him in a way, lean and athletic, quick and bright, but arty rather than pop-starry, interesting rather than handsome.

His mother had died of cancer in December 1993, which was a great emotional blow. To the surprise of Ken, and his sister Christine, she turned out to own the house they had lived in, which Ken had always presumed was rented. 'As she was dying, she asked me to look after Christine. I think she said much the same to Christine. She is a year older than me.'

When everything was sold, and Ken got his share, he bought an attractive Victorian terrace house in Fulford, south of York. He was doing it up himself, being a handyman, from the electrics to the tiling, with a view to letting it out to students. That was why he happened to be living at Julie's house at the time. Both of them were working hard, with a reasonable lifestyle, sound finances, able to enjoy themselves and afford skiing holidays. 'There was nothing really we were short of; nothing we were dreaming about.'

On the Monday of the first week of the Lottery, they happened to run out of biscuits, so they decided to walk round to a little local supermarket, Jackson's Family Food Store. Until then, they had not been aware the Lottery was starting, but inside the shop they noticed a new Lottery counter. 'Why don't we have a go?' said Ken. He had only £3 left in his pocket, so he bought three lines. He based his first line on birthdays – his sister Christine's is 3 July, Julie's is 5 November, his best friend Pete is 14 November and his own is 30 October. He threw in his mother's house number, 44, and then at random picked 22 as his sixth number, for no reason, really.

He worked most of Saturday, as he often did, then ended up in the early evening at the local pub in Copmanthorpe, downing two or three pints with some friends, including his apprentice. 'He was just a young lad, who was working with me, travelling around in the company's Transit van, which I drove. I said to him as we left the pub that I wouldn't be picking him up on Monday. "Why not?" he asked. "'Cos I'll be a millionaire by then." I said.'

He went home to Julie's house, and was having a shower, preparing to go out with her for the evening, when she shouted from the living-room that the first Lottery programme was on. 'I didn't really hurry, just finished having the shower, then I came out, half-naked, with a towel wrapped round me, and sat down beside Julie to watch Noel Edmonds. She'd bought one ticket, which she was holding, but hadn't got one number, so she asked where mine was. I had to go off and find it. Turned out I had all six numbers: 3, 5, 14, 22, 30 and 44.'

Ken tried to ring the Camelot number as printed on the ticket, but couldn't get through. He tried again, then realised he and Julie had agreed to meet their friend Ashley at the local pub, and he was now running late. 'I rang Ashley and said I was going to be late as I'd won the Lottery. "So have I," he said, and hung up on me. He presumed it was a practical joke, the sort we were always playing on each other.'

It took him about two hours to get through to Camelot and establish his win, but it was the first week, with new systems being operated. Eventually a Scottish voice was on the phone, someone called Alasdair, who said 'Congratulations!' Another Scotsman called Rik Dalglish would be on the way to see him on Sunday. 'When I finally got to the pub, I told everyone. Why keep it a secret? And I got drunk. Why not, when you have a good reason to celebrate.'

Next morning Ken woke up pretty groggy, then he remembered he had promised to do a 'guvvy' – the local name for a private job – for a friend in the village. 'I didn't really fancy crawling over his roof, but I'd promised him. I also needed the £30 cash in hand. I'd blown all my cash in the pub and didn't have a penny in the house, and I fancied going to the pub again at lunchtime.' He did the job, then remained housebound for the rest of the day, unable to go out to the pub, waiting for Rik. 'It was the first day for Rik as a Winners' Adviser. He was in a hired car, an automatic Granada, which he hadn't driven before. He had a mobile phone he didn't quite know how to use. He'd also got lost.'

Meanwhile, the press were desperate to track Ken down. He'd told everyone at the pub, so the news had spread quickly, but there was the complication about where he was living. His address in the phone-book was the one he was converting, which proved to be empty when the press got there. Julie's house, where he was living, was in her name, but her phone was ex-directory. Seems strange, for a secretary to be ex-directory? 'I didn't want to be cold-called by people trying to sell me double glazing,' Julie said. 'We did a bit of that at work, with insurance offers, and I know how annoying it can be.'

When Rik eventually arrived, one of the first topics he brought up was whether to go public or not. Ken immediately said Yes, why not, no sweat, no problem. In that case, said Rik, everything must be done at a press conference, all in one fell swoop, make an event of it, which means not telling any reporters beforehand. Almost as he spoke, the first gentleman of the press, in the form of the *Daily Mirror*, arrived at the front door. 'I've only just discovered some of the press were offering huge amounts of money for tip-offs,' said Ken. 'If I'd known, I would have rung up and grassed on myself. I'd have claimed the reward by saying, "I know exactly where he is."' The *Sun* then arrived, and voices could be heard shouting through the front letter-box. Rik and Ken crept out of the back door, over a garden wall and escaped, while Julie went out of the front door on her own, saying the house was empty.

They all met up at Stakis York Hotel, where they spent the night. Ken had been given the choice of holding his press conference in the north, at Leeds, or in London. He chose London straight away.

Next day they drove to Watford in Rik's hired car. 'Rik also had a pager, which he wasn't very used to. In the end, when messages started coming through for him, I rang Camelot on his mobile. "Hi, it's Ken Southwell here, we're now at Junction so-and-so, be with you soon." Rik also had fun finding Camelot's HQ at Rickmansworth. Turned out he'd only been there once. It was all a good laugh, really. When we got to Camelot, I had to change my clothes in the toilet. I bet

winners are being better treated now. Not that I'm criticising
Camelot – it was early days. Or Rik. He's a lovely bloke. Been
awful if we'd had to spend all that time with someone we
didn't get on with.'

The first National Lottery press conference to announce
any winners was held at a fashionable golf club, Moor Park,
Rickmansworth, very handy for Camelot's HQ. It was chaired
by David Rigg, the De la Rue representative on the Camelot
board, who had become Director of Communications.

'When we walked in, it was wall-to-wall TV and press
people,' said Julie. 'I was completely fazed, so I decided to stay
well out of it. I realised I didn't like publicity. I stood at the
back, and then Sarah Linney from Camelot saw me obviously
not liking it, and took me out of the room.'

'I loved it,' said Ken. 'I was on Sky News, GMTV, Channel
4, and I got to be interviewed by Selena Scott. That was
good . . .'

'Ken is more extrovert than me. He can handle all that,'
Julie added.

Ken cracked a joke, several times, about having wasted £2
– because he'd won with his first line, yet he'd spent £3.
Afterwards, Tim Holley, Camelot's chief executive, put his
hand in his pocket and gave Ken back his £2. What larks.

Ken and Julie stayed the night at the Kensington Hilton,
then had a walk round London in the morning with Rik.

'It was funny being recognised in the street,' Ken said. 'At
least sort of recognised. People would look at you and think,
Now, did I see him on GMTV or what?' They returned to
York by train on the Tuesday, with people still looking at him,
so Ken imagined. 'Glancing over their newspapers, to check
it was me, whoever I was. I could sense they felt they'd seen
me somewhere.'

Julie went back to work on Wednesday, saying she had no
intention of giving it up, despite Ken's win. She enjoyed her

# NEWS

For immediate release on 21 November 1994

**THE NATIONAL
LOTTERY**

## NATIONAL LOTTERY JACKPOT WINNERS

## CELEBRATE IN STYLE

.

Two of the National Lottery's first ever Jackpot winners celebrated the combined £5.9m Jackpot with champagne today (Monday 21st November) at Moor Park Golf Club in Rickmansworth near operator Camelot's headquarters.

George Snell and his daughter Tricia Marden of Edmonton and Ken Southwell of York were amongst seven people to each scoop £839,254 for matching the six winning numbers correctly. Ken Pilton of Hillingdon, Middlesex was also a winner. Two other winners had their tickets validated and were given their cheques this morning but do not want publicity.

George is a 69 year old retired miner who has also served with the army and the RAF. He arrived at the celebrations with his daughter, Tricia Marden who, because of rocketing mortgage payments, recently went back to school - as a cleaner - in order to save the family home for her and her husband, Stewart who is a plumber and their three year old daughter, Katie. Father and daughter bought the ticket together and will be sharing the winnings.

**Contacts**

The Rowland Company

London
Tel: 071 436 4060
Fax: 071 255 2131

Hall Harrison Cowley

Birmingham
Tel: 021 236 7532
Fax: 021 236 7220

Bristol
Tel: 0272 292311
Fax: 0272 299984

Cardiff
Tel: 0222 344717
Fax: 0222 344630

Edinburgh
Tel: 031 226 7348
Fax: 031 226 4915

Maidenhead
Tel: 0628 416100
Fax: 0628 777472

Manchester
Tel: 061 437 4474
Fax: 061 437 7085

Southampton
Tel: 0703 226361
Fax: 0703 331585

The National Lottery
is operated by
Camelot Group plc

Contact

Brunswick Public
Relations
Tel: 071 404 5959
Fax: 071 831 2823

CAMELOT

*Press release on the first winners*

Ken Southwell who is single and aged 35 is a Communications Engineer who was sub-contracted to install some of Camelot's terminals in stores. He plans to buy his girlfriend, Julie a car and to spend some time thinking about how to spend the rest of the money.

Ken Pilton, a 64 year old Cockney says he still feels the same, despite his big win and does not plan to be lavish with his winnings, but thinks that he will treat himself to a new Skoda car. Twice divorced Ken is also going to avoid gold-diggers and has no plans to marry again, choosing instead to spend some of his winnings on a visit to his brother, Ron, in New Zealand and on taking his 19 year old son, Colin, on a world cruise.

David Rigg, Communications Director of Camelot commented:

"We have over 1.1 million happy winners after the first draw. We are delighted to be paying seven people a share in the Jackpot and we are still waiting for the seventh winner who is from Essex to come forward. We look forward to many more winners in the coming weeks".

job too much. She also wanted to retain her independence. Ken went back to work as well, but only to give in his notice. 'I'd gone as far as I could in my job. I'd been thinking of leaving anyway. I want a thinking period now, during which I can work out my master plan. I'm still thinking.'

A couple of weeks after his win, he was still taking stock, but had no regrets about going public. 'I'm still enjoying it. In a way, I've won your money – some of the one pounds which everyone has put in. So I feel I should share it. Not share the money, certainly not, but share some of my pleasure. That's why I'm willing to talk to you or the media. I don't intend to act like a dog who keeps a piece of meat to itself. I haven't won such an enormous amount of money that it becomes obscene. It's a good sum, enough for life, but I might easily blow it or lose it by investing in the wrong things. I'm sure the press would like that . . .

'I expect the begging letters will soon be rolling in, but I've discussed it with Julie. She's going to open them all. No, I don't intend to give any money away or go around treating my friends. Why should I? I don't expect any enmity from them. I'm sure some friends are jealous, of course, but amiably jealous, the way I would be if it happened to them. I'd go around saying, "Oh, you lucky bugger", which is what I'm sure they're all doing now. It's been a learning curve, so far. I've experienced what it's like, in a minor way, to be a bit of a celebrity. Almost all the stories about me so far in the papers have managed to get at least one fact wrong. Imagine what it must be like to be really famous and written about all the time! That's one thing I never appreciated.

'In a year's time, I'll tell you what else I've learned.'

# AUDREY AND ANDY, HARTLEPOOL

On the evening of Saturday 18 March 1995 Audrey Jenkins, aged twenty-eight, was at home in her council house in Hartlepool with her friend Brenda, watching the Lottery programme, as she had done most weeks since it began. Her partner Andy Voss, with whom she had lived for eleven years, the father of her two children, Carl, nine, and Claire, five, was away from home that day. He had gone south to Norwich, looking for work. For the previous eighteen months he had been unemployed. His last job was as a taxi-driver, part time, but he has never had proper full-time work since he left school aged sixteen. All four of them were living on £70 a week unemployment money.

Audrey had picked four of her numbers from the family's birthdays, as she had done for the last three weeks. She chose 19 for her own birthday, 19 January; 18 for Claire's, 18 May; 24 for Andrew's, 24 December and 31 for Carl's, 31 January. Then she had chosen 9, as it was Carl's lucky number and finally 41, for reasons she can't remember. Andy had suggested 44, for reasons he can't remember either. 'But she'd ignored me, as she usually does, and chose 41 instead.'

When the numbers started appearing on the TV screen, Audrey's first thought was that she had got five of them right – the ones she could remember choosing. It was only when she went to check her sixth number, that she found she had got all six right. 'I was shocked. I couldn't take it in. I didn't believe it.'

Her friend Brenda rang her husband, who came straight round to celebrate. Audrey then rang some of her own family, and they too came round. One of them brought a bottle of wine, which led to some problems as they didn't have a corkscrew in the house. Andy, when at home, only drinks lager straight from the can. Audrey has been known to drink wine and she did have a bottle in the house that evening, but it had a screw top. So they had to borrow a corkscrew from a neighbour.

Round about nine o'clock, Audrey thought she would wake the children, to tell them the good news, so she went into their bedroom and put the light on. She woke Carl first, as he was

*Audrey and Andy*

the Lottery fan, telling him she was a winner. 'You're telling me lies!' he said.

Meanwhile, Andy and three of his friends were about a hundred miles away in an old van on the A1, returning from a pointless journey to Norwich, having failed to find work. He'd switched the radio on at eight for the results, and was sure he recognised at least four of the dates of family birthdays, knowing Audrey usually based her numbers on them. So he made them stop the van at the next service station, somewhere near Doncaster, and went into a phone-box to ring Audrey, but the line was engaged. When he got home about eleven o'clock, he could see all the lights on and the house full of people. His first words, when he opened the door, were 'How much?' They didn't go to bed till about 3.30 in the morning, both in a state of shock.

Before going to bed, Audrey had contacted Camelot to say she'd got the six numbers, but heard only a recorded message at first. She became confused by the recorded instructions, hanging up when she should have held on, but eventually she got through to a real voice and told them she thought she was a winner. She was one of just two jackpot-winners that Saturday, each of whom would get about £4 million. Next morning a Camelot official, who said he was one of their Winners' Advisers, Rik Dalglish, rang from London at 9.30 in the morning to say he was on his way to see them, but probably wouldn't arrive till the afternoon.

Throughout the Sunday, there were endless callers and telephone messages at Audrey and Andy's council house in Endrick Road on the Owton Manor estate – relations, friends and neighbours, all asking if it was true. Both come from large families: Audrey has six brothers and one sister, Andy has three brothers and one sister. By mid-morning, the news was probably half-way round Hartlepool.

Around midday, a representative of the *Sun* arrived, having been phoned by someone about all the rumours, then some local pressmen knocked at the front door, asking if it was true. Andy denied it, having been instructed to do so by Rik on the phone.

Rik finally arrived in the early afternoon, with the press calls still growing. It seemed pointless now denying it any further; the media attention had turned into a bombardment. When Rik explained the pros and cons of going public, it took Audrey and Andy very little time to decide. They felt besieged, trapped in their own house. Rik suggested that they could, if they liked, go to London and give the press conference there, and they immediately jumped at the idea. 'I just wanted to get away for a while,' Andy said. 'And the thought of giving one press conference, talking to everyone at once, seemed the best way to get rid of them all.'

They left almost at once, hardly giving themselves time to pack a suitcase and get the kids ready, and all bundled into Rik's car. 'I thought reporters were following us,' said Andy. 'In fact, I'm sure they were. When we stopped at a service station, I felt people were looking at me. I was becoming paranoid. We went into this hotel for lunch and a man opened the door for us. "He must know," I said to Audrey.'

They spent Sunday night at a Hilton hotel near Watford, not far from Camelot's HQ, the first time Andy and Audrey had ever stayed in any hotel. On Monday they arrived in London, where Rik booked them all into the Savoy Hotel, a family suite for them, and a connecting suite for him. He gave them strict instructions to tell nobody in the hotel who they were or what had happened, and to reveal nothing to anybody until the press conference. And then, during the press conference and afterwards, they must not say which hotel they were staying in. It was obvious that such a nice, clean-looking, well-scrubbed, happy family, young and outgoing, clearly deserving – Andy might be unemployed, but he had got on his bike and been looking for work – would make a perfect family as far as publicity was concerned.

Since the dramas and confusions and bad publicity over the hounding and outing of the 'anonymous' Blackburn Asian factory worker in December who had won over £17 million, which had led to some criticism of Camelot's handling of winners, more and more of them were opting for privacy, turning down the excitement of a press conference and the delights of a hotel. The Savoy might seem a strange choice, unnecessarily luxurious and possibly intimidating, but it isn't the sort of hotel where you might expect to find Lottery-winners, or one that has staff who might leak information to the tabloids.

'Oh aye, I'd heard of the Savoy, like,' said Andy. 'I knew it was posh. It was a bit hard to relax, especially for the kids. We hadn't brought proper clothes, or a tie, so we weren't allowed to eat in the hotel dining-room. We had to eat in our rooms.' Next day they did some shopping, spending £1,000 in Oxford Street, getting rigged out for the press conference. Audrey bought a very smart black tailored suit, Andy a double-breasted dark blue suit, white shirt and patterned tie. Carl was in a white shirt, buttoned to the top, and black trousers, while Claire wore a floral frock.

Almost from the moment Audrey had heard the news, she had felt ill. Nothing to do with her win, so she thinks. Just chance that she had a terrible sore throat and an aching head, sure she was getting tonsillitis. The thought of the press conference began to terrify her, and she wondered if she had made a mistake. But Rik said not to worry; the press conference could be delayed for another day or two, no problem. Still she didn't sleep properly. The press conference was preying on her mind. But on Wednesday morning when she woke up, her throat felt much better, so Camelot's press department quickly confirmed the details. It was to be held at

11.30 on Wednesday morning at the Waldorf Hotel in the Aldwych, a middling smart London hotel used by Miss World contests in the old days, or for business conferences, not one of London's élite hotels like the Savoy.

Before the conference, our happy family all had their hair done in the Savoy, including nine-year-old Carl, who had arrived in London with what appeared to be a skinhead haircut, but he managed to get it trimmed even shorter, at a cost of £17. 'I couldn't believe the price,' Andy said. 'Camelot paid, mind. I just had to sign the bill. We were charged £17 each. It was the first time any of us had ever been to a hairdresser. My sister does it for us. The barber I had kept on trying to make conversation. He asked how long we were staying in the hotel. I said three days, probably, but I didn't know. Then he asked what sort of work I did, and I said, None, I was on the dole. He couldn't work out how we came to be staying there. Of course I couldn't tell him, could I, in case anyone found out before the press conference.'

When the conference started, there were about fifty press, TV and radio people present, almost filling the room, plus a dozen Camelot officials and half a dozen hotel flunkeys standing along the walls, ready to serve light refreshments to the hacks. Audrey, Andy and their two children arrived through double doors with David Rigg, Director of Communications at Camelot, and walked the length of the room before taking their seats at a long table set with microphones. Claire and Carl sat at either end. They looked bright and cheerful, staring around, their eyes wide open, giggling at each other, but as the conference progressed, they seemed to lose energy and interest and began to slump deeper into their chairs.

David Rigg did the introductions, smiling and beaming, saying who Audrey and Andy were, then asked for any questions. There was a slight pause. Few reporters like to ask the first question. 'Oh, there aren't any,' said David Rigg.

Then at last someone shouted out the obvious question: 'What are you going to do with the money?'

Audrey looked at Andy. Andy looked at Audrey. 'We're still in a state of shock,' said Andy. 'We haven't decided.' He took the lead in answering the questions, unless they were specifically aimed at Audrey, and seemed unfazed, cheerful, amused, honest and open, and to be enjoying himself. Audrey looked more ill at ease, but then she had not been feeling well, but when asked a question, she too answered coherently and sensibly. She explained how she heard the news, how at first she thought she'd got only five numbers. Andy was asked if he had a job, and said he'd been a taxi-driver, but not for some time. They were asked why they had agreed to go public, and Andy said they wanted to get it all over. 'If we'd stayed in the house, like, we'd have cracked up. We'd have been prisoners.'

Someone mentioned a story in one of the tabloids that they had invested their last £1 on the Lottery. 'I never spoke to no newspapers,' said Andy, 'so that was a load of lies.'

'I think what Andrew means is that the report was not strictly accurate,' David Rigg beamed.

Andy then said he'd been upset that one paper had described his house as run down. 'We never thought that. It was our pride and joy.' So would he get a new house? someone asked. 'We'll have to. Ours is run down, isn't it?' They'd like a three- or four-bedroom house with a garage, but not far away from where they live. Not in a posh part of the town, just near their old friends. 'We don't want to be snobs and leave our old friends. I'd also like a greenhouse.'

One reporter, referring to the fact that Andy had been out of work for most of his life, asked him, if he could have chosen between getting a job and winning the Lottery, what would it have been?

'What do you think?' Andy replied. 'Would you carry on

working if you won the Lottery?' Yes, said the reporter, rather self-importantly. He would, actually. He liked working. 'The best I could have been offered,' said Andy, 'would have been a job on £200 a week. I don't want to sound snotty, like, but I'm not taking that, now, am I?'

There had been a hint, from one or two of the more superior reporters, of condescension towards this young, out of work, working-class couple, but it had soon begun to fade. The hotel staff lining the wall showed no such feelings. They were openly gaping, wishing it was them, hanging on every word, even those who had not understood Andy's north-east accent and had to have whispered translations.

Andy was asked if he feared he might lose contact with his friends, through all this happening. 'No, I think I'll gain friends.' Everyone laughed. Asked about his future plans, he said he'd like to take his children to Disneyland. That seemed to be his only definite decision so far. Almost on cue a Mickey Mouse figure appeared, who pranced around with the children. One of Camelot's neat little tie-ups.

A photo line-up was then arranged for the cameramen, the whole family being grouped together with Mickey Mouse. Then they all went outside into the early spring sunshine for more photographs. By now, there were almost a hundred reporters and photographers, all pushing and shoving. 'Audrey, smile this way,' one of them shouted. 'Oi, that fucking TV camera is in the way again. Andy, can you put Carl on your shoulders? Audrey, give us a bloody smile!'

Carl and Claire were in turn carried aloft, then held by hand, then walked up and down. A large cardboard cheque appeared, as if by magic, carried by a Camelot official. It was a Royal Bank of Scotland cheque for £3,987,786, big enough for even the most short-sighted cameraman to capture and let the world enjoy the National Lottery logo and the Royal Bank's full name.

Audrey and Andy had done well and were now enjoying themselves. The questions had been fair, with little edge, except for a couple which tried to suggest that Camelot might have encouraged them to come out. They denied this nicely, without appearing to be aware of the undertones. It was obvious to everyone they were there of their own free will.

One question was about why they were not married, to which Audrey had replied, saying they hadn't been able to afford it. Would they now? 'We haven't decided,' she said. This line of questioning might have revealed more about their personal relationships, but it was not pursued. The press were content with a nice happy story about a nice happy couple, and Camelot were delighted to have delivered it.

After the main press conference and the photo-call, several carefully chosen media people were allowed brief one-to-one interviews. The longest was given to a young female reporter and photographer from the *Hartlepool Mail*, Audrey and Andy's local paper, who had come to London for the press conference. They seemed as excited as the winners to be in the Waldorf Hotel.

The reporter began by asking what pubs and clubs Andy normally drank at in Hartlepool. Andy told her, and said he'd still be drinking there as he didn't want to be a snob and drop his old friends. Then she asked what he thought of London, as it was his first visit. 'All these meals,' he said. 'All these people. There's no way I'll be doing all this again.'

She asked about the reaction back home, what his friends and relations were thinking. Andy said they'd been ringing home regularly since they arrived, and everyone was pleased for them, but there were a couple of rumours going round the town he'd like to squash. It was not true he was getting any money from all this. He wasn't charging for interviews or selling his story to anyone. There was no money in this. Camelot were paying for everything. He'd spent nowt so far.

She asked what schools they had gone to, and what schools the children were at. Would they now be sent to a private school? Audrey thought for a while, as if she hadn't considered this before. Camelot officials had gone over the sorts of questions they would be asked and all had come up, over and over again, but not this one. 'Well, they're happy at school, why should I take them away? I suppose if other kids got on to them about the money, well, then we might move them, like. I want us all to carry on living a normal life. We won't be normal, of course, but we'll treat our friends as normal. I won't not talk to people just because I've now got money.'

She then asked Andy if he had any hobbies. He said he played football every Monday on the Rec. Audrey was asked about her hobbies, and Andy replied for her. 'Nagging at me!' 'I'm not writing that down,' the reporter said, rather virtuously.

I wondered how she would survive in Fleet Street if she always made moral judgements on people's answers. But then she probably didn't want a London job, judging by her keenness to hear Andy's views on the awful London traffic and the funny food.

'Eee, I dunno what we've been eating half the time,' he said. 'We have this menu in the hotel, and I don't know what most of the stuff is. On the dole we're used to going to the chippie or the Chinese.' The reporter persevered, wanting to know exactly what he had tried. 'Lobster. We did try that. Oh, aye, it was nice enough, but I could only eat half of mine. I've felt full all the time since I came to London. I feel hungry enough, but then when I sit down, I feel full. I don't understand it.' The reporter wrote this down, perhaps seeing it as some sort of metaphor for London life.

The next day they all went on GMTV, but turned down another morning TV programme as it would have meant going to Liverpool. They were then invited to appear on

BBC 1 on Saturday evening, during the Lottery programme. Andy didn't really want to stay in London much longer, finding hotel life uncomfortable and constricting, but Audrey fancied it. After some discussion with Rik, they decided to stay in London but to move out of the Savoy. 'I'll be able to boast when I get home I stayed there, but it's been a bit hard on the kids. They haven't been able to run down the corridors.' So they moved to the Kensington Close Hotel, less formal and more touristy, handy for Earls Court where the BBC Lottery programme was to come from, live at the Daily Mail Ideal Home Exhibition.

They also decided to invite some of their relations down from Hartlepool, for a day in London and to be part of the audience for the Lottery show. Andy made several phone calls about hiring a twenty-seater coach and found it would cost £455. 'They asked for a deposit, to be paid in Hartlepool.' However, they scratched around and the money was found, with Andy promising to pay them all back.

Before they returned to Hartlepool, I got them to sit down quietly in a corner of their hotel and look back on a rather strange week in their life, starting with the press conference.

'My mouth was dry before it began,' said Andy, 'but I'd calmed down a bit by the time it started. They asked the questions we expected, so I enjoyed it. I could do it again, like.'

'When I first walked into that room,' said Audrey, 'I was very worried, but it wasn't as bad as I expected. Andy did enjoy it because he enjoys talking ...'

Neither had any regrets about going public. 'I felt worse in Hartlepool,' said Andy. 'Getting right paranoid, being hassled in our own house, closing the curtains and locking the door to keep the press out. I was right pleased to get away. Rik was brilliant and really looked after us all week.'

The best thing of the week for all of them was the GMTV appearance. 'That was brilliant,' said Andy. 'They really looked after us. Audrey talked to Mr Motivator and I talked to the weather girl. They were all so nice.'

The BBC Lottery show was OK, but they were on only briefly and hardly allowed to say anything. On the whole, they'd enjoyed London, but wouldn't like to live there. 'The size is brilliant,' said Andy. 'You get all sorts down here, but the traffic, phew, I couldn't drive here. We saw the sights – Buckingham Palace, Trafalgar Square. I kept on pointing out to Audrey places I recognised from Monopoly, such as Mayfair. We even saw Prince Charles. We were in a taxi, leaving the Savoy, and he was going down the Strand in a big car. The taxi-driver pointed him out. We all saw him. It was brilliant. After we'd been on GMTV, we got recognised in the street quite a bit. "There's the Family of the Week," people kept on saying. Sometimes they'd just whisper, or look nervous, not quite knowing who we were, but knowing where they'd seen us, so I'd wave back, to let them know it was us. Some people came up and congratulated us. I enjoyed it, but I wouldn't like to be famous, with that sort of thing happening all the time.'

'I just want to get back to normal life,' said Audrey. 'The financial people are coming to see us in a couple of weeks. We just want to listen to all the advice, then think about it.'

They had been thinking about their £4 million at various points during the week. Going off to Disneyland, which they'd boasted about, might be a problem, as none of them had a passport or had ever been abroad.

Another slight worry was how they would be treated on their return. Would people be friendly, and let them get on with their normal life? Audrey wondered if they would get begging letters. 'We'll just not open them, pet,' said Andy. 'They'll just be full of lies, anyway, that's what Rik says.'

As for the more distant future, they had hardly thought about that. 'We might start a business, you never know,' said Andy, 'so that the kids can have something, do something with their lives when they grow up, instead of having nothing, as I've had. I hope when they grow up there will be work for people, that they won't have to struggle.'

Most mornings, lying in bed in their London hotel room, they had found themselves discussing what to give their respective families. 'What worries me is any of the relations coming back for more, later on,' said Andy. 'I just want to say, "Here you are, this is what you're getting", then let them get on with it. I don't want anyone moaning that we've still got so much.'

It was, of course, Audrey's money, won in her name. She smiled, and said she didn't think like that. 'I look upon it as our money, to help all our families.' Did it worry Andy that she might, in some argument in the future, claim it back? 'I hope not. She hasn't crowed about it so far.'

I then asked if they'd had any arguments or differences in the past. 'All couples do,' said Andy. What over? 'Money. That's what we've usually rowed over. Having no money means we can't go out and enjoy ourselves. That's the pressure you get, with having no job. It means you're stuck inside with each other, all day long. So we had arguments, but just over money, mind. Nothing else. It should be all right, now...'

They left, hand in hand, late on the Saturday night, going back in the coach to Hartlepool with their friends and relations after the BBC show. It was hard to estimate how their lives would change in the next year. They did appear genuinely nice, sensible, solid people. It seemed astonishing that someone so presentable as Andy should be on the dole without ever having had a proper job. Yet this is the nature of unemployment in the 1990s.

Camelot had been lucky with such an attractive couple, but various cynical thoughts did linger at the back of my mind. What exactly had Andy been doing in that van, looking for work in the south? Why had they never got married, when they seemed in some ways so old-fashioned in their values? With such big families, would there be rows to come with their numerous relations? And what will happen to their children, especially the lively extrovert Carl with his shaven head and ready wit, now that his mum is a multi-millionaire?

Audrey and Andy and their family were the first – and possibly the last – winners Camelot booked into the Savoy Hotel. It did seem an unsuitable choice. They were also the first and possibly the last winners to take their young children to their press conference, exposing them to the full media attention. Could that be a mistake, which might rebound when they got to school? But they all seemed happy and well adjusted enough as they set off towards Hartlepool and home.

'If I ever get a job,' said Andy to Rik when they said goodbye, 'I'd like your job, Rik.'

**5**

# BARRY, EAST LONDON

Money or health, which matters more to you in life? Health, most people would immediately respond. Yes, but if you already had poor health and not much money, wouldn't wealth help to make you healthier, or at least life a bit more bearable?

Barry, disabled from multiple sclerosis, became a millionaire when he won the Lottery in April 1995. A few months earlier he had finally been declared unfit for any more work, pensioned off and put out to graze.

He was thirty-seven, married with two young children, living in a modest terrace house out in the unfashionable flat lands of east London, a solid upper-working-class area, filled with families who have lived there for generations. Barry's street is perfectly neat and respectable, many houses with modern windows and Spanish-style double-glazed porches, but very narrow, which often leads to minor disputes between neighbours about parking. Families in work, these days, often have two or three cars per house, so it's not always possible to park your own car outside your own house. Which can be tough if you are handicapped, hobbling on two sticks.

Barry sits on a large couch, his sticks beside him, short fair hair, very hefty, very tough-looking, broad Cockney accent, not a person to mess with, despite his MS and the fact that he is only 5 feet 6 inches tall. His weight has shot up since the onset of his MS, restricting his activities. He is now 16 stone, much to his regret.

Hard to believe that when he left school just a few weeks before his sixteenth birthday, he was only 4 feet 10 inches tall and weighed just $7\frac{1}{2}$ stone. It did at least help him to get his first job – as a bellhop boy at the Mayfair Hotel on £10 a week. He stuck it only a week, until through family contacts – an uncle who worked at the Bank of England as a messenger – he was taken on at the Midland Bank as a boy assistant in their executive dining-room in the City, on £16 a week.

'I started there on 6 August 1973.' He has the date off pat, having filled in so many forms these last few years. It was a job for life, so everyone told him, working for the Midland Bank, and he was suitably proud and grateful. For the first four years he enjoyed it very much. 'I saw the other side of life, which I didn't know nothing about, fine wines and food, fancy décor, that sort of stuff. I'd never seen a silver plate before. No, I wasn't envious; I've never been that sort of person. I was very happy to have a good job.' Until he had words with his immediate superior on the dining-room staff. 'It was the time that the West India docks were closing and he was sounding off, blaming the dockers for being greedy, always striking. He turned to me and said, "Isn't that right, son?" I should have said, "Yes, Alf", and let it pass, but I said No. That didn't go down well. We didn't get on after that, so I put in for a move. I've never been good with this,' he says, pointing to his head. 'I'm not much good at reading or writing. I'm much better with these,' he says, pointing to his hands.

So he managed to get a move to the Midland Bank's bullion room, where for two years he humped bags of coins. It was this which first started to build up his strength and muscles. He helped his physique further when he became very interested in physical fitness and started body-building. He was then promoted to the security side, becoming a guard on Midland Bank vehicles taking money to the branches. 'In seven years doing that, I got mixed up in three raids. Once when I was on the pavement as a look-out, once in the vehicle and once when I was the bag-man. Oh, they got away with the money each time. You just drop the bags and let them have it. It's a natural reaction. Then there's no violence. The Midland was getting a lot of raids at the time, 'cos we were still carrying £100,000 bags. The other banks had reduced to £25,000 bags. So we got hit more often.'

In his spare time, he joined the Parachute Regiment as a volunteer – much more arduous than the Territorials, he says, and he spent three weekends out of four jumping out of planes, living rough in the wild. He first got married when he was twenty-seven, but it didn't last. He was doing endless shift work at the time, and his marriage suffered. He got remarried in 1990, to Chris, who was a cook in the City at the offices of an insurance firm. They have two children – Glen, aged five, and Karen, two. He bought his house nine years ago for £43,000, thanks to an advantageous staff loan from the Midland.

Until 1989, his health had always been perfect, so he believed, no complaints, no worries, and he lived a very active life. Apart from body-building and training with the Paras, he had taken up scuba-diving and skiing, having a skiing holiday with his friends every year.

But now, looking back, he does remember one strange incident when he was nineteen, which he had long forgotten. 'I suddenly lost the sight in my left eye for six weeks. Something had attacked the optic nerve. It cleared up just as suddenly, and no one said anything at the time. I just thought, "That's one belt, and I won't get hit again."'

But, in about 1989, his eye started to go funny again and he was sent for treatment to Moorfields Eye Hospital. At the same time, something mysterious went wrong with his leg. After endless medical inspections and tests, going from expert to expert, hospital to hospital, he was given three different tests, including a scan. These indicated he was in the first stages of MS. 'It didn't worry me too much. I was only just thirty, and felt fit enough, able to do most things I'd always done, so I shrugged it off. I don't dwell on things. I decided just to get on with life.'

Two years later he felt there was something wrong with his running. 'I was used to running ten miles with the Paras, no problems, run all day if I had to. I just put it down to getting older. Then my balance seemed to get poorer. It was just my legs which were suffering, the lower part of my body, not my upper half. Something seemed to be wrong with the messages. The docs eventually told me that the main problem was now in the lower part of my spine. When this sank in, I felt terrible. All of a sudden, all the things I'd dedicated my life to were out of the window. That's when I had to give up the Paras. And I realised I'd eventually have to give up work.'

In 1994 he went on sick leave, which lasted a year, remaining housebound, while he tried to work out what sort of future lay ahead for himself and the family. 'See that corner under the stairs? Used to be cupboards there. I took them out so's I could have a bed downstairs. We did the work, but then I thought, Sod it, I'm not moving my bed there. I refused. I'm a bugger really for refusing to accept things. I still manage, just, to get up those stairs every night to bed. In some ways it still hasn't sunk in. I still bend down to pick up things, thinking I'll be able to do it. I'm a stubborn bugger. I won't take any drugs, none at all. I sometimes wonder how my wife puts up with me!'

During that year at home on sick leave he devoted himself to the children, helping to look after them. 'I've put my life into my kids and the relationship with my wife. You have to work at that sort of thing, if you're going to be together twenty-four hours a day. She gives me a kick if I begin to feel depressed. I did go through one belt of depression. I worried about the kids. I've never been one to say No, and always had the money to say Yes. Now I was looking at little money, and no holidays ever again.'

He tries to do some work in the house, though all he can manage on two sticks is a bit of gentle dusting. That day he was babysitting Karen, an incredibly blonde little girl, who stood in a corner, watching. His wife had taken Glen to school. Barry was still managing to drive his car, an E registered Montego. 'I have some power in my legs, though I clunk the gears a bit. I want to keep driving as long as possible. When you sit in a car, you look and feel normal. Nobody knows the truth. My main worry was my wife. How was she going to cope with an invalid husband and two young kids, on a greatly reduced income?'

When he was finally paid off, his pension was worked out at a third of his salary. 'It comes to £11,000 a year.' So your pay must have been £33,000? Sounds a lot for a security guard. 'Oh, it was, but you should have seen the overtime I put in. About £7,000 of my annual pay was overtime and shift work. And I had worked for the Midland for twenty-two years. They looked after me very well. I've had lots of help from them. The funny thing is, the department I worked with has just closed. I wouldn't have had a job for life after all, not in that department. Who would have thought twenty years ago that something like the Midland Bank, or any bank, would be laying off staff. You never can tell . . .'

Barry did the Lottery from the beginning, spending £5 a week on tickets. He picked his first five lines at random, then stuck to them, keeping his old ticket so he would know which they were. He has also done the football pools for many years, investing £2.40 a week. Twice a year he went to the dog races at the nearby track, Walthamstow, mainly as an outing for the kids. He doesn't consider himself a gambler.

The last week in April was a roll-over week, so it was known the jackpot would be big – not that Barry was taking much notice as he never watches the Lottery draw. 'I don't watch a lot of television anyway, and I hate game shows. I prefer films, if I'm watching anything. Chris had the telly on that evening, watching Cilla Black's *Blind Date*. That's my idea of yuck!'

On 29 April Barry was out in his back garden. It's sixty feet long, a surprising length for a little terrace house. He was shooing his children's two pet rabbits into their hutch after they'd had a little run in the garden. It was proving quite difficult for him, hobbling around. He was using one of his walking-sticks, plus an old pole for support. The children had already gone inside. Karen was in bed, and Glen was watching *Blind Date* with his mum.

'Chris had switched to watch the numbers being drawn, and I could hear her shouting from inside the house. "You've got one, Barry, you've got two, Barry, you've got three ... Oh my God, you've got four..." Then she came out into the garden, looking like a gibbering wreck. "Can you check these, Barry? I think you've got all six!" I thought she was just getting me going, but she said No, look, I've written them down. She'd taken them down as they appeared, so they weren't in the right order. When I put them in the right order, I could see they were the same as mine. I started to shake, so I said to her, "Hold on, let me get in and sit down."

'When I sat down, my first thought was she'd copied them down wrong from the telly. We rang her mum and dad, knowing they would have written them down – and we had them right! I checked it on Teletext, and then phoned all the family, to tell them the good news.

'I rang Camelot, and they took down my details, saying

they thought several people had got the jackpot, but they couldn't confirm anything yet. They rang back in an hour to confirm I had a winning ticket and that an adviser would be coming to see me next morning. Chris went out that night with her family, but I stayed at home with the kids. I'd given up going out. I find it physically too hard to go to places like pubs. I never drink beer, anyway. Never liked the taste. A whisky, that's about the only thing I enjoy.

'Then we discovered on the Teletext that the jackpot stood at £18.9 million ... I must be one of the few people who knows what eighteen million pounds looks like. Oh, I've seen that, and more. I knew how big a million pounds is to carry. I also know what that sort of sum can do to you. It was the scariest moment in my life, really it was. Scary. And I've done most of the scary sports you can think of. Jumping out of aeroplanes, that sort of thing. I was really, really scared. I honestly didn't want to win that sort of money.

'That day I'd been reading something about Lady Di and her money settlement if she got divorced, and it said she would only end up with £6 million. There was me, Joe Muggins, going from nothing at all to that sort of status. It was unbelievable. I'd only been on the pension a month, dead worried how I was going to cope from now on. I hoped I wouldn't be the only winner. I worked out that at most there might be seven jackpot-winners, as they'd never had more than that. I told Chris when she got back that we'd probably be looking at £3 million. I didn't sleep well that night. In fact I don't think I slept for three nights ...'

In the event there were fourteen jackpot-winners, the second highest number so far. Not counting the freak week with 133 winners, the average number of people sharing the jackpot in the first twenty-three weeks had been between two and three. Fourteen winners brought Barry's slice right down. Each got £1,355,975. Was he disappointed?

'Not at all; I'm very happy. It's more than enough to allow us to do everything we want to do. I'm pleased there are so many winners spread around the country. It takes the pressure off us. If I'd won the £18 million on my own, life would have been unbearable, what with me being a good sob-story and that.'

When the Winners' Adviser came next morning, it was she who used the phrase 'good sob-story', explaining that the tabloids would love it. 'She said they'd probably soon hear, as we live in London. But she also said that, because of the fourteen winners, she didn't expect huge publicity. It could be done on a small scale. But it was up to us. We should have a think. Chris wasn't keen on publicity, and didn't want to be involved or let the kids be involved. I decided to do it, if it could be done fairly quietly. I was pretty worked up, like a champagne bottle that had been shaken, but not yet popped. That was me. In the end we decided just to have a photo-call, not a proper press conference. It was going to be on the Tuesday, but Camelot were announcing their new scratch cards that day, so it was organised for the Wednesday. We were told to speak to nobody from the press till then.

'On Monday we had to go to their Trafalgar Square offices to do the validating, but just as I was leaving the front door at five past nine, the phone rang. I thought it might be some press tracking us down, and nearly didn't answer it, but it was the Social Services. Eighteen months ago, at that time when I definitely knew I had MS and was going to be housebound, I'd applied for a special stair-rail and various bits of tackle for the bathroom. They were now ringing to say they were coming round that week to install it. I said, don't bother, mate. I won't be staying here long. I've won the Lottery...'

Barry's photo-call was held at Walthamstow dog track. About twenty photographers turned up, plus local television. He did his bit, going outside among the spring flowers and dutifully shook his champagne bottle. 'It wasn't as bad as I'd feared. The day was fine, with fluffy clouds, and of course it is a nice setting. I felt quite relaxed and quite enjoyed it. I didn't regret it, but that evening, after all the excitement, I felt pooped. I didn't want to do any more. Next day Camelot rang and said *The Big Breakfast* show wanted me, but when I heard the time I had to be there, I said, No thanks. I haven't done anything else since then. I want to get back to normality as soon as possible, and get the kids back to ordinary life.

'We're going to have a holiday in a week or so. I've hired a villa in Menorca. I don't want to go anywhere too popular or busy. I think the publicity has faded already; at least I hope so. People's memories don't last more than two weeks. I was recognised by a stranger when I went into Sainsbury's last week, but not this week. People in the street know, and have congratulated me. There's been no malice or envy, but that's because of my condition.

'I'm still waiting for my disabled parking bay to come through, so I can always park outside my own house. I've waited a long time for that as well, but I bet it'll come too late. Oh yes, we'll be moving. Chris doesn't want to move too far, about ten miles away, say, in Essex, so we'll still keep in touch with all the family, but I'd like to go a bit further out. I've explained it all to Glen. He's gone back to school today. I've told him we'll be moving, and he'll be going to a new school. I believe in always explaining everything to kids. He says he's looking forward to it.

'I'm not going to use Camelot's panel people, the ones who advise you about the money. I've rung the man who was in charge of personnel in my department at the Midland Bank. I'm gonna use their advisers. I might get a better deal, being ex-staff. I've paid it all into my local Midland Bank branch. They're working on a portfolio for me. We are going to help all our family, but we haven't decided how much yet. No, I'm not going to donate to any charities. I'm not even a member of the MS Society – I've never been interested. I have had one professor on the phone, from some medical school, asking me to donate to some research thing, but if I started giving to him, where would it stop? I haven't got enough to give money away. If I had won £18 million, then of course I would. The professor heard about my win because our photo was on the front page of *Disability Now* – a paper I'd never heard of.'

Barry insisted on hobbling to a cupboard to get a copy, along with some other newspapers, mainly local, such as the *Walthamstow Guardian*. In one of them he was quoted as saying he was going to take his family to Disneyland in Florida and buy himself a Mercedes, because 'that's my dream'.

Outside his front door, his old car was still there, even though he had had several weeks of wealth. 'My Montego is bashed to buggery, but I don't think I'll buy a Mercedes, not at the moment. But it still is my dream. Can you understand that? Because I now can buy it, there's no reason to buy it. I'd like to keep it as a dream. Can you follow that? People use their cars as status symbols, don't they? Well, I don't need that now. I know I can buy one any time, so I don't have to.

'Yes, I was asked if I'd rather have my health than the money. The answer's obvious, isn't it? Anyone would want their health. I've also been asked if I think the money will change my life – and that's a really stupid question! Of course it will. A month ago I was looking at a life of drudgery. All Chris had to look forward to was looking after an invalid husband. The kids had to look forward to a home with very little money. Our lifestyle is not going to be that now. There will be no drudgery from now on . . .'

## THE FIRST WINNERS' ADVISERS

The National Lottery, as a new phenomenon, created a new activity and also created some new professions, most notably that of Winners' Advisers. They are the first people from the National Lottery to arrive at the home of a big winner, to explain what will happen, what might happen, perhaps calm them down, answer their queries, listen to their worries, then advise them on what to do next.

It's not a job, as yet, which has a career structure, as no one has done such work as a full-time occupation in the UK before, so Camelot had to decide what sort of people would be the most suitable temperamentally, and what sort of previous employment might best equip them for this new job.

Camelot chose two people – Alasdair Buchan and Rik Dalglish – to organise this work, giving them a contract for the first six months. Both are in their forties, i.e. of an age which conveys experience of life, and both are Scottish, i.e. with accents, and a persona which rarely gives offence. Combined with smart clothes and a plausible manner, such people usually find it easy to deal with people from all regions and all classes.

Perhaps more important was their background. Each is an ex-journalist with many years of experience, mostly on popular newspapers. This was possibly their most vital attribute.

Tabloid journalists know very well how other tabloid journalists will react. One of the biggest problems for all the major winners in the first few months was handling the *Sun* and the *Star*. Good tabloid journalists are also experienced at walking into the lives of unknown strangers, making contact, making friends, but at the same time, like policemen, they are very quick to observe things which don't quite make sense, things which are possibly being hidden and might come out later leading to complications or embarrassment.

Alasdair, the senior man, went to Strathclyde University and comes from a political family: his mother, Janey Buchan, was MEP for Glasgow and his father Norman was a Labour government minister. After twenty years in Fleet Street, Alasdair left full-time journalism about five years ago and set up a PR company with his friend and fellow journalist, Rik. They applied to Camelot, before Camelot had won the franchise, offering to do their PR. In his application, Alasdair added that at one time, when he was on the *Daily Express*, he had been the minder who looked after that paper's million-pound competition-winners. It was this experience, he thinks, that helped to secure them the job. For the first six months of the Lottery, he and Rik divided the jackpot-winners between them – which meant they had handled about twenty millionaires each.

'Not one of mine so far has lived in a high-rise block,' said Alasdair. 'On the other hand, not one of them is professional middle class. The majority were living in council houses, many of them out of work. Only about three would you put into the middle class, because they were running their own small business. I've found these the hardest to deal with. Some of them tend to be more self-centred and try to triple-think every question, displaying all their own insecurities, making things far too complicated. The working class don't feel the need to play fantasy chess games with the future, but take each step as it comes. About 80 per cent of them decided on no publicity – far more than happens abroad. I think it's to do with British folk culture and the history of the football pools. You don't have to have ever filled in a football coupon to know you put X for No publicity. So that was most people's immediate reaction. The other folk perception is that journalists are barracudas, so I never reveal my background until a friendship has been established.'

Alasdair or Rik normally arrive at the winner's home around Sunday lunchtime, having got up early and driven for four hours. 'We couldn't do it on the Saturday evening, after the draw, as we'd arrive in the middle of the night,' Alasdair said.

'Early on, I did liaise with the winners' hot line. I made a few calls to claimants, to get the feel of it. It's not usually known until about eleven which outlet the winning ticket was sold at, so, till then, they have to listen to everyone who thinks they have won and take down all the details. Some people are just totally mistaken – getting their numbers wrong. Some are mad – mentally ill – but genuinely think they have won. Some are liars. God knows why they are doing it. I wrote the original script for the telephone people to take all the calls through a series of questions and assess the callers. Once the retail outlet is known, it is always clear who actually has won, so we ring the winner back and arrange to call the next day, telling them to do nothing, tell no other people, till we arrive.

'Often I arrive to find up to eight adults all sitting waiting, plus up to a dozen kids. It's always a very crowded sitting-room – and pretty tense. My nerves are usually jangling, anyway, having driven four hours, and probably got lost, trying to find their house. The first thing I usually say is, Can I take my jacket off? Their first thing is to offer a cup of tea.

'It's vital to take your time, go very slowly and repeat everything several times. They are looking for something solid to stick in the middle of their minds, which have overnight turned to jelly. You must appear to be in control, let them see you know what you're doing, give them confidence that you are confident. If you can't answer certain questions, you say you'll soon find out a specialist who can. Twenty years of working in Fleet Street does give you general counselling skills. Almost everyone has said afterwards it was a pleasurable experience, that Rik and I did help. But I suppose the big thing is to know if they'll still say that in five years' time.

'The first real question I tackle is how they get the money. They are always surprised when I say "Tomorrow", thinking it will probably take weeks, as if we have a little van going round all the shops picking up the pounds before they can be paid. I explain they can take their ticket to Camelot's local regional office on Monday and have it validated, then they'll get the money at once. They usually want me to see their ticket. I say that's not my job, that's technical, using the computer, but I look at it, out of politeness. We know by then that they have won, because they are the only people who have bought the right ticket at the right outlet.

'I explain my main job is to be available for them during the next week, to help in any way with advice. When we come to the subject of publicity, I make it clear I have no view on this. It is up to them. I just point out the pros and cons. I go over the chances of keeping their win secret, whether they want to or not. I ask how many friends and families they have told already – which is usually lots – and of course they say, Oh no, our friends and family won't leak it. They don't like it when you explain that in that case it probably will come out somehow. The *Sun* and the *Mirror*, after all, were at one time offering £10,000 for such information.

'A few Asian families have won, and they were always adamant that "their community, their people" would certainly not go to the press. If enough family and friends know, I always warn that the chances of keeping it completely secret, not just out of the press, is almost non-existent. To their credit, with Asian families, it does take longer to leak out – two days as opposed to two hours.

'I use the same phrase – that it's like a pebble causing ripples in a pool. If they tell lots of people, then they've dropped a bloody huge rock in the pool and the ripples will be enormous. I also explain that people gossip about their win not necessarily for envious or nasty reasons but because they are happy and excited for you. I try to establish some foundations in their mind, before it has leaked out, to prepare them, so they won't feel hurt and blame their community for letting them down.

'I tell them to ask me any other questions in their mind, however stupid they might seem. That's when they usually ask, "How do we bank the cheque?" They have realised by then that taking a cheque for £5 million to their local branch is going to have the cashier shrieking – and it will be round the town in minutes. I ask where they bank, and explain that we can arrange for it to be paid into the head office, not their local branch, so no one locally will know. If they haven't a bank, we suggest they leave it with the Royal Bank of Scotland, which is Camelot's bank, who will open a secret account for them, or at another bank, if they want.

'My first visit usually lasts two hours. Then I leave them to it, giving them a little handbook we've prepared, "Out of the Blue – It's You!" They don't read it, but they feel that by holding it they have established some sort of bond. I hope by then I have appeared an avuncular figure, the only one in the room who is not all screwed up and shaking. I check into a local hotel, leaving them to talk among themselves, then I return about five or six in the evening. I usually have to go over all the same points again, as they still can't take things in.

'That's when certain problems start to come out. They'll

have been thinking of what to give each member of their family, and probably discussed it with me already. Perhaps £50,000 to each of their children, if they've won, say, a million. The biggest family gifts I've dealt with were a couple who won £6 million, and immediately gave £500,000 to each of their two brothers, and to her mother and his father, which meant they gave away £2 million at once. But more often it drags on and gets complicated. It often happens that one of their family, say a grown-up child, is about to get divorced, or has been left by their partner, which they haven't mentioned earlier on. They don't want that person getting their hands on any money. So we discuss how that can be done, how it must be

*'Out of the Blue' – Camelot's guide for winners*

put in the daughter's name. I tell them not to go around promising money to their family until they've thought it all out, but of course that's usually too late. They've been promising people money from the beginning. I do explain that it's not my job to advise on handling the money, usually by telling them that if I was an expert in handling money I wouldn't be skelping up and down the motorways in the snow and rain every Sunday morning; I'd be off on my yacht. But, of course, they still want to talk about things like that, so I let them.

'My second visit usually lasts no more than an hour, then I'll go back to my hotel and have dinner. Next day I take them for validation, and stay by them until there is a press conference, or as long as they want me to.

'As a generalisation, the more the money, the more swings of mood there are. Winners can burst into tears, when the press doorsteps them or some member of the family has let them down. If I'm there, still in the house, I always go to the door and deal with strangers or the press. In many ways, it is similar to a sudden death in the family. Everything has been immediately changed. There's sudden confusion and emotional panic, the normal constraints in life have gone, they don't know what to do next, what the future will hold, how to behave, where to go. Bereavement is actually easier. It really can be, in that there are basic steps to go through, with the funeral and the forms. Winning a big amount is a total shock to the system.

'The behaviour of the big winners in the first week is fairly standard: the same symptoms and reactions. They won't be able to sleep, they'll pick at their food. They won't remember what I told them, so I'll have to say everything again, every day. Their mind has gone numb and they can't retrieve their memory. Then there is usually some form of guilt. "I didn't really want to win this much ... I would have been happy with much less ... Why did it happen to me?" It's understandable. Most people buy lottery tickets for the fun of it, never thinking beyond winning £10, or £1,000 at the most. Then the complications happen, and they realise their life will change for ever.'

If it happened to you, Alasdair, knowing what you know, having observed what you have seen, would you go public or not? 'Oh, I would. With luck and some organisation, you can control the publicity. That's where we help. Otherwise it will leak out and you will have no control. But the main reason I would go public is to avoid the pressure of living a false life.

'We keep in touch with those who have decided not to go public, and their problems can be far worse. One of the big winners was in a mountain rescue team in a remote area. He loved doing it, and his dad had done it before him. But he gave it up because he was scared that, if people found out, there would be tensions and jealousies in the team. You can't have tensions when rescuing people, and it could be his fault. He perceived it would come out, so he moved right away from the area. It meant that his wife had to give up her job as well, which was sad. She'd just been promoted, and was about to do something new and exciting, which she was longing to do.

'The neighbours of another secret winner still haven't found out, nor have any of his relations. So he's done well, keeping it secret – but mentally he's in a terrible state. He's scared to buy a new car, or people will ask questions. He thinks people are following him. He suspects all strangers. He can't sleep for ghastly and ghoulish dreams. He rang me just the other day, and said he knew I'd been calling him – which I hadn't. His life has been turned upside down. He's gained nothing, except money in the bank. There was a younger bloke, who won early on, who didn't tell anyone. He was in a club when suddenly a reporter and photographer came up to him and said, "Can we interview you?" He nearly had a heart attack. They were from the local paper, doing a survey on what fashions people wear in nightclubs. It was a false alarm, but that's how he leads his life now, always worried that people will find out.

'The ones I know who have come out have not regretted it. Ken Southwell in York did everything he was asked, and became well known, so that people ask him to do things, such as test-drive cars, which he loves. I'd say he's enjoyed the whole experience, up to now.

'So if it happened to me, I'd come out, lie back and enjoy it for that week, then try to get back to normal life.'

# 7

## STEVE AND HELEN, LANCASHIRE

After I had made that first brief visit to Steve and Helen in rural Lancashire, I wondered all the time if they had managed to stick to their aim of telling no one, neither their own children nor family and friends, that they had won £2.8 million. How could they possibly carry it off? So I went back just two weeks later, ostensibly to hear their life story, but also to find if their secret was still intact.

Steve's mother was again upstairs in her room, the telly blaring away, and still unaware, said Steve, that her son had become a millionaire. What about his father? He hadn't been mentioned on my last visit. That was a longer story. Steve's father was Scottish, born and bred in Motherwell. He had moved about fifteen years earlier to rural Lancashire with his family, looking for work, having been paid off from the local steel works. He never did find a new job, then he fell ill and died, probably a result of his steel-working days. His widow, Steve's mother, has not been in good health since. Smoking thirty cigarettes a day has not helped.

When Steve was aged twelve, his Scottish accent long gone, and in theory attending the local comprehensive, he started work part-time on local farms, at evenings and weekends, then during the day during the harvest season, bunking off school. His education was therefore rather limited, but at sixteen he none the less got into a local college to do a two-year City and Guilds course in livestock. 'I got a prize one week, for being the best livestock student. It was a book. I don't know where it is now.'

He left at eighteen and has worked on farms ever since; sometimes driving tractors, ploughing, ditching or fencing. Sometimes looking after cattle and sheep. A lot of it has been seasonal work, but he has been rarely unemployed, being hard-working and cheerful, willing to have a go at most agricultural jobs. At the time of his Lottery win his job was collecting bulls' semen. 'You get the bull to jump up on another bull which is normally standing in a hole. As one bull mounts the other, you put its penis into an artificial vagina and collect the sperm in a test-tube. It goes to the labs to be diluted, and then gets packed and sent all over the country. All over the world, I'm told, 'cos it's good stuff.' For this he was getting £3.57 an hour, working three days a week. 'You don't go into farming to make money. But I've always enjoyed working with livestock.'

Helen, his wife, was born and brought up locally. They knew each other vaguely at school, but she was in the year above – being eight months older – and they had no contact. He was hardly at school anyway, and her school career was also rather curtailed.

'We're both thick, really,' said Steve.

'Speak for yourself!' said Helen.

She wanted to be a nurse, when she was at school, and did some biology, which she liked, but they wouldn't let her do chemistry, which was needed for a nursing course. Her main problem at school was fighting, for which she was expelled when she was sixteen. She then left home, going to live with an aunt in a nearby town, working on a stall in the market. Then she did some picking on a mushroom farm before deciding to go back home. Like Steve, she has four brothers and sisters, mostly out of work.

At nineteen, Steve got married to a woman fifteen years older, by which time she was pregnant with Lee-zette, who is now nine. At the age of twenty-one, Steve was a widower. His wife died in a car crash, aged thirty-six. 'We'd been living apart and getting divorced by then, anyway.'

Steve kept his daughter, whom he had been looking after, and in June 1989 he married Helen. She'd got to know him again through his mother, whom she met when she was doing a part-time job in a bingo club.

'When I was younger, I'd been a bit of a bad lad. No angel, you might say, especially where women were concerned. We were just friends first of all, then it sort of developed – and we've been happy ever since. Our wedding was a grand affair, and cost me £3,000. I saved up for it, and I got a loan. I've always been a good saver. If I want something, I save up for it. I've got good credit. I borrowed £5,000 for the car, which I'm still paying off. The wedding was in a church, the full thing, though I'm not religious. I don't believe in it. You might find out there is something else when you die, like, but I don't intend to find that out for some time. I paid for it all 'cos Helen's dad couldn't, could he? The photos cost £500 and the wedding dress £1,500.'

It seems an enormous price for a dress, living on a small wage as an agricultural labourer, but presumably it's been used since?

'No, I haven't got it no more,' said Helen. 'I lent it to a girlfriend for her wedding. When they got divorced, her husband tore it up in a temper.'

They booked a week's honeymoon in Blackpool, but after just two days on their own, they came back to pick up Lee-zette from Steve's mother, who was looking after her, and took her back on their honeymoon. 'We just missed her so much.

I've always loved kids. We've brought them all up as our own. They don't know any different.'

Helen was also working at the time of the Lottery win. She had decided in January that though she loved their three children, she was fed up with being stuck at home all day, so she got a job in an old folks' home, working three nights a week, caring for people with Alzheimer's, for £20 a night. 'I was getting an NVQ. No, I'm not sure what it means. Nursing something.'

Steve had been unemployed at the time Helen started work, as it was winter, with no farm work on offer, and was a bit alarmed, and confused, to find that they would lose money by Helen's getting a job. 'All the bills were being paid by the council – the rent, the council tax, school meals, everything, and we were getting lots of benefits 'cos we were unemployed and with three children. I wanted to work, always have done, but that's the way it happened. But Helen's getting a job meant we lost all our allowances, and were worse off. I had to find a job quickly, to make it up, which is why I got into bulls' semen. Yet we were still getting less than when not working. I don't understand it. Don't ask me how it works.'

At the time of their Lottery win, they had had a very exhausting five months, each working at their respective jobs. Helen was doing a twelve-hour night shift at the home, from nine till eight in the morning three days a week, going straight to bed when she got home. Sometimes it clashed with Steve's work, with him going out as she got home, so she then had to stay up and look after the kids till he got home, and then go to bed.

They have done the Lottery from the beginning, spending £5 a week, always sitting up as a family on Saturday evenings to watch the results. Five times they had won £10, but nothing more. The thought of winning big money had never crossed their minds. Never? 'It was just a game, an amusement, which the kids enjoyed watching,' said Steve. 'Lee-zette did once say that if she won, she wanted to buy a car. I told her she couldn't drive, so what was the point of that? She said she'd keep it till she was grown up, and then drive it.

'I'd never thought of what I'd do, personally. I don't have those fantasies. I'm very philosophical. If the bills are paid and the family's got enough food, I'm content. We're not great goers-out and we don't drink. I've got a crate of lager in the kitchen left over from Christmas. Have a drink now if you want. Me, I'd rather have a cup of tea.

'The family matters most to us. We're sort of turned in, I suppose. I never let the kids play out on the street. They play in the garden, that's why all that stuff is there. That motorbike is real. I got it for them for £60. They can all ride it. I can as well, despite my weight. They're not allowed to swear, and we don't swear either. The most important thing is telling the truth. If they do something wrong, break something, like, then they might get disciplined – that means a smack, no telly or straight to bed. But if they tell the truth at once, they never get punished. Just told off, told not to do it again. As a kid I got hit all the time, for anything, and I don't believe in that. Only if they tell lies. That's how we've brought them all up. I suppose it's old-fashioned, if you like.'

On 13 May 1995, the day of their Lottery win, it happened to be a day when neither had to go to work, so they had packed all the kids into Steve's 22-year-old Dormobile, used for a myriad of agricultural purposes, but still going strong, and went off for a day out. Helen packed a picnic – crisps, sweets, egg sandwiches and meat pies. Steve is a great meat-eater. He prefers that above any other sort of food. 'I hate greens, never touch them. Spinach or cabbage or lettuce, yuk! The only vegetable I'll touch is carrots. I knows greens is good for you, so we make sure the kids get some, but me, I never touch them.'

They went to visit a famous church, whose name now escapes them, and then a stately home, once used as a location in a TV drama. The weather was good and they had their picnic in the open air. They'd set off at midday, and didn't get back till 8.30, by which time the younger children were fast asleep in the Dormobile. All the kids went straight to bed when they got home.

Steve and Helen sat watching Sky TV, which they have on full time, except for the Lottery programme on BBC, but that night they had missed it. Later on, Sky did give out the winning numbers. 'I think I've got four of them numbers,' he announced, getting up to look for his ticket. Each week he chose four of his five lines at random, and usually forgot them. One line, his winning line, was based roughly on the family's birthdays. 'No, I've got them all,' he said when he came back with his ticket. His winning numbers were 7, 16, 25, 26, 28 and 41. He'd chosen 25 by mistake. They haven't got a birthday on the 25th, but one on the 24th, which he'd meant to pick, but got it wrong.

'Liar,' said Helen.

'No, I have got them all. Here, have a look.'

Helen, according to Steve, was pretty shocked, but he didn't feel anything at all, so he says. 'I always stay calm. I'm not a person who goes about shouting and screaming.'

They rang Camelot as directed on the ticket, but were confused, as so many have been, by the automated instructions. 'We had to ring three times before we understood it. Then eventually we spoke to someone who said they would ring us back later. That was when the Winners' Adviser rang, congratulating us, and saying he'd come and visit us in the morning.'

Did you celebrate on Saturday evening? 'Not really, apart from having a bacon sandwich.'

But they did discuss what might happen to their children

if it came out they had won all that money. They decided they would keep it quiet, for fear of one of them being kidnapped. Then they went to bed at their normal time, about 11.30.

'I slept fine,' said Steve, 'but a certain person tossed and turned and kept me awake . . .'

'I got up in the end and made myself a cup of tea,' said Helen.

'Did yer?' said Steve. 'Never heard nothing. So I must have slept after all.'

They were all awake at 6.30, when the first child got up and started charging around. Steve's mother slept in as usual, staying all morning in her room.

'We still haven't told her. It would be like telling the press. She'd tell everyone.'

When the Winners' Adviser left, he gave them a copy of Camelot's brochure, 'Out of the Blue – It's You!' The first line in the booklet reads: 'Congratulations on becoming a Big Winner in the National Lottery – you're probably still wondering when your feet are going to touch the ground again!'

Steve's mother might not be very observant or a great reader, but even a cursory look at this booklet, with its full colour and screaming headlines, might, well, give her a little clue as to what had happened?

'She won't see it,' said Steve, ''cos we've hidden it.' He led me to a metal cabinet in his bedroom. 'It's approved for use in Northern Ireland,' he said, tapping it. Yes, but what is it? 'My gun cabinet. I've got two shotguns inside. I've used them on farms when I've had to shoot rabbits, clear vermin, that sort of thing. It's got hidden hinges, an anti-pick lock and it's bolted to the main wall. No one can get inside it. That's where I've put the Lottery booklet . . .'

On Monday they were driven by the Winners' Adviser to Camelot's regional office in Liverpool, going in by a side door, part of the strategy to keep their identity secret. Steve had to produce some form of identity, and had taken with him both his driving licence and his shotgun licence. He was photographed twice, front and side view, and told that the photo would never be published or released. It was purely for security reasons, just in case anyone at any time might try to impersonate Steve. Then he was presented with the cheque for £2.8 million. On hand was an official from the Royal Bank of Scotland, who then took back the cheque, as Steve had elected not to have it paid into his own bank. He was offered a photocopy of it to keep as a souvenir. Most winners, public and private, are delighted to receive it. Public winners have it framed for their living-room; secret winners hide it away, secretly.

'I said No, thanks. Why would I want a copy of the cheque? I'd seen it, paid it in, so that was it. Seemed pointless to me, wanting a copy. Daft, I call it.'

Before he left Camelot's office, two of their officials made the same remark to both Steve and Helen: 'This must be the best thing that's ever happened to you ...' Again, Steve declined to go along with their presumptions.

'The best thing that's happened to me in life is him,' he said, giving a gentle kick to Darren, the sleeping baby lying on the floor at his feet. 'I delivered him. He was supposed to have only one kidney, that's what the scan had shown. Earlier on, they'd seen no kidneys at all, then they found the one. We'd been told, the minute he was born, he'd have to go straight into an incubator, 'cos of only one kidney. Right? About a week before he was due, at 3.15 in the morning, Helen shouts from the toilet that her waters have broke. She can feel the head coming out. So I gets her in the living-room, and I delivered the baby, right here. I cut the cord meself. And the baby turned out champion. Both kidneys intact. So much for their scan! And he was a ten-pounder, just like the rest. All mine are big 'uns ...'

Helen's best moment in her life so far was marrying Steve. She couldn't possibly see winning £2.8 million comparing with that.

'I wouldn't say we've always been happy,' Steve explained. 'The kids have had a few little problems. Lee-zette was born with a hole in the heart, but turned out OK. Glen's a bit deaf in one ear. Darren's now got something wrong with a tear-duct which will have to be seen to. Apart from them little things, they've all been fine. Losing one of them, that would be the worst thing in our life. No money could ever make up for that.'

There was a knock on the front door. Special postal delivery. A letter for each of them from the Royal Bank of Scotland. Inside each was a gold credit card. Steve smiled as he held his up. 'I've always had a credit card, but this looks a good 'un.'

In the two weeks or so since they'd received the cheque, they had spent only £500 – paying off some outstanding debts and having a day out, taking all the children to the seaside. Just the sorts of things they would normally do if they happened to be in funds. They have bought no luxuries, no special items, or acted in any way that might suggest to outsiders – or even insiders such as Steve's mother – that something unusual had happened.

'We've made no decisions yet about the money,' said Steve. 'We're waiting for the panel, the experts from Camelot, to hear their advice. The Winners' Adviser told us that if it's all invested in something simple, we will have an income of £3,000 a week after tax. The most I've earned in my life has been £200 a week, and that's been at harvest time, working seven days a week. The money's in three bank accounts at the moment – £100,000 we can draw on instantly, and then £2.7 million split between two longer-term accounts.

'I've been back to work for a couple of days. They were

stuck, and I didn't want to let them down. Now I've given in me notice; I said I was going to a new job. Helen also went back to work, then gave in her notice, saying that we're moving. I was quite sad to give up my job; I fair enjoyed it. Perhaps I'll go back to work some day.

'So far, we haven't really told any lies, not really. Just not told the full truth. I have this mate at work, and when he heard we were moving, he says to me, "You must have won the Lottery." I said Yes, smiling, like. He said £57 probably. I said, You're not far off wrong. I've seen him several days this week in the street, and he still makes the same joke, that I haven't got a better job, that I must have won something. He doesn't believe it, of course. It's just his joke. He doesn't want us to move, 'cos I'm the one who helps mend his car . . .'

It is true that they will soon be moving, and they have been considering either Scotland or the Lake District, one or the other, they're still thinking. They fancy a large house out in the country. At present they have three bedrooms – one for them, one for Steve's mum and one for the three children. To have enough for all, when they grow up, they think they'll need a six-bedroom house.

It is also true, in a sense, that Steve has something new to go to, which is what they've told friends and people at work. In his life so far, as an agricultural labourer, he has moved around from time to time, from job to job, so there will be nothing unusual in another move. 'I've told people I've been offered two jobs, and I'm deciding which one to take.'

Will he have lots of land in his new place, so that he can run his own farm at last? 'I don't think so. Farming's a very responsible job. Lots of worries. I think a couple of acres at first will be enough. Enough to have a pony for the kids, perhaps a few pigs for myself, as an amusement. We'd rear them, get them slaughtered, then put them in our deep-freeze. I like the idea of that: eating our own pigs. I don't plan to work any more, except for odd jobs around the new place, doing things for myself and that. Oh, I'll soon find things to occupy my time. But the best thing will be seeing the kids all the time, watch them growing up, like.'

They've made one trip to Kendal so far, to look in at an estate agent, but decided nothing. 'It was funny the reactions. When I said we were looking at something about £100,000, they were a bit off-hand, not interested, like. Perhaps the look of us made them treat us that way. Then when I said we might go a bit higher, up to £500,000, say, they couldn't do enough for us. Their attitude suddenly changed.'

Scotland is Helen's idea, not Steve's, despite having been born there. She hasn't ever been there, only seen it on TV, but she thinks it looks very pretty. They hope to have found something, somewhere, within a month.

They have no qualms about moving to a different part of the country. They feel no special connections with their present town. 'The kids want to move as well. Lee-zette's best friend at her school has just moved away, so she's keen. It's a good time for her to move, anyway, before she starts second-ary school. I want them all to go to private schools now. I don't expect our life will really change, but their life will. They'll have a chance of becoming doctors and lawyers. You need to go to private schools for that sort of thing.'

'But I don't want them to go away to school, to boarding school,' said Helen. 'I'd miss them too much.'

'It all depends where we end up,' said Steve. 'There might not be a good private day school near by, so we'll have to see. Perhaps five days a week at school, then they would come home weekends. We'll have to see.'

What about your mum, Steve? What will happen to her? 'That's up to her,' he said flatly, seemingly bored with the subject. 'We've told her I'm moving to another farm in about a month probably, and left it up to her whether she wants to come or not. She can stay here, no problem, if she wants. She's said nowt so far. It's her option. We're not pushing her.'

But if she comes, she'll find you've moved to a luxury six-bedroom mansion with at least two acres. Won't she make some sort of comment? 'We'll cross that bridge when we come to it.' Yes, but she'll want to know where you've got the money from. 'I'll think of something. I might say I've inherited something . . .' But she's your mum. She must know your relations? 'OK, I'll say Helen's inherited it. Some old woman she was looking after has left her a house. Or something. As I said, we'll face that when it happens. Same with the kids. We don't plan to tell them either, unless we have to.' If your mum does decide to stay here, on her own, then presumably you'll never tell her? 'Probably not. I don't expect we'll have much contact. She won't write or ring us, probably, if she doesn't come with us. So she might never know.'

Do you or don't you want her to come with you? 'Really, I'm not bothered. She's me mum all right, but all our family, on both sides, have always leaned on us, taken advantage, like. We're looked upon as the soft ones, the only ones who can ever manage any money. The rest can't do owt. We're always the ones bailing them out, paying their debts. We paid all me dad's arrears on this house when he was alive. And then me mum's. It's her house, in her name as the tenant, but she was being chucked out for her debts, so we moved back in to help her, which we have done. So she can stay here OK, now we've got her straight. They don't deserve anything, our family. They can't manage anything. They've never helped us. Why should we help them now?'

Surely one of them will be bound to find out eventually, even if you do move a long way away and lose contact? 'And they'll be right furious! If they knew now, they'd be all over us, our best friends, saying they'd done this and that for us. They'd be sticking themselves right up our bums now, if only they knew. So we're not telling, and we're not giving them anything. I think it's your relations that can cause you misery when you win the Lottery. That's what happened with that Blackburn bloke, so I've read. We want the money to last us for our life, and for our kids' lives. When we've got that sorted, in about a year's time, then we'll see.'

So far, they've not found it too hard, not letting on. They tend to keep themselves to themselves, anyway. When the subject of money or the Lottery has come up, they've managed to bite their tongues and say nothing.

'When we move, I'm going to start driving lessons,' said Helen. 'We haven't been able to afford that till now. We'll both go and get passports, so we can go abroad, if we want to, as we've never been. The kids are dying to go on a plane, but we're not really bothered.' Steve plans to buy a better car, an Espace, second-hand. 'You buy new, and the value drops at once. We'll still watch the pennies. Helen's done packed lunches for the kids all week, even though we can now afford to pay for school lunches. We'll still put £5 on the Lottery every week. We like watching the numbers coming up.'

Their children, once they go to private schools and lose their local accents and attitudes, are likely to change quite a lot. Isn't that a worry? 'You mean in a year's time they'll all be stuck up? I hope not. But yes, their lives will be very different. I don't envy them. I'll just be glad they're getting a better chance in life. We'll also change. People who say they won't, well, it's an utter lie. When you can buy anything you like, it's bound to change you, but I'm not going to end up with two Rollers. Well, one, maybe . . .'

He smiled, looking almost smug for once, then returned to his normal, calm, relaxed, low-key, laid-back self. 'When people know you've got money, they let you have a two-week trial on any car you like. I've read that somewhere. So what I'll do is drive a Roller for one week, then a Merc, then a Porsche, then I dunno, just to see which I like best. But I won't buy a new one. I'll always go for second-hand, perhaps ex-demonstration model. That's the plan, anyway...'

Helen has one minor hobby, to which so far she has devoted little time. She collects teapots in unusual shapes, plastic or china, it doesn't matter, just anything silly. She's also a bit of a reader, and usually has a Mills & Boon love story on the go. Steve only reads DIY books. Both of them smoke, around twenty a day, but once they move, so they say, they're going to stop. 'It's a bad example for the kids.'

That evening they were going to drive overnight to Scotland in a hired Espace to look at houses. No estate agents had yet been contacted, or an area decided on. They'd just drive off, then stop and look around when they saw somewhere nice. All the children were going with them. The school attended by the older ones had been informed they would be having three days off for house-hunting. Again, no lies had been told. 'The kids and Helen will sleep in the wagon during the journey. Tomorrow night we'll find somewhere nice to stay. A little farm, bed and breakfast, perhaps even a hotel. I've never stayed in a hotel before. Nothing posh, mind...

'The thing about winning the Lottery is that it means all your dreams can come true – but it depends what your dreams are. We've never really had any. All we wanted was to be content, and the kids to be happy and healthy. With each pregnancy, I didn't worry about the baby's sex, just that they'd be healthy. We might have another kid. I always fancied six kids anyway. We'll have to see...'

'See you next year,' I said as I left, but found it impossible to see anywhere ahead. How could they keep it a total secret, just the two of them? It was fortunate that Steve's job did give a reasonable cover for a sudden move, but then what? Wouldn't their new neighbours soon find out? Then what would his mother and the rest of the family do?

## MARK AND PAUL, HASTINGS

At first it appeared that nobody was going to claim Britain's biggest ever jackpot prize, the reassuringly genuine-looking, genuine-sounding sum of £22,590,830. (Random numbers tend to look like that but, by the same laws of chance, someone surely must win a neat round number, say £1,000,000 or even £10,000,000? Not so far. There is a nice oddness, an attractive quirkiness, in these long strange sums, and it gives Camelot's sign-writers something to do, filling the figures in on their three-feet-long reproduction cheques.)

The jackpot was big because 10 June 1995, week 30 of the Lottery, was a roll-over week, there having been no jackpot-winner in week 29. This was the sixth time there had been no winner, which was roughly in line with what the statisticians had forecast. What they hadn't forecast was that phenomenon of week 9, 14 January 1995, when those 133 jackpot-winners, i.e. 133 people (or groups of people), had each picked the same winning six numbers. How disappointed, even cheated, they must have felt, confidently expecting to win £2 to £3 million – which is what a normal jackpot-winner, sharing it with two or three others, might expect – only to find they had to share with 132 other winners. Each had to be content with £122,510.

Before the draw on 10 June, it was known the jackpot

would be high, but of course no one knew how many, if any, might pick the right numbers. It is one of the minor phenomena of the National Lottery – and of other lotteries round the world – that after a jackpotless week, when there has been no publicity for any big winner, public or supposedly private, even more people rush to buy lottery tickets the following week. Yet if more people take part, the chances are you will share your prize, whatever it is, with more people. There is therefore, strictly speaking, little logic in hoping for better luck in a roll-over week. It would suggest either enormous greed on the part of the public, attracted simply by the unusually enormous prize, or that news of a roll-over week in itself generates more publicity and therefore more punters. More research, please.

On the evening of Saturday 10 June, nothing happened. No claimers, no chancers, no jokers, no fakers, yet two hours after the televised draw there are usually dozens of such callers. It was the quietest night so far for the Lottery hot line in Merseyside and for the team of Winners' Advisers standing by, as ever, on red alert, ready to zoom off. And rather puzzling. Why was no one claiming to have bought the lucky numbers 12, 15, 26, 44, 46 and 49? The computer knew that one ticket with those numbers had been bought, and where and when, but so far there had been silence. Perhaps, since it was summer, the winner or winners might be away on holiday, and not hear the good news till their return? Or perhaps it might never be claimed?

Every week there are many unclaimed prizes. The biggest single win going begging at the time was £342,000 for a Lottery ticket bought on Christmas Eve. It lay unclaimed for five months until late May, which was just within the deadline. The rule is that, after six months, any unclaimed prizes go to the five good causes. Most of the unclaimed prizes in Britain are very small, about £10, but after nine months of operation the total had risen to £22 million, exactly the size of 10 June's unclaimed jackpot. Well, unclaimed on 10 June.

About eleven o'clock in the morning on Sunday 11 June, Camelot heard from the shop in Hastings they knew had sold the winning ticket. A pleasant-looking, slightly greying man in his forties had been in to check his numbers, hardly able to believe his luck. His name was Paul Maddison, though he had not given his name to anyone in the shop, so he says. He had merely been checking his ticket, which he had bought with a friend.

What happened next has to be considered a world-class achievement for the tabloid press, up there with some of the greatest ever exposure stories. Never has so much dirt – sorry, information – been gathered in such a short time by so many hacks working on the same story at the same time, yet all starting from scratch, on a Sunday, with so little to go on. What they revealed in the next forty-eight hours about two hitherto unknown men, without any help whatever from the men themselves, has to be called remarkable.

The police, with all their legal powers and official resources, could not possibly have competed. The army? Well, they would have been left gasping. It was in a way a Fleet Street Falklands war, a Wapping World War III, with battle honours given out accordingly. The *Daily Star*, for example, had eleven names in their campaign honours list on Tuesday morning – nine reporters and two photographers – who managed to fill five pulsating pages that day. The *Mirror* and *Sun* also devoted five pages, plus several the day before. Even the *Independent* led its front page on the Tuesday with titillating news of the £22.5 million Lottery-winner Mark Gardiner and his rather complicated love life.

The basic, unvarnished facts are that the winning ticket was bought jointly by Mark Gardiner, aged thirty-three, and his friend Paul Maddison, forty-five. Together they run a glazing and replacement window firm in Hastings called Croft Glass Ltd. They were late to claim their ticket because Mark had left it at work, and they didn't check it until Sunday morning. He is still adamant that he told nobody about the win, apart from Brenda, a supervisor in an old people's home, with whom he was living. Paul told no one except his wife Ruth, a teacher. They can only suppose that someone in the shop heard what had happened and recognised Paul. Camelot immediately started their own investigation in case the retailer or his staff were at fault. Whatever the source, within an hour the national press had been tipped off. Within two hours, there were forty press and photographers outside the rather small scruffy premises of Croft Glass Ltd in a back street of Hastings, desperate for details, any details, of the two owners.

Two of Camelot's new Winners' Advisers, Jack and Maggie, set off from the Camelot HQ near Watford. They were meeting Mark and Paul at a hotel at about the time the first reporters started appearing. It was quickly agreed that, as secrecy was going to be impossible, they should hold a press conference. Until then, they must stay in hiding and speak to no one. So Mark and Paul and their respective partners, plus the two Camelot officials, fled from Hastings and booked secretly into a hotel.

By this time, the great and hungry mills of the tabloids had already started grinding, exceedingly quickly, exceedingly graphically. They were initially handicapped because the story broke on a Sunday, when offices and official bodies are closed, making it difficult to check public services or follow up documents, but they were helped by the fact that enough people were quickly ringing in with information, hoping to make a few bob or settle a few scores. The *Sun* and the *Mirror* had each offered £10,000 for information when the Blackburn winner was being hounded, which had later been withdrawn after much criticism. But it is common folklore that the tabloids pay for tip-offs. They also of course have their own investigative skills, contacts and methods. The results, over the next two days, were several fascinating stories and allegations about our heroes, particularly Mark:

- His name, for a start, had been Mark Gardiner only for the last year. Before that he had been Mark Cresswell.
- He was an adopted child, brought up by Irene Cresswell, who took him as a baby and gave him her surname.
- His 'best friend' from school, where his nickname had been 'Oil Slick' or 'Oil Rag' because of his greasy, unwashed hair, described him as 'the scum of the earth'.
- This 'best friend' said he was pleased Mark had won the Lottery. 'He'll now leave Hastings and we'll all be shot of him.'
- Mrs Cresswell, his adoptive mother, was heartily sick of his behaviour as a 'feckless drunkard, womaniser and thief'.
- His adoptive mother also predicted his future: 'I hope he drinks himself to death with the money ... I wish he was dead. He has been nothing but a curse to this family.'
- It was alleged he had debts and court fines amounting to £10,000, mostly for non-payment of bills in connection with the window-glazing business.
- At the age of thirty-three, Mark was reported to have been married three times already, and the tabloids had not only tracked down each wife but got exclusive family snaps, wedding photographs and lurid quotes.
- The *Sun* had even managed to show his third wife – to whom he was still married – lying half-naked, spreading herself across their famous page 3.
- The wives alleged, *inter alia*, that Mark had not paid maintenance, had been a wife-beater, a thief, a drunk, and generally an out-and-out 'bas—'. (There is a tradition in

most tabloids that while any dirt can be dished out, rude
words must sometimes only be hinted at.)

- Wife number two alleged that, during their short marriage, he had had ten mistresses.
- One of several mistresses interviewed and quoted at
length said, 'They say Mark Gardiner is a professional
glazier. He is not. He's a professional git.'

Do please note that I am quoting these allegations only as
examples of the interest the newspapers showed in our two
heroes – they are not necessarily true. But you didn't have to
plough through the pages of riveting revelations and titillating
tit-bits to get the main message. The headlines summed up
Mark Gardiner very simply: 'Lotto Rat', screamed the *Sun*.
'He's a prize cheat, says hubby . . . Ratalogue of his Rottery . . .
Ten Lovers in 18 months . . . My Cheat Ex should use Win to
buy Harem . . .' In the *Mirror* the headlines were equally
emotive: 'I adopted Mister Nasty . . . Life and Loves of the
Lottery Rat . . .', while in the *Star*, the headline was 'Lucky
Bastard', followed by 'Drunken Monster Made Life Hell for
Three Wives'.

While the hacks hacked away at their stories, Mark and
Paul and their respective partners spent a fairly sleepless night
in their luxury hotel, too excited to sleep, unaware of the
millions of pages of newsprint about to be devoted to their life
story. Well, Mark's life story.

The press conference was called for 2.30 on the afternoon
of Monday 12 June. It had all happened so quickly that
Camelot had not had time to arrange a famous hotel or an
interesting venue, which is what they usually try to do, and
decided to hold the press conference at their own HQ near
Watford, not the most fashionable of rendezvous, nor in the
most salubrious of their hospitality suites. Because of the large
crowds expected, they booked their own canteen.

The winners had left home in such a hurry that they were still in their ordinary Sunday casual clothes, including shell suits. (Remember them, from the summer of 1995?) So their first object on the Monday, when they left their secret hideout, was to buy new outfits for the press conference.

There was a large turn-out of press and TV, but not enormous, considering the scale of the win and the size of the scandals in Mark's life (alleged, of course), but the conference had been called at very short notice. I counted about a hundred people in all, plus Camelot officials. Sitting at the back, in a shirt, was Tim Holley, Camelot's chief executive, the first time I'd seen him at a press conference. Lottery press conferences are meant to be happy affairs, so Camelot hopes, congratulating and sharing in the joys of a new winner as he or she is unveiled for public gaze whom, until that moment, they know nothing about. On this occasion many of the reporters present already knew a great deal about Mark's alleged life story so far – from what they'd read or written themselves. Naturally they were hoping to ask him some personal questions, or at least get him to confirm some of the more colourful allegations.

The conference was chaired ably and affably by David Rigg, who is well versed in giving little away, but doing it charmingly and smoothly without ever being ruffled. He was ready to protect Mark, should some of the questions become too personal, though Mark himself was willing to respond when some of the allegations made by his ex-wives were put to him.

'There's two sides to a story,' he said. 'When all this calms down, some nice things will be said.' He denied he had two daughters. 'Only one daughter. I don't know where you got that from, unless I was asleep.' He would not say whether he would give any money to his last wife – to whom he was still married – or comment on the critical remarks of the woman who brought him up, except to say it was all very sad. He refused to divulge his debts, but said he expected a cup of coffee from his bank manager next time he met him. Asked if he would buy a car, he said Yes. Asked what sort, he said, With wheels on. On the whole he was jokey, amused, confident, and had clearly begun to enjoy himself. Asked about the future of their firm, he said they might buy a new van and take on more staff. 'We'll let them fit windows while we sit in the office picking Lottery numbers.' Was £22 million perhaps too much, and a trifle obscene? 'Nar,' said Mark. 'It's not enough.'

Their respective women, Brenda and Ruth, who sat with them at the main table, said almost nothing. Paul Maddison, Mark's partner, appeared as relaxed and as confident as Mark and replied to questions when asked, but there were not as many personal points put to him. By comparison, little had come out about Paul, except that he had been married before and had two teenage daughters. His wife Ruth, about whom little had been revealed, was said to be a teacher and very popular. 'All who know the couple believe Mrs Maddison has been the making of her husband,' wrote the *Daily Mail*.

After the conference, the four winners were ushered out of the canteen, through a locked door and into a private winners' suite from which the media were excluded. The TV technicians were left to pack up their wires and entrails, the reporters sat dictating their thoughts into mobile phones or their considered pearls into lap-tops while around them the canteen staff started rearranging the chairs and tables, ready for normal Camelot life to resume.

The winners' suite was comfortable and luxurious, in that anonymous, atmosphereless, featureless way beloved of airline executive suites. There were sandwiches and fancy cakes already laid out, most of them grown crisp and dry with waiting, but there was real champagne to be opened and jugs of real orange juice ready to be poured. David Rigg was mine

*Paul and Ruth, Brenda and Mark*

host, plus several Camelot officials, including the leader of the Winners' Advisers team and all three of the new Winners' Advisers who had taken over in March, including the two who were personally looking after the winners.

Mark and Paul couldn't sit down, walking round, babbling away, over-excited like actors who had just come off stage, hyped up, unable to come down, going over some of the questions and answers, remembering incidents from the madness and strangeness of their last twenty-four hours, taking little sips of champagne, starting stories, then returning to half-finished anecdotes and observations.

I went across to Ruth, Paul's wife, as she and Brenda were both sitting down. Brenda looked a bit stunned and bemused, but Ruth was all smiles. Mark and Paul came over now and

again, but mostly they wandered round and round the room.
They both appeared pleasant, polite, affable, nice enough
blokes. Hard to believe Mark was the nasty rat as portrayed in
the newspapers; but then what do nasty rats look like? They
also looked very smart, which helped, in their immaculate
casuals. From time to time they suddenly became aware that
they were wearing brand-new clothes, and stood to admire
themselves, or each other. 'Doesn't he look smart!' said Ruth,
catching sight of her husband across the room. He was in a
soft black jacket and a fashionable collarless shirt.

Paul, the elder, lean and bespectacled, with a greying crew
cut, appeared the more mature. I could imagine him on the
doorstep, doing a very convincing and sincere spiel for the
latest window improvements, while Mark, also wearing specs,
but plumper and less handsome than in his newspaper
photographs (all taken when he was much younger), seemed
more boyish, more jokey, more like an eager but popular
junior clerk than an ace glazier and demon lover.

Paul and Mark did most of the talking. The Camelot
people listened, making appropriate responses, giving the
right smiles, knowing that, in this situation, winners are totally
self-obsessed, unable to take in or receive what people are
saying or doing. It's like the winning team in the Wembley
dressing-room after a Cup Final, knowing the facts, the final
result, but not taking in or savouring what is happening to
them. I leaned across and tried to talk to Brenda but didn't get
very far. She was four months' pregnant, so it had all been a
physical, as well as an emotional, strain.

Ruth said she was glad to be out of the press conference
but, like the boys, she too was burbling away, her mind
tumbling, her head teeming. She looked very elegant in a
well-cut light cream linen suit with a short skirt, showing her
good legs. A bit like a younger Sue Lawley.

'I'll tell you a funny thing. I had dreaded this press

conference, and Paul had been very worried, but it wasn't how I imagined it would be. You see interviews on TV, or read them in the papers, but I hadn't realised that the person being interviewed is actually in control. *You* decide what you say or what you let out ...'

Yes, I said, very true. But you can't control how they write it up afterwards, or what they add, or what they suggest. 'They haven't discovered yet that I've been married before,' she continued. 'So that's something they don't know.' Well, with Mark to go on, they were a bit preoccupied and had enough marriages to investigate. 'That was a factor in deciding to go public, knowing they would get on to Mark's life. But it was too late by then to even think of staying secret. The press were everywhere. We had to go public and get it over with. I was at work at the time, when Paul rang me, and of course I didn't believe it ...'

At work, on a Sunday? But I thought you were a teacher? 'I'm deputy head. The head is away this week, and I'm in charge, so I went in on Sunday morning to prepare for the week. Then this happened. I haven't told the head yet. He's somewhere in Wales. I wish I'd spoken to him. I wonder if he'll switch on the TV or read a paper and find out what's happened. What a shock he'll get! Perhaps he won't know anything till he gets back. He's a Methodist, by the way, a lay preacher, and is against gambling ...' She smiled at the thought, but then added quickly that she too was against gambling.

'Oh yes, ethically and morally I'm against the Lottery. I also think the odds are so enormous that it's stupid to try to win it anyway. That's what I've told Paul all the time, that he and Mark hadn't a chance. Now I've had to eat my words ... If it was my money, which of course it isn't, I would give almost all of it away. I don't want that amount. I certainly won't give up my job. I'm back to school on Wednesday, whatever happens. I don't know what it will do to the boys.

They are, well, very interested in spending. I'm not interested in money, but they're pretty materialist. There was a time yesterday when I was already regretting what had happened. Last night they totted up what they'd like to buy, and only got to £1 million. Goodness knows what they'll do with £22 million! I do wonder...'

She looked towards them still moving round the room, gabbling away, as if she feared for their future, and what it would do to their personalities and their lives. I wondered how she, a teacher, had come to meet a window glazier. 'In a pub,' she said, 'about seven years ago. I was working behind the bar, getting extra money at weekends. Teachers don't earn much unless they get promotion. I recognised Paul by his order before I got to know him. Then we discovered we'd both recently been divorced, were living alone, and it developed from there.'

They married and moved near Perth in Scotland, near Paul's sister, to start a new life in a new place. They sold up their respective homes in Sussex, which was a mistake, because when they returned to Hastings as Paul's new job had not worked out, prices had rocketed and they could afford only a small, basic modern semi. 'I've always hated it. It hasn't even got a chimney. Now I will at least get a new house...'

But what Ruth really wanted to talk about was the big excitement in her life, something she had long hoped for. 'I've just been accepted for an MA course.' Is that good? Not just good, she said, but vital in her case. She trained as a teacher in Reading, but did only three years for her certificate, not a fourth for a degree, which she should have done, another mistake, but now at last she was about to make up for it. 'It's hard to get on and to get the funding, but I've done it. I'll be doing it in-service, not going away to college. It's run by the University of Sussex. I was so thrilled. Oh, far better than winning the Lottery!'

But now, with £11 million in the bank, will there be much point in doing the course, or carrying on teaching? 'Of course there is. I love teaching. I was thrilled to be made a deputy head and even more thrilled to get on the MA course. It starts in September. I can't wait.'

I asked what Paul thought. Presumably he won't see much of her once she starts the course. Has he been supportive, so far? 'He doesn't really understand. He doesn't know about education, having had very little himself . . .'

She has had no children, and doesn't expect to have any now, at the age of forty. 'I think it's too late for that, but there are other things I might try to do in the future.' Such as? 'Singing lessons. I did look around locally for a voice teacher, but couldn't find one.'

I asked how Paul and Mark had met. She made a face, which I couldn't interpret, either thinking hard, or thinking hard about something she didn't want to think hard about. They originally met some years earlier when they were both working for the same glass firm in Eastbourne. After Paul had returned from Scotland, he found that Mark had begun his own business, and he eventually joined him as his partner. It hadn't been doing too well in recent years, apparently, thanks to the recession and other problems.

Paul was standing near, so I asked him if that had been the reason for doing the Lottery – to help the firm. 'Exactly. We've put on between £30 to £50 each week. All I really wanted was about £20,000 to clear our debts and overdraft. Yeah, Ruth always did say it was stupid. We've had a few small £10 wins, and we put that into more tickets. We usually sent one of the lads to buy the tickets, which was what happened last week. The tickets had been left in the office, under the fax, which was why Mark didn't check them on Saturday night.' Why was one of the staff sent each week to buy the tickets instead of buying them eight weeks ahead? 'Because we've never had enough money to buy more than a week ahead,' said Paul. 'But we will now.'

'His shirt does look smart, don't you think?' said Ruth, as Paul moved off round the room. I complimented her on her suit. She lifted up her jacket to show me her blouse. 'I got a discount on this,' she said. 'I found there was a fault in it, so I pointed it out at the counter. Then I thought, What am I doing, asking for a discount! At the counter, we discovered that Brenda's credit-card limit was too low for her things, so I had to help her, but she promised to pay me back. That made us laugh as well. We were dying to tell people, but of course we couldn't say a thing to anyone till after the press conference. The girl in the shop was obviously intrigued that Brenda and I were buying complete new outfits, including shoes. "Going somewhere nice? Is it a wedding?" I asked Maggie [their Winners' Adviser] if we could tell her, and she said yes, as we were by then on the way to the press conference. Oh, the girl was so thrilled for us.

'I've enjoyed it all so far, better than I expected. It is nice and a bit different to be the centre of attention. Camelot have been great and put no pressure on us, but I can't wait to get back to school on Wednesday. I don't know how the kids will react. I'd like to buy them all something, or do something for the school, but of course it's not my money. It belongs to the boys. We'll have to see what they do with it . . .'

After an hour in the winners' suite, they eventually gathered up their things, clutching Richards and Next carrier bags containing the clothes they had left home in. They were then driven away in separate cars by Maggie and Jack, the two Winners' Advisers, heading for another secret rendezvous, in another hotel, for another night of seclusion, then back to real life on Wednesday. Some hope. How could they experience real life ever again?

Meanwhile, a burglar was breaking into the flat Mark

shared with Brenda, no doubt knowing they were away giving a press conference, and aided by the handy photographs showing their house and the street, which had appeared in the tabloids.

Back in Wapping, the press conference snaps were quickly developed, and the picture desks were delighted to see that in the pictures of the four of them, kicking up their feet in a supposed dance of delight, you could clearly see the labels on their new shoes. Perfect material for captions.

Next day there were further revelations about Mark's life. His real, biological, mother, with whom he had tried to establish contact some years earlier, had been discovered. She was furious that after thirty-three years of privacy and a new marriage, with no one knowing she had ever had an illegitimate baby, her secret had come out. 'Her life has now been wrecked,' so her new husband was quoted. 'I have a vision of Mark finishing up with a Ferrari and going into a brick wall – and I hope it is tomorrow…'

Mark and Paul had provided the greatest coverage so far of any Lottery story – filling more space than the Asian man from Blackburn. But then it was the biggest single win. And the juiciest story. It had one predictable after-effect. The following week there were seven jackpot-winners, all of whom said, No thanks, definitely not, no publicity, no press conference …

# LENNY LOTTERY

Which of course was a shame for Lenny Lottery. Yes, there is such a person. He is one of the many unusual creations, bizarre by-products, interesting side-effects, amusing ancillary industries, unexpected happenings and strange developments caused by the birth of the British National Lottery.

Lenny Lottery is his legal name, as every reader of the mighty *Sun* well knows. His arrival, three months before the Lottery even began, was the earliest manifestation that the *Sun* was not only well aware of the importance of the National Lottery but was tooling up, preparing itself, long before its rivals and long before the world at large had taken in the possible consequences.

In Fleet Street, using the term in its generic sense, a legend is already attached to the birth of Lenny Lottery. One day, it is said, a young struggling freelance, desperate to join the *Sun*, rang up and pleaded for work. OK, my son, he was told, you can join us, but there's one condition. You must change your name.

Like many good legends, there is a lot of truth in it. In fact it's almost totally true, except that the reporter in question was already on the staff when the call came that changed his life – well, changed his name. 'In the office, there is a variation of that legend,' said Lenny himself. 'The story is that the news editor was looking around the newsroom for someone to turn into Lenny Lottery, and I was the only reporter in the room at the time, so that's how I got the job. Good story, but not quite true . . .'

Lenny is a rather serious, stocky, young man with an open countenance, a countryside face and a strong Liverpool accent. Nothing flash or sharp or clever-clever, so the first impression is that here is an ordinary bloke you could trust. Neat and tidy in his dark green suit, carrying his attaché case. Perhaps an insurance salesman, or a higher grade clerk. Certainly not what many people expect a reptile from the tabloid press to be.

He was born Aidan McGurran in St Helens, Merseyside, thirty-two years ago, one of four children of a poor Irishman who arrived in Lancashire aged nineteen with only ten bob in his pocket. He got a job in a car factory, married and raised the children, all of whom went to university. Aidan's two brothers went to Oxford, his sister went to Salford and became an accountant while Aidan himself studied politics and history at Manchester. As a postgraduate, he did a year's course in journalism at Preston. His first job was on the *Oldham Chronicle*, before he joined a Liverpool news agency. For a while he worked in Manchester on the *Daily Sport*, part of his CV he'd like to forget. 'Yes, that was a bit embarrassing. It wasn't quite, shall we say, a newspaper of record, but there were some fine journalists working on it.' He then moved to the *Sunday People* and from there, in 1993, to the *Sun* in London. He is married to Deborah, formerly a BBC journalist in Manchester, who is five years older than him and has four children by a previous marriage. Together they have a son, Conor, aged two, and they live in Essex.

He is clearly proud to work on the *Sun*, defends it stoutly, even when I give him examples of Lottery winners who allege that the *Sun* hounded them. 'That would just be young local reporters. I don't want to sound snobbish, but a lot of them act the way they think *Sun* reporters act. Do you think we would last more than six months on the paper if we made things up or did things illegally? Of course not. We might print things people want to keep quiet, but we don't fabricate. We are professionally accurate. I don't know why people think the BBC News is accurate and trustworthy when they use ten-second soundbites totally out of context.'

Sorry about that, Aidan; I mean Lenny. So what's the real

*Lenny Lottery*

story? 'I was out on a job one day, the Craig Charles rape acquittal story, as it happens, when my bleeper went, from the newsdesk. Nothing unusual about that. It goes at least eight times a day. It was the news editor. There was a long pause, then he said, "Would you mind changing your name?" Being a trained journalist, I naturally asked the obvious question – Why? He explained about the National Lottery starting, adding that I could always change it back in the future. Apparently you can change your name by deed poll every day, if you want to. So I said Yes. No, it didn't surprise me. When you work for the *Sun*, you expect surprises, things not to be quite normal. You can go in and be told that today you are dressing as a woman.'

Aidan, as was, was an ordinary reporter at the time, one of many. In the nature of things, most ordinary reporters are hoping one day not to be so ordinary, perhaps becoming a specialist, a feature writer, or even a star columnist, so turning into Lenny Lottery meant he was moving up the ladder, having his own specialist subject to write about.

'It costs about £100 for the deed poll, but I didn't pay. News International's lawyers did it. When I rang my wife in Manchester, there was a long silence. Her first words were: "Will it affect the life insurance?"'

Lenny does not wish to be too specific on how exactly his change of name has affected his personal life, or whether he has notified all the relevant authorities. 'My mother and father, and my wife, still call me Aidan, but most people at work now call me Lenny. I can respond to either name. I don't notice the difference. Journalists outside the paper think it's all a joke, and don't believe I changed my name, but I did. And it was worth it. I became a specialist, looking after an important subject.'

He became Lenny three months before the Lottery began, with space to fill in the paper, so it took quite a bit of research,

and some imaginative journalism, to create regular Lottery
stories, when Lottery there was none. 'You have to hand it to
the editor, Stuart Higgins,' says Lenny, a tad creepily, I
thought. 'He recognised long ahead that this was going to be
an enormous story with enormous effects on the country.

'When it did start last November, we went to town. There
was a Lottery story on the front page on five out of the first
six days. For three months we were doing a four-page pull-out
on Lottery-winners, plus of course tips and numbers and how
to play. Camelot have always been very helpful. Let's say it's
been a fruitful relationship, though our aims have not always
coincided. We have revealed winners whom they wanted to
keep quiet. The whole business of the Blackburn Asian being
named was not Camelot's fault. All they did was to confirm he
was a factory worker with three children, living in the North,
which they did with his agreement. That did help us to
eliminate some of the other possibilities. Some of our rivals
think that at times we must have had special help from
Camelot, but that's just jealousy. We've had no more help
from them than any other paper. We've just put in more effort
and had better contacts.

'When we doorstep someone and say Congratulations,
they are usually amazed we've found out. But if you think
about it, we couldn't possibly have found out if they hadn't
told someone. That someone tells someone, it gets round
locally, and we get to hear very quickly. Don't forget, we have
twelve million readers and the vast majority are Lottery
players. It's their culture. It's mainly the working classes who
play, and they are our readers. You don't get many middle-
class winners, which is why the *Daily Mail* rarely gets any
Lottery exclusives. We get them because they're our readers
and they ring us. Working-class people are more inclined to
tell the truth and admit things. They don't have the problems
with privacy the middle classes have. I remember when I was

at university, I did some canvassing for the Labour Party. On the doorsteps, the working classes would give a straight answer about whom they were voting for, but the middle classes wouldn't. We even get Lottery-winners themselves ringing us up.'

Really? When asked to name them, Lenny was forced to admit that it hadn't happened for a while, not in fact since back in November 1994, when two of the jackpot-winners contacted the *Sun* in person, so he says. 'They did. Ken Pilton in the first week and Fred Baker the second week both rang us. That rarely happens now. In fact I can think of only a couple of smaller winners, one of whom won just £900,000.'

So what the *Sun* now relies on is relations or neighbours to ring them, tip them off, hoping of course for a fat fee? 'Oh no, that's not always the case.' Come on, Lenny, they do it for money. 'Honestly, money is not always an issue. I don't say money is never mentioned, but they do it because they are pleased, they want to pass on good news.

'The calls can start coming on Saturday evening, after someone at the pub has been heard boasting or celebrating, and we make enquiries, often before Camelot has got to them, or before the person concerned has decided they want publicity. With experience, I can often tell which are the wild tips, based on nothing, and which sound likely.'

And if they prove correct, how much would someone get for a tip-off? 'I don't know,' said Lenny with a smirk. 'No, honestly. I just put them down for a tip-off fee. Others decide how much. It's not a huge amount, not as big as some people think. If it was my decision, I think all winners should automatically be named. There should be no secrecy. When you buy a ticket, it should be written into the agreement. That's what happens with some of the state lotteries in America. It would keep it much more open. But I don't think the jackpot should be capped. The bigger the possible win, such as a roll-over week, the more interest is generated.'

Since the Lottery began, it has been a full-time job doing Lottery stories every day, though now and again he has had to help out on non-Lottery news stories. 'In the beginning, I did think the Lottery fever pitch would begin to fade by Christmas and I would be back in the newsroom, but now, who knows how long Lenny Lottery will go on for. Perhaps for ever. It shows no signs of fading.'

His Lottery stories are not just about winners, but about the good causes, charities, Oflot and Camelot. To get into the *Sun* as a winner these days, and get lots of column inches, you have to have had a huge win, be a really big Lottery rat, or have a very touching story. 'In that first week, with the five front pages, the wins were £840,000 each. Now I don't think we'd be interested in a winner under £4 to £5 million, not for the front page, anyway, unless it was a really good human interest story. If the person was boring, it wouldn't matter if he was a millionaire. But if it was a good story, then a £50,000 win would be enough.'

A good story, in *Sun* terms, of the touching sort would be someone dying of cancer. Of the colourful sort, a criminal record helps, or a lurid sex life. Mark Gardiner scored heavily on his interesting personal life, as did Lee Ryan, aged thirty-two, whose girlfriend Karen Taylor won £6.5 million in March 1995. He later received an eighteen month gaol sentence for a car theft. 'I've liked most winners I've met – even Lee Ryan. I'd call him a lovable rogue, not a low-life toerag.'

From his experience of winners, he has found all are shell-shocked at first, most try to get away for a while, then there is a period of adjustment before life goes on. 'Most of them do not go in for ostentatious display, apart from Lee Ryan. They treat their family and friends, get a bigger car, nicer house, and that's it. It's early days yet, of course. In the long term there might be more surprises. I can see in the years to come one or two winners becoming big businessmen or women, turning a £1 million win into £5 or £10 million, realising the financial clout they have acquired.

'I don't expect many marriage break-ups unless there were deep-seated problems there already. And if there were problems, at least you won't have the Child Support Agency on your back in future. Most people I think will continue with their lives and be happy. I resent it when some upper- and middle-class commentators say the prizes are too big because working-class people won't be able to cope with a big win. This is very patronising. If you have had to cope for years with not knowing how to pay the next bill, or buy shoes for the kids, then you are good at coping. Most people can cope with sudden wealth. There are far worse dilemmas in life. I haven't yet heard of any winner being carted off to the loony-bin ...'

Lenny hopes he can cope with being Lenny Lottery for a while longer. He is on nearly £40,000 a year, not bad for someone of thirty-two, with good expenses, though, unlike some specialists, there are few perks associated with his job. 'All I've had out of Camelot so far are a couple of meals and a short trip to the USA. They took three reporters to Georgia to look at their lottery. We got amazing help and facilities in Georgia. The woman in charge of their lottery couldn't do enough for us. She even took us home to her house. Imagine David Rigg doing that. As for Tim thingy, I've never met him. Dunno what he looks like.

'I'm still enjoying the job, and the *Sun*. I've no desire to join a broadsheet. I can't quite see the *Daily Telegraph* poaching Lenny Lottery. I still get a bollocking from the news editor if I miss a Lottery story which one of our rivals has. When that happens, which is rare, my professional ego and self-esteem as a specialist is at stake and I sulk all day. This might be self-deception, I suppose, thinking that the Lottery matters . . .'

He paused, and then looked at me as I closed my notebook. 'What did you write down there,' he said, suddenly rather worried. I suppose not many *Sun* reporters do get interviewed, and have to face the possibilities of their chance comments being taken out of context. So I read him back his last remark. 'I didn't mean the Lottery doesn't matter. It certainly does matter, and most of the country agrees on that after what's happened in the last year. It's important to the paper, as important as bingo, but perhaps not as important to readers as, say, the sports pages. The culture of the paper is a gambling culture, with bingo and other games, so the Lottery ties in with the promotion of the paper as a whole. That's why it matters to the *Sun*.

'What we do also matters to Camelot. I think it's fair to say we have helped to create the national frenzy for the Lottery.'

## JOHN, DURHAM

During that same week in June 1995 as our window-glazing friends were enjoying themselves and their £22 million frenzy, six other winners across the country were also coming to terms with new-found fortune, if not quite new-found fame.

Only one ticket had won the jackpot on 10 June, but at the next level – five correct numbers plus the bonus number, or Match 5+ as Camelot likes to call it – there were six winners, each of whom received £628,947. Quite enough to start the odd flutter in the odd breast for anyone unaccustomed to handling such a sum.

Beneath them, in levels of winnings, and perhaps, who knows, even in levels of excitement, were 535 people who had each won £4,408 for getting five numbers right. Next, with four correct numbers, came 37,157 people who won £139 each. Finally came the vast bulk of 'winners', 890,537 of them, who got three correct numbers and received £10. In all, £42 million was distributed in prize money, but it was an unusual roll-over week. The total sales had been £72 million, the second highest so far.

Three of those Match 5+ winners decided to stay anonymous. Only their nearest and dearest know who they are, always assuming that by now they have got round to telling them. But three winners, for various reasons, decided to go public.

One was 29-year-old Tony Lloyd of St Helens, Merseyside, an officer at Walton Prison in Liverpool, the first known prison officer to win. Will there be soon, or has there already been, a winning prisoner? Unlike the rules for general elections, prisoners, lunatics and members of the House of Lords are all allowed to enter the National Lottery. If and when a prisoner does win, will the Home Office allow a press conference in his cell? And what happens if he wants to buy himself out of gaol? Mr Lloyd, a single man, night-clubber and sports-lover, immediately agreed to a press conference which, to his delight, was held at Central Park, Wigan, the home of the Rugby League champions, his favourite team.

'I was out clubbing on Saturday night and I couldn't be bothered to check my numbers when I got in at two a.m. I have never won anything in my life, not even a raffle, so I didn't think I was in with a chance. It was only on Sunday when I saw the numbers in the paper, and had an idea that I might have four or five of them, that I checked and discovered I had won. I couldn't believe it. It's a brilliant feeling.'

At the press conference, Mr Lloyd said he planned to buy a house, a Mercedes or a BMW, and take some fifteen of his mates on a holiday for a week to Benidorm, or similar. He sounded interesting, if by now a little conventional, as most winners seem to like BMWs and Benidorm. Instead, I chose to follow a winner who sounded decidedly uninteresting, one of the many you rarely hear about, who would never make the pages of the *Sun*, either as a Big Win story or Sexy Shock Horror story. After the excitements and mass coverage of our window-glazing friends, it seemed time for something more low-key and perhaps more typical.

On the evening of 10 June this winner was sitting in a lodging house in Durham City watching the draw on television along with four other people. 'Lodging house' gives slightly the wrong impression, for it is a comfortable, cultured, cluttered family house with three bedrooms, built in the sixties, on a middle-class estate just on the outskirts of Durham. It has lots of books, paintings and photographs, ethnic items and ornaments from Africa and assorted religious inscriptions. On the door as you go in is a carved wooden notice which says: 'There are no strangers here, only friends we have yet to meet.' Very welcoming.

In the main living-room is a framed scroll which reads:

CHRIST is the HEAD of the house.
THE UNSEEN GUEST at every meal.
THE SILENT LISTENER at every conversation.

Rather alarming, and a bit confusing? Well, it confused me when I first saw it, trying to work out the logic behind the capitals.

The landlady, Miss Sheila Shearburn, aged sixty-nine, is a jolly, indomitable well-spoken London-born lady, a cross between Margaret Rutherford and Joyce Grenfell, though smaller and cosier than either. She looks upon her lodgers as part of her family, and treats them as such.

With her that evening watching television were two young Spaniards, a girl called Carmen, and her brother, working their way round England, and a Spanish woman who teaches Spanish. Sheila herself speaks Spanish and used to be a teacher, hence the Spanish connection. The fifth person sitting watching television was John, employed by Durham University, but not in any academic capacity. He is a kitchen porter. They were watching *Seaquest DSV* when Sheila suddenly remembered that they all had Lottery tickets, including herself. She had bought two lines for £2. She knew that John had invested £5, so she asked him to change the channel to BBC 1 and the Lottery show.

'I don't like all the silly, frightful games on the Lottery show,' said Sheila, 'but I do like to see what the winning numbers are. John wouldn't change it at first, so I shouted at him, telling him we'd miss the numbers if he didn't hurry. When the numbers came up, I didn't have one, so naturally I moaned and groaned. The Spaniards had won nothing either, but John was sitting there, looking dazed. So we all shouted at him to hurry up and tell us how he had got on. He was trembling slightly, but at last he said, "I think I've won something ..." Naturally, we all jumped round the room, wanting to celebrate John's good fortune. He just looked stunned. We don't have any drink in the house, but I said to him, "Why not go out and have a few beers?" but he said no. So he sat in his chair all night, with the same dazed expression. We later watched a film, as we usually all do on Saturday evenings, and went to bed about 1.30. John had still said nothing and done nothing. But that's very like John. He is easily embarrassed and absolutely hates any attention. He also tends to mumble. It took me about two years to understand what he says. But he's a very kind man, helpful to everyone. I'm very fond of him.'

It wasn't until the next day that John rang Camelot to tell them he'd won some money. And it wasn't until several days later that he agreed, reluctantly, that Camelot could hold a small informal press conference to announce his news to the local media.

It was surprising, in a way, that he should agree to anything at all, but that is to forget the importance in his life of the outgoing, extrovert Sheila, his landlady and faithful friend, who has played such a part and been such a support during the last eight years of his life. She encouraged him to come out and get it over with. 'And, for goodness' sake, I do hope you'll try to *smile*, John!'

The press conference was held on the Thursday morning

at Collingwood College, Durham University's newest college, founded in 1972. The university itself dates back to 1832, the third oldest in England, a collegiate university modelled on Oxbridge, very desirable, very hard to get into, with some very distinguished graduates. (Yes, I was there in the 1950s, when it was very small, just 1,500 students, most of them northern grammar-school boys.) Today there are 10,000 students, almost half of them women, with a large percentage of public school and middle-class students.

Collingwood, despite being so new, has already got an air of tradition and affluence, with its award-winning buildings set in 40 acres of mature woodland near the Botanical Gardens, a couple of miles outside the ancient part of the city which encloses the cathedral, castle and older colleges. Collingwood has 550 students and offers every undergraduate a room of their own, complete with carpets, central heating and, in half of these rooms, an en-suite shower, toilet and washbasin plus tea- and coffee-making facilities. In my day in Durham, living in the castle, we didn't even have a washbasin in the room. The kettle was on the landing and it was always bloody freezing.

That day, the day of John's press conference, it happened to be Collingwood's June Ball, so there was bunting and flowers and marquees going up and young men and young Sloaney girls getting excited about the evening's posh events. They took little notice of John Heaton, one of their college's kitchen porters, going about his normal business. He had insisted on going in and doing his usual working day, though it had been agreed, with the head chef's permission, that he could take a short break when the time came for his press conference.

Camelot's regional officer, Alan Drummond, had come from Sunderland, while Sally Evington from the press relations company Hall Harrison and Cowley, who handle

Camelot's regional publicity, had arrived from Liverpool. She got out of her car, carrying a brand-new pair of yellow rubber gloves and a little red brush. They think ahead, these publicity gels. She'd had it agreed with the college bursar that it would make a marvellous photo opportunity if John were to be snapped in the college kitchen, washing up. If, of course, any photographers turned up. If, of course, John agreed to be seen washing up.

Only five newspaper reporters and two photographers did turn up, all from Newcastle and the north-east, but none from the nationals. There was no TV or radio presence. Tyne Tees TV had been invited, and expected, but never appeared. One local radio reporter did later get him on the phone, but John refused all further requests.

John stood in a corner of the dining hall, where the press conference was to take place, wearing jeans and a green sweatshirt, looking terribly embarrassed and worried, waiting for proceedings to begin. He is forty-four but looks somehow older, being so thin. Sitting on their own at a far table were his father, two brothers and his sister, who had taken time off work to come and witness the press conference, whatever that might be. In the event there wasn't one, as such; more of an informal photo-call. There was no David Rigg figure chairing the show, no microphones, no walking in, no sitting in a line, no questions being taken in turn, nothing of the London or Watford media presentation that has now become almost standard. In fact, nobody seemed to know what to do next.

A Newcastle photographer asked if he could take his photographs quickly, to catch the *Evening Chronicle*'s next edition, so the Camelot officials agreed. Another photographer suggested that it would be better to go outside, because of the sunlight, rather than in a dark kitchen, so John was led outside, followed by Sheila Shearburn carrying her own camera. She was wearing a tartan skirt and a tartan jacket with a shiny WVS badge in her lapel. The five reporters followed the photographers and had to content themselves by asking a few questions in between the photos.

Sally from Liverpool carried her rubber gloves and the brush, plus the traditional photo-call elements as seen in all Camelot publicity pix – a bottle of champagne, only one on this occasion (and they'd forgotten to find a glass), plus the inevitable three-feet-long, ever so corny, reproduction cheque made out to J. Heaton.

I was standing beside John as the photographers decided on the best location, and waited for some plates to be brought from the kitchen as an extra prop. At last they were ready and John reluctantly pulled on the rubber gloves, clutched the silly little red brush and perched on a dangerously piled stack of plates, holding the reproduction cheque. He was clearly hating what he was being put through, unable to pose and pretend he was enjoying it. 'John, could we have a jump for joy?' shouted one of the photographers. At last he did manage a thin, tight-lipped, scowl.

'You'll be very lucky to get a smile,' Sheila told them. 'Come on, John,' she shouted to encourage him, 'do try to look a bit happy, John!'

A glass was found and stuck in his hand, then he was instructed to shake the champagne bottle and make it fizz. He appeared to enjoy that more, and shook it several times, emptying most of the bottle into the air. At last his mouth had opened, his teeth could be seen and, lo and behold, there emerged definite traces of a smile. Sheila cheered and clapped, then got up close with her camera to take advantage of this historic moment. I offered to snap her with John, using her camera, so she moved forward, getting very close to John, but the photographers shooed her away. They hadn't finished with John yet, if she didn't mind. But she laughed out loud and started taking more snaps. Eventually she got into the picture, and some of the photographers did take her, standing with John.

When the photographers had finished, the reporters moved in to ask a few questions. John confirmed his age, that

*John Heaton*

he had bought his Lottery ticket at Safeways and that 44 was one of his chosen numbers because of his age. He couldn't remember the reasons for his other numbers. They were chosen at random. He admitted he had been divorced some years ago. None of the reporters cross-examined him on that, as they were more interested in how he felt on hearing he had won. 'Stunned,' was the best he could manage. He was asked how he would spend the money, but didn't answer, simply shaking his head. A new car, perhaps? He hadn't got a car, he said, and couldn't drive, but yes, he might take driving lessons in the near future. When asked, he said Yes, he intended to buy his mates in the kitchen a drink, but no, he didn't intend to give up his job at present. What do you normally drink, John? 'Scotch,' he said. This was solemnly written down by one reporter as whisky, till it was pointed out that he meant Scotch beer. Someone asked how much he earned as a kitchen porter. He said his basic wage came to £110 a week.

That was about it, really, and those few facts had had to be ground out of him. No one pressed him further on his personal life. The *Newcastle Journal* next day said he was aged forty-four and divorced, described him as a shy kitchen porter, said he planned to keep working, but they did use a nice smiley photograph.

I felt sorry for him having to go through even such a harmless, kindly interview. If he had won that £22 million, the tabloids would have torn him apart. The ex-wife would already have been found, and probably every woman he had ever spoken to in his life.

The press then departed, but Sally, the press officer, decided she still wanted a photo of John inside in the kitchen, for Camelot's own purposes, such as *Jackpot*, the monthly magazine that goes to the retailers who sell Lottery tickets. One of the five photographers had been hired by Camelot, for their use, so he led John into the kitchen and propped up the

Camelot cheque beside a sink. A new pair of working overalls, still in a plastic cover, were brought out, and John put them on. The kitchen was large and modern and incredibly clean. Some of the waitresses, getting ready for lunch, came to smile and shout to John as he posed for the photo. Several chefs then appeared, in their uniform. The other kitchen porter, a much younger man, shouted something about John being lucky, getting to wear brand-new overalls. 'Oh, he's a canny lad, John. Very quiet, mind, but a good lad.'

The head chef arrived, large and jovial. He had been out in the grounds, checking some of the marquees. He said he was called John Herring. 'Like the fish,' he said, probably for the millionth time. His staff consisted of six chefs in all, plus the two kitchen porters. John had been with him nine months, since last October. He was a good worker, but very quiet.

'We advertised the position in the JobShop, you know, the council place, and interviewed seven people. The previous porter was in a band and had given in his notice, saying the band was turning professional. John was one of the people I interviewed and I thought he seemed fine enough, and I'd let him know. Then, a few days later, the previous porter said he was leaving immediately after all, as his band was going abroad, so I was stuck and needed someone at once. I drove to John's lodgings myself, and offered him the job. He said he could start at once, which he did. He's a good porter. They both are, two good lads. They see jobs that have to be done without needing to be asked.

'I'm pleased for him, like. We all are. He rang me on the Monday morning to ask if it was all right not to come in that day. I said, "Fine, but what's the matter, John?" "Personal business," he said, then he hung up. I thought, Now, what's he done? Two hours later he rang up and said he wanted the day off as he'd won the Lottery. "How much?" I asked. "A lot," he said. "Yes, but how much?" "A lot." "More than a thousand pounds?" "Aye, a lot more." In the end it sounded as if he'd won £60,000, so I said, "Congratulations!" I told everyone in the kitchen that John had won £60,000. It was only when he came into work on the Tuesday that we discovered it was £600,000. I thought we'd lost him when I heard how much he'd won. I hope he'll stay on, till the end of term anyway, but you never know. I don't think he's the sort to vegetate, as he likes working; on the other hand I don't think he's the sort to start a business. I'd do the same, if I won the Lottery. I'd keep on working, not start a business. I've only got seven years before I retire, anyway. I certainly wouldn't start my own business.'

The Camelot photographer then wanted a photo of John with the entire kitchen staff, plus the eighteen waitresses. They all crowded round, smiling at the camera, while he looked very embarrassed. 'Hurry up, man!' shouted one of the waitresses to the photographer. 'We only get a twenty-minute break.' At last the photographer had finished and everyone went back to work. John's hour of, well, not glory, not fame, but attention, was now over. Judging by his face, suffering would be the better description.

Sally was on her mobile, reporting back to base. John's father, brothers and sister had been forgotten in the rushing around, with the media taking over John. They had been sitting all this time at the back of the dining hall. Sheila made them stand on the steps of the college entrance with John, so that she could take their photo for the family album. John's father, plumper, solider than John, but grey and tired-looking, was as ill at ease as John, but his two brothers, both factory workers, and his sister looked smart and well turned out. Once the snaps were over, they rushed away.

I got John on his own at last. He was clearly glad that it was all over. The only word he could muster to describe what had happened was 'embarrassing'. I asked why he had told the head chef he had won only £60,000. He stared at me, thinking carefully, as if bemused by his own action. 'I thought I did ... I couldn't get the words out ... the lines were a bit crossed ...' Because the sum was so big, so obscene, or because the figure itself is hard to say? 'Aye, it is a mouthful, mind. Hard to get your tongue round it ...'

I turned to more harmless questions, such as where he was born. In Durham City, he said. He left school at fifteen. 'I went straight into the pop factory.' This was Wood and Watson, a factory making lemonade and soft drinks. He was eventually paid off, had various other jobs, but they petered out, till seven years ago he became unemployed. He went on various government schemes, some of which were to train as a painter and decorator. 'I passed a couple of City and Guilds, but I failed the advanced craft on the written exam.' He hated being unemployed and was willing to do any job, or train for anything. 'You lose your pride, being out of work. That's why I don't want to leave this job. I know what it's like not having a job. Anyway, I like doing it. It was the best thing in my life, getting the job, at my age and with few qualifications. When the chef came to the house for me, that was the best moment. Now that was good luck. I've never been a lucky person, not in anything. But my luck changed when I got the job ...'

Was he by any chance regretting having won the Lottery? He stared at me for some time, half sighing, half turning away, as if trying to convey his feelings of confusion without actually using any words. 'It's a worry,' he said at last. 'An awful lot of pressure's on me. I don't know what I'm going to do. I'm not sure ...' With that, he said he must get back to the kitchen. He had work to do.

I gave Sheila a lift home. She was bubbling and excited, saying how much she had loved the morning. John had done well, considering that he's John. It was good to see him smile, for once. At home, she insisted I shared her snack lunch.

'Delicious M & S crackers with onion and sesame seeds. Do you know them? Oh, they're awfully good. Then on top I put just a smear of Primula dip. You'll love it ...' Then she asked me to sign her visitors' book, a posh, leather-covered affair inscribed 'Commander and Mrs Shearburn and Sheila'. She asks all lodgers and visitors to sign it, something she's done for decades.

Her late father was an officer in the Royal Navy. She went to Southampton University, travelled and worked abroad, teaching English in Ethiopia, among other places, then came home to London to look after her widowed mother. They had a big house in Ladbroke Square and took in lodgers to make ends meet. 'Lovely house and situation, huge communal garden. Kenneth More used to live next to us, and Ken Russell. The two Kens, I called them. They don't live there any more, of course.' In 1987 their landlord wanted their house and offered to buy them out. After long discussions and negotiations, she and her mother accepted £36,000. It seemed a huge amount to them, until they discovered all it would buy in London at the time was a grotty one-bedroom flat in a not very desirable area.

Her only brother, who had gone to Oxford and had become a Jesuit always known as Father Algy, had moved north to Durham where he was the RC chaplain in Durham Gaol. He said they should come to Durham, where for £36,000 you could get a really good house, and be near him. So they did, and soon began taking lodgers again.

John arrived in March 1988. 'I'd put an advert in the parish bulletin, St Joseph's. No, John isn't a Roman Catholic, but his sister-in-law is, and she'd seen my notice. John was living locally, on the Sherburn Road estate, with his father. Father Algy decided he was suitable, no problems he could see, even though he was unemployed. So John moved in. The council of course paid his rent. Father Algy was very good to him. He got John three months' work once, in London, painting and decorating at the Jesuit College in Stamford Hill. Do you know it? John still kept his room on here and came home alternate weekends.

'Over the years he's done endless government training schemes. On one painting scheme, all he got was £10 over his dole money. Only £10 a week! Yet he worked so hard, very long hours. He's never hung around. He's done painting and decorating for many of my friends. He helps people all the time without charging. He did this room. Isn't it good?' John left at one time, moving into a flat, and Sheila let his room, but he returned after a few months.

John usually accompanies Sheila round the town, now that she uses a stick for her arthritis, helping her with shopping or going with her to meetings. 'Algy used to call John "Sheila's minder" – behind his back, of course. I suppose I do embarrass him all the time, but we get on very well. We're jolly good friends. He complains when I'm untidy. He's not very keen on gardening, that's the only job he hates, so I have to force him. Otherwise, he's marvellous. He doesn't like my African statues at the front door, the naked ones. "You shouldn't have that sort of thing around for bairns to see," he told me the other day.'

The previous week, John had made arrangements to see an insurance rep, thinking he should start a modest pension scheme for his old age, now that for once he is in work. He's also been contacted by an adviser, through Camelot. At the moment, though, everything is staying in the bank until he decides what to do with it, if anything.

As good friends, they had already arranged a foreign holiday together, going to Spain in September, staying at the holiday flat of a friend of Sheila's from Durham, a fellow lodging-house-keeper. John had never been abroad in his life, but felt that now he's in work, he'd be able to save a bit each week. 'We're still going, but John insists he will pay for me! We'll see. I speak Spanish, of course, which will help. It will give John a chance to get away for a while, away from the pressures of the press!' She gave a hearty laugh. The media pressure has been exceedingly light, compared with what it could have been.

'John only goes out once a week, on a Sunday to play snooker and have a few beers. Otherwise, he's at home watching TV, if he's not at work. One of his interests is the American Civil War. He reads everything about it. I have been to Gettysburg myself, visiting friends, and I've promised to take him there one day. Perhaps we'll do that now, as he has the money. I'll help him get to places he'd like to see.'

Sheila's mother died in 1987 and her brother in December 1993, so her reasons for coming to Durham, or staying there, have gone, though she feels settled and has no plans to leave. She can't predict what will happen to John now. 'He was so unsure of everything on the Sunday. For two days he hardly ate. His life has been turned upside down and he worries about the future. But I've told him straight, "Money gives you power, John, power to help people." So we'll have to see what he does from now on . . .'

# RONALD AND DIANA,
# THE NORTH-EAST

Ronald and Diana chose to be anonymous and to remain
anonymous for ever, so they hope, which meant that when I
first spoke to Ronald on the phone, all I knew was his first
name. I did not know his age, surname or any personal details
apart from the number of his red Escort car, and that he would
be waiting for me outside the station when I got off the
London train. He'd sounded very soft-spoken on the phone.
Either naturally quiet and hesitant or someone deliberately
keeping their voice down to disguise it. He had agreed to meet
me on neutral territory, and then we would take it from there.

I should have thought of a password, or some secret sign,
to make recognition easier, but none was necessary. The
moment I left the station I spotted him standing by his red
Escort. Late thirties, solid-looking, with a management air,
despite his casual clothes of windcheater, polo neck and grey
flannels, very neat and immaculate. Could be a bank manager
or a comprehensive headmaster on his day off. Inside the car
sat his wife Diana, about five years younger, looking grave and
serious like a Sunday-school teacher. It was a fairly old car, W
registration, but in spotless condition. They would be getting
another one soon, but not brand-new, perhaps a year or two
old. No need to draw attention to themselves. No need for
anyone to suspect.

We drove for about forty minutes to an old mining village, now landscaped and tidied up, all signs of the pit removed. We stopped outside a row of Edwardian terrace houses with bay windows and little porches, modest but quite attractive, the sort a junior colliery manager might have had in the old days, when Coal was King and this area of the North-East was pulsating with industrial life.

Inside, the house was gleaming. Fitted carpets, central heating, modern kitchen at the back and, beyond it, a new bathroom which Ronald had done himself, extending it into the spacious back yard. He had used seasoned pine wood, very Habitat, and there were lots of indoor plants and pot pourri and little ornaments. No garden as such, but plant tubs on the concrete slabs in what was left of the back yard.

It was now two weeks since they had won the jackpot. It couldn't have come at a better time in their life, but from day one they had been determined to take things very slowly, very gradually, doing nothing flash, nothing showy. They wanted to make sure none of their neighbours ever found out what had happened, said Ronald. He was standing in the back kitchen while I was being served coffee and shortbread by Diana in their living-room. I wondered what he was doing, talking from the kitchen, then I realised he was smoking, standing with the back door open. He smokes only ten a day; never in the living-room, and never in front of the children.

Ronald is exactly thirty-six years and two weeks old, born locally, the oldest of three brothers, in the village they still live in. His father, a miner, died aged forty-seven of lung cancer. Ron left school at fifteen and worked as a van-boy delivering for Rington's Tea. Next he was employed as a van-driver for a confectionery firm. When they began to notice how neat and presentable he was, he was promoted to salesman.

It was while he was a salesman that he met Diana, who was working in one of the shops on his rounds. She was only sixteen at the time, and had just left school. 'I did do GCEs, but I didn't do very well. "Could do better" was on all my reports, that's why I ended up serving in a shop.' She comes from Newcastle, the big city, and has two sisters and a brother. Her dad worked in the shipyards before retiring. From selling to shops, Ronald was offered a job in a shop, a large old-established grocery in Newcastle, with a promise that they would give him some management experience. He became assistant manager, and Diana joined him there, as an assistant on the counter. He was eventually made manager of the shop, in charge of a staff of twenty-three, including part-timers.

'It was hard work, but I did very well at first. Our shop won a prize in trade promotion and Di and I got a free weekend in Paris, but the big supermarket chains were undercutting us and offering special bargains we couldn't match. It became a right rat-race. Then the Metro Centre opened, and we lost many customers. The owners decided to sell up, as the site was worth a packet, and I was made redundant.

'I stayed at home for a year. I had my redundancy, and there were lots of things I wanted to do. That's when I did the bathroom. When the money ran out, I tried to get another job, but there was none. I didn't want to go into shop management again, as I'd found it far too stressful. I was willing to try anything, but there was nothing for someone of my age with no qualifications. All I've got is my driving licence, so I started helping out with a mini-cab firm. Nothing regular, like, just when they were stuck. On the day of the win, I'd done no work for several months and was on income support of £108 a week. Scraping the bottom of the barrel, you might say. Di was thinking of going back to being a shop assistant to help us out. But we'd kept the house going, the mortgage was part paid by income support and the kids were not suffering. We were managing – just.'

They have three children, twins aged eight, Tom and Tara,

and Luke, five, all at the village school. 'I remember at the beginning of the year,' Ronald said, 'looking at the calendar and noticing that 22 July was going to be a Saturday this year. That's my birthday, my thirty-sixth birthday. I said to Di, Well, after 22 July, we'll have no more worries. Why's that? she said. 'Cos we'll have won the Lottery, pet. It wasn't a joke. I really did think we would win it on my birthday. I've always felt I'm misplaced in this life – that I'm destined for better, different things. Not necessarily to be richer, because I feel rich in my family, with Di and the children, but I felt something would happen to me. And, from the beginning of the year, I felt sure this was our year.

'As 22 July got nearer, I suddenly realised something else – that my thirty-sixth birthday was also the thirty-sixth Lottery. Well, that clinched it. It's my lucky number anyway, 22. Not just my birthday, but it's the number of our house and the date we got married, 22 June. Everything about 22 July was spot on.' Came the day itself, 22 July, Ronald restricted himself to his usual £2 on the Lottery. That's all he has been able to afford since it began, though there was a spell when he was doing a bit of mini-cabbing that he upped it to £4 a week. He has had the same numbers since the beginning, based on a complicated code that involves two alphabets which translate the six letters of his first name, Ronald, into six numbers – 2, 3, 21, 22, 23 and 40. He did explain it to me, using paper and pen, but I didn't understand it. 'Perhaps I should sell the secret, now it's come off!' You can't, you're a secret winner. 'Oh, yeah . . .'

As ever, on a birthday morning in their house, the birthday person gets their breakfast in bed and the presents ceremoniously opened. From Diana, Ronald got a shirt and trousers. From the children, socks and a scarf, plus of course home-made birthday cards from each of them. They had made no other plans for the day, but Diana's mother suddenly rang, as the weather was still so hot and tropical, to invite them all for the weekend to the Northumberland coast, where they had retired to a bungalow, to celebrate Ronald's birthday.

'We hadn't planned to go anywhere, as we had no money to spend,' said Ronald. 'I had to take £20 from the housekeeping money to buy petrol for the car. As we drove to the coast, wondering if the car would last, as it was making funny noises, I was thinking about the Lottery, thinking that if I got five numbers right and I won a couple of thousand, that would help us through the rough patch till some job turned up. It might even be enough to dump this old car and buy something a bit more reliable.'

They had the day on the beach, swimming and sunbathing, and mostly he forgot the Lottery. In the evening, Ronald and his father-in-law decided to go to his club, the Conservative Working Men's club, have a few beers and a game of snooker. 'We were in the snooker room on our own, just the two of us. From the bar, I could hear the telly on for the Lottery. I half-caught one number but I didn't recognise it, so we carried on playing. In fact I shut the door, to keep the noise out. I then had a premonition that someone would open that door and call for me. It wouldn't be for something bad, to make my heart sink, but for something good.

'At 8.40 the door opened, and someone asked if either of us was called Ronald. I was wanted on the phone. I went into the bar and picked up the phone, which was behind the counter. It was Di, saying we had won the Lottery. I said she must be joking. She said she wouldn't have rung if she was joking. I said she must be wrong then, she'd made a mistake. She said she had checked. I said, Then double-check. She said she would, and I said I'd ring her back in ten minutes.

'I'd spoken as quietly as I could, so no one in the bar could hear. I put the phone down and went calmly back into the snooker room. When I'd closed the door, I punched the air and said, We've won on the Lottery! My father-in-law gave me a hug. He asked if I'd got five numbers right, or what. I said No, all six, the jackpot. He gave me another hug. I still can't believe what I said after that. "Whose break is it?" We had fifteen reds on the table when I'd left the room. We played for another fifteen minutes, and there were still fifteen reds. We were doing it automatically, in a daze, getting not one of them in a pocket. "I can't take any more of this," I said at last. "Let's pack it in." I had said to Di I'd ring her back, but instead we just went straight home.'

At home, Di and her mother, plus Tom, Tara and Luke, had been watching the Lottery programme on TV. 'I heard the number 22,' she said, 'and I thought, Yes we've got that, our lucky number. Then 21 and 23, then 2 and 3. Then I heard 40 and thought, No, we haven't got that, so I went to get the ticket, to check. We had got 40, after all, which I'd forgotten. I came back, holding the ticket in the air, which confused my mother. She's never done the Lottery and she thought I was holding up a biscuit-wrapper for some reason. I was jumping about and saying, We've got all six! We've won the jackpot! I checked it on Teletext, in case I'd made a mistake, and rang Ron at the pub. I could hear his voice changing slightly when I told him, but he said he didn't believe it. I had to check, and he'd ring back in ten minutes. After twenty minutes he hadn't rung, and I was beginning to think he'd fainted or something.

'I got Luke to bed. Being so young, he didn't really understand what was going on, but Tom and Tara did. I played a game with them on the floor, to occupy them, with mice which you move around. Tara had taken it all in and was very excited. She got out her pen and paper and started to make a list of things we'd do, now we'd won the Lottery. We'd have a new house and a swimming pool, she could have a rabbit, Tom a dog, and their dad could buy eight cans of beer. The day before, she'd gone shopping with Ron and he'd picked up a four-pack of beer, put it in his basket, thought about it, then put it back, knowing we couldn't afford it. So Tara in her fantasy list was letting her dad buy eight cans. I tried to calm them both down, saying we didn't know at this stage how much we would get.'

Ron and his father-in-law eventually arrived home. Ron was by this time very excited and unable to stop talking. So much so that he started ringing round his family, telling his brothers and then Di's brother and sisters. 'My first call was to my brother, and I said, What's it like talking to a millionaire? He said I'd been drinking, and was just trying to wind him up, so he hung up. I then realised what I'd done. Two minutes later I rang him back to say it was all true, but on no account should he tell anyone. When I rang the rest of the family, I told them the same – to keep it secret. They were the only people I told – just our own families, brothers and sisters. No outsider was told.

'The hardest part of the Saturday evening was deciding where to put the ticket, as we were in single beds at my in-laws' house. I put it under the mattress at first, then I noticed the mattress was a bit worn. I thought the springs might disfigure the ticket, so I put it under the bed, on the floor. Di said, What about mice – they could eat it in the night. Clever dick, I said. I don't think they have mice, but then I thought she had a point so I got it out from under the bed. This time I put it in a drawer, and took it out again. What if Luke got up early in the morning and was looking for something to draw on and found the ticket? It had to be put well away from any of the kids. I can laugh now, but I was worried. All our future was tied up in that one ticket. In the end I went into the kitchen and put it high up, above a cupboard. Once I'd done that, I was asleep in ten minutes. No problems, I slept like a log.

'On Sunday, I tried to find out who to ring. I found the instructions on the ticket confusing and misleading, saying contact your retailer first. I didn't want to do that, as it would draw attention to us, so I thought I would try and ring Camelot direct. I decided not to ring from my father-in-law's house, as that could be traced if some operator was being nosy, so I went out and looked for a phone box. I'm surprised I did that, I mean thinking ahead, being so careful. I felt like James Bond on a mission. In fact that's how it's felt for the last two weeks – the mission is to keep it all secret, a challenge I've set myself.

'I rang Directory Enquiries and asked for Camelot. They gave me the Watford number first, but I told them to look for a regional office, they must have one in the North-East. As I was speaking to the operator, his voice changed. Mine probably did as well. He could tell I was excited. I knew by then that we'd won two and a half million pounds, and so had three other jackpot-winners. I eventually got through to the regional office and gave my details, and Maggie, a Winners' Adviser rang me back. She said she would come and see us next day. I made it clear when she arrived that we did not want any publicity. She asked how many people I'd told, and I gave her the list. She put no pressure on me to go public.'

So far, he thinks there have been more pressures on their brothers and sisters to keep the secret than on themselves. 'It's a burden for them, I realise that, but we are a very close family, we do stick together, so I know I can trust them. Di and I have got each other to discuss it with, which we do, endlessly, and with our brothers and sisters, but each of them is scared to mention it to their in-laws and relations.

'I have used a sort of cheap psychology, saying that if it gets out, we're going away at once and they'll be left with the press hounding them. I've made it clear I am going to treat each of them, when things have been sorted out, when I've seen the experts and got the tax settled.

'That in itself caused a bit of worry. One of them rang and asked, if it got out, but wasn't his fault, would the brothers and sisters get nothing? I said No, of course not. I wouldn't chastise them. I would still give them all something. It would just be better, for all of us, if it was kept secret. If it comes out, we all lose. That's how I've left it. It's not really been a conscious effort, for us, keeping it secret. We had never discussed it before. When it happened, it was just our immediate reaction – to keep it totally quiet. For the sake of the children, that's the main reason. We just want them to have normal, ordinary lives.

'There was nothing wrong with our normal, ordinary life before this happened, except that we had no money. Now the whole object is to keep our lives on an even keel, to keep them the same. I'm willing to forfeit my dreams of having a brilliant new car, a four-wheel drive, which I've always wanted, for the sake of protecting the children. I could go out now and buy several, but the moment I parked it outside, the whole street would know. It wouldn't be worth it. My selfish pleasure is not to be compared with the future lives of our children.'

But surely Tara and Tom know? They are aged eight, after all. They heard the programme, took in the news and made that list. It could be all round their school by now. 'I don't think so. For a start, we did try to calm things down after that first excitement. They still don't know how much. We said it had turned out much less than we first thought. We made it clear we're keeping it quiet and being very calm. We haven't bound them to secrecy, as such. That would probably have the opposite effect, knowing kids. On the Tuesday we had a bit of a party back here for the brothers and sisters. I went with Tara in the car to buy some champagne, along with one of the cousins who was coming to the party. I could hear them talking about the party in the back of the car, and I told them both it would be better if they didn't talk about it any more.

It wasn't a warning. Just that it was better not to tell people.

'If we didn't have any kids, that would be different. I'm not saying we'd have had a press conference, as that's not our style. Last week was great, exciting enough, really, just inside the family. The whole week, I couldn't stop talking. My sleeping was fine, and my eating. It was the talking. I couldn't stop. A friend of mine, a few months ago, long before the win, said something really good to me. He has got a flash car and nice flat, but I've never envied him. I don't envy anyone. But he said he envied me because I've always got pleasure out of simple things. Our best thing is having a picnic up by the Roman Wall, just the five of us on our own. That will still be the best, whatever we decide to do with all this money. Without any kids, I suppose we would be off by now, having a luxury holiday, or buying a posh car. On the other hand, we'll have as much pleasure in the end by taking things stage by stage. We have had to struggle, the last few years, so old habits die hard.'

I asked if they had ever been tempted by the example of Lee Ryan, who had captivated half the nation and filled many pages in the tabloids with his spending exploits. In March, his partner Karen Taylor had won £6.5 million. They had bought a five-bed Tudor-style luxury home and Lee had indulged himself with a £45,000 Jaguar and a £130,000 Ferrari Testarossa, despite the fact that he was awaiting trial for allegedly handling stolen cars.

'Yes, I've read all about Lee Ryan and his flash cars. I said to Di that his spending makes us seem poor. I am prepared to spend, when the time comes. But not now...'

## BOB AND ANNE, ALLOA

I got to Alloa earlier than I expected so I parked in the middle of the town and had a look around. Although it was a Sunday, it seemed quite busy. No sign of Alloa Athletic, the town's only claim to fame in most English ears, but I could see the brewery, well known to many Scottish mouths. Nice, affluent-looking town of some 15,000 citizens, clean and proper, solid and prim, about thirty miles north of Glasgow, not far from Bannockburn. The Highlands are within sight and provide stunning views to the north.

It had started to rain, so I sheltered in a supermarket called Somerfield's, a name new to me, but it's part of a large chain formerly called Gateway. At the entrance was a blue and white banner: 'WE SOLD A WINNING JACKPOT TICKET!' This must be the very place Bob had bought his ticket. 'Aye, and we haven't seen him in since,' said a supervisor. 'You'd have thought he'd have bought us a wee box of chocolates ...' I asked the duty manager if their jackpot win had improved Lottery sales. She didn't know, but went into a back office to check. 'Not at all,' she said. 'It's made no difference. We might as well take that banner down now, I suppose.'

Four weeks previously, on 29 July, Bob Westland had won Scotland's biggest Lottery prize so far, £3,791,092. He was still working at his old job, so I had to see him on a Sunday, his day off, at his home in Alloa. Handsome house, grey stone, very sturdy, very Scottish, semi-detached, five bedrooms, some nice stained glass windows, pretty porch, worth around £100,000, judging by the local estate agents' windows. My first middle-class couple, by the look of the house and location. (On reflection, Ken Southwell owned his own house, and so do Paul Maddison and his schoolteacher wife, though I hadn't actually seen it yet. Let's forget social classifications.) Any middle-class effect was ruined slightly by a couple of old cars in the front garden, neither of which looked as if it had been driven recently. Bob and Anne Westland have four sons, which could explain the old cars.

Bob is fifty-seven, bearded and burly in appearance, but very soft and gentle in manner. He was born in Tillicoultry, about five miles away, and his dad was a motor mechanic. He went to Alloa Academy, where he met Anne, his wife, who was in the year below. He left school at seventeen and a half, after his Highers, and went into Alloa brewery as a chemist in the labs, earning four guineas (£4.20) a week. After three years, he moved to BP Chemicals at Grangemouth as a trained industrial chemist, where he worked for the next twenty-three years until 1982, when he was offered redundancy.

At the age of forty-four, he decided he'd do something different with his life. A man he met while on holiday in St Andrews recommended running a post office, a job for life, he said, and very secure. With the help of a bank loan, Bob paid £25,000 for the village post office in Plean, not far from Stirling. Since then, he has worked hard to build it up, selling groceries and general goods. He's the sub-postmaster and employs two women part time to help on the shop side.

Anne went from Alloa Academy to Moray House teachers' training college in Edinburgh and has been teaching ever since. Her present job is deputy headmistress of Claremount primary in Alloa, which has 240 pupils. She took only two years off in all for the birth of her four sons, thanks to the help of her mother.

Their oldest son, Mark, is thirty-two. He left school at sixteen, refused to go to college, became an apprentice in the local glass works and studied for his HND to become an engineer, then did some more studying and became a teacher. For a while he taught in Botswana and then moved to Abu Dhabi in the United Arab Emirates. He is married to Lesley, a local Scottish girl, and they have two sons, Philip, six, and Tom, two – Bob and Anne's only grandchildren so far.

David, twenty-nine, went into Somerfield's from school (yes, that supermarket), moved around and became a manager, and is now manager of Pet City in Edinburgh, the biggest pet-food shop in Europe, part of what is planned to be a national chain of pet shops. 'He's always telling me my shop is a mess,' said Bob. 'He says I should organise it properly with computers and stuff. He says if he had it, he could turn it into a goldmine. Och, but I'm quite happy the way it is.' Chris, twenty-four, is a lorry-driver, heavy-duty stuff, mainly whisky. Robert, twenty-two, works in the offices of the Scottish Amicable insurance company in Stirling. He is the only son still living at home, but he spends a lot of time at his girlfriend's in Edinburgh.

In the last four years or so, since their boys left school and started work, Bob and Anne have become relatively well off and been enjoying themselves a bit more, taking two to three holidays a year. A package holiday to Greece in the summer, a long haul at Easter, such as to Botswana to visit Mark, then sometimes another quick trip to Europe in the October half-term.

Anne earns £25,500 as a deputy head. Bob earns £25,000 from his post office, plus another £5,000 from the shop. Altogether, a pretty decent income. 'Yes, but it's never seemed a great amount,' said Anne. 'We have spent quite a bit over the years, helping the boys, such as on car insurances.' All the same, they recently bought an ex-council house as an investment, getting a bank loan, with a view to doing it up and renting it out.

As the long hot summer of 1995 began, both of them were enjoying their jobs with no immediate thoughts of giving them up, though retirement was looming. In his mind, Bob was hoping to find a buyer for his post office in the next year. Anne was naturally pleased the school holidays had begun, but she was intending to stay on another four years until she was sixty, then take her pension.

'Teaching is not as much fun as it used to be. In the old days, they were desperate for teachers and would bend over backwards to keep you. I remember teachers being encouraged to bring their babies to school, they were so desperate you'd leave. I used to finish at 3.30 sharp in the old days, and be home for the boys coming in from their schools. These days, I'm lucky to leave school before five in the evening. It's all this paperwork. The government has gone mad. You have to do such detailed reports, write out what you plan to do and how it went. It never stops.'

But surely it's improved standards of education, as we are told? 'I don't think so. It just tires out the teachers, and I don't think the kids gain by it either. I suppose the only improvement is that it might make some teachers more focused. You do have to think out ahead what you are going to do. But I've always known what I'm doing. The paperwork is not necessary. It just demoralises teachers. Having said that, I still like the teaching. And I still like the children. That hasn't changed.'

Bob, in his post office life, thought that things had become easier, if anything, thanks to computers, but doesn't care for some of the bureaucracy. 'I was a bit annoyed when all sub-post offices, all 19,000 of them, were told to balance up on a

Wednesday instead of a Friday, just to be in line with Crown post offices – the big ones. There's only 1,000 of them, so it seemed a bit pointless. It ruined our Wednesday afternoons, which used to be our half-day off. Sometimes we have to stay behind till two or three, balancing the books. Oh, it's rarely exactly right every week. I can live with up to £20 out, as it usually balances out over a year, but if it's over £20 out I have to stay till I get it right. It's usually something simple, like a figure written back to front. Apart from that, I enjoy the work. Still do. I like meeting people. I like the banter.'

When the National Lottery started, Bob confidently expected they would choose his post office as an outlet, but it never happened. To his fury. 'I phoned them several times, but never got anywhere. No explanation. I know I was on their original mailing list, because they wrote to all sub-post offices asking if they would stay open till 7.30 on a Saturday just for the Lottery. We normally close at 12.30 on Saturdays, like most post offices. I wrote back and answered, Maybe, which I think most people said. Then I heard nothing. My post office is on a main road and I do motor vehicle licences, which most sub-post offices don't do – so you'd think I'd get the Lottery. Cowie has it, in their village post office, about one and a half miles away, yet they don't do motor licences. It's all very strange, and annoying. I can only assume it was done on postal districts, as Cowie and Plean are both FK7. They got it, and we didn't. I suppose they just want one in each area.'

It would have made a big difference to his general trade, and his income. Retail outlets receive 5 per cent of Lottery money, the same proportion as Camelot itself. Not at first sight a huge slice, but as the cake as a whole was proving so very much bigger than anyone expected, it has become a good income. 'You're a bit wrong on the figures,' said Bob. 'Normal shops and supermarkets might get 5 per cent but sub-postmasters get only 4 per cent. I've checked. That's another mystery. I can only assume the Post Office itself is taking a cut . . .'

Despite his professional annoyance, Bob personally has been a keen participant and so far had won twenty times. Only £10 wins, but it proved to him he had a winning touch. 'Oh, right from the beginning I was sure I was going to win. No question about it. I always knew. I'm a lucky person. I buy tickets for a charity lottery called Club 100, and I'm always winning.' Most weeks, he has spent £10 on Lottery tickets.

Anne also plays the Lottery, but never more than £5 a week. She had become fed up with Bob's passion for the Lottery and had banned him from telling her the results on Saturday evening. 'I don't want to know. I'd rather find out slowly on Sunday from the papers that I haven't won. Bob can't wait, of course. In Turkey, he went on and on about it. On holiday, I forget everything about home completely, but about 8.30 on a Saturday evening, wherever we are – Greece or Turkey – he starts saying, Oh, Chris hasn't rung. This is because Chris knows Bobbie's lottery numbers and been told to ring him if he's won anything.'

Anne has always been a bit embarrassed by their Lottery expenditure, especially whenever she has been the one buying the tickets for the family – for Bob, herself and perhaps one of the boys, which often comes to at least £20. When this has happened, she has gone to three different outlets. 'Just to spread the money around.' Out of shame? 'I suppose so. I don't want folks to think we have so much money to spare. The first time I put it all on at one place, the woman on the counter asked if it was the school's money, presuming it was a staff syndicate. I said yes. After that, I went to three places, though I don't know why I bother. The Lottery queues round here on a Saturday are huge. Most people look as if they haven't got two pennies to rub together, and I want to say to them, Why don't you go and buy food and groceries for your family instead?'

On Saturday 29 July, it so happened that Mark was home on leave from Abu Dhabi with his wife and sons. Bob went to buy the tickets after lunch, from Somerfield's, driving there in his J-registered Cavalier, along with Mark. 'I bought eleven lines for myself and Mark bought one line. I ribbed him about that, spending only £1. It was the first time he'd been home since the Lottery started, so I had to explain it to him. He still stuck to his £1. He said you're just as likely to win with one line as with eleven.'

In the afternoon, Bob and Anne had a drive into the country, towards Stirling, and on the way home went to Safeways to buy some food for a barbecue they were planning for their son and grandchildren. 'I like Safeways' barbecue things better than Somerfield's. They do funny chicken and unusual sausage things.' It was the height of the heatwave, which Scotland enjoyed just as much as everywhere else, and the barbecue in their back garden went on till nine o'clock, when Lesley decided it was getting a bit cold, so they started to bring their drinks inside.

Bob was not supposed to watch the Lottery programme, not when they had visitors, and he had stuck to the agreement, but about 9.30 he sneaked into their lounge, knowing his grandson Philip was watching a children's video on the television. He asked Philip if he could interrupt him for a few moments, just so grandpa could check something on Teletext. He saw that the jackpot numbers were 28, 34, 41, 45, 46 and 49. 'I looked at them, and didn't recognise any, but my immediate thought was, Hmm, bound to be a roll-over week with such high numbers, four of them in the forties. Nobody will have them. I checked Mark's ticket first, and he had one number right. Anne had none right, so I then looked at my tickets. None of my normal numbers had come up, and I usually keep the same five lines. But one of my random lines had three right, so that was £10. Then I noticed that another of my random lines had all six numbers right . . . I went into the breakfast-room, where Anne was sitting drinking with Mark and Lesley, and said "I've got six numbers . . ."'

Bob stopped in the middle of his story, and leaned back in his chair, smiling but saying nothing. I presumed he was either still overwhelmed by what happened, or perhaps bored by going through it all again. 'You tell him, Anne,' he said.

'Well,' said Anne, picking up the story, 'I said, "What numbers?" I'd forgotten all about the Lottery, because he wasn't supposed to tell me anything about it till Sunday. He was standing in the doorway, leaning on the post, white as a sheet . . .' Bob groaned and made a face at this. 'Oh, you were, you were so,' said Anne quickly. She has grey hair and spectacles, and looks at first sight rather school-mistressy, but she has very bright eyes, thinks quickly and is clearly a sharp and strong personality.

Bob speaks more slowly, as if lost for words now and again, but he took up the story. When he had composed himself, he rang their sons, Chris, David and Robert, to tell them his news. David was out for the night, in Perth, and they couldn't contact him, but the others had watched the draw and thought the same thing: bound to be a roll-over, no one will have those numbers. 'I then tried to reach Camelot,' said Bob, 'but all I got was some answering machine, where you have to answer yes or no, give certain details, then it goes on. I gave up before I reached a human voice. I remember thinking, "Am I paying for this call or not?" That was probably when I gave up.'

Chris and his girlfriend came round and insisted on staying the night, and they all sat up chatting till two in the morning, still without having got through to anyone at Camelot. They'd learned from Teletext, however, that there were three winners who would share an estimated £8.5 million.

'We didn't sleep at all,' said Bob. 'I was worried about my ticket, and didn't want to lose sight of it. I'd read somewhere about an Irishman who'd won the Irish Lottery, who put his winning ticket in the attic for safety, then couldn't find it. I put it safely in my wallet, and slept with it by the bed.'

'I couldn't sleep either,' said Anne. 'I had a funny feeling in my chest which made me think, Oh no, I'm going to die before we've even got the Lottery money!'

Next morning, Bob was still very worried about his ticket, beginning to wonder if it might somehow be wrong, a mistake or a misprint. From his phone call to Camelot, he had picked up that the ticket would have to be validated, so on Sunday morning he went to the post office-cum-store in Alloa – not Somerfield's, where he'd bought the ticket – and asked them to put it through their machine.

'You've won,' said the assistant, 'but I can't pay you out this much.'

'I know that,' said Bob. 'I was just checking.'

'You must be one of the three jackpot-winners,' said the man. 'Can I take your photograph?'

'Certainly not,' said Bob, leaving the shop.

Eventually he did get through to a real voice on the Camelot hot line and told them his details, quoted the code number on his ticket, and they said they would ring back.

'At four o'clock there was a knock on the door – it was someone from the *Daily Record*. He said, We know you're the winner. Can we take your photograph and have a few details? He said I was Scotland's biggest winner. As they already knew, I agreed to a photo, but I still don't know how they knew. I can only suppose someone in the post office must have seen me. The news was round the town in about two hours, so I gather.

'Someone rang back from Camelot to confirm I'd won, and said a Winners' Adviser would be with me next morning, catching the first plane from London to Glasgow. In the meantime, I had to tell no one. "Too late," I said. After they'd rung, there was another knock at the door, and it was someone saying he was from the *Sun*. I refused to talk to him, saying No comment. He said he'd been told by Camelot, but that must have been a lie.'

Bob went to work as usual, first thing on Monday morning. 'The following Monday was a Scottish bank holiday, so I was paying out double the usual pensions. I couldn't not be there for that. Anyway, I couldn't get anyone to cover for me.'

It was still the school holidays, so Anne was at home waiting for Maggie, the woman from Camelot. 'When the subject of staying private came up, I said it was too late. We could never have kept it secret anyway, not with four kids. We would have had to stay indoors all the time, worrying that it might come out. I'm glad it did. When I went into the town, people were so nice, coming up and congratulating me. I even got cards with best wishes.'

They agreed to go to Glasgow next day for a press conference, which they enjoyed. 'The questions were all much the same, over and over again,' said Anne, 'so we just answered a load of rubbish. Oh, you know. How do you feel? Will it change your life? You have to tell them something about what you're going to do, so Bob said he'd buy a Jaguar. At first I said I'd like to take a trip to the Okavango Delta in Botswana, but they hadn't heard of that, or could spell it, so I changed it to a world cruise. That's the sort of thing they want to hear.'

'They took us outside for the photos,' said Bob. 'And I was asked to sit on top of a post-box, but I refused. I didn't want to fall off it! In the end I agreed to lean against it. But they were all fine. I enjoyed it. Later on, when we were walking down a street in Glasgow, a window-cleaner came up to me. "Hello, Big Man," he said. "Can I give you a wee rub for good luck?" Amazing, wasn't it, that you should be recognised after one fleeting moment on TV...'

*Bob Westland*

At the end of the week, Bob took Friday afternoon off work, having found a replacement, and they went to London for the *Lottery Live* show. Camelot put them up at the Kensington Hilton. 'Have you been there?' Anne asked. 'A bit touristy, I thought, nothing special. Don't think I'll stay there if we go to London again.'

'They rather did the dirty on me in the programme,' said Bob. 'We did have a wee rehearsal, but on the show itself an executive from the Post Office suddenly appeared and presented me with a large key and a shield. I didn't know it was coming, so I was left a bit speechless. Trust the Post Office to go to town, getting some publicity for themselves!'

He went to get the shield, which thanked him for his services to the Post Office, making a face as he handed it over. He also bought the newspapers that had carried his story. His grandchildren had mixed them up, so he had trouble finding the right pages. The bit he liked best was in the *Sun*. An editorial said, 'Well done to Bob the Postie, the Lottery-winner who went to work next day, not wanting to let down his customers.' 'The newspapers were fine. I didn't spot any mistakes. I've got no complaints, except about the reporter who said he had been told by Camelot, which I still don't believe.'

'I think the Lottery is a good thing,' said Anne, 'because it does help good causes. My only complaint is that they ought to widen the causes. It should go to hospices, children's homes, the homeless, people like that . . .'

So what are they going to do with their money? Some people might say they were already rich, before their win. 'I'd like to make sure that my children and grandchildren have security for life, that their future is assured,' said Bob.

'Oh, I'm not so sure about that,' said Anne. 'I'm more worried about them ending up as playboys or on drugs. This may be my schoolteacher's mind, but I'm not going to encourage people not to work. We've worked hard all our lives, and so should they. Robert said the next day that he was giving in his notice at the Scottish Amicable, as he's never liked it, and I said, "You are not. Do that, and we won't give you a penny." "So you're making me go back to work," he said, just like a wee boy of five. "You only give up your job," I said, "when you have another job to go to."'

So far, they have made no financial plans. The £3.79 million is lying in the Royal Bank of Scotland, earning 7.5 per cent in a ninety-day account, while they decide how to spend it. 'I've taken two friends out for dinner,' said Anne, 'as my treat, of course. Nothing fancy, just a local hotel. We got a taxi afterwards which cost £1.20, and I gave the taxi-driver a £2 tip. For a £1.20 fare! My friends thought I'd gone mad. So do I, now I think about it. That's been one of the little problems, wondering what to tip in places like the hairdresser.'

Bob said he had faced the same problem. The first time he'd gone to his golf club after his win, he was worried about how to behave. 'Should I buy drinks all round? But then people think, What a show-off. Should I therefore just buy a round for my friends? Or should I take turns, as usual, even though people would then say, The greedy bugger, him with all that money! You can't win. In the end, I bought one round for my friends, and carried on as usual. You haven't got to worry about what people think. Just get on with life.'

'I don't expect any problems,' said Anne. 'I'll just say it's not my money, it's my husband's. I've already met a few of the kids in the street, and they all know. There was one six-year-old yesterday, only this size, who stopped me and said, "What about that £3.79 million, Miss?" He got the figure exactly right, which surprised me. Shows it has helped his maths!'

They did worry about burglars, as their win had been so well publicised locally, and hired a house-sitter when they went to London for the Lottery programme. 'But that's a problem we've always lived with,' said Bob. 'That's why we have our two killer dogs. With being a sub-postmaster, you always worry about being robbed or held hostage in your own house while they go off and raid the post office.' Heidi is an

Alsatian and Jess is a collie. Neither had taken the slightest bit of notice of me since I'd arrived.

'So far, we haven't decided what we'll spend the money on,' said Anne. 'We're still thinking. But we will give some away.' A box of chocolates, for example, for the staff at Somerfield's? When I told them the story, Anne said that would be the last thing she'd do. Bob said they were wrong anyway. He'd been in the shop that very morning. In fact he'd been in a few times since the win, buying more Lottery tickets. More?

'Oh yes, I'm still doing them,' said Bob.

'But I don't see why,' said Anne.

'Apart from greed,' said Bob.

'I accept what has happened to us, right enough,' said Anne. 'What I haven't done yet is understand it. What does it mean? What will the money do to us?'

**13**

## NEIL DICKENS,
## CAMELOT'S HEAD OF SECURITY

Sub-postmasters have to worry about security, about stick-ups at the counter or being held hostage for their keys. At any one time they can have several thousand pounds about their premises. Think of the possible haul from Camelot if you could somehow crack into its system. Each week, each normal non-roll-over week, it has on average £65,000,000 flooding through the organisation, all in cash.

Naturally, when it all began, it looked for a top man to organise security, so it hired Neil Dickens. He retired from the Metropolitan Police on 10 July 1994, aged fifty-five, after thirty-eight years in the force. He had joined, aged sixteen, in Watford, his home town, where he rose to the rank of Chief Superintendent before being transferred to the Met in 1982. There he was made National Co-ordinator of the Regional Crime Squads. Later he became Deputy Assistant Commissioner, the highest-ranking detective in the country.

On his retirement, he had not intended to take another job but just to enjoy himself, but Camelot offered him the position of Director of Security, a job he felt he couldn't refuse. 'It just sounded so exciting, getting into something totally new.' He had to learn about lotteries and went on visits abroad, particularly to Canada, and also about computer systems, which he didn't know anything about.

'So far, the level of crime has been nothing like the stuff I used to deal with. That involved major criminals and international drug traffickers. In fact it's all been petty crime – up to now. But I am sure there are many criminals out there who are slowly working out how to crack the National Lottery...'

At first the main problems were attempted fraud, with people trying to forge winning Lottery tickets, all very simple, and very naive. Their first prosecution occurred in August 1995, nine months after the first draw, and concerned a couple who, after the winning numbers had been announced one week, bought a ticket with the same numbers and then tried to obliterate the date. 'Their defence was that their baby had chewed the ticket in the corner.' Several people have tried

*Neil Dickens*

variations of the same trick, either altering or cutting off the date, or sticking two together. All pointless, as there is a secret code which gives the date and time of purchase. Camelot felt it had to prosecute as a warning to others, and one person has been found guilty and fined.

Another type of fiddle concerns some newsagents, or their staff. When you buy a ticket, you have fifteen minutes to cancel it. If you do, the first ticket is cancelled and a new one issued. What a few newsagents were doing was cancelling tickets at the moment of issue, and pocketing each £1. People would then end up with a ticket which had been cancelled, but were not aware of this until when by chance they had some winning numbers. They then tried to claim, only to be told they held cancelled tickets. 'It was when nine people wrote and complained to us from the same area about their cancelled tickets that we investigated and found out what was going on. Now that we've been going for some time the computer has a profile for each outlet. Any unusual number of cancelled tickets will show up very quickly.'

When the scratch cards started in March 1995, some newsagents thought of another trick to cheat the public. By scratching a certain part of the card, which has a code, they could find out if the card was a winner or not. They would then claim the prize themselves, or sell the card to their friends, and sell the useless ones to the public. When scratch cards first appeared on the market, they managed to get away with it, as people didn't quite know what a tampered card looked like. Since then, several newsagents have had their terminals withdrawn – and the public are warned to buy no card which has been touched or damaged in any way.

There was also a case of a real winner, who had won £100, who asked for his cheque to be posted to him rather than collecting it from his regional headquarters. When the cheque arrived, he altered it to £50,000 and went along to a building society and opened an account in a false name and address. The staff congratulated him on his win. 'All our cheques are double-checked against a list we give the Royal Bank of Scotland, so the fraud was spotted before any money went into the new account. The man had also been caught on the building society's security video, so we knew what he looked like.' Observations were kept on several cashpoints in the area, but the man himself never turned up, presumably realising he had been found out. He was eventually caught, convicted and sentenced to three years' imprisonment.

Judging by the experience of foreign lotteries, there will soon be a bit of money-laundering taking place, if it hasn't already happened. With the ordinary on-line weekly Lottery draw, the odds are so stacked against anyone winning a big prize – one in 14 million for the jackpot – that it's not worth someone with dodgy money investing in a few thousand tickets, in the hope of winning. But with the scratch cards, the odds are much more favourable. 'If you spent £10,000, you should recover between £3,500 and £4,800 in prizes, depending on the type of game. A criminal normally gets only one-third of the value of his stolen goods, so a return of 48 per cent is very good.'

By spending his ill-gotten money, made from drug dealing or selling stolen goods, on £1,000-worth of scratch cards, a criminal could probably provide himself with £480, perhaps even more, but, best of all, he has a perfect explanation when the police come and question him about his cash.

It has also been known for people with dodgy money to buy winning cards. 'Say, for example, someone has won about £1,000 or even £100,000 one Saturday evening. He goes to the pub and boasts about it, as people do, so it gets around. He might then get a knock on his door on Sunday and a local thief offers him £120,000 in cash for his £100,000 winning ticket. That would be worth it, to the thief, to go and claim on his winning ticket, saying he bought it, and providing himself with a good explanation for having so much money. And the real ticket-holder is happy, as he's made even more. That has happened abroad. It's possibly happened here, though we haven't had evidence of it yet.'

It would not, presumably, be illegal to sell your winning ticket to someone else? 'True, but we would try to stop such a thing, as it reflects badly on the image and integrity of the National Lottery.'

Counterfeiting a winning ticket is impossible, so they say. Tampering or doctoring is always going to be found out, so they also say. Fiddles on the retailing side, worked by those selling tickets? Well, they think they have got a grip on all the possibilities. But one day, surely, there is bound to be a real National Lottery fraud? With such big sums around, big criminals will find a way. Out of Camelot's 550 employees, one day, one of them, by the law of averages, will either be bent, or susceptible to temptation or blackmail, and will reveal the secrets of the system?

Mr Dickens looked pensive. From day one, this has been a major concern. Hence all the internal security devices at their Watford HQ which always baffle me every time I want to go from one room to another. Hence the intensive security screening that every employee has to go through. It's called Schedule Ten, and involves an exhaustive questionnaire, similar to the Official Secrets Act. A full personal history has to be revealed, driving offences admitted, bank and tax records given, including clubs joined and charities contributed to – not only by prospective employees, but also by their partners.

Camelot's Security Department organises the question-naires but the answers are sent to Oflot, the government's supervising body. Their investigators do the final checking. This resulted in six people being dismissed in the early months when the system was being set up, because of discrepancies in their records or worries about their profile. There are forty people in Camelot's Security Department, half of them uniformed security guards, patrolling and guarding the premises, while the others include investigators in plain clothes. The building itself keeps a low profile, situated in an anonymous-looking business park outside Watford, which you could easily pass without noticing the discreet Camelot flag. The front door is round the back of the building. There is no sign over the entrance. The staff need a special key to move from room to room or floor to floor.

So far, there have been no reported cases of Lottery-winners or their children being kidnapped, though, from my experience, it has entered the thoughts of several of them. Mr Dickens didn't think this was likely, not in Britain.

What about computer fraud? An outsider might infiltrate them one day, just as many supposedly secure companies have had their systems cracked. Mr Dickens, naturally enough, would not say what measures they have taken to secure the computers. On the other hand, he was very keen to boast about the way in which the arrival of the National Lottery has helped to combat crime in other fields. All of which I found fascinating.

Because on average 30 million people, or 65 per cent of the population, play the Lottery every week, it means that 65 per cent of dead bodies, stolen cars, abandoned flats or abandoned suits are likely to have a Lottery ticket on their persons or their premises.

The other week, said Mr Dickens, a very expensive car was stolen in London. It was later found dumped, but on the back seat was a torn-up Lottery ticket. The ticket was checked, the precise place and date and time of purchase established (which is recorded to one-tenth of a second) and by chance it turned out to be a garage forecourt. This garage, as most do, had a closed-circuit video system. When it was wound back to the precise day and second, they were able to see who purchased the ticket. It was a known petty criminal of that area, who was arrested and convicted for the car theft. In another case an old woman was mugged. Her handbag and purse had contained only a few pounds, but also her Lottery ticket. Two kids were later arrested, on suspicion, in possession of a similar-looking purse, which they said they had been given. They were then asked about the Lottery ticket, which they said they had bought. They were asked where and when. They gave the name of a newsagent – which didn't tally with the code on the ticket. The ticket tallied with the place and time the woman said she'd bought it. Hence they were lying, and arrested.

'So far, eight bodies, all murder victims, have been found to have Lottery tickets on them. The ticket proved invaluable in helping to establish the victim's movements in place and time.'

So, hurrah for the National Lottery. It has become part of our national life and, in a way, part of our national security system.

# 14

# THE PRESTON SYNDICATE

Walne's chemist shop in Preston, Lancashire, is on the Larches council estate about three miles from the centre of town. A rather pleasant council estate, as council estates go, with its own large park and a scattering of private houses around the edges. And as chemist shops go, they have had their fair share of break-ins, with bricks and missiles thrown through the front window and attempts made on their drug supplies. The worst spell was in 1993 when there were four break-ins in just three weeks. This included a dustbin through the front window and the theft of some of their choicer perfume selections. They now have an internal iron grille, which their young manager, Andrew Hall, puts up every evening, cutting off the back dispensary from the front shop. They also installed iron bars on the back window and a burglar alarm. Since then, the shop has on the whole been pretty secure.

It stands in the middle of a modern row of shops, small, cheaply built, functional, rather drab. On one side is a fish and chip shop called Harbour City, and on the other is a family butcher. Further along the row is a post office, a newsagent and a hairdresser – the usual line-up of suburban shops, all trying to make a living in hard times, struggling to compete with the big boys in the mega out-of-town superstores.

The front window of Walne's boasts a poster offering FREE FILM and a notice, in rather less glaring headlines, announcing EMERGENCY CONTRACEPTION. It describes a certain sort of pill which can be taken up to '72 hours after sex'. On the front glass door of the shop a sliding notice reveals to the world of the Larches estate whether the chemist is CLOSED or OPEN. It also reveals that it has been printed by 'SUDOCREAM antiseptic healing cream'.

The shop has four female part-time assistants, who average two and a half days a week, for about £55. Each lives in a council house on the estate. I arrived just three days after their syndicate of five – the four assistants and Andrew – had received the money. All five were still a bit stunned by what had happened, going through the usual stages of shock, wonder, doubt and amazement but, none the less, each had returned to work, going about his or her normal pharmaceutical business. For the moment, anyway.

The youngest assistant is Sarah Bradley, twenty-eight, a single mother of two children: Christopher, aged ten – born a couple of months after Sarah's eighteenth birthday – and Matthew, two and a half. It was Sarah who bought the ticket that changed their lives. Well, will change their lives. She left school at sixteen with few qualifications and worked as a clerk in an office for a while, till she had her first baby. She then got a job at the chemist shop, but gave it up for a few years when her second son was born. She returned to the shop six months ago. 'I enjoy it. It's a good laugh. We all get on well and it's good fun teasing Andrew.' Her £55 weekly wage has of course been the vital attraction, enabling her to survive with two small children and an out-of-work partner.

She lives with her partner, John, a welder, laid off because of a back injury. They have been together for five years and he is the father of Matthew. They don't have a car. John can't drive, and though Sarah did pass her test some years ago, she has never been able to afford a car, or anything else, come to that. 'It's always been a struggle. My ambition has been the obvious things – to own my own house and have a car. I'd love to be independent and not have the hassle of taking two kids everywhere on public transport.'

Sarah is the joker in the shop, along with Linda. Both of them think up silly little practical jokes to play on young Andrew. Despite being only twenty-seven, and therefore younger than any of the girls, Andrew is the only trained pharmacist, so he is in charge, he is the boss, the shop manager. But because of his age and his boyish, open personality, he does come in for quite a bit of teasing.

Linda Ford, the other joker, is thirty-eight. She also has two children, Lisa, eighteen, and David, sixteen. Her husband David works for a second-hand car firm and his hobby, passion even, is Grand Prix races, which Linda herself has grown to enjoy. Not driving, just watching, especially if the races happen to be in England. Her first job, after leaving a local school, was at Boots the chemist in downtown Preston, then she took ten years off to have her children, returning to work at Walne's, her local chemist, when young David was eleven and starting at the local comprehensive. David has an apprenticeship at British Aerospace just outside Preston, where Lisa is already working. She is training to be an engineer. Linda and her family have lived on the Larches estate for seventeen years.

They have a family car, an A-registered Vauxhall Cavalier, rather modest for a Grand-Prix-loving husband. In his fantasy, he has always been driving a Williams Renault. Lisa, their engineer-to-be daughter, had a car, a Nova, till very recently. 'She'll kill me for telling you, but she was coming back from Blackpool, visiting her boyfriend, driving on her own, when a wasp flew in through the window. She mounted the pavement and went into a lamp-post. The car was a write-off, but she was OK.'

The sorts of jokes that she and Sarah have pulled on young Andrew have of course all been harmless and affectionate. Hardly worth repeating, really, but I said, Oh, go on. 'Andrew was waiting for a phone call one day from a Mr Lyons,' said Linda. 'Then he had to go out, delivering. When he came back, we told him Mr Lyons had rung, and he had to ring this number at once. We gave him the number and all stood around, pretending to be busy. We could hear him saying he had to speak to Mr Lyons immediately, then there was a lot of confusion. We'd given him the number for Blackpool Zoo! And he was asking for Lions! Eeeh, worra laugh! Another time, not long after he came here, he was on the phone, putting in some orders. One of them was for more Radox bath salts and he was shouting at us, asking us what fragrances we needed. I said we should order some more River Deep, then I paused, saying we could also do with some Mountain High. They do have names like that. Well, we could hear the girl at the other end of the line laughing ... It was some time after that before Andrew did any more telephone ordering!'

Linda is also known for her creative imagination; at least the others think she is being creative when she gives excuses for being perhaps two or three minutes late in the morning. A fresh-fish van had overturned on the Dock Road, that was one explanation. Next morning, she was two minutes late again, so Andrew asked what the problem was this time. Linda said it was a flock of seagulls on the Dock Road, eating the fresh fish. Well, it amused the other girls when they heard this story.

The third woman in the shop is Hilary Williams, tall and extrovert, who always likes a good laugh. She is forty-two, married with two children, Jennifer, eighteen, who is a hairdresser, and David, ten. Her husband Ricky is a lorry-driver working for a fruit and vegetable firm. They too have had a struggle in life, always being hard up. The latest drama was over their car, an ancient Vauxhall Cavalier which cost only £150 to buy, but they had to spend £275 to get it through its MOT. 'Then it still wasn't right, and we had to lash out another £300. It worked for a bit, but last week we were told it was knackered. It wasn't worth repairing any more, just fit for scrap. We've had to dump it.'

At about the same time, Hilary broke her spectacles. To save money, as she couldn't afford a new pair, she bought a cheap pair off the peg. 'They were useless. So I've been stood here these last few weeks, with a spyglass, looking like Sherlock Holmes, trying to read the prescriptions.'

The fourth and final female assistant is June Cross, fifty-four, the oldest and longest serving. She is small, bespectacled, rather serious-looking, the quiet one of the foursome. She is married to William, formerly a labourer on a building site, but for the last eleven years he's been working for the police as a traffic warden. They have two daughters, Annette, thirty-two, and Maria, twenty-seven. They both went to college and now have good jobs, one as a hospital liaison officer, the other a teacher.

June herself left school at fifteen and became a shop assistant in the local Co-op, giving it up when she had a family. 'When Maria was eleven, I got a part-time job at her school as a dinner-lady, helping with the children. The school was just opposite here, but it's now been closed. One day I happened to see an advert for this job in the window, and applied for it. I was interviewed by Mrs Walne herself. She said many people had applied, but she would let me know. Twenty minutes later, when I was back at school looking after the dinner queue, Mrs Walne came over, right into the dining-room, and she said I'd got the job . . .'

She paused, for effect, and I said, Heh, that was good, June. She smiled, her rather serious expression turning to a girlish glow. 'I started here on 10 September 1979, doing seventeen hours a week for £18. I still do the same hours, two days' work really, but now I get £51. There's been quite a change over the years. We used to have more young mothers in those days, because of the school opposite, but now we have a lot more older people.'

One of the most recent changes in the lives of all assistants working in the nation's pharmacies is that they must all go through a Pharmacy Assistants' Training, equivalent to an NVQ. This is regardless of whether they actually handle drugs or medicines, which has rather bothered June. After sixteen years in a chemist shop, she feels she is already qualified to do what she does. 'I've always worked at the front, in the shop, with the perfumes and things. I don't deal with the medicines at the back.' So June, in her quiet way, has been worrying a bit about doing the eighteen-week course, which includes a series of multiple choice questions.

Andrew, as the resident pharmacist, supervises her work. 'June has really nothing to worry about,' he said while June was at the front, helping a customer. 'So far she's got full marks. She really is a lovely woman ...' Andrew, of course, thinks they are all lovely, and vice versa.

Andrew can look very young, in a fresh, innocent, open way, but on the other hand, after just a few moments' concerned conversation, he does strike you as solid, sensible and mature, someone you could trust for expert and wise advice, despite his youth. I watched from the back pharmacy as he attended to an elderly woman who was worried about her asthma inhaler. Andrew was standing almost to attention behind the front counter, his arms clasped behind his back, square shoulders, very clean in his sparkling white shirt, neat tie, suit trousers and shiny black shoes. The girls all wear the traditional white coat, but he wears executive civvies. He has dark hair, which is neatly cut, with strong streaks of grey – despite only being in his late twenties – which add to his look of youthful distinction.

The woman was worried that her inhaler was giving her a sore throat and bad cold which didn't seem to go away. Andrew took her through her asthma routine, the strength of her inhaler, how often and when she used it, and came to the conclusion that the sore throat was caused by the dry hot weather, but a simple cough medicine would ease it. He appeared to know about her job, adding that working in a smoky atmosphere was not helping. When he came back into the pharmacy he was still wearing his concerned expression. No faces or sighs about the length of time he'd spent talking and calming the woman down. 'This is the worst place for asthma I've known. I can't understand it. It's worse than some inner city places, yet we're near the countryside, not far from the coast. Perhaps it's the hot dry summer. That's been bad for asthmatics everywhere.'

Andrew was born in Leigh, Lancashire, and his father works as a pharmaceutical rep, which he says had nothing to do with his choice of career. He went to the local comprehensive, where from an early age his hair started to show bits of grey. 'Boys behind me in class used to pull it out. The grey bits were very thick, like fishing wires. No, I wasn't worried about going grey. I was more worried at the thought of going like my dad – he's hardly any hair at all . . .'

He got good science A levels – three Bs in chemistry, maths and physics – and a place at Manchester University. He had originally thought of taking some science degree, but decided on pharmacy, doing something which would lead to a specific career. 'It turned out to be a fairly old-fashioned traditional course. We did things like chromatology, extracts from plants and pharmacognosy, all of which is irrelevant to this job. It made me more qualified to work in industry as a chemist than as a pharmacist, so in my first job I did worry a lot and had some sleepless nights. For about six months I walked round the shelves with the *BNF* in my hand.' This stands for the *British National Formulary*, the standard work which lists all drugs, plus their side-effects. 'I have made mistakes, of course. You wouldn't be human if you hadn't, but on the very rare occasions it's happened, I've managed to catch the person before they've got home.'

He did his first, trainee, year in Leigh, moved to Liverpool, then on to Bolton, where he first became a manager. The reason for so many moves in a short time was because his father tipped him off about vacancies which he heard about on his rounds. He came to his present job, however, through Lynn, his wife, whose home town is Preston. She is an E-grade staff nurse, on £14,000 a year, at the Royal Victoria Hospital in Blackpool.

When they set up house together, they chose a brand-new house in the smaller village of Wesham, equidistant between Blackpool and Preston. Andrew said: 'It was after we got the house that I looked round for a local job, and heard about this one. I started here on 5 October 1992. I love it. The people are the friendliest bunch I've ever known. No, really. Perhaps it's because people have more time here than they have in inner city places. You don't get any abuse. Oh, it happens in some chemists. When you run out of stock and ask people to wait till tomorrow, they can give you a right mouthful. Here, they're always prepared to wait.' Andrew himself does personal deliveries in his own car in his lunch break, taking medicines to the elderly or housebound. He wouldn't ask the girls to do it. Anyway, none of them has a car. 'It's also good for business,' he explained with a smile. Meaning PR-wise. Customers like chemists who deliver.

His salary is £25,500, which he admits, with a blush, is pretty high. It includes a bonus deal dependent on the 'scripts', which is how they refer to prescriptions. When he took over as manager, the monthly total of prescriptions was 2,000. Mr

Walne promised that if he got more than that, he would be paid 10p per script. Now it's up to 2,500, so Andrew is doing pretty well. 'Yes, but it makes me so guilty.' Why? 'Well, I see people in here coppering up, counting every penny, really hard-up people, struggling to keep going, and here's me, only twenty-seven, yet I'm earning all that money, have my own house, a new car, and my wife has a new car, it just doesn't seem fair...'

'Oh, come on, Andrew,' said Linda. 'You've studied hard to get where you are. You've worked for it and you deserve it.'

'That's what Lynn tells me when I start saying I feel guilty. She just tells me to shut up.'

Their house cost them £60,000, and they got a mortgage of £57,000. 'The £3,000 we put down was really Lynn's savings. She's good with money. I tend to fritter it away if I have anything in my pocket.' Since their marriage eighteen months ago, they have been saving hard. One savings account is earmarked to start a family. They want to have children in the next three years, before Lynn is thirty, but they know it will mean giving up her salary, as she wants to bring the children up herself. 'We were discussing it only the other week; deciding how much we'll need to save before she can leave.'

The other piggy-bank is a longer-term ambition. Andrew has always dreamed that one day he will own his own chemist shop, with his chosen name up front, if not quite in lights but in some tasteful lettering. Just a few weeks previously he'd heard that Mr Walne, the shop-owner, who runs another, bigger shop elsewhere in Preston, was thinking of retiring. It turned out he was thinking some time ahead – in fact on 1 January 2000. 'That's when he'll reach fifty-five. I spoke to him about it, and he told me yes, that's when he intends to pack it in. I asked him if, when the time came, he might give me first refusal on this shop, and he seemed agreeable. What he actually said was, "When you're ready, Andrew." So, that was reassuring.' Andrew took this to mean that he therefore had five years to save up and make some sort of bid, if of course they could manage to save anything at all, what with starting a family.

'It's just been a dream, of course. Something to aim for. I don't even know how much the shop is worth. That wasn't discussed.' Pushed to give an estimate, he thought £150,000 might be the price, seeing that the business had been doing well since Andrew came. A huge sum for someone of his age to contemplate, already lumbered with a house mortgage, which could easily turn into a lump of negative equity, given that house prices have slumped in the three years since they bought. 'It probably has gone down in value, but we haven't dared to think about that. We bought it to stay there for life, so the value in a way hasn't worried us.'

The thought of his own shop might have been a fantasy, something to realise in the years ahead, but it hasn't stopped Andrew and Lynn discussing it in idle moments. Lynn, so they decided, would be a partner in this fantasy shop, by which time their fantasy baby would probably be at school. Lynn's nursing experience would enable her to set up a little clinic as part of their own chemist shop, in which she would offer pregnancy tests, cholesterol tests, measure blood pressure and asthma levels, teach first aid and baby care, monitor asthma. This would be done while you wait, something no chemist shop has ever done, as far as Andrew is aware. 'I'd also like a proper baby department, with all the foods and stuff, even selling prams. Of course we couldn't do it in this shop. We haven't space. Anyway, it's all just been our idle fantasy, as of course we haven't had any money...'

Until, that was, the night of Saturday 26 August. They have been playing the Lottery, all five of them, in a properly organised syndicate, since April. All rather modest, as big winners go, contributing just £1.20 each, enough for six lines. They stick to the same six lines, one of the girls going each Saturday to buy the ticket. So far they have twice won £10. On the night in question, three of the girls were out, with none of them watching the *Lottery Live* show. Andrew had taken Lynn for a surprise treat, picking her up from her Blackpool hospital and taking her to the Winter Gardens where he had got tickets for *Joseph*. Afterwards, he had planned to take her to dinner in a restaurant.

Linda and her husband were out visiting relatives. June was at home, but watching *Colombo* on another channel. Hilary was out having a drink at St Bernard's, the estate's Roman Catholic social club. Sarah was also out having a drink in a pub on the estate, having left her fiancé John at home with the children.

It was John who actually saw the programme and checked the numbers. Sarah had bought the ticket that week, so he knew where it was. He immediately rang her at the pub, the Savick, telling her to come home, they'd won the jackpot.

'I didn't of course believe him,' Sarah said. 'I thought it was a joke, but then I thought he wouldn't do that. It would be too cruel.' When she got home, she started ringing round the girls, leaving messages for them. Linda came home early, so she got hers first.

'My first worry was that Sarah hadn't actually bought the ticket,' said Linda. 'She can be a bit, let's say, forgetful.' Linda in turn ran round the corner to June's house to tell her personally. Eventually they all gathered at Sarah's house, still trying to contact Andrew. They'd left a message on his answer phone, but without saying they'd won the jackpot, just asking him to ring Sarah.

'I don't know why we didn't tell him,' said Linda. 'I think we were worried that because we were always playing tricks on him, he would think this was just another practical joke.'

Meanwhile, in Blackpool, Andrew and Lynn decided after all not to go to a restaurant after the show. Instead they stopped on the way home to pick up a take-away from their favourite Indian restaurant. 'The phone rang just as we got through the front door,' said Andrew, 'before I had even listened to any of the messages. It was Sarah who told me the news. She knew by then roughly how much we would each get – about half a million was the estimate. Well, it was a shock. I had to sit down. I even had a bit of a cry. We didn't go to bed till 1.30, by which time we'd forgotten all about the Indian take-away. So we threw it out. I didn't sleep, of course.'

On Sunday, a Winners' Adviser, Francesca, arrived from Liverpool. They quickly agreed to go public, which was fairly academic, as the news was all round Preston. With five people, and messages left all over the town, it was bound to leak out.

'When Sarah rang me at the pub,' said Hilary, 'I couldn't hear for all the noise, so they shouted it out: YOU'VE GOT SIX NUMBERS! Naturally everybody in the pub heard as well. Over at the Labour Club, so I'm told, someone came on stage and announced that we had won.'

'No!' said Linda and June in unison, who had been carrying on serving. 'I never knew that.'

'That's what I've been told,' said Hilary. 'You can't keep many secrets in this place.'

Their Winners' Adviser told them to give no interviews, tell no more people, until after the validation and the press conference. Because Monday was August Bank Holiday, it didn't take place till Tuesday, so they had two days in which to keep quiet.

'The pressure was terrible,' said Andrew. 'Not being able to talk to anyone. Monday was hell, though I was the luckiest one. I live well out of town, and my street isn't even in the

*A–Z*, so no one could track me down.'

The *Lancashire Evening Post* was OK,' said Hilary. 'They were very discreet in their report, not giving away too many details, but one of the national tabloids was terrible. They sent people round the estate, knocking up people late at night, asking for our addresses, which was awful of them. They never spoke to any of us, but they implied that they had. We only won a relatively small amount, but the pressure was terrible. Imagine what happens to people who win £20 million! They must get hounded.'

'The *Sun* also implied that there was a row between us and Mr Walne,' said Andrew, 'suggesting he was upset because he wasn't part of our syndicate, which is totally untrue. He probably didn't even know we had one. Anyway, he is thrilled by our good luck.'

They validated in Liverpool, Camelot's regional HQ, where each received their cheque for £446,952, then gave a press conference in the Victoria and Albert Hotel, Manchester, beside the Granada TV studios. All were in their best and newest clothes. Andrew had on a brightly coloured striped shirt instead of his usual white. June, Hilary and Linda were in smart summer suits. Sarah wore a white broderie anglaise blouse.

'We were very nervous,' said Andrew. 'But it went OK. The funniest bit was a live interview afterwards, on BBC Radio 5. The interviewer discovered that Sarah was the only one not married. He said he had a decent job, good prospects, but he didn't have what Sarah had, which was money – so, live on air, he proposed to her! That was very funny.'

At the end of the week they went down to London for the Lottery TV show, which again made them very nervous. 'Beforehand, I looked around and I could sense we were all thinking the same thing – what are we doing here?' said Andrew. 'But it was fine, and we enjoyed it. The only disappointment was that when I've watched the show, I've thought it was spontaneous. It's not at all. It's not only all rehearsed, but we were given our script. They'd written down the questions we would be asked and our answers.'

'But we all enjoyed it,' said Hilary. 'I thought Camelot were brilliant, the way they looked after us.'

Now, three days after their fleeting moments of national exposure, they were all back at work. The four women repeated, once again, that they intended to carry on working. Well, for the time being. On the little noticeboard in the back room I could see a dozen cards and letters of congratulations, sent from friends and customers on the estate. From time to time I could hear people in the front shop saying 'well done' to June, the longest serving and therefore best known of the assistants.

*The Preston Syndicate: Andrew Hall, centre, then, from the left, June, Hilary, Sarah and Linda*

It was Linda's numbers, not June's, which won them the Lottery, as it was her line which came up, all based on her family's ages and birthdays. 'If you had said to me I would win the Lottery,' said Linda later, having a mid-afternoon cup of tea and Kit Kat, provided by Andrew, 'I would have said I'd be off like a flash, sitting on a tropical beach the next day; you wouldn't see me for dust. But that's not real life. In real life, when it really happens, you have commitments. You don't want to let people down. You take things slowly. I've never won a thing in my life before. I considered I wasn't lucky. But now we're already looking for a new house on the outskirts of Preston, something nice and detached, perhaps up to £100,000. Then we'll invest the rest for our old age. We won't go overboard. My husband David has already found out you can't actually buy a Williams Renault even if you have the money. There's a huge waiting-list. But we will go and watch all the Grand Prix races in future. So far, all I've spent any money on is a new outfit, the one I wore for the Lottery show. Our children think, of course, it should be Spend, Spend, Spend. They can't understand our caution. Lisa [the trainee engineer] is already committed to her career, so I don't think it will affect her too much. She had her first flying lesson on the day we won, so I might help her with that. But I worry that David [aged sixteen] will now think he's made for life, that everything will be easy. He's got a big shock coming to him . . .'

Hilary was very pleased by the reaction of her eighteen-year-old daughter Jennifer. 'She said she was very happy for me, after all the years we've had to struggle. She said I should put all the money in the bank and forget it. That's what we have done, though I am going to buy a new computer for David [aged ten] as he's mad on them. And of course we will buy a house. I'd like to treat Ricky [her lorry-driver husband] to a holiday in Australia. Thirty years ago, his sister emigrated on a £10 passage, when she was twenty-four and Ricky was only eight, and he hasn't seen her since. But really, it hasn't sunk in yet. I keep veering between thinking, Well, it's not a lot, we're not exactly millionaires, then thinking, Yes, it will change our life. If it was a lot more, I would give some away, to animals, or Bosnian children. I think I'll keep it all. Nobody helped me when I was hard up.'

June, the quiet June, aged fifty-four, was still in a state of shock, so she was telling customers all afternoon. 'If I pinch myself any more, I'll be bruised all over!' She hasn't been pestered as much as the others, being so quiet, but also because she is the only one who is ex-directory. Despite the money, she thinks she still won't learn to drive, but she will buy a bungalow on the edge of the town. 'We have never had any capital in our whole life, but this will mean we won't have to worry any more about paying the bills. We've always had good health, and that's the most important thing. People talk rubbish when they say money won't change their life. I won't change, as a person, I've been this way a long time, but your life is bound to change by having fewer worries.'

She might even, she said, start dancing lessons. Dancing?

'Yes,' she said. 'I've wanted dancing lessons all my life, but could never afford them.'

Sarah, the youngest, was already looking at houses away from the estate. 'I want somewhere really quiet, but I hope not too far away, as I want to keep working here. I'll have a car by then, just a small one, nothing expensive. That's all my dream ever was – a house and a car.' In one of the local newspaper reports of their win, Sarah was quoted as saying her first treat was going to be a 'roast beef dinner'.

'I didn't quite say that. I was just joking amongst the girls and some reporter overheard me. What I actually said was, "Well, it won't be a frozen chicken this Sunday for lunch!"'

Andrew, the lovely Andrew, had of course already got his

master plan lined up, if only in his head. Will he now do it? 'Well, Lynn will probably leave work earlier than planned, but that's about all. We won't change our house, as we're happy with it, though if and when children come, we might move somewhere bigger.' He is now contemplating private education for his children, if and when the time comes. 'I've nothing against comprehensives, as I went to one, and nothing against the teachers. It's just the funding. The way things are going, state schools won't have the money for anything.'

And the shop? Will he now buy his own?

'Yes, I could make Mr Walne an offer this very moment, but I'm still thinking about it. The dream has come true, but I'm holding back. There's no hurry. We're off on holiday in a week's time, our first holiday for eighteen months, since our honeymoon. It's just a bog-standard package, an apartment in Cyprus. I suppose I could up-grade us now I've got the money, but I won't. I've never actually fancied exotic holidays.'

Will he change, as a person? The corny question, but also the corny thought which strikes every winner at this stage. 'We're all bound to. It'll probably make us a bit more self-confident, I suppose. But human nature being what it is, I'll still be a worrier. I won't have to worry about money any more, but I'll doubtless find something else to worry about. I'll probably turn into a hypochondriac.'

Having his own chemist shop could be handy.

**15**

# ALAN AND LINDA, MARGATE

Alan Baker and Linda Hill won the jackpot towards the end of the National Lottery's first year, in week 48 of Camelot's rule, as they always like to describe it, or 14 October 1995 according to the calendar. And straight away they decided to come out, go public, enjoy the experience to the full. They opted to come to London for the validation, instead of Reigate, Camelot's regional office for their area. They arrived on Monday evening and checked into the Charing Cross Hotel, nice and handy for the validation next morning at Camelot's Trafalgar Square offices. The Savoy Hotel would have been equally handy, but by now Camelot were not lashing out as often on the luxury treatment. Alan and Linda were paying their own hotel expenses.

The moment they got up on the Tuesday morning, Linda started making the bed, putting the curtains neat, tidying the room, until Alan told her to stop. After twelve years as a chambermaid at Butlin's at Cliftonville, Margate, she was understandably finding it hard to cast off her working habits. Not that she wanted to. She was determined to carry on with her job, and had gone to work on Sunday and on Monday, despite their win. Alan on the other hand had given in his notice on Monday, finishing at 3.30 – for good.

Linda is forty-seven, originally from Coventry, and has five sisters and three brothers. She is trim and slender, bubbly and attractive, open and friendly, showing few signs of some of the tough periods she has had in her life. She has five children and has been married twice, but was hoping that would not have to come out. She joined Butlin's as a chambermaid in 1973 and has been with them since then, with only a couple of spells

*Alan and Linda*

off. She enjoys the job, despite the low wages. Over breakfast in their hotel they read the *Sun*, which had a front-page story about her – though she personally had not spoken to any reporter, neither had Alan. But they were not upset. In fact they were both pleased to see the space they had got – front page, continued on another page. Linda was only slightly annoyed that the *Sun* had put her salary at £125. Black mark there, Lenny Lottery. Linda says she has never earned £125, even for a six-day week. Her normal wage, doing a six-day week, is £90, which comes to about £75 in her hand. (Lenny Lottery, with whom I took up this mistake later, says it was someone at Butlin's who gave him that information. Next day he corrected it. Well done, Lenny.)

Alan is fifty-four, tall and rather burly, with greying hair, spectacles and a cheerful disposition. He comes from Ramsgate, has been married, and has three children. All his working life has been spent in the betting business – his dad was a bookmaker and so is Alan. At one time he had his own little business as a bookmaker, standing on race courses, both horses and dogs. For the last few years he has been the manager of a Tote betting shop in Herne Bay, a senior manager, which means that apart from running his own betting shop, he has to supervise seven others. Seems a lot of responsibility for a basic salary of £13,000 a year.

He has been in a front-line position to see the effects of the National Lottery on the gambling business. During the year, many betting shops have closed, staff laid off, turnover down by up to 20 per cent, so the industry has been complaining. 'Some of our shops have been badly hit, losing up to 45 per cent of their customers. But, on average, we've had just a 10 per cent drop. Depends on the area you're in, and the sort of customers. I've noticed in my shop we've lost a lot of our morning trade.'

Alan and Linda first met ten months ago, in February.

They were both living alone, each getting over a divorce. Linda was in a bed and breakfast establishment, Alan in a small flat. She had a boyfriend, who was a friend of Alan's, and that was how he first caught sight of her. 'This bloke always maintained I was his best friend,' said Alan, 'but I wasn't really. In fact, I didn't really like him. When I saw him out with Linda, I used to think, "What's a nice girl like her going out with him for?" When I heard they'd split up, I wanted to tell her I wasn't really his best friend. So I was looking out for her, to tell her. By chance on Thursday evening, when I was playing cards in this pub I go to, the Dane Valley Arms, she came in with her brother Mervyn. She was wearing a black mini-skirt, and I thought, Hmm, she is tasty. But you know what it's like with the lads. When you're playing cards, you think about the cards. But I did manage to go across and say to her, Hello, remember me? She said Yes, and I said I'd like to see her again. I got her phone number. This was on 2 February this year. I rang her on 3 February, and went out with her for the first time on 4 February and that was it. We just clicked.'

On 11 June they set up home together, renting a small council flat which Alan has been busy decorating and furnishing ever since. In his life, there have been times, he says, when he has been quite wealthy, running his own betting business for a while, but his divorce was expensive. In recent years he has had very little money. Linda has never had money. For her, life has been one long struggle. She has never had a holiday abroad, never been in an aeroplane. She hasn't a car and has never learned to drive.

They were together in their little flat on Saturday evening, 14 October, watching the Lottery programme as usual. Alan puts £7 on each week, usually sending one of his staff to the local newsagent to buy the tickets for him on Saturday morning. Five of the lines are his and two are Linda's, numbers she has chosen. 'We always said we'd share every-thing, if we ever won. I did have four numbers once, and won £91.'

'As I was watching the programme,' said Linda, 'I heard Mystic Meg say that she saw someone in blue winning this week. My Butlin's uniform is blue, so that was good. I don't think Alan took it in. We were talking through the pro-gramme, as we always do, waiting for the numbers.'

'I wrote them down as they came up,' said Alan. 'Mine were all useless, but Linda's second line had got five right, so I shouted out loud, "You lucky cow!" Then I shouted, "Now you can get your front-loader!" That's what she's been wanting for the flat – a front-loading washing machine. I worked out five numbers would bring her about £1,000. Then I said that if only this number 38 was 30, she'd have all six numbers right.'

Linda took the ticket to check, and saw that Alan had misread it. It was a number 30, not a 38. He had been confused by the computer typeface. 'Well, we both felt funny then. Very strange. The next thing we did was start ringing people – family and friends. In fact we were on the phone for hours, and didn't get to bed till 12.30. We also had quite a few drinks,' she said. 'In fact, I went to bed quite drunk!'

They had managed, with a struggle, to ring Camelot. 'I didn't know their number,' said Alan, 'so I rang Linda's dad to see if it was on Teletext. He gave me a number which I rang and it turned out to be a tipping agency, tipping Lottery numbers. I didn't need that, did I, having won? But I got through in the end and was told Maggie would come and see us on Sunday afternoon.'

Linda insisted on going to Butlin's first thing on Sunday morning to do her normal chambermaiding shift, which Alan thought was silly. She left him instructions about their Sunday lunch, about what to do with a piece of pork she'd bought, which again he thought was silly. 'We never argue, never have done,' said Alan, 'but one of the things we'd said the night before, the moment we won the money, was that whatever happens, we must not fall out. So there we were, having a silly argument about the lunch with me telling her not to bother about it, now we're rich. She gave in – and binned the pork. It went down in the rubbish sack. Later that day, when her brother came round, we brought it out again, cleaned it up and put it in the deep-freeze.'

By the time Maggie, the Winners' Adviser from Camelot, arrived, news of their win was all round the town, as so many friends and relations had been told, but they would probably have agreed to publicity anyway. 'We were happy with the win, and thought, Why not? We have nothing to hide. Maggie also explained that if we get it over with at a press conference, the press will be happy and they won't pry into our lives too closely.'

So on Tuesday morning they walked from the Charing Cross Hotel to Camelot's London office, where Maggie met them. They were taken below to a suite in the basement, where Rachael Hudson, head of the London regional office, went through a list of questions – names, address, ages, family details – writing down the answers on her clip-board. There was some slight consternation when Alan discovered he had forgotten his driving licence, the proof of identity he had meant to bring with him. However, he had also brought his passport and three credit cards. Rachael checked them and then asked for his Lottery ticket.

'Here you are,' said Alan. 'You can have it for £1,000.'

'Do you mean it?' said Rachael, taking the ticket from his hand. 'This is worth £1.9 million!'

'No, really, it's yours, for £1,000. We've decided we don't want to be millionaires.'

Rachael turned the ticket over, wondering if this could be

true, and noticed that the ticket had not yet been signed.

'You have to sign here.'

Maggie came across to look at the ticket. 'It was the last thing I told you to do, Alan,' she said.

'Ha ha, just a joke,' said Alan. 'I would have let you have that ticket for £1,000 – because it's not the right one! I've got the real one here in my wallet.'

Well, it made a change from bursting into tears or going totally silent, which, according to Rachael, is what often happens at this stage.

Next came Sarah Linney, Camelot's press person, head of their newsroom, who went through a similar list of factual questions, getting enough information for a hand-out she would have to write at once and give out at the press conference. She also went through the format of the conference, what things they might be asked, such as their plans for spending the money. She told them to reveal nothing they didn't want to reveal, but at the same time to talk as much as possible, tell little stories. 'You don't have to worry about them. They want to see you happy.'

They couldn't think of what they intended to spend the money on, apart from the usual things, such as a house and a holiday. 'We can't go till January,' said Alan. 'Linda's daughter Caroline is having a baby on 12 November, so she wants to be here for that. Then it will be Christmas, so I think we'll wait till January. I'd like to take Linda to Spain, to Benidorm. I think she'd like that, but of course the weather won't be so good in January. Perhaps we'll go to Florida instead . . .' He was emptying his head, rather than talking, and the Camelot officials smiled and nodded as he burbled away.

When Linda, however, happened to say that there was also her work to think about, she wasn't going to give that up, Sarah interrupted. 'You must say that at the press conference,' she said. 'The press will love you being a chambermaid and not giving it up. But don't say you went to bed drunk on Saturday evening. That could come out badly. Just say you had a few drinks. What about you, Alan? Are you carrying on work?'

'Oh, no, I've already given in my notice. Why work if I've got £1.9 million? I don't have to rely on anyone else from now on. But I won't do nothing for ever, because I'd get bored. I might open my own book again. You meet all sorts on the race track, but everyone is equal. There's no side in gambling. The Queen Mother loves it, you know, and so do ordinary people.'

Sarah asked if he had any strong views about the effects of the Lottery on betting shops. 'Well, it hasn't helped, has it? Some have lost 45 per cent.'

'Oh, no,' said Sarah, clutching her head in mock panic. 'You're not going to attack the National Lottery, are you?'

'Don't worry, I'll keep my opinion to myself. But it's not a good gamble, is it, the National Lottery? The odds are terrible.'

'You'll probably be asked if the prizes are too big.'

'They are,' said Alan. 'Twenty million is ridiculous. Two million is quite sufficient. Though now I've got my two million, perhaps three million would be better!' Everyone laughed.

While we waited for the next official, Alan demonstrated tick-tack signs, the hand gestures used on race courses to signal the odds. Endless cups of tea and coffee were drunk. Alan and Linda beamed non-stop. From time to time she touched his knee while he gave her a cuddle.

The next official personage was a Scotsman in a dark suit from Drummond's Bank, part of the Royal Bank of Scotland. He had with him the actual cheque, made out to Alan for £1,891,543. He explained that advice about possible investments would come later, when they met Camelot's panel. For now, he suggested that they left all the money with the Royal

Bank of Scotland, and he would open an account for them. He had brought with him £2,000 in cash, for them to have at once, as spending money. In a few days they would get a gold card. They could have access to more of the money at once, and the rest would be on deposit for a month, while they decided what to do next.

This was all said very quickly and matter-of-factly. I didn't hear him say that the money could of course be put into their own bank accounts, if they happened to have any, but it is true that Alan and Linda, like most winners, did appear a bit over-excited and perhaps not taking everything in. It is therefore easier to keep everything simple at this stage. 'Actually, we're having two separate accounts,' said Alan. 'We've already decided that. Half in her name, half in mine.'

There would be no problem about that, said the Scotsman. That could all be done. 'Do you want a calculator to work out the exact halves?' said Alan, smiling.

'No, I think I can divide by two in my head,' said the banker.

When he'd gone, I asked Alan his reasons for two accounts. 'If we want to buy each other presents, the other will always know the details if the money's in the same account, so it's best to keep them separate. I love Linda dearly, and she loves me, but you never know what might happen in life. And whatever does happen, she'll have £900,000 in her own name.'

The press conference was held again in the Waldorf Hotel, but in a slightly smaller function room. The room was full, with about fifty press men and women, plus three or four camera crews. The previous week, when a £2 million winner had been unveiled, no TV crew had turned up. Linda had already made the front page of the *Sun*, a story which had given the impression she was a deserving person, i.e. a humble, poorly-paid Butlin's chambermaid. So that was an attraction.

The questions were standard – how had they picked the numbers, what were they going to do with the money. They admitted they were each divorced and had grown-up children. 'Will you get married?'

'No,' said Linda emphatically.

'You have been married?' someone asked.

'Yes,' said Alan.

Linda smiled, appearing to agree, so she didn't actually lie. Before anyone could get further details of her marital history, Alan was asked where they were going for their holiday.

It was all over in fifteen minutes. After the obligatory photo session outside, they withdrew into a private suite for champagne, where they were joined by Linda's brother Mervyn, aged forty-three, his arms covered in tattoos. He looked rather sad and forlorn. He explained he took pills for his nerves and depression, but wasn't on them today. You weren't allowed to drink while taking them, and he did intend to have a few glasses of champagne with his sister, with whom he had always been very close. 'She's a lovely girl,' he said. 'And when you think what she's been through, she deserves it. In fact, it couldn't have happened to a nicer couple.'

**16**

## PETER DAVIS OF OFLOT

Looking after Britain's National Lottery during its first year was Peter Davis, Director General of the National Lottery, a follow-up job in a way. It was he who granted the licence to Camelot in the first place. If anything went wrong he could get double the blame, for giving it to them in the first place and for not regulating them enough should they in any way transgress.

He is an accountant by profession, aged fifty-three, tall, rather hefty, wears glasses, looks solid and establishment, but is usually rather affable and un-pompous. It was a surprise to most people, and himself, when in 1993 he was appointed by Peter Brooke, then the Secretary of State for National Heritage. 'I'm just a boring, middle-aged chartered account-ant,' he was quoted as saying. 'I had never met Mr Brooke before. I don't know why I have been chosen.'

He lives in Wimbledon, likes football and fly-fishing, and is married with two sons. Alexander, the older, is at Lincoln College, Oxford – Peter's old college – while Timothy is at Bradfield School. Peter himself went to Winchester College. At Oxford he read law, then decided he would prefer a more practical profession and qualified as a chartered accountant. He worked for Price Waterhouse for several years, becoming a partner, before moving sideways into industry, joining the carpet empire run by Phil Harris, Harris Queensway, whose accounts he used to look after. Peter, as deputy chairman, remained more in the background, cautious and careful, looking after the financial side, while Mr Harris – later Sir Phil and now a Lord – was the energetic public figure who became one of Mrs Thatcher's favourite entrepreneurs in the 1980s. He was paid well and had some valuable shares in the company, but its growth continued too fast, so in 1988 he moved on to Sturge Holdings, insurance underwriters and stockbrokers, where he was finance director. At about the same time, he became deputy chairman of Abbey National.

*Peter Davis*

In 1993, when he was approached about the Lottery job, it came right out of the blue, so he says. He has no Tory party connections, social or otherwise, nor had he ever done any government work. 'I was head-hunted, that's all there was to it. A head-hunter rang me up, someone by chance I had met before, but that is irrelevant. He was working through a list of people and asked me if I might be interested. My first reaction was No. I don't know anything about gambling or lotteries of any sort, and I had never worked for the government in any capacity. But the more I thought about it, the more interesting and exciting the project sounded.' So he agreed to go on a long shortlist, which was whittled down to three or four, all of whom were interviewed personally by the minister. Looking back, he assumes they were looking not just for a solid, reputable accountant, which of course he was (on the Council of the Institute of Chartered Accountants since 1990), but one who had had some sort of mass market commercial experience. Thus his years in the carpet business, not exactly the most socially prestigious of industries, had proved to be a vital factor.

He was given a Civil Service grading but not an official car, a salary of £80,000 a year, an initial staff of six, and told to get started. His first and main job was to appoint the licence-holder, with only the Act of Parliament and some very hazy wording (see Chapter Two) to guide him. 'You are quite right. It was left to me to decide what to do and how to go about it. But no one leaned on me. The government left the choice to me. And if I had mucked it up, I would have carried the can.'

He travelled to the USA and elsewhere, and his researches into lotteries around the world showed him that the UK Lottery was going to be different in two important ways from almost every other government or state Lottery. 'First of all, ours was likely to be run by a company from the privatised sector, not by a government department, as in almost every other country. We were not going to have Civil Servants running it. I suppose that is traditional Tory thinking, to let private commerce run it, and I have no views on that. Secondly, it was laid down from the beginning that specified good causes would share equally the money raised, which would go direct to them. In North America and in Ireland, lottery money goes to the state first of all, and then they themselves do the sharing out. In Britain, the amounts of money would always be known – and always be absolutely visible.'

Before the bidding process started the only known factor in the dividing up of the total Lottery income was that 12 per cent would go in tax to the government. Applicants for the licence were asked to bid the percentage of total sales which they would commit to the good causes and to prizes for the players. 'In looking at the bidders, I had several broad criteria in mind, including which would raise most for the good causes, which would keep the least for themselves, and which would be the best company to run the Lottery and meet its commitments.'

All the eight bidders suggested slightly different percentages and variables, so it was hard to compare like with like, especially when the size of the possible income was unknown, and estimates varied enormously. Mr Davis, being a trained accountant with modern computer facilities at his disposal, along with his fountain pen and a sheet of paper, created fifteen models, fifteen revenue scenarios, based on various estimates of what the Lottery might bring in, including those which the various bidders were proposing.

'Camelot clearly came out top as the company which would provide most for the good causes across the range of different revenue models. I'm not saying it scored the top mark in every case – in some scenarios another company would have done better – but, overall, Camelot was the company most likely to

# NEWS

**THE NATIONAL LOTTERY**

## THE NATIONAL LOTTERY:

## BACKGROUND MEDIA BRIEFING

**Contacts**

**The Rowland Company**

**London**
Tel: 071 436 4060
Fax: 071 265 2131

**Hall Harrison Cowley**

### Introduction

**Birmingham**
Tel: 021 236 7532
Fax: 021 236 7220

Britain's National Lottery is on track for launch on the 19th November 1994. When

**Bristol**
Tel: 0272 292311
Fax: 0272 299084

fully operational, it is expected to be the world's largest lottery and Britain's biggest

brand. It is projected to raise more than £9 billion for good causes over the next

**Cardiff**
Tel: 0222 344717
Fax: 0222 344630

seven years, create a millionaire nearly every week and generate hundreds of new

**Edinburgh**
Tel: 031 226 7348
Fax: 031 226 4915

jobs throughout the country. Between now and the launch, a massive logistics effort

is underway to ensure a punctual and smooth start-up. This document is designed to

**Maidenhead**
Tel: 0628 416100
Fax: 0628 777472

give you the background to one of the most ambitious and exciting commercial

**Manchester**
Tel: 061 437 4474
Fax: 061 437 7055

ventures ever undertaken in the United Kingdom.

**Southampton**
Tel: 0703 226361
Fax: 0703 331585

### The licensee

Under the National Lottery etc Act 1993, eight consortia submitted competitive

tenders to run the National Lottery on behalf of the British people. After months of

rigorous evaluation, the Director General of the National Lottery, Peter Davis,

announced that Camelot is the preferred applicant. Camelot submitted the lowest bid

- that is to say it seeks to retain the lowest percentage of sales to cover all operating

The National Lottery
is operated by
Camelot Group plc

**Contact**

**Brunswick Public
Relations**
Tel: 071 404 5959
Fax: 071 831 2823

costs and any profit.

*Press release on Camelot's victory in the tender race*

secure most for the good causes, and in every case to keep the least for themselves.'

So Branson's percentage must have been more than 5 per cent? 'I'm not saying, but Camelot retained the least.'

Have you still got the sheet of paper? 'Yes, but you are not seeing it. It is there, and has been seen only by the National Audit Office.'

Camelot, Mr Davis said, also scored highly on the quality of its management, the commercial experience and stability of the various partners and the strength of its technical systems. That they could start in November – which Camelot still thinks was a vital factor in their win – was less relevant. 'They all said they could start in October or November, though frankly, I had some reservations about whether some of them could. Overall, Camelot seemed to me to be clearly the best. One of my jobs now is to see that each Tuesday the right amount is transferred from Camelot direct into the Bank of England, into an account specifically for the good causes.'

During his first two years in office, two annual reports were published, so we could all see what Mr Davis and Oflot were doing. His 1993–4 report revealed the interesting fact that the submissions from the original eight bidders for the licence came to a total of 160 volumes containing 800,000 pages of information, tables and charts.

Oflot's 1994–5 report, which was published in October 1995, was full of praise for Camelot and the millions rolling in. 'A remarkable achievement,' Mr Davis wrote in his introduction, 'and all concerned at Camelot, and its suppliers, should be congratulated.' In reacting to widespread specula-tion about why Richard Branson's consortium did not win, the report made clear that their 'contribution to the good causes chosen by Parliament was lower than Camelot's'. It revealed that Oflot's staff was now up to thirty and was costing £3 million a year to run. (But this money comes from Lottery

proceeds, not from the government.) This report also mentioned, in passing, that the National Lottery logo – fingers
crossed in a smile – had been officially registered in the name
of the Secretary of State for National Heritage, although I had
always presumed it belonged to Camelot. All they have is the
right to use it, and authorise its use for Lottery purposes while
they hold the licence. If and when they cease to hold the
licence, the logo can be used by National Lottery operators in
the future.

The National Audit Office also produced a report in July
1995 evaluating the applications for the National Lottery. It
praised Oflot's conduct as 'comprehensive, consistent, logical
and properly controlled'. It said that Branson's plan to give
away his own profits was 'not a relevant consideration under
the Act'. But aiming to be an utterly fair organisation, the
National Audit Office did give each of the seven failed bidders
a chance to air their views on the story so far. This revealed,
incidentally, that each bidder had spent at least £1 million on
their application. Only Branson had a really serious grumble
– saying that more money would be coming in if he had won,
because his researches had shown that more people would
play, knowing all profits were going to good causes. Oflot's
Director General dismissed this research as inadequate.

The National Audit Office report included some interesting figures which Camelot and the other bidders gave as
their forecasts of Lottery revenue, back in 1994. All such
figures are now hard to pin down, because there were so many
bandied around at the time, in print as well as in speeches, by
both Camelot and the government, all of them working in the
dark, of course.

With hindsight, both Camelot and the Department of
National Heritage want to be able to boast about the Lottery's
success, showing how well they have done, but on the other
hand, excessive success and excessive profits could suggest

naive predictions and obscenely high rewards. So it pays to choose the original prediction that best suits your case. You can find some very modest estimates, by both government and Camelot officials in 1993–4, which can now be used to prove that the Lottery did twice as well as expected in its first six months. However, the National Audit Office's report gives the success at just 40 per cent higher than the applicants had forecast. It says Camelot's principal revenue forecast, in their application, was sales of £850 million up to 31 March 1995. In the event it was £1,191 million. All the same, a tremendous success story, for the government and Mr Davis of Oflot.

But there were two minor problems for Camelot during the first six months of operation. The Oflot 1995 report found them guilty of a minor breach of their Section 5 licence when there was a breakdown on the first day of the instant scratch cards. This was a technical failure, quickly put right, and not exactly a hanging offence. 'That did concern me,' said Mr Davis when I asked him about it. 'One of my jobs, as the independent watchdog of the National Lottery, is to monitor Camelot's technical services as well as their handling of the winners.'

The other could have been more serious and did lead to questions in the House of Commons. This concerned the anonymity of the £17.8 million Blackburn winner of 10 December 1994 (named by the press as Mukhtar Mohidin). Peter Davis's published report on this incident reprimanded Camelot for committing a 'technical breach' by giving out general information about him. (David Rigg had confirmed that the winner was from the north of England, worked in a factory and had three young children, facts given out with the winner's oral permission, but deemed to be unwise.) But Camelot were cleared of causing his identity to be leaked to the press. Peter Davis interviewed the editors of the *Sun* and the *Daily Mirror* and believed what they said – that it was their

NEWS RELEASE

OFFICE OF THE

**NATIONAL LOTTERY**

<u>**LOTTERY WINNER ANONYMITY: REVIEW PUBLISHED**</u>

The Director General of the National Lottery, Peter Davis, has today (April 3) published his review of the arrangements for the protection of the anonymity of the winner of the jackpot drawn on Saturday 10 December 1994.

Mr Davis said "In the first 20 weeks the National Lottery has created 30 new millionaires and a further 295 people have won prizes of over £100,000. It is important for future public confidence in the National Lottery that winners who wish to remain anonymous can continue to rely on Camelot's professionalism to help protect their privacy. The measures which I have asked Camelot to introduce should help to achieve that aim."

The Director General conducted a thorough review of the events surrounding the draw on 10 December 1994. He found no evidence that Camelot, the licensed operator, breached the terms of its operating licence, which requires it not to disclose the identity of a winner without written consent. Camelot committed a technical breach of the Game Rules by announcing general information about the winner, falling short of his identity, without consent in writing. This is not a matter of serious concern.

The Director General found no evidence that Camelot issued any information, publicly or privately, which helped others to discover the winner's identity.

2 Monck Street, London SW1P 2BQ
Tel: 0171 227 2000; Fax: 0171 227 2005

*Press release on the 'technical breach'*

own investigations and contacts that led them to the winner.

There were also two running topics in the press as 1995 progressed and Camelot came under more and more criticism, neither of which had had any coverage when the Lottery first began: were Camelot's profits too high and were the jackpot prizes too big? I asked Mr Davis for his reaction. 'I have my own private opinion about Camelot's profits but I do not regulate profits and it is not in my powers to dictate how much profit they earn. Camelot have said that their profits will not exceed 1 per cent of total revenue. Camelot was the cheapest operator of all the applicants for the licence, in terms of how much they retain out of total revenue for operating costs and profits. It was always likely that the operator would retain a higher percentage early on, to cover their setting-up expenses. Over the seven years, they will receive only 5 per cent of the total income for costs and profits, while the good causes will get five and a half times as much at 28 per cent. And the good causes will receive their 28 per cent without having any expenses whatsoever.

'I am delighted that the National Lottery has done so well and that Camelot has proved so successful. The point of using a private sector operator was to maximise the income, and it has worked.'

On the subject of capping the jackpot prize, he said that the Heritage Secretary could issue a Direction on the subject to the Director General if he or she thought fit, depending of course on the policy of the government. He himself could probably also insist on a change, if he decided that this was in accordance with his statutory objectives and in the interests of the National Lottery. In those circumstances he could legally put a cap on the prizes. 'But I have no current intention of doing so.' Research and experience abroad shows that any cap will depress turnover because it is the desire to win a big money prize that excites and motivates players to buy tickets.

This is confirmed by experience in the UK, where, in a roll-over week, bigger prizes bring in 15–20 per cent more money.

'Our biggest jackpot prizes may sound enormous, but you should think back to 1826, when we last had a National Lottery, before some Treasury person ran off with the money. In those days the big prize was £20,000. If you translate it into today's terms, that comes to about £92 million. And if you look abroad, in a place like Spain, their El Gordo can pay out a top prize of well over £100 million. Yes, it's usually divided between a whole village, but our big prizes here are usually shared, too. In fact for the average jackpot-winning ticket since the launch, and taking syndicates into account, I believe the figure is around £800,000 for the average win.'

The Director General's salary has increased marginally since the Lottery began, now up to £83,000, and it is not tied to its success, unlike Camelot's income. He has had the privilege of meeting a few private and public winners, some of them when observing Camelot's panels at work. In October 1995 he travelled to Australia at the expense of Interloto, the world lottery body, to give a paper at a world conference of lottery organisations. His wife went with him. 'But I paid for her, of course.'

He himself has never bought a ticket. It was his own decision, to ban himself and his own family from entering, to the annoyance of his two sons. If he ever did enter and win, when his term of office finishes, he would spend the money on buying some exclusive fishing rights in Ireland and in Scotland. 'Then I'd do something frightfully boring and invest the rest to provide a nice secure income.'

Would he go public, or stay private, should he win? 'The problem of anonymity is not as great as it was in the first few months. I don't think people are being hounded as much. Lottery-winners are becoming part of life.' In the early months, when everyone was talking about the Blackburn winner, Mr Davis had his own imagined scenario of what he might do, as a jackpot-winner, to secure total anonymity. First, he wouldn't claim in the week he'd won, but keep the ticket for a few weeks, if not months. Then he would hire an extremely dour Scottish accountant to act on his behalf. People don't realise this can be done, though it is a bit complicated. He would then send his accountant to receive the money and put it at once into a numbered bank account in Switzerland. It would all be invested, and he would slowly improve his standard of living by spending the income. That was the sort of story he used to tell people at dinner parties.

'Today, my view has changed. If I were to win the jackpot now, I would go for it. I would attend the press conference. Why be embarrassed about one's good luck, even if it might mean putting up with a lot of press attention for a few days? After that, there will be new winners, you'll soon be forgotten and can get on with your life. One of the difficult parts of secrecy is not being able to share the truth and the money with family and friends.'

Very true. But can you ever really get on with your own life, whether you have gone public or stayed private, after you have suddenly won an enormous amount of money? We shall see.

## PART TWO

# LIFE AFTER THE LOTTERY WIN

## KEN SOUTHWELL, YORK

Most public winners, after they have had their moments of publicity, retreat into their shell, a new shell usually, and want nothing more to do with the public or the press. Ken Southwell of York was the first public winner, having his fifteen minutes of fame in week 1 of the National Lottery back in November 1994. A year and a bit later it would still be relatively easy to track him down, should you be so minded, or mean enough to want to interrupt his happy and contented life.

It is true he has gone ex-directory, into a new house in a different village, and he now uses Camelot to sift all requests, refusing most media approaches these days, but he is still living in the York area and makes no secret about who he is. If approached by a stranger, he'll still say, Yes, I am that bloke, the early one who won £839,254 on the Lottery. He even offers the world at large a pretty good clue. One of his two new cars is a Range-Rover with the number plate KWS 800. (Walter is his middle name.) The number cost him £1,900; a little present to himself.

His house is modern and detached, in a little hidden-away enclave in the heart of a very desirable village on the banks of a river. Barges and pleasure-boats glide up and down. The most desirable parts of the village have river access, with their own wooden bridges and piers directly on to their own little harbours. Ken hasn't quite got that, but his house does have good access to the river bank, handy for Julie when she takes their Alsatian for a walk. They've got the dog for security, not because of his Lottery win but because they are in a village known for its wealthy residents – many of them, probably, a lot wealthier than our Ken. So far.

He is still living very happily with Julie, in his house this time, not hers, which was the case when he won his money. She is still working. They are still not married. He bought the house in 1995 for £165,000. 'It was £190,000, but this couple were getting divorced so I steamed in and made my offer in cash, outright, and of course they took it.' He made a half apologetic, half smiling face. That's what happens when you have money. You can steam in anywhere if you have it.

His hair was still fairly spiky on top, long and straggly behind. He was wearing fashionably baggy trousers and boots, and appeared relaxed, confident, at ease, smiling through his rimless spectacles. The house was comfortable and middle class, with books, paintings and nice bits of furniture. Professional, rather than nouveau riche, but then of course he wasn't poor when he won his money. He had a proper job, as an engineer, and owned a terrace house.

He hasn't worked since his win, not in the normal being-employed sense. Instead, he has been very careful to make his money work for him. 'One of the first things I did was put almost all my money, £800,000 of it, into a ninety-day bank account. I can recommend this to any Lottery winner. It stops you making hasty decisions. You have three months to think it out and consider all the best investments. And, at the same time, you're getting a high interest rate while you make up your mind. It took me about four months to get my portfolio organised. I listened to the advice of Camelot's experts, and thanks to them I have a person who manages the portfolio for me, from day to day, but I approve or decide the main lines. It's mainly in the obvious things, stocks and shares, gilt stuff, managed funds. The idea is to go for capital growth as well as income. I have about £400,000 in stocks and shares alone and they went up by £25,000 last month. They can of course go down as well as up. I have also three other houses, apart from this one. My master plan is now in place. I have got projections for the next five and ten years. Let's see, in five years, since winning the Lottery, I should be worth £3.2 million. I've forgotten the ten-year projection; it's in the office. That's not too ambitious – turning £1 million into £3 million in five years. Don't forget I started with a little bit of my own. The Lottery win nudged me just over the £1 million mark.'

What he has done is an extension of what he was planning to do anyway. At the time of the win, he'd bought a terrace house in York which he was working on. 'So I bought another two. Nice houses, lots of room. I've been quite cute, really. There will always be a need for student accommodation in York. That won't decrease ever, thanks to the university. I decided on the houses myself. It was nothing to do with my advisers, it's with being a stoic Yorkshireman. If the bottom falls out of stocks and shares, I'll always have my houses. If house values fall, I will always have a cash income coming in from letting to students. Altogether we have five houses, because Julie now rents her house out.'

He did all the conversion work himself on the three houses, and that's been his main occupation in the last year. He's enjoyed doing it, working on his own, making his own hours. At the maximum, when every unit is completed, he should have ten lots of students, giving him a very good weekly income. 'I've been pretty cute,' he repeated.

Yes, but ten students means ten people moaning on about the roof leaking, fridges not working or, even more likely, complaints from neighbours. What's the point of being worth £3 million if you've got to put up with all that annoyance?

'I've thought about that, and I think I can cope. That's why I have what I call my office, here in this house. It has its own phone, answerphone and fax, and I don't go into the office or answer anything after five o'clock. I only do office hours, which I dictate. Our own phone is ex-directory, and no one can get that, only close friends.'

He doesn't expect that his tenants, mostly students, will know who he is or how he got his money, and sees no reason why he can't keep that part of his life totally separate. In the village, though, people know who he is and his background. 'I've known this village for twenty years. I used to play in the pub's darts team when I was younger.'

In York, when doing his shopping, he still occasionally gets recognised in the main street and he quite enjoys it, but he has become much tougher on media interviews. 'That's why I get Camelot to handle everything. They tell me who wants to talk to me, and I accept only about one out of ten. Just the occasional broadsheet. I don't do tabloids any more; they never did get all the facts right. I suppose that was always going to happen, with the complications over my address, on where I was living. But they never even managed to get Julie's name right.

'It's been in the papers that the Range-Rover is Julie's, with quotes from her, which is all wrong. It's mine. What she's got is a new Suzuki Vitara with a soft top, which I bought for her. That's what she wanted. I call it a tart's car. I've also got a Porsche. I bought that recently, a present to myself. It's a Porsche Super Sport, an old one, 1987, cost £21,000, a collector's item. I treated myself to the sort of car I drew as a boy. You know, in your exercise book, you drew your dream car without its having a name. This is it. I really wanted to have a motorbike, a big one, but I didn't have the bottle. On the whole, the press have been kind, but their licence has been unbelievable. Anyone with less resilience than me might have got pretty upset.'

He never did get any begging letters, which is surprising. 'Not one. Perhaps they couldn't find my correct address, or people knew what my answer would be – No. I do have a bit of a reputation for having a sharp tongue and the image of being pretty tight.'

Ken doesn't think their life has basically changed, only their lifestyle. 'Our house is bigger and better, and it is very nice to come home to a beautiful house. And, of course, I have more houses and more cars. I did have one car, especially for the dog. A bit silly, really, but I don't like him mucking up my Range-Rover.' He still does the Lottery, spending about £3 a week. 'Not every week. The shop's often closed by the time I get there, but I've done well. Since my big win, I've had three numbers right four times, and won £10 each, and I've twice had four numbers, with the bonus number, not that that matters, and got £70 and £90. Not bad, eh?'

He still goes to the pub, and drinks and chats and argues with his friends, but not about politics or religion. 'If you were to stand beside me in the pub and get talking about religion or politics, I would agree with you, whatever you said. I wouldn't care. I've never voted and I've no religion. I have no views on either subject, because they're both bollocks.'

I noticed a copy of *The Times* lying around. Had he taken that up since his new-found wealth and status? 'I always read *The Times*. I get it for the facts. I don't want opinions in newspaper stories.

'Inside the house we don't live much differently. We have the same friends, drink the same, eat the same, go on the same sorts of holidays. I went on that skiing holiday which we'd booked, but also took another one later, thanks to the Lottery money. But our day-to-day spending is much the same as it was. I've done no wild spending.'

Or given anything away, to friends or family? 'No, not yet, but I've made arrangements so that Julie and my sister Christine will be set for life, whatever happens to me. Christine is a teacher, unmarried, content with her life, but of course I'd help her if she needed it. When we go out with friends, I don't treat them. Everyone pays their way as they always did. I don't intend to give away any money because the point is to reinvest it, to manage it properly, so that all three of us will always be sure financially, whatever happens.'

At that moment Julie came from work, looking smart and elegant in her black tailored skirt and jacket and crisp white blouse. She still works for the same financial firm, but is no longer a secretary, having been promoted to Personal Assistant. She went to change into her jeans and Barbour jacket, ready to take the dog for a walk and throw off the working day.

'Oh, I still like work. I'd miss it if I gave it up. I think I'll do it for at least another five years. The people at work were all thrilled by what happened. They all crowded round the TV when Ken was on. There's been no ill-feeling. But I suppose I would like to have my own independence. I might in a few years run my own little business. A flower-shop, perhaps. I don't like to live completely on Ken's money. I do have more money now, but it's thanks to Ken. I live in a lovely house and I also have the rent from my own house. I don't have the domestic bills to pay, as this is Ken's house. I still do the Lottery, but only £5 a week. I suppose I'd like to win some money myself, in my own right . . .'

How about getting married? She looked at Ken, waiting for him to answer. 'I don't think so. We've got no plans to get married. Someone would have to convince me it was a good idea . . .'

And children? Ken shook his head, but Julie gave a thin

smile and said, Perhaps, one day. Then she went off for a walk with the dog.

Looking back, Ken has no regrets at all about coming out and going public, and still says he enjoyed his moments of fame, and would recommend it to any winner if they have the right temperament. But there was one down side, something rather annoying which would not have happened had he kept his name out of the papers. On 6 December 1994 a woman from his past came back to haunt him – a date he was very aware of. 'It was on 6 December 1993 that my mother died. I'll never forgive her for that.' She was a woman Ken had lived with for three years, though their relationship had finished in 1990 before Julie came into his life. He had a son by her, a piece of information that naturally had not come out in any of his media-friendly interviews or publicity at the time of his Lottery win. 'Her story was in a newspaper – and they ran screaming headlines, making me look like a rotten bastard, saying that she was now claiming £100,000 from me now that I'm a millionaire ...'

Was it true? 'The son is true, but I've been paying her £80 a month maintenance, which was our agreement, every month since we parted, and I haven't missed once, whatever some people might think. I've had no contact at all with her, or the boy, since we parted. And I don't intend to. It was all a mistake, and ended badly ... I was very upset, but I decided to say nothing in reply, just shrug it off. After all, I'm the wealthy one, and she's not, but I came out looking a right bastard. By not saying anything in reply, of course, some papers kept on repeating the same lies. There was one local paper I could have closed, taken to the cleaners, if I'd decided to sue them for getting things wrong and libelling me. I decided to say nothing, knowing it would just be tomorrow's chip papers.

'She was using a solicitor, so I hired a top barrister. It's up to them now to sort it out and reach some sort of settlement. She's been quoted as saying she wants £100,000. I think it's irrelevant that I'm better off now than I was, but I'm prepared to increase the maintenance, to help with the boy's education. I don't know how much; whatever is reasonable. It's up to the lawyers to agree it. They're still working on it. She seems to have gone quiet at the moment. I have made some allowance in my will for the boy, but I'm not telling her that or revealing any details. It's her I don't want to help, after what she put me through.'

Hasn't this incident made you regret going public? 'Not really, but I now know how the tabloids work, which is why I won't talk to them any more. They build you up in order to knock you down. I've seen it happening with Sting. They're desperate for me to blow it all. That's why I've taken a lot of time and trouble about what to do with the money, making sure I keep control. I much prefer managing my houses on my own. As I say, I think I've been pretty astute and I hope I'm now set up for life. My only regret is that my mother wasn't here to see it.'

Ken has taken up some of his old hobbies again, such as clay-pigeon shooting. They still have regular skiing holidays, but have so far not travelled much. Julie would like to go to Australia, but Ken doesn't fancy the long trip. 'I hate being cooped up on aeroplanes, or anywhere. That's why I don't like the cinema. I still do the Lottery, same as Julie. She watches it, but I don't, now that I'm a millionaire.' He smiled self-mockingly. 'Actually, I hate the word "millionaire". I don't usually use it. You get no title when you're worth only £30, so why should you get one when you happen to have a million? I hate pigeon-holing people.'

Have people been nicer or nastier to you since the win? 'On the whole, people have been nicer than I expected. They still stop and say, Well done. I've enjoyed it all. I've got no worries. All I have to do in life now is worry about my health . . .'

Julie had returned from walking the dog, and was listening to Ken boasting about his lack of worries. 'Yes, but you did worry about the stocks and shares, didn't you? The investments have been a worry.'

'I'd call them a learning process,' said Ken. 'Of course they cause worries at times. In the old days I worried about getting to jobs, or false ceilings, or having enough diesel. I got those financial worries because I knew nothing at all about stocks and shares. But they're not long-term worries. The priorities are all different now. I took off one cap and put on another cap, and in the process I had to learn new things. If you are a worrier, then you'll presumably still be a worrier, whatever happens. Julie is actually the worrier, not me. She worries enough for both of us, so that's nice for me.'

If it's been a learning process, moving into new fields, what have you learned about life itself? Ken didn't answer, but was pleased to think for a while. He does have a confidence about himself, able to give up one career in the police and start an entirely new one, but becoming a millionaire – sorry, becoming rather wealthy – has made him even surer of himself.

Before I first met him, I'd been told by several Camelot people that he was one of their favourite winners, how they all loved him, he was the one with no problems, no phobias, no moans, the one who could be relied upon to be helpful. I'd therefore imagined him as a much older person, already semi-retired, with little else in his life, perhaps even a bit pathetic, who had turned being a Lottery-winner into his only activity. That was the image I'd picked up. Wrongly, of course.

Ken is younger, stronger, tougher, sharper than I had expected. He has not only won the Lottery, but beaten it, made himself its master. And master of the media, in the sense that he has risen above it, got it in proportion, got out of it what he wanted, not caring about public perceptions – something that real celebrities rarely get right. Inside his life, he is also in control. The money is not controlling him, or causing the problems so many winners experience. Well, apart of course from the mother of his child. It seems reasonable to expect he will still be in control in ten years, and worth £10 million.

I asked about happiness, and whether the Lottery win had made any difference to them. It can't be graded, of course, but if they were forced, could they give points out of ten, before and after?

'The Lottery hasn't made much difference to me,' said Julie. 'I was happy before, so I suppose that was ten out of ten. I am just as happy now. The Lottery hasn't affected me, compared with Ken. I've kept out of it, avoided all the publicity. Ken has loved it, most of the time. So I've left it to him.'

'Julie, how can you give happiness ten out of ten?' said Ken. 'There is no such state. You can't ever reach it. I never have, at any period of my life. Before the win, I was fed up with my previous work, going round sites all the time, driving all over the country, and I was about to leave. So I'd say eight out of ten. Today, yes, I am very happy, but my top mark is nine out of ten.

'Money does not necessarily buy happiness,' he said as I left. 'That's what I've learned. What it buys is time, time to make decisions, time to make the right decisions. This relieves you of a great deal of stress. Stress is a killer, so if you have less stress in your life, you live longer. So I would have to say that yes, in that sense, money does buy happiness . . .'

# 18

## AUDREY AND ANDY, HARTLEPOOL

I feared I had lost Audrey and Andy. Of all my ten big winners, they proved the hardest to keep in touch with. There is of course nothing in it for them, no advantage to be gained, no reason to talk about themselves and their lives, once the initial excitement has worn off. The last thing most people want is any more publicity, even in a serious book, not once they have become multi-millionaires.

Yet they had seemed so nice, so happy, so well balanced when they appeared with their two children at their London press conference in March. Something seemed to change once they got back to Hartlepool. When I rang Audrey a few weeks later, she said she was fed up with the whole thing and wished people would leave her alone. Then they disappeared, to stay somewhere secret, I was told, and even Camelot lost track of them. Over the next few months I sent messages and letters and got no reply, and had decided that was it. Not much use doing before-and-after interviews if you don't get the after interview. I would have to dump them, never knowing what happened afterwards.

Had something gone wrong with their relationship? That thought did strike me. Or could it be something to do with the children – Carl, nine, and Claire, five? It was rather unusual to have exposed such young children to the media, having them sitting in at the press conference, taking them to the TV studios, letting them enjoy the delights of the Savoy. Since then, all public winners with young children have taken great care to keep their families apart from any publicity. Perhaps the children had suffered in some way on their return, or been picked on at school.

Then in November, ten months after their win, I got a call from Audrey. Yes, she had been driven mad, but now they were a bit more settled. She gave me their new address and phone number, but I had to cross my heart never to reveal it.

I got a taxi from Darlington station and made the driver's week. The previous day he'd made only £1.50, taking someone to the local shops. My journey took for ever, as we couldn't find a certain new estate, by which time the fare was £30. Well, when you are dealing with millionaires, it does help to act like one.

Their house turned out to be detached and modern, with green fields to one side, and houses still being finished on the other. A rather raw estate, yet to be completed and landscaped, with the show house still doing brisk business. Their house is right at the end, nice location with a rural aspect, but not at all extravagant. Quite modest in a way, for someone with £4 million to spend.

A new car was in the driveway, but again nothing too flash. A £20,000 Vauxhall Omega, two-litre. New conservatory at the back, but an off-the-peg mass-produced one, not a designer model. Smallish garden with not much growing, but then it was winter. Fully furnished, fitted carpets throughout, all spanking new. I was surprised to find they had been in this house over six months, since May.

They both looked healthy and tanned. Audrey's hair had been restyled, cut fashionably short, and she was looking well, but a little bit plump. She groaned. Since the win she had put on a stone. Andy had put on a stone and a half and was now

13 stone. 'I keep getting told I've eaten my shadow,' he said.

They had indeed been unhappy on their return from London, but not for any of the reasons I had suspected. It was simply the press. 'We thought by giving the press conference, it would all be over, that's what Camelot led us to believe,' said Audrey. 'But when we got back to our house, there were reporters and photographers waiting outside for us. They wouldn't go away, and for about three weeks they pestered us – and all the neighbours, going round the doors, asking questions. I didn't mind ordinary people stopping us in the street, like, and congratulating us. Oh aye, that happened a lot when we went up the town centre. They'd say "Shake my hand, rub some luck on us", or come over and say "Give us six numbers". That didn't annoy us, not really. It was just the press, chasing us and getting everything wrong. The local *Mail* was fine, but every time a national did a story they got something wrong or made it up. There was a story that on the night of the win, Andy had gone running down the street, begging for coppers to make a phone call. That never happened. We always had our own phone in our house.'

'We couldn't escape, or get away anywhere,' said Andy. 'I'd given away my old car the moment we won the Lottery. It was a B-registered Cavalier, which I gave to a friend. In the end I had to hire a car just to escape the press.'

'Our mistake was going back home,' said Audrey. 'We should have gone straight into a hotel or rented some place till we'd bought something.'

After a month, they couldn't stand it any longer in their old council house, so they moved in with Tony, one of Andy's brothers, hoping the press would not find them. They stayed with him for another month till they moved into a new house of their own, the one they now live in.

'It only cost £90,000 altogether, with the extra bits we had done,' said Andy. 'Some people think that isn't much for people in our position, but we think it's a canny house. The only problem is the clart on the road, with all the building work still going on. I didn't think it would last this long. We should really have waited till the estate was finished, then bought the last house instead of taking one of their first. It means my new car is always dirty, with the mud and that. Just look at it!' He was staring out at his car, which looked perfectly clean to me.

The move, however, has generally been a success. Their nearest neighbours include a bank manager, a teacher, a nurse, a hairdresser, all of whom have been friendly, with no sign of snobbery. 'They've all been spot on,' said Andy. 'We all went out recently to a Chinese restaurant in Middlesbrough, and at the end I said I'd pay, the bill was on me – but they wouldn't have it. I was followed to the till with them all throwing money at me. In the end we all had to sit down and get out bits of paper and divvy it up. Usually, like, when I'm out with me brothers or me football mates, and I say I'll pay, they all let me.'

They kept their move as quiet as possible, not even giving Camelot their new address, hoping the local press would never find out. Then one evening there was a knock on the front door. 'It was two people from Radio Cleveland,' said Audrey. 'Nice enough. They said they wanted to do a fifteen-minute interview with us, once a month for the next year. I sent them away, of course. I wasn't having that. I never found out how they knew we were here. That's still a mystery.'

Their immediate neighbours all know they are Lottery-winners, and there has been no attempt to hide it from them, but their privacy has been respected. 'A friend was in the post office one day,' said Andy, 'at the time that Lottery family got burgled when they were in London for their press conference. [The Bensons from Hull, who won £20 million in July 1995.] They could hear someone at the top of the queue saying, Well, they can replace what's stolen, now they're millionaires, so what's the problem? Our friend thought someone would then start talking about us, but they didn't. Instead a woman said, "Well you wouldn't like your house burgled, however rich you were." Which was good. We were never mentioned.'

Andy does have a fear of being burgled, which is one reason for keeping a low profile. Audrey's main phobia is still the fear of being pestered by the press, feeling she has a right to be left alone and not pointed out. Their instant celebrity has been random, not worked for or earned, not dreamed about and hoped for, as with sports or show-business stars, who might equally dislike being pestered, but they knew in advance it was part of the price to pay. Lottery-winners have fantasised about spending the money, but not about being famous. Many, like Audrey, find it hard to cope with even passing fame.

Local life became a bit easier when another Hartlepool resident won half a million and distracted some attention. But then, in early September, on the day after their return from a holiday in America, Andy was opening a letter that had been passed on from an old address. It stated that Audrey was to appear in Court that afternoon at 2.20. 'It was too late for her even to get there on time. So I said she'd better get her chequebook out, quick . . .'

'I couldn't believe it,' said Audrey. 'Andy thought it was funny. I was gutted.'

She was being summoned for an unpaid council tax bill of £41.44 due for the last month of residence in their old council house, which they had vacated four months earlier. 'I rang the council to complain,' she said. 'They said they'd already sent two reminders, but I'd never got them, as they'd been sent to our old address. Yet they knew our new address. We've been here since May and paid council tax here. I explained that of course I wasn't avoiding paying, not in our position, and I'd pay at once, but I didn't want nowt in the papers. "It's not our business to inform newspapers," said a voice. Ten minutes after I'd hung up there was a call from the local papers. And that started everything, all over again.'

The *Hartlepool Mail* devoted the whole of its front page to the story on 7 September, with the headline 'That's Rich!' Audrey said they got all the facts right, and she gave an interview to their reporter, Alison Jesney, the one who had interviewed them in London. She has no complaints about them. But naturally the tabloids descended, seeing a good funny story – and cartoons. In one, the Camelot finger is pointing at Audrey, as a tax-dodger. Once again poor Audrey was driven mad by reporters and photographers, door-stepping her or pestering neighbours, just when she thought that was all behind them.

'We thought of fighting the court case, blaming the council. One of the problems was that letters to Andy and his brother Tony both get sent to A. Voss, so that was part of the mix-up. But we decided that would just bring us more publicity, so I paid up. I had to pay court costs, as well. The bill was £74 in all.'

For the next few weeks, it brought renewed attention, and led to various rumours going round the town, which upset Audrey.

'Quite a few came back to us. Friends and relations told us what they'd been told . . .' Such as? 'Well, we were said to have employed a nanny for the children, which is rubbish. That we had minders to take them to school. We were supposed to have our own security guard. Then there were stories about us being tight with our money, and that we were splitting up. That really hurt. All of it was untrue.'

Perhaps the most remarkable thing about their win is the lack of any apparent ill effect on their children, despite taking them to London for the press conference. 'No, they've been fine,' said Audrey. 'No trouble at all. We kept them off school for a week when we got back from London, but then sent them the following week. Kids did say to them, "Oh, we saw you on the telly", but no one was nasty. Carl still knows about it, and understands, but I think Claire, being younger, has begun to forget about it by now.

'When we first moved here we wanted them to stay on at their old school and finish the term, as the summer holidays were coming up, but Carl said he wanted to go to the new school at once. He went on and on about it, so we agreed. Claire wasn't so keen to move, as she's much shyer, but in the end we moved them, both at the same time. Claire cried for a day at the new school – well, perhaps two days – but that was it. She soon settled in. They both love it.'

And do the kids at their new school know about the Lottery? 'Why, aye,' said Andy. 'It was Hallowe'en last week, and all that day at school kids said to Carl, "If we come to your house, how much will we get?" That evening we got about thirty kids knocking at the door, some as old as sixteen. We gave everyone £1 each, so they were well pleased.'

Despite some vague thoughts at the time of their win about possibly sending them to private schools, they have now decided they will go to a local state comprehensive with everyone else. 'They're happy at school, doing well, and have good friends, so why should we take them away?'

'If they want to go private later,' said Andy, 'then we'll see how it goes. I just wouldn't like them to turn out as thick as me . . .'

'Speak for yourself!' said Audrey. 'Andy's mam keeps on saying we should send them private, but I don't want to. They would sort of change socially if we did, mixing with different people.' Her main object is not to spoil them. They have had a new bike each, and they've recently bought an expensive CD-Rom computer package which cost £1,500. 'That's for all three kids,' said Audrey, nodding towards Andy. 'He plays on it most.'

Carl has got a Newcastle United shirt, something he used to beg for in the past. 'In fact, he's got all three tops. I couldn't afford one in the past, but I don't think that's spoiling him. Most of his friends have got them all. If you're in work, that's what folks spend their money on, their bairns.' The idea of a live-in nanny or any minders appalled Audrey, suggesting that she had become some sort of dilettante mother. She would never let anyone look after her kids. 'After all, what else have I got to do?' she said with a half sigh.

The rumours about being tight worried both of them. In making decisions about gifts to their family, they had been striving in their minds to be generous. They made all these decisions on their own, not relying on outside advice from either Camelot or accountants, so they didn't know what might be considered normal and fair as far as other Lottery-winners were concerned. One problem was that each comes from a large family, with thirteen brothers and sisters between them, plus parents, none of them well off. They bought a new house for their respective parents and gave money to the rest of their family and friends. They don't want to be specific, as some needs were greater, some families bigger, but altogether they have given away £800,000. 'Do you think that's enough?' asked Audrey. 'Have we been fair?' asked Andy. More than fair, from my experience. (Proportionally, they have given away more than any other of the winners I followed.) The £800,000 also included some smaller amounts to friends. When they left their old council house on the Owton Manor estate, they went down the street and gave between £3,000 and £5,000 to each of twelve neighbours. 'They were over the moon,' said Audrey. 'They just didn't expect it. One woman even burst into tears.'

'Looking back to the beginning of the year, it's not just our lives that's changed,' said Andy. 'All our brothers and sisters now have their own homes. No one lives in a council house any more. We've had no problems with anyone in the family, no jealousy or moans. The only pressure, as we say, has been from the press.' How about charities? 'Oh no, we're not starting that. If you do one, you've got to do them all.'

Their personal spending has been modest. Andy's new car cost only £20,000 and he now wishes he'd perhaps got a top-of-the-range model, but he'd still go for a Vauxhall. 'I can't see myself in a Mercedes, not in my jeans and sweatshirt.' Audrey has just got her own car, a Peugeot 306, despite failing her test for a second time. 'I was a bag of nerves first time, so it wasn't a surprise. Second time, I was quite pleased with myself. I only failed on a couple of small mistakes. So next time I hope I'll get through.'

They have had two foreign holidays since their win, the first time abroad for either of them. The first was in August to Disneyworld in Florida, fifteen nights at a cost of £5,000. 'I came back more tired than when I went,' said Audrey. 'It wasn't very relaxing. There was nothing to do in the evening, so we just trailed around and the kids argued with each other.' Before they left, they warned both Carl and Claire not to reveal to anyone that they were Lottery-winners. They managed to keep it quiet, though they had a near escape when they were taken to see a film set at MGM.

'The film they happened to be making was about a woman who wins a lottery, so the guide taking us round asked people to put their hands up if they had ever won a lottery. I managed to grab Claire's hand and keep it down and Andy got Carl's, just in time. Quite a few people did put their hands up, American and British tourists, but they'd only won £10 or so.'

Their second holiday, again with the children, this time at half-term, was to a hotel in Spain, which they enjoyed much more. 'Oh yeah, Spain was great. There was a nice pool and the kids played round it all day while we could sit and sunbathe or have a drink. It was much more relaxing.' They made friends round the pool with two other couples, who naturally asked what Andy's job was. And Andy, without thinking, said he didn't have one. It then came out in conversation that they'd already been to Florida in the summer for fifteen days, so the friends enquired again about Andy's work. How come at twenty-eight he wasn't working? Andy hadn't actually thought out an explanation. He still hasn't, even though he says he doesn't want to go round telling strangers about themselves. 'On the last day, one of them says, "I know – you must have won the Lottery!" It came out that quickly we admitted it. But I didn't say how much. They shook our hands and were delighted for us, so that was nice.'

Andy enjoyed the holiday in Spain, but is not pining for another one. 'It's the foreign language, not understanding what's going on. I'd rather stay at home, me, with my feet up watching the telly, even if she does nag at me ...' Audrey would like to have more holidays, especially in the sun, and would like to travel, but wouldn't go without Andy and the children, so that's been one minor bone of contention.

Meanwhile Andy has taken up golf, and now plays two or three times a week – badly. 'I started in the 140s. Now my best score has been 99, but I enjoy it. I go to the pub afterwards with a couple of mates. The barman did ask me the other day what I did – meaning how could I afford to play golf two or three times a week – but I didn't answer him. Aye, it is a worry, what to say. Yesterday I was on the phone about Audrey's car insurance. We've insured her car in my name, till she passes her test, so they wanted to know what my job was, for the forms. I can't say unemployed, can I, as that's not right. On the other hand, can you be retired at twenty-eight? That just makes folk wonder.'

Apart from those minor worries, Andy appears perfectly happy not having an occupation. He also plays football once a week with his brothers and some friends. Recently he broke his arm in one of their matches. 'After the game we always have a few drinks, so I ruin all the good of playing football. That's probably why I've put on weight.' He still drinks beer, and didn't like the fizzy lager stuff in Spain. Audrey, when she is out, will now drink wine, and finds she enjoys it. Andy also has his garden, his conservatory and his greenhouse to amuse him, plus Carl's computer, and he's about to decorate the front room and kitchen. 'I could pay someone to do it, but I want to do it myself. It'll keep me doing something. Friends are always saying I haven't bought many big toys for myself, no daft luxuries. They say, How about a speedboat, and we could go water-skiing with you. But I've no interest in water-skiing. They say, Buy a Ferrari, but I'm happy with this car. You can only drive one car at a time.'

One treat he did fancy for himself he was unable to buy, even with his £4 million. 'I'd always wanted a season ticket for Newcastle United, but you just can't get them. There's a waiting-list for years. Carl was very disappointed.' Instead, he bought five season tickets for Middlesbrough, to take Carl and his brothers. They were easy enough to get at the time, at the beginning of the new season; now they have turned out a good and even a glamorous investment. No one knew of course that Juninho was going to arrive from Brazil.

Audrey, apart from her driving lessons, has little to occupy herself and is now beginning to feel a little frustrated. 'I've now got to the stage of being bored. I know it doesn't make sense, really. After all, I never had a job before, but I wasn't bored then. Just running the house, feeding the children, making ends meet, that seemed to take up all my time. Now I can do what I like, as they're both out at school all day, but sometimes I don't know what to do, and time hangs heavy. All my friends are out at work, so I've no one to do things with, the way Andy has his friends to play golf with.'

How about pottery classes, art classes, learn a language? Audrey made a face. Voluntary work? Another face. Wasn't there something, when she was younger, that she always wanted to do?

'I did want to be a hairdresser, but I left school with no qualifications, so it's now too late.' You could go to evening classes and learn hairdressing for its own sake, even if you never run a salon. 'Oh, I don't know. If I walked in, someone would be bound to point me out and say she's won the Lottery. I'd need to go with someone . . .'

Eventually, says Andy, he would like to start a little business, to do something with the rest of his life apart from sitting in front of the telly with his feet up. 'It would need to be the sort of business I could do with Audrey. Be no use me getting tied up with something on my own, and leave her with nothing. It has to be a joint thing, but I don't know what. One of my brothers suggested a pub, which I'd quite like, but the rest of my brothers and friends would probably come and drink up all the profits. So I haven't got a clue, really. Friends keep on suggesting things like buying property. Go into property, they say, but I don't fancy that. I don't want secretaries and directors. Someone else said I should buy Hartlepool United. That would be canny, but I haven't quite got the money to turn them into Newcastle United!'

They have no intention of getting married, as they can see no point, or in having any more children, but they say their relationship is fine, no problems. Audrey received the cheque in her name, as she was the winner. She chose the numbers and paid her £1, but their money is held in their joint bank account at the TSB. What about the investments, the portfolio – is that jointly owned as well? 'We haven't got none,' said Andy. 'We didn't see anyone from the Camelot panel. They took a long time contacting us, but I suppose that wasn't their fault as we kept our new address private. But when they did, we couldn't be bothered meeting any of them. We left it in the Royal Bank of Scotland at first, after we got the cheque, in two accounts there, which was what Drummond's arranged for us, but when the statements started coming in, we couldn't understand them. I couldn't work out what was going on. There's no Royal Bank of Scotland round here that you can go into, like, so we transferred everything into our local TSB account. We can understand the TSB stuff.'

And is it in some special long-term investment account?

'No, it's all still lying there.'

How much?

'All we've got left, after buying the house and that.'

That comes to just over £3 million. Surely every penny is not lying in the same place? They both nodded. What about Tessas and National Savings Certificates or PEPs, all those safe, tax-free investments which are easy to understand?

They looked blank. 'Yeh, I have heard of that National Certificate thing,' said Andy, 'but we're not bothered. We have a current account and the rest is getting 6 per cent. I don't know if we're being conned or not, or being stupid, but it suits us. The bank itself has said we could get better rates. But we didn't fancy meeting any advisers. These people just tell you what you already know...'

But you don't actually know a great deal? They just smiled. I then pointed out they'd need some help in the end when filling in their tax forms, as they would have to pay a higher rate on their unearned income from the bank. Andy said, 'Yeah, I'd heard of that. Someone told me there were two rates, 25 per cent and 40 per cent. So I know we'll have 65 per cent to pay.' Not quite, I said, it doesn't work that way. It's a sliding scale. But I could see he was already becoming bored. In a way, through mental laziness, they have probably saved themselves quite a lot of time and aggravation, given their temperaments. Ken Southwell did admit that his complicated investments caused him quite a bit of worry. And they can go up or down.

Perhaps keeping it simple is best for them. The £3 million they have left invested at 6 per cent means £180,000 a year, or about £100,000 after tax. More than enough for them to live on for ever in some style and luxury, judging by their present rate of spending. Having a portfolio of some fifty different investments, even handled by someone else, can be a head-ache, causes worries – and creates charges. They and their children's future is assured, whatever happens, without any worries or meetings or paperwork, as long, of course, as they manage to remember to fill in their tax returns every year, and don't wait till there's a court case. They have at least made a will, using the solicitor who handled their house purchase.

They have never bought a Lottery ticket since their win, having no interest in winning more money. 'I wasn't really into the Lottery anyway,' said Audrey. 'I'd only done it for three weeks before I won it. And I only spent £1 a week . . .' She didn't think she'd changed, as a person, since their win. 'Just the lifestyle has changed. I don't think I have.' More confident, perhaps? She didn't think so, though it was nice being confident in shops, able to fill up the trolley without looking at prices.

Andy, on reflection, thought he had become more con-fident in himself. 'I tell people off, which I never did before.' He then told a long saga about a row with the conservatory people, about some faulty pointing which he wouldn't pay for till it was redone, then a row over a damaged roof which they said wasn't their fault. 'I wouldn't have had a go at such people in the old days.'

He thinks they will move house again in about five or six years. 'Next time we'll stay here till the other house is all finished and perfect. And we'll have it specially designed for us, with a swimming pool this time.' He smiled at the thought of pleasures to come.

Are they happier, since their win? They both said Yes. Even though Audrey had admitted becoming bored and still feared the press pestering them again, she had no regrets about winning. 'All I regret is going public. The press didn't leave us alone afterwards. So we didn't gain by having the press conference.' Before their win they rated their happiness as seven out of ten. Now Audrey gave it eight out of ten. Andy thought a little bit higher.

Were they happy with each other? 'Apart from her nagging all the time,' said Andy laughing, the third time he had mentioned it.

This time Audrey didn't laugh. 'I wish you'd stop saying that,' she said. 'We'll probably have a real row when you've gone. But no, I'd say we are happier than we were. Life's not perfect, but we do have fewer rows. In the past, they were often really to do with money. That's all gone now.'

**19**

# THE NEW WINNERS' ADVISERS

After the first six months of the National Lottery, a new team
of Winners' Advisers had taken over. Alasdair and Rik had
been working on a six-month freelance contract to help create
the system and get it operating, using some of the skills and
experience they had acquired as journalists. They then
returned to other activities. Camelot decided the new team
should be in-house staff employed by Camelot. None of the
new team came from journalism, though two had had media
experience. They appointed three new Advisers permanently
out in the field, plus one in charge, based in Watford, who also
went out to see winners when necessary. She had worked for
Camelot from the beginning, in public affairs, and before that
for a charity. With Alasdair and Rik I used their real names,
now that they have moved on. As I write, the three new ones
are still hard at it, so I will not use their real names.

The oldest of the new Advisers is Jack, aged fifty-three. He
had no connection with Camelot until he got the job in March
1995. For thirty years he had been a policeman, rising to the
rank of Detective Superintendent. On his retirement, he
worked for a short spell for a bank, on the investigative side.
'I didn't want to do a job that was depressing. I wanted a good-
news job for a change. I've spent enough years going out on
Sunday mornings, knocking on doors, bringing bad news.'

The two other Winners' Advisers are women. Maggie is in her forties and was in TV for a while before doing a degree in psychology as a mature student. She worked for ICL (one of the firms behind Camelot) before joining Camelot. 'It wasn't such a great help, already working for Camelot. The interviews to be a Winners' Adviser were the most gruelling I have ever had.'

Francesca is the youngest of the four, aged thirty, with a degree in social sciences, specialising in psychology. She is small, quizzical, with an open face and a concerned expression. Jack is big and beaming and always looks hearty and affable – it's hard to believe he's spent a lifetime bringing bad news. Maggie is rather extrovert, with flashing eyes and expressive mannerisms, betraying perhaps her television past.

To the outside eye, there appears to be no obvious common denominator, no single personality, which makes a good Winners' Adviser, but then winners come in all types. What an Adviser needs is the ability to fit in and adapt to all circumstances. Getting on with people is what matters; some sort of management experience also helps.

Francesca's first job was working for a video firm which made training and promotional films for industry. She started as a scriptwriter, then moved on to be the manager of the creative department. She loved the job, but after six years the firm closed and she was out of work for three months. In July 1994 she saw by chance an advert in a local paper, saying that Camelot were recruiting. She got through three successive interviews, and was offered a job. 'I was thrilled. It was so exciting to be in at the beginning of something so historical.'

Her job was as a team leader on the National Lottery line. There were three teams in all, nine people in each, who answered phone calls and dealt with letters. During the week it was mostly players asking about the rules or the systems, but on Saturday the winners started ringing in, or people thinking, or pretending, they had won. 'Nobody had ever worked for a Lottery before, so we were all starting from scratch. But it felt dynamic. Everyone worked so hard. We did expect a fall-out because people were hired so quickly, but out of the three teams, I can think of only one person who left, and she left of her own volition.'

In March 1995, after six months on the hot line, one of her superiors mentioned that there were going to be some vacancies for Winners' Advisers, and suggested she should apply.

'I had various interviews, singly and in groups, the usual sort of thing, to see how you relate with other people. Once we were given a hypothetical situation and asked what we would do. I remember mine was to do with a jackpot-winner, whom you've gone to see in his house, with his family, all celebrating. One of his family comes up to you privately and tells you that the winner is actually a drug pedlar who's been selling drugs to schoolchildren. The press conference has already been announced. What do you do?'

So what was your answer, Francesca? 'Well, I said I would talk to the winner privately, then determine the next move. Even if he admitted it, I wouldn't necessarily cancel the press conference. I'd discuss it all with the press department, to hear their advice, before helping the winner to decide what was best for him.'

And was this the correct answer? 'I don't think there is a right or wrong answer. Every situation is so different.'

Jack, the ex-policeman, was given the same situation. 'My first reaction was that it might have happened a long time ago. Perhaps he's been rehabilitated. People do silly, irrational things when they're young, which adults often forget. He may have turned over a new leaf. Anyway, that's what I said . . .'

Francesca and Jack both gave positive reactions to the hypothetical situation, which probably impressed Camelot, meeting a problem head-on, dealing with it constructively.

'I don't know what the right answer was,' said Jack. 'But I felt very pleased to get the job. I presumed it was my background and experience which did it.'

Maggie had a different hypothetical scenario concerning a sixteen-year-old girl winner who had a dominating boyfriend. 'I'm sure there were no "right" answers. I think all three of us were chosen because we don't make value judgements about people.'

Francesca's first big winner was a family syndicate which had won £2,442,406. 'The adrenalin was buzzing. I was very nervous, but we all got on very well. It was also fortunate that their daughter lived adjacent, with their gardens backing on to each other. That was handy when we came to make a quick escape. The press had found out, and I got there only minutes before them and was able to move the family into a hotel. I had memorised some of the cars that had been in their street – the last three numbers of the registrations, and the colour and make. When I got to the hotel, I checked to see if any of the same cars were there. My worry was that if any national papers had been on the scent, they would have checked into the same hotel. But there was none. It all went off very well. They're a lovely couple. I still get postcards from them when they go on holiday. They gave a press conference and went public because the press had already found out, so there was no escape. When I go and see a winner, I always explain the pros and cons of both going public or trying to remain anonymous, and the decision is always the winner's.'

The first thing she says to every winner, when she speaks to them on the phone, is to stress that they mustn't tell anyone. 'It's a natural instinct to tell people, and they're bursting to do it. If they've already done so, they don't like to admit it, because they feel they have done something wrong. I once spoke to a winner on the phone who swore blind that nobody, but nobody, even his own family, had been told – yet I could hear a party in the background, all obviously celebrating, with people shouting Congratulations!'

On arrival, she tries to get safely inside their house before showing her ID card. 'I've told them on the phone I'll be carrying one, and what sort of car I'll be driving, so they're looking out for me. When I arrive, some of them won't have eaten or slept. Some are still hung-over from Saturday night. Some are still drunk. Some are very low. Some high. They are half thinking it's not true, anyway. You see all emotions – and you have to respond to them. Some just need a hug, so I do that, or squeeze their hands while we talk. What I'm really trying to say is, Hello, I'm here, don't panic.

'The first thing I get round to, after the initial chat, is to explain validation. The winners are in a state of shock, and it is important, in order to help them keep their feet on the ground, to explain that the ticket cannot be finally confirmed as a winner until validation. That's usually during the following week. They are often surprised to hear they will get the money next day. Some think it will take weeks, or they'll get it in instalments, spread over years.'

She then returns to the topic of who has been told, stressing the fact that if families and friends know, the press may soon find out, and will probably be interested in their story. 'That's when we start talking about staying private or going public. It often depends very much on the personality of the winner. Some people enjoy the attention and it helps them to celebrate their win. During that first day they are in an emotional turmoil, a constant change, up and down all the time. There is a sense of relief when I arrive. If they are staying private, they may worry about secrecy. It is a big shock to them, the biggest they'll probably ever have, so naturally they may veer between ecstatic laughter and floods of tears.'

Francesca's first experience of a press conference was with

Audrey Jenkins and Andy Voss. Rik had looked after them, but she was there to help out, to see how it worked. 'As we entered the main room at the hotel there were scores of press and cameras. It was extremely exciting, and the winners both enjoyed the experience far more than they thought they would.

'One of the worst moments was when I was driving some other winners back home. They were a lovely couple and everything had gone well, but we'd had a very gruelling day and they'd been up very early to do GMTV, so we were all very tired. We stopped in a motorway café, Watford Gap I think it was, and a message came through for them on my mobile. I didn't have to tell them the bad news myself, luckily. Jack broke it to them – that there had been a minor fire at their home while they'd been at the press conference. Oh, I really felt for them. They were very good, considering. Their first worry was for their dog – was she all right? That showed that they had the right sort of perspective.'

The hypothetical situation, of a winner being a drug dealer, has not yet happened to her in real life. 'No, even now, I still don't know the "right" answer. Every situation is different. When we first meet them, they can be emotional and unable to concentrate. We try to pick things up rather than ask questions directly. It is important to build a relationship in order to provide the most appropriate advice and support.'

In the six months so far, Francesca has personally looked after thirty jackpot-winners, approximately fifteen of whom have remained private. 'Some of the private ones do suffer from a bit of paranoia at first, but most get over it. I am always surprised by how cool they can be. You do need a lot of self-discipline to tell nobody. Six of my private winners have spent nothing at all. They are still living in the same house, so there are no visible signs of their new wealth. Sometimes they move after six months or so, usually within a fifty-mile radius. I've only had one who has moved right away. I have had only one person who tried to tell literally nobody at all. The norm is to tell at least your partner, and perhaps a couple of your nearest relations – but swear them to secrecy. This was a young girl living on her own, who for four weeks told absolutely nobody. She did find it a strain keeping it a secret, so after four weeks she told her parents, and they didn't believe her! Now they do, and she's moved back in with them. They all seem very happy and are coping well.'

Maggie has had a number of syndicates and large families, which has resulted in a high proportion of public winners – about 50 per cent. 'With syndicates, someone is more likely to let the cat out of the bag, even if they want privacy. You hope they will be logical enough to sit down, tell the truth about who knows, and realise it can't be kept secret.'

Francesca, for some random reason, has had a high proportion of retired people among her winners. Out of her thirty, she could think of only one professional, an accountant. Jack, on the other hand, has had four professional winners – two lawyers, a doctor and an accountant, all of whom have stayed private. 'They find it fairly easy to hide it because they have the social skills. One of them bought a new Jaguar, and his neighbour's first remark was, "Oh, I see you're treating yourself again." In a different neighbourhood, the question would have been, "Where did you get the money from?" The professionals can always say an insurance policy came up, or they made a good investment. They can find plausible explanations for any new purchases.'

None of Jack's winners, professional classes or otherwise, has gone mad on a spend-spend-spree, unlike Lee Ryan who appeared on TV with all his new cars and toys. 'Most winners are very sensible. They are delighted with their good fortune and are determined to manage the money properly so they and their children can enjoy it for the rest of their lives.'

The Winners' Advisers are accumulating more winners every week. Their main personal contact is in the early days – meeting them, taking them to validation, to a press conference if they are having one, then perhaps to meet Camelot's legal and financial panel. Camelot plans to keep in contact with big winners, if desired, for up to five years. Each regional office also helps to look after local winners.

I asked all three Winners' Advisers what they had learned about the human race, and about themselves, by doing this unusual job.

'I now realise how lucky I was to have such a loving and supportive family,' said Francesca, 'now that I've experienced how difficult some people's lives can be. As a student, I liked to think I was not judgemental, but I probably was. Now I am genuinely open-minded. I never stereotype people by their appearance or their education. Money and situation is no clue to a person's real life and personality. I now know you can't judge a book by its cover.'

'I am still struck by the strange sort of shock which winners go into,' said Jack. 'It's as if they are in shock from shock, surprised by their own surprise. I'm talking about when we first meet them, on the Sunday or Monday. They have of course dreamt about winning, but they never knew how they would feel – and that shocks them. I've also noticed how education and social background has nothing to do with how people go on to cope and enjoy their win. You just can't tell. Steve and Helen [Chapters One, Seven and Twenty-one] amazed me by how they have coped. I just never expected it when I first went to their house. I think the first time I really realised how bright Steve was, was the day I went with them to meet the panel – the lawyer and the accountant. Most people come out reeling, but Steve was so perceptive, so intelligent. It struck me then that he was nobody's fool, but also what a wise, lovely bloke. I don't think I've ever seen such well-cared-for children in any family, anywhere.'

Maggie says she was not too surprised by the sometimes complicated lives people lead. 'When I was in TV, I saw many environments. I knew how differently people live. I'm still aware of it, of course, when I arrive to see someone, yet at the same time I'm also struck by how similar we all are. Deep down, everyone wants the same – a roof over their head, to provide for their family and live a decent life. We're all protective people, battling out there to earn a living, but then we come back to our own nests. I must say I'm always happy to get home to my own little family.

'I do worry about all my winners, and feel protective towards them. Some you have more in common with, but they all need and get our support and understanding. I would say most people are happier since their win; certainly I haven't met one who wants to give the money back. When there are problems, it's not really the Lottery money which causes it. The problems are already there. People's relationships are finely balanced, and it just needs some shock, some change, to upset them. For example, people can have control over others through money, or lack of money. A Lottery win can upset this. It's like other major changes in your life – changing houses or jobs, retiring, deciding to have a baby, things you think at the time will make things better, but they can be stressful. Sometimes they only open up cracks already there.'

Maggie has still to come across a spend-spend-spender among her jackpot-winners. 'They are all so sensible, even with their investments. They think stocks and shares are risky, unaware of course that their PEPs, their Tessas and insurance bonds are all linked to the stock market. I have only had one who got mixed up in a dodgy investment, talked into it by a so-called whizz kid, and his solicitor is now sorting it out. The ones who are more likely to go on a spending spree are the Match 5+ (plus bonus) winners. To some of them it's like a nest-egg which they might as well enjoy, so they have a dream holiday or buy the car they have always wanted, knowing life will then carry on as normal. If your win is only a few hundred thousand or even half a million, and you're still young, you couldn't actually live on the income for ever, not if you buy a new house and car. With a jackpot win of a million pounds or more, your old life won't go on; it's altered for ever. You won't need to work again, you can live easily on the income. That somehow makes people take things slowly and sensibly, not rush or be flash.'

Almost all winners are very generous to their family and friends, but tend not to donate to charities. Maggie, though, does have a couple of big winners, both private, both elderly, who have left huge donations in their wills. 'Being private, of course, and anonymous, you'll never know about them . . .'

Winners' Advisers themselves have a hectic, stressful life, driving around 4,000 miles a month, putting in around fifty-five hours a week, giving and endlessly listening, hardly seeing their own families. Who will advise the advisers, should they ever have problems? It is hard for them to start a new domestic relationship, unless they are already in one, because of the nature of the job. They can be rung up at any time of day or night if winners are worried. They have to take Saturday evenings quietly, as they could be up at the crack of dawn to drive hundreds of miles. They find it hard, because of security reasons, to talk about the precise nature of their job, even with their friends. If it comes out they work at Camelot, they will usually say they are in public affairs, which is technically true.

'The job is unpredictable,' said Francesca. 'You couldn't exactly call it nine to five. You have to be there for the winner when they need you, which can sometimes cause havoc with your private life.' Luckily she does have an understanding partner.

'Ours is an invisible job in some ways. We can't talk about

it. Even colleagues back in the office don't realise everything that's involved. It's not just driving around, meeting big winners, and staying in hotels. It's very demanding. I think another couple of years will do me. But I have loved it. Everyone is fascinated by the National Lottery. I've been in a very privileged position. It will always be something to tell my grandchildren ...'

## PLAYING THE NATIONAL LOTTERY

### 1   CHOOSE YOUR NUMBERS.

The National Lottery playslip has a number of boxes on it. These boxes are called "boards".

You select your six numbers by marking them on a board.

If you want to pick another six numbers use another board.

Only use a pencil or a blue or black pen. Put a clear, bold, vertical line through each number you've chosen. If you make a mistake, mark the void box and use another board.

### 2   LUCKY DIP–THE EASY WAY TO PLAY.

With Lucky Dip the terminal randomly selects a set of six random numbers for you. All you have to do is:

• Simply ask your National Lottery retailer for a "Lucky Dip". (You can have as many Lucky Dip selections as you like).

OR

• Mark the Lucky Dip (L. Dip) box on each of those boards on which you wish to play Lucky Dip. (Note: you should not select a set of numbers and mark the Lucky Dip box on the same board.)

### 3   PAY THE RETAILER.

Next, give your playslip to the sales assistant and pay £1 for every set of six numbers and Lucky Dip selections you have chosen.

### 4   GET YOUR TICKET.

When you've paid, the retailer will enter your selections into the terminal and give you a National Lottery ticket. It will have your chosen numbers (including any Lucky Dip selections) and the draw date(s) printed on it. **You must check** that the numbers you have selected, the number of selections and the draw date(s) are correct and that the barcoded serial number is clearly readable. Then write your name and address on the back. Keep your ticket safe, you'll need it to check off your numbers in the draw. Don't lose it! You'll need it to claim your prize, as it is the **only proof** that you are a winner.

### 5   LOOK OUT FOR THE WINNING NUMBERS.

If six numbers on one of your printed selections match the six main numbers that are drawn – in any order – you are a jackpot winner. You also win a prize by matching five, four or even three out of the six.

There will also be a seventh 'bonus number' drawn. If you already have five matching numbers, look out for it. The bonus number gives you the chance to win the second highest prize.

As well as the televised draw, you'll find the winning numbers in national newspapers and clearly displayed in all National Lottery retailers.

**20**

# BARRY, EX-EAST LONDON

Barry hasn't moved far from his old terrace house in east London, not as the crow flies. His new home is hardly ten miles away but the changes are immediately obvious – social, architectural, geographical and physical. His spanking new £280,000 detached four-bedroom house is situated in a semi-rural enclave in Essex. East London seems light-years away. He now lives in an area of public schools and prep schools, village commons and ancient ponds. But perhaps the nicest thing about his new house, which Barry appreciates every day as he takes his son back and forward to prep school, is something that helps his physical condition – the parking.

Parking was hell outside his old terrace house, fighting for any space in his own street, especially for an MS sufferer, trying to manage on two sticks to get in and out of his car. 'The winters were worst. I would be totally exhausted, getting the frost and snow off the windows before I'd even got into my car.' The week before he left the old house in July, his special disabled parking bay was finally agreed, after eighteen months of waiting. Too late to do any good, so he ignored it. Now, in his new house, he has a double garage, with electronic doors he can operate from his car. There's also a door straight into his house, so he need not worry about the winter weather.

It took them longer than they expected to find what they

wanted. 'We looked at lots of posh houses, expensive places owned by people with lots of money, or so you would think, but while the living-rooms looked nice and their kitchens were good and that, we kept on finding their upstairs rooms, which people don't normally see, were all horrible. They didn't look after them. I was surprised, really. So in the end we decided to go for a brand-new house.' It's in a small development, just twenty-nine houses, vaguely mock-Tudor, very exclusive. So exclusive that after six months' living there, there is still only one other resident. Builders are still around and the roads are still very muddy. 'You need at least a quarter of a million to buy one of these, so you have to be well off.' The recession has, of course, not helped. Barry and his wife Chris bought first, and got the best pick, so he thinks, tucked into a corner, well out of sight. He doesn't mind the empty houses all around. They are not desperate to have matey neighbours.

The glare of the fitted creamy-white carpets and the white leather suite made me shade my eyes for a few moments, and I wondered about the wisdom of such light colours, with two very young children bringing in muddy feet and muddy hands. Barry just smiled. 'It was what we fancied.' Then I remembered that in the main room of their old terrace house they had gone for an almost white fitted carpet.

Glen, aged five, was with his mother Chris at the kitchen table, doing some sums when I arrived. It was the first day of his Christmas holidays. Karen, aged two, was doing head-stands on the leather sofa. Glen soon joined her, then together they piled cushions on the floor and did more headstands. Barry sat back on his chair, clutching his stick, enjoying their enjoyment, telling them off from time to time for shouting or fighting, but not very seriously.

He looked well, though still the same weight, 16 stone. He originally soared in weight when his MS first began to restrict his physical movements. He had of course been a body-builder and keep-fit fanatic. But what he thinks did the real damage was leaving work and being at home every day with the kids. 'It meant I ate their meals with them, the things they love, like burgers and chips. When I was working, I'd eat in the evening with Chris, and we had better food, with spices and stuff. After Christmas, I've been told by a certain person I'm going on a diet. I haven't lost anything in the last six months; on the other hand, I haven't put anything on.'

He pointed with a smile to his single stick – a battle of mind over matter, he thinks. On the day of his Lottery win he was in the back garden using two sticks, his normal routine at the time. 'I think it's my training in the Paras. You're climbing a mountain and think you can never take another step, but you do. I told myself I will get down to one stick, and I have. I still have good days and bad days, but I think I'm in remission at present. I'm never going to get better, but I haven't got any worse in the last six months. I think the Lottery has helped. The financial worries I used to have caused a lot of stress in my head, a lot of strain. They've all gone. I'm still with the Neurological Hospital in Holborn. They see me once every six months, or sooner if I have problems. There's no medicine you can take. Nothing you can do. It seems to belt me every five to seven years, you know, just comes up and belts me one. First it was my eyes in my twenties, then later it was my legs. The last belt was in my back, two years ago.'

I looked around the room for any signs of disabled facilities. In his old house, he had cleared a space under the stairs for use as a downstairs bedroom, but never used it, forcing himself upstairs to bed every night. 'I still do that. I'm determined not to let it beat me. It's easier here, because the stairs are wider. I come down the same way, bumping on me bum. I've put nothing special in – no extra rails or supports or anything – but one of the reasons for buying this house is there's an extra room downstairs, and a downstairs WC. I can have my bedroom here in the future. Everything is better here, for me and the kids. We've all benefited.'

Glen had just completed his first term at his prep school – fees £1,300 a term. As he paused from his headstands, I asked him how it had gone. He paused, thought, and said, 'Fine,' then went back to playing. Barry took me through the details of the boy's school uniform: red blazer, mustard shirt in winter, white shirt in summer, grey jumper with red and green edges, grey trousers in winter, grey shorts in summer.

Are trainers allowed? 'Certainly not. Must be black shoes.'

Glen had a part in the school Christmas play as an elf, a non-speaking part, but he did get to sing. Barry and Chris have attended several school functions and have felt no social unease. 'There's them that will not talk to you and think they're a class above, and those who will talk. But that's most places. It doesn't worry me, either way. I haven't told any of them about us and the money. No one has asked. I don't want people to know, just to take us as we are. I'm not really into socialising. We never were ones to live in other people's pockets. But I'm very happy with the school, and Glen's progress. There's been a tremendous change in him. He would never sit down and do things before; now he sits and reads without being told. His reading has come on so much. Tremendous. No one told him to do those sums in the kitchen when you arrived, you know. He'd just decided to do them.'

'I won a prize,' said Glen, getting up from rolling on the carpet with Karen.

'That's right,' said Barry proudly. 'A merit badge, it was. You get to wear it for one week. Glen got it for good work and also for honesty.'

They have honesty tests? 'He found some money in the playground and took it to the headmaster. I've also noticed he's more polite. And his speech is slowly changing; just certain words. I dunno. Oh yeah, yesterday I heard him talk about gar-age, whereas we say garridge. That was funny. He's not aware of it, of course. Certain people he refers to by their surname, but I haven't got the hang of that. When you come in, I didn't know whether to tell him you was called Hunter or Mr Davies. I know at school the teachers are all Mr or Miss, but the helpers are all called by their first name.'

Any little friends?

'Oh, yeah, he's been to a girl's party, his first ever party. And he goes to tea alternate Tuesdays with his friend Kirit. Dunno how you spell it. He's Indian. Very nice little boy. We've met his parents, and they're very nice too.'

Chris had come in from the kitchen and I asked her about Kirit's parents. She repeated that they were very nice, and added that they were the only people so far who knew about the money.

'Oh, yeah, I forgot that,' said Barry. 'What happened was that Glen told Kirit we'd won £300 and bought the house with the money. His mother thought this was a bit strange. You can't buy many houses with £300, can you? So I told her.' The truth?

'Yeah, I said £1.3 million. If asked, I don't lie. I just don't want to be asked.'

Altogether they have given £310,000 to their parents, brothers and sisters, roughly £50,000 each, plus their old house to one of Chris's sisters. 'She was living in a one-bedroom flat, on her own, with two kids, so she's thrilled to have her own three-bedroom house with her own garden.' Another sister was in a negative equity situation, so her £50,000 has greatly helped. One relation had just been made redundant. So the money has transformed the lives of all their family.

For themselves, they have bought two new cars, an Escort Ghia at £12,000 for Chris and a Vauxhall Cavalier at £17,000 for Barry. 'I did look at a Mercedes, even though I told you last time I didn't want one. When I found what the insurance would be, I said, No way! Because of this [pointing to his legs], they wanted £3,500. Next time I won't buy any new cars. You get a better bargain if they're one year old. Chris hardly drives hers anyway. Mine's automatic, with power steering, which is brilliant for me. The gears on my old one were getting too much.'

After all their purchases and gifts, they were left with £700,000, all of which has been invested. Barry did not make use of the Camelot panel, or the kind people at the Royal Bank of Scotland, but went back to his old employers, the Midland Bank. 'They did a portfolio for me, all very low risk. No, it's not all in Midland Bank things. I've got stuff in Abbey National, shares in BP, all sorts. It hasn't been a worry. They put the portfolio together, and I agreed. I just said, nothing risky, that's all I said. The idea is that in three to five years the £700,000 will grow to £1 million. They tell us every month how it's going. In the last six months it's gone up to £760,000.' He has not given anything to charity, so far, but says he will eventually, when his investments have matured. 'I'm going to give something to the Neurological Hospital. Definitely.'

Looking back, he wishes now he had not gone public, low-key and local though it was. 'We still meet people, especially when we go back to where we used to live, who come up and congratulate us and that's very nice, but really, I'm trying to forget it. They won't let you. I want to move on. No, I haven't been hassled. It's in my head, really. That's just how I feel.'

'I never wanted to go public in the first place,' said Chris. 'So I was proved right.'

'I suppose I was selfish,' said Barry. 'Maggie from Camelot did say we were a good story, me with this, and the two kids, and the press would soon be after us, but I did it for my sake, thinking I'd enjoy it. With hindsight, I should have thought of the children, not myself. What I don't want to happen is kids in the playground saying to our kids, "Your dad got your money by luck." It's not that I want them to think I must have made my money in the City, I don't want that either. I just don't want it to be talked about. The kids themselves will forget very soon. I think Glen has already, and of course Karen never took it in at all.

'Karen is going to Glen's school in January, in the nursery department, and that will be the only school she'll ever know, just as this house will be the only house she'll remember. Glen has already forgotten his old school. Soon he won't remember it at all. I want them to grow up thinking this is their normal life, as it's always been. That's been the big advantage of winning when they were young. They won't know about our life before. And with me just being pensioned off, it couldn't have come at a better time in my life.'

They themselves don't expect to change. They eat the same sort of food, still use the same Chinese take-away in east London, still don't drink or even have drinks in the house for visitors. Chris still smokes, perhaps even more than before, but Barry has not smoked for ten years. He still does the Lottery, £5 every week. 'It gives me something to do on a Saturday evening. I've won £10 once and had four numbers once and won £30.' Barry's only personal extravagance has been a new suit by Boss costing £500. 'It was to go out to a do with Chris's brother. I'm a hard fit, and always need arms and legs altered, so I thought I'll buy one good suit, have it ready in my wardrobe, in case I ever go out anywhere smart again. I found it easy to pay the money. I think it's worth it, to have my one good suit. But a certain person, she's terrible! She can't spend a thing on herself.'

'I know,' Chris giggled. 'I just can't do it.'

'I keep saying, Go out and spend money on yourself, gel, but she won't. Buy some new clothes, I say, but she won't. She doesn't like jewellery or anything like that. She can spend £200 on something for Glen or Karen, but spends nothing on herself. "Ooh, it's too expensive." That's what she always says. She will think of negative reasons. I think deep down what she fears is that if she starts spending, we won't have enough left to leave for the children. Which is stupid. I keep explaining to her, listen, we have made £60,000 in the last six months, doing nothing, in interest. That's more than twice as much as I earned in two years, working all hours. But she doesn't get it. We often turn on the Teletext to see how our shares are doing. Sometimes they go up by 10p and sometimes down by 10p, which worries her. I tell her all the time, that's what shares do. It don't matter, I say. Over five years, our portfolio will go up. We've got *no* worries.'

Chris listened to all this without speaking, just making little childlike faces. She has a rural, innocent, ruddy glow to her, not at all the stereotyped east-ender; more like a character from Arnold Wesker's *Roots*. She started getting ready to go out, to take Karen to a friend's, and was putting on a Barbour jacket, which I admired.

'That's mine,' said Barry. 'You see, she'll wear my new clothes rather than buy her own. I said yesterday she should buy a new car, automatic, because she prefers driving mine. "Oh, no," she said, "don't be ridiculous, we can't afford another new car." I have changed, in that I can spend money. She hasn't.'

They have spent some money on good holidays. Not long after their win they went off to Menorca. A few months ago, they went to Disneyland in Florida, taking her sister and family, a party in all of eleven, for which Barry paid. 'Menorca was nice, but a bit quiet,' he said. 'But Florida was really good. We all loved it. But I'll tell you what, we was sitting the other day, thinking about our next holiday, and I asked Glen where he'd like to go – back to Menorca or Florida? What he really wanted, he said, was to go back to 62. That was the number of the caravan we took at Great Yarmouth last year, before the win. He prefers that to going abroad. So I've made enquiries. We're going to book it for next summer.'

There is no doubt that Barry and Chris are much happier since their win, more than most couples. Living with MS is clearly easier with money. Before his win, he had been pensioned off and his future looked bleak: each gave it a rating of five out of ten. Today Barry gives it eight out of ten. 'I'm not just a lot happier for myself, but for all the family – parents, brothers and sisters. My children are secure and will never be hard up.' Chris gave it even more points, nine out of ten. 'Oh, everything is better!'

'There are no negatives,' said Barry. 'It's nice to know that when the time comes we can hire a nurse full time. Chris doesn't have to worry about looking after me.'

Being stuck at home all day, housebound, has not had quite the effect he expected. 'It's funny how my role has changed. Dads normally go to work, don't they, and the wife says to the kids if they've been naughty, "Just you wait till your dad comes home." Chris never says that, 'cos I'm here all the time. I'm on a par with Chris now. We both tell them off, if we have to, and we back each other up. I like it this way, squaring the roles.'

At thirteen, Glen will probably go on to public school, or at least an independent school. 'No way would we send him to boarding school. Chris is very much against that. Mind you, if he gets to eleven and says he wants to go to boarding school, and puts up a good case, then we'd think about it. I look upon it this way. He's going to have a greater social standing than me, so we might as well get used to it. At the end of the day he'll have to decide for himself what he does in life. If he ends up as an executive or a dustman, then it's his decision.'

There is one minor, piddling, un-serious worry lying ahead

in the future, which Barry talked about after Chris had gone out. She is becoming bored. That's the reason, he thinks, why she's smoking more. After six months, the house is now in order and there is not a great deal of domestic work to do. Next term, Karen will be at nursery school. What will she do then. Another baby? 'We have discussed that,' said Barry. 'But we've just left the nappy stage with Karen. We don't want to go back to all that. Also, I'm thirty-eight. I don't know how many years I've got ahead – fifteen, perhaps? I'd like to be up and around for as long as possible, till Glen and Karen are say eighteen and twenty. At the moment I still drive him to school every day, take him to gym classes, do as much as possible. When you leave, we're going to play computer games together. I want them to have memories of me as an active dad. I want their memories to be of me doing things, not as some invalid. Having another child, well, he or she might not see me so active. And there's another thing. With two kids, we can leave them half each. With three, they only get a third. So we've decided we're not having any more.'

If Chris does become seriously bored, what then? 'She has talked about opening a shop, but she doesn't know anything about shops. So I've said to her, you get yourself on a course, learn about business studies, then you can run a shop. Another idea is that she'll go back to cookery. She used to be a chef, as you know. She fancies going to college and learning about cake-making. That's another plan. Oh, I'm all for it. She can do anything she wants, if she can think of something. I want her to fulfil her ambitions in life, even if I'll never be able to . . .'

# STEVE AND HELEN, LANCASHIRE

One year later, 28-year-old Steve was no longer a collector of bulls' semen, but he and his wife Helen, and their three children, had not in fact moved to Scotland as they had originally intended. They had hired a Renault Espace, as planned, piled all the children in, and went off on a quick visit to the Scottish Highlands to look at possible properties. After three days, all sleeping overnight in the vehicle, they had returned to their Lancashire council house rather disappointed. 'Scotland's too hilly,' Steve told me on the phone. 'I could see the kids having trouble on their mountain bikes. They'd have to have the brakes on all the time, which would soon ruin their shoes.'

Audrey and Andy had proved difficult to keep contact with, when I had assumed they would be easy, but right from the beginning I had expected real problems with Steve and Helen. How could they possibly keep their win secret, and not even tell Steve's own mother, living in the same house with them? Eventually, so I imagined, it would come out, there would be family squabbles, Steve and Helen would do a bunk, and I'd never hear from them again.

But they were punctilious and polite every time I telephoned or wrote to them, though I was worried I might let slip some remark, some reference, which might reveal their secret, so I restricted myself to generalities. I rang as an old friend from the past, never asking direct questions, which of course I was dying to ask, such as 'Does your mother know?' – just in case she was in the room, listening.

When they were about to move, Helen rang and gave me the new address and phone number. No signs of paranoia, no need to sign the Official Secrets Act. I rang when they moved in, and Steve told me it was a big house, like, in nice countryside. They had not moved to Scotland after all but to the relatively flat foothills of the southern Lake District, an area where their Lancashire accents would obviously not stand out as much as they might have done in Scotland.

I got a taxi from the station in their nearest town. The driver, a young woman, knew the name of the village, but had never heard of the Manor House I was looking for. We drove round the village several times, and in the end I rang Steve to ask him for precise directions. He said it was up a lane, which he described, with no name at the end, but he would drive down and wait for me at the roadside.

He was there in the Renault Espace, along with Helen and all three kids. I followed them, still in the taxi, up the lane and into the courtyard of the Manor House. It was very impressive, with several barns and stables and assorted outhouses gathered round the walled courtyard, leading to a side entrance to the Manor House. All the outbuildings were in spanking condition, the stonework clean, the paintwork gleaming, the blue slate roofs all pristine. In one corner was a clothes-line hung with children's worn jeans and cheap T-shirts, rather contrasting with the affluence of the surroundings. Steve and Helen got out of their car, followed by the kids spilling out into the courtyard. They immediately started grabbing their bikes or racing round the courtyard, all screaming. Then they started throwing chestnuts at each other. Steve has six very ancient chestnut trees, so he explained, very well known and much admired in the locality.

Steve's Gazza-type haircut had long grown out. It was neither bleached nor shaven at the back any more and looked quite normal. His weight looked much the same, as did his earring. Helen's complexion appeared much less grey and ashen. She was wearing a pale cardigan and trousers. They both looked well, healthy and happy. Neither was smoking.

They had all just come back from the school run, and Helen took them inside for tea while Steve gave me a tour of the estate before it grew dark. The house is Georgian, Grade II listed, he said, with eight main bedrooms and 60 acres in all. I admired the lawns and the gardens, the line of trees opening out into the distance from the main entrance, the walled garden given over to vegetables and soft fruit, the tennis court, the ancient yew tree, the topiary garden going back to the eighteenth century, the trout stream and small tarn. He took me to one side, and pointed out the fence he had put up to keep the younger kids from falling in the tarn. It was made of old bits of wood and packing-cases. 'We're going to build a jetty at that end,' he said. He was letting out most of 50 acres for grazing to a local farmer, having no use at the moment for the fields, though eventually he would get a pony or two for the children. 'Look at them crows,' he said, pointing up. 'They treat those trees like a rookery. It's gorgeous in this courtyard when the full moon is up. The kids love it. They've never had such freedom.'

We then toured the house itself, down into the massive cellars which Steve is going to turn into workshops, then round the eight bedrooms and three bathrooms and the assorted reception rooms. On various landings I kept seeing some of the kids spying on us, then disappearing down corridors or crossing in the distance, into staircases I couldn't see. Steve kept on opening doors into pantries and minor rooms, saying each of them was bigger than the bedroom they used to have. Not boasting, just remarking.

The whole house was carpeted throughout in best Wilton, and yet the main impression, apart from the kitchen, was that they were squatters. There was so little furniture, hardly any personal ornaments or decorations, no signs at all of any books or paintings, that it did seem as if it was somebody else's house. Even the children's bedrooms were bare and spartan, apart from their beds and Mickey Mouse duvet-covers. They had brought all their old stuff from their council house, but it was so meagre, so skittery, that it had all but disappeared into just a couple of rooms. So far they had not got round to buying many new items, or at least anything which would signify their new social position. The kitchen, the only place which did seem equipped, was filled with a large rather nasty-looking plastic table and six chairs. 'All MFI,' said Steve proudly. 'I put them together myself. Not bad, that chair, for £19! We're cheapskates, we are.'

The property had been advertised for sale at half a million, but Steve got it, for cash, for around £400,000. 'I can't actually remember how much exactly. The previous owner had spent a fortune on it for his daughter, but then he'd lost his money in Lloyds and had to sell quickly. All the floors and windows and electrics and roofs have been redone, so that was one of the big attractions. It meant we had no major work to do. There's a cellar that still needs a new floor, which I might do myself, and the walled garden needs to be dug out properly. I might do that as well. Hire the machinery, drive the digger myself.'

Despite the size of the house, the bills so far had not proved excessive. 'The council tax is only £900 – we're not in the top band, which surprised me. The oil tank for the central heating has just been filled, which cost £333. Four of those should do us each year. I estimate our outgoings on the house will be no more than £5,000 a year, which is nothing when you think we've got over £100,000 in unearned income coming in every year. There's tax to pay on that, of course, top whack at 40 per cent. But we still won't be spending it all.'

We then went in, and joined the children having their tea. Helen offered me a plate of biscuits and a cup of coffee in a plain white cup. She used instant coffee powder. When the children had gone off to play, I asked about Steve's mother. The last I'd heard was that they planned to tell her nothing, but give her the option of moving with them, or not, when the time came. 'She decided to stay,' said Steve.

So she still doesn't know anything? 'Not about the Lottery, but yes, aye, she knows about the house. She came with us when we were moving, didn't she. She was very useful, helping to look after the kids. Cheap labour!' But didn't she wonder about this amazing house, and how you come to be living here? 'We've told her it comes with the new job. We live here rent free. She's accepted that. I said in five years' time, if all goes well my new boss says I can buy it off him. She's accepted that as well.

'We've even had one of our old friends to visit us, and I told him the same. Actually, I didn't tell him anything; I just waited till he'd looked around, then he started asking a few questions. Rent free, I said, goes with the job. He then said, "Yeah, of course, I understand – insurance. Your boss wants you to live here, to keep the place safe and keep the insurance down." It all made sense to him. He said he knows about rich people wanting other people to live in their houses for them. I didn't have to lie at all. He estimated the house was worth only £200,000, because he said it was too big. He'd heard these sorts of big houses are hard to sell these days, since the recession.'

So their Lottery win is still really secret? No friends or relations or neighbours know about it – just the two of them? Nobody else at all? 'Well, our solicitor knows, and our accountant knows, but that's all. I suppose one or two other people in their offices must know as well, dealing with all the papers. If they ever let the secret out, I'd sue them for breach of contract.'

Looking round the house, I could see why any visitor might not immediately suspect what had happened, accepting that it was someone else's property in which they are living rent free. Steve and his family don't really seem to have taken it over or fitted in. Their personalities, so far, have not been stamped on the house or the gardens. Their own belongings seem cheap and meagre by comparison with their surroundings. A visiting burglar, not just a visiting friend, would assume the present occupants have no money at all. This does not seem deliberate, carefully and cunningly worked out by Steve and Helen to disguise what has happened to them. It's simply how they want to live. They are not into ostentation or conspicuous consumption. Never have been. Probably never will be.

'I've only bought one luxury thing, apart from the house,' said Steve. 'I got this mobile phone. I wanted to keep in touch with Helen when I was going up and down the M6, moving our stuff.'

The house goes with his job, so he explains to people, and I can see that being accepted by most people, but how does he explain the job itself, and what he actually does for his new boss? 'I don't go into details. I say he is a landowner and big farmer, but he's also into property and investment, and I'm his finder. I have to track things down for him, property and things, and I get 10 per cent of what I find for him. It's not really a lie. Because that's what I am doing these days. I manage my investments. And I hope to get 10 per cent, if I'm lucky.'

When the children were safely out of sight and sound, he got a large briefcase off a shelf, opened the security lock and took out a mass of papers and folders. He couldn't find what he was looking for at first, and asked Helen to help. She eventually found it – the master plan. This gives the details of his portfolio and the strategy behind the fifty or so investments which have been made on his behalf. In all, it was decided to invest £2.4 million, the sum left after the purchase of the house, while keeping some money in cash for emergencies.

'The bank put up a proposal which would gain the persons handling the portfolio about a quarter of a million in bonuses and commission. I didn't realise that till the accountants at Ernst & Young pointed it out. So, instead, we've got them to handle it; they will charge only the normal accountancy fee, by the hour, plus expenses, not taking any commission. Any commissions that do come in will belong to us, and they will take their fees out of it. Oh, we've been learning about money. The accountant suggested half in no-risk investments, giving a guaranteed income, and the rest with some risk, but I said No. I wanted three-quarters no risk, and just low risk on a quarter. So this is what we've done.'

He then flicked through bundles of policies and documents and statements from a variety of insurance companies, building societies and other financial institutions. 'It was a good job we left the old house when we did. We were getting that many financial letters arriving, dozens of them, and it was beginning to look a bit suspicious.' He locked the briefcase and put it safely away on a high shelf, out of reach of any of their kids. He admitted it had taken some time, making all these financial decisions, but no, it had caused him no worries, no headaches. 'Even when we were both on the dole, we had a system for paying all the bills on time. We even managed to save a bit. It's just good management, that's all you need, regardless of how much you've got.'

They have given nothing away to any friends or relations, and nothing to any charities. 'Charity begins at home,' said

Steve. 'We've got most of it tied up in trusts for the children. You never know what happens to the money, when you give to charity. It might go to abroad, to help poor people there, which is good, but they should stop their own wars first. That's what causes all the trouble, fighting over religion and that.'

But both of them are considering doing some voluntary work themselves in the future. Helen would like to go back and work with old people and Steve is thinking of becoming a Special Constable when the kids get older.

How about a fourth child? That was always their aim – hence the space left on the T-shirt. 'That's been a big decision,' said Steve. 'But we've now gone off that idea. The wife does get broody when she sees babies, but I don't think we should bring any more children into this world. We've realised that now Darren is two, we'll be more mobile soon, but if we have another baby, that could put us back. It's a big world, and we'd like to see a bit of it. We've got passports for the first time. We intend to do a bit of travelling in the next year or so. We fancy a safari in Africa. Instead of having another ourselves, we're gonna foster. Not adopting, just fostering, for a few months at a time. We'll ask our kids first, like, if they agree, because we want them to be for it and realise that taking in other kids doesn't mean we don't love them.'

The two older kids have settled at the local primary school, and Steve and Helen take them in by car every day and pick them up afterwards. 'Lee-zette loves the school, better than her old one. She even likes the school dinners, which she didn't before.'

Their daily routine revolves round their children, running them back and forward, then they all eat together, about 4.30. 'I don't tell them off as much for shouting now, as we've all got all this space, and there's nobody next door to worry about, but I teach them manners and courtesy, keeping their elbows off the table, that sort of thing. I do worry that they're a bit molly-coddled, a bit over protected. In the other house we didn't let them on the street, 'cos of the traffic and the dangers. Before we left, our street was invaded with druggies selling their stuff in the open. Helen rang the police, but they weren't at all interested. Round here they have acres of space to play in, and they love it, but we still keep a close eye on them all the time. No, they haven't had any friends home for tea yet, but I'm sure they will. I make sure they all have jobs. Lee-zette helps her mum with the cooking and cleaning, Glen and Darren bring the wood in.'

When she is twelve Lee-zette, their oldest child, will go to a private school. That's still the intention. 'There's tons round here. We'll vet them and pick the best. Not boarding. Helen wouldn't stand for that. But they'll all have the best private education possible. I don't worry about them turning out snobs. It will be better for them. They'll have a better start in life and more chance of being a lawyer or doctor.'

Their own social life has not changed. They are still basically turned in, not interested in going out or meeting other people. 'We keep ourselves to ourselves. We're not bothered about other folks. I haven't joined anything, and don't want to. Helen has been on a school outing, a sort of sponsored thing, and we're going to the Christmas play, but that's about all. One woman from the village did call not long after we moved in. Sort of posh county type, nice enough. I wasn't in at the time, just Helen, so she went away. The next day we called on her, all of us, in the Espace, just to say hello. We were invited in, but I didn't go. I said we were on the way somewhere and couldn't stop. I haven't seen her since, but I have rung her once. I thought I saw some lad hanging around her property, so I rang her, but it was all right. It was someone working for her.'

They still do the Lottery, £5 a week as before, and have twice won £10. 'It's just an amusement. The kids like watching the show.'

As people, they don't think they've changed because of the money. Any changes would have happened anyway.

'When I was younger,' said Steve, 'I was very self-conscious. In a strange town, for example, I couldn't ask anyone the way if I was lost. Now that wouldn't worry me. But it's nowt to do with the money. It's Helen, really. She brought me out of myself. A few people have changed towards us, but not many, because people don't know. I think the estate agent got a shock when we went in to ask for an eight-bedroom country house. We didn't say anything, of course, about the Lottery. I notice when I'm giving our address to people in shops or whatever, if I give the full address and say it's the Manor House, then their expressions do change, so I just usually say Manor Cottage. We do have one, part of the outhouses. I suppose a farm labourer lived in it at one time, but the previous owner couldn't get permission to convert it. The Lake District Planning Board are right buggers. It's just used for storage now.'

They haven't spent anything on clothes. Helen says she'd never buy designer things. Waste of money. They don't drink wine or eat better food. 'The only thing that's changed is that we eat at McDonald's more, which we didn't use to. There's one in Kendal, and we often take the kids there as a treat when we've been shopping.' They have got private medicine plans for all the family. 'And we've had an Aids test. We had to have it for the insurance. So we now know we're Aids-free. There was one cheeky nurse who said I should lose weight, but I ignored her. I don't care about my weight.'

Steve is about to take up a new hobby, but a very cheap and modest one, making model soldiers out of plaster. He's got the kit and is going to start soon. 'I love war games, but I've no

one to play with. I can't get any of the kids interested so far.'
Helen has taken up driving, and has had two lessons. Going
well, she says. They have both given up smoking, not wanting
to set a bad example to the children.

Steve doesn't miss work at all. He finds the house is enough
to occupy him. 'I cut the grass yesterday, knowing you were
coming, and again this morning, as I thought it didn't look
good enough. It's a sort of incentive, trying to make everything look good. Because it's your own, you want to look after
it. I did think about getting a ride-on lawnmower, a sort of
little tractor thing, till I saw the price. I got a second-hand
petrol mower instead, but I might eventually get a bigger one.
I do find it hard to spend money. We look for bargains, as we
always did. Helen's got a dishwasher now, which she never
had, so that's new. When we were buying it, they said that a
five-year guarantee would be £100, so I said No way. Then
they reduced it to £80, so I took it. A saving is a saving.'

They now have three cars, but none of them flash or
extravagant. 'I treat cars like junk-boxes,' said Steve. Their
biggest expenditure was on the Espace, second-hand, which
they got for £14,000 and still think it's a lot of money. They
have an old van which cost only £350. Steve bought it to move
their furniture, which he did all by himself after he found out
how much it would cost to either hire a van or get professional
movers. 'The van will soon go, or fall to pieces. We'll probably
just dump it, but it did serve its purpose.' Instead of his
22-year-old Dormobile, he now has a Jaguar – but an old and
battered X-registered Jag. It was a straight swap with a friend,
and no money changed hands.

'I watched that Lee Ryan on the television the other night
– the Lottery-winner who is now in prison because of his car
dealings. I saw him driving around in his flash Rolls-Royce,
but I wasn't envious. I could buy one, of course, if I wanted to,
but I never would. What struck me, watching him driving it,

was insurance. God, it must cost a bomb! I'm just a simple, common person and I want the simple common things in life. I don't want those sorts of luxury items. I don't look upon the house as an extravagance, not really. We've got three children, so we need lots of bedrooms. I look upon it as capital, not as an expenditure.

'The main thing in my life is still the same – Helen. When I found her, my life changed. If I had to choose between losing Helen and giving the Lottery money back, I'd give it back at once, no problem. She's still the best thing that ever happened to me.'

**22**

# THE ACCOUNTANT, PHILIP PLATTS, MANCHESTER

Every big winner gets offered the services of what Camelot calls its professional panel – an accountant and a lawyer. The Winners' Advisers are there to give hand-holding, personal and emotional help and assistance. The professionals' advice is meant to be hard and factual, legal and financial. Most winners avail themselves of this free opportunity. Andy and Audrey declined it. Steven and Helen took it.

Philip Platts is an accountant who serves on their northern panels, though he was not the one who advised Steve and Helen. He heads Binder Hamlyn's financial planning services in Manchester. They are right in the middle of the city, in a tall modern building with a swish modernistic reception area, two well-groomed receptionists and a series of discreet glass-walled meeting rooms which are named after English lakes. The biggest is called Windermere, as it should be. We sat in Grasmere.

Philip is forty-three and comes from Manchester, dapper and bouncy, a keen amateur actor and singer. He's said to have been very good in Hyde Amateur Dram. Soc.'s recent production of *The Winslow Boy*, but alas I missed it.

He's been with Binder Hamlyn for seven years, specialising in financial planning for private clients. 'In accountancy language, we call them high net worth individuals. Other people call them mega-rich.' Until 1994 they had all been either self-made millionaires or those with inherited wealth. The arrival of overnight Lottery-winners somewhat changed their profile.

Philip likes to think he has always given his clients a full professional service. Since the advent of Lottery millionaires, he has found himself giving a much more personal service. They all arrive new to the world of high personal wealth, and many have never met an accountant before, so he likes to establish a personal relationship from the beginning and hopes to become a friend, not just their accountant.

Binder Hamlyn are openly proud of the Lottery connection. In the firm's glossy brochure, which I studied in his waiting-room, there is a whole page complete with National Lottery logo which is headed, 'It's you – now what do you do?' It boasts that they and Arthur Andersen – to which they are joined – won their Camelot contract in open competition. 'We are different from lawyers,' Philip said, 'in that there are five or six accountancy firms which are national, and multinational, with branches everywhere. You don't usually get that with lawyers. I personally didn't come on stream till about March 1995, when I went on my first panel. Since then, well, my success rate has been rather striking.'

He estimates that 90 per cent of the jackpot-winners he has met since that first panel have ended up as clients of his firm. In six months, therefore, he had acquired twenty major winners, from all over the north of England and Wales. 'Yes, it is astonishing. I don't think many others have had this rate of success.'

With the big winners, the panel is usually held at Camelot's regional office – i.e. on neutral ground, so they won't feel intimidated. The Winners' Adviser may be there as well, to help translate anything into layman's language. 'I usually start the meeting, as I'm more garrulous, opening it for the professionals. I introduce who we are and what we do, but I do that very quickly. The most important single thing for every winner is to make a will – so I hand over to the lawyer for fifteen minutes or so, and let him speak. If I decide he's going above their heads and frightening them to death, I might butt in. Otherwise, it won't do me, or them, any good.

'When it's my turn, I usually start by saying that investment plans are simple. Some advisers I know say investments are complicated, so you must use me – that's their theory. I say the opposite – that it's all very simple. Then I say I have only two investment aims for them, regardless of the size of their win: to provide a reasonable income and for the money to grow at least in line with inflation. I assume they will want their money to pass down in their family, through the generations, so if they just leave it in the bank and do nothing with it, then in twenty years it could be worth only a quarter of its present worth, judging by the last twenty years.

'The panel usually lasts for between an hour and an hour and a half, and in that time I don't give any specific details. It's just a chat, to get to know them, hear their desires and worries, and tell them my general investment aims. If they decide to appoint my firm, I will then draw up an investment plan for them. They get this first meeting free, and then a free letter from me, which simply goes over what I have said. Sometimes they come back to me before they've had the first letter, wanting an immediate meeting. They say they've not slept for seven days, since they won, worrying about the money. That can put pressures on us. Everyone has different needs and problems, so it can't always be done quickly.

'One problem is the obvious one – their family and friends and their expectations. It's usually not been all sweetness and light since they won. With the self-made and the inherited wealthy, you don't get those family problems. You do with

Lottery-winners, so that has to be sorted out.

'At the second meeting, I usually assume they will be giving a certain amount to family and friends, and perhaps a quarter of a million will go on a new house and car. During this second meeting, I then work out what sort of money will be left for investment. If for example there is £10 million left to invest, I will explain that a modest return of, say, 3 per cent after tax will bring them in £300,000 per year, or £6,000 a week. They usually say there's no way they could spend that every week, so we discuss what sort of income they would like to live on. The smaller the income, of course, the better off they should be in the future, as their investment grows. I had a young woman in the other week, a student, and I worked out that investing her money would bring her in £2,500 a week. She exclaimed in amazement. That was what she had already been living on – for a whole year!'

After the second meeting, he sends them his investment plan. There is then a third meeting, when they come in and he explains it all and does some fine tuning. 'People are scared of stocks and shares, so when I suggest, say, £1 million in shares, they might reduce it to a quarter of a million. The problem is that the general public hear only the bad things about shares, and prices falling. But you have to go along with their feelings.'

Philip has dealt with some of the biggest winners so far, roll-over winners, including a £20 million winner and two £11 million winners. The latter have both remained private, even though they live not too far away from each other. One has taken Philip's advice completely and gone along with his investment portfolio, while the other has left all his money in the bank. Much to Philip's agony. He hates to see what he thinks is waste. 'Just think what happens when you leave £10 million in the bank, or a basic building society account! It just needs the interest rate to go down by 1 per cent, which it does all the time at present, and your income has gone down by £100,000 a year! And, with a bank, you are also paying 40 per cent tax on the interest. With a building society, it's not even totally safe. I'm not saying any of our building societies are going to collapse, but the building society protection limit is only £18,000 per account.'

Fortunately, only two out of his twenty big winners have done absolutely nothing with their money. 'I suppose it's a mixture of fear, worry, lack of understanding and a belief that they've won so much that there's no need to invest and earn more.' The rest, in the main, have followed most of his advice. For which, of course, he charges, once they have had the initial panel meeting.

What are in fact his fees? 'Er, that is a sensitive subject. I don't really want to go into it. An hourly rate can be very off-putting. It all depends – on how much I work on it, how much other people do. And the rates can vary.'

But winners themselves must ask, so what do you say? 'As a rough guide, I quote what our annual charges would be if, for example, we were handling a portfolio of £3 million.' And? 'In that case it might be around £3,000.'

What about commission? 'That is another sensitive area, so I must make it clear we do not take or charge commission. We work purely on a fee basis. When we are investing on someone's behalf, in, say, unit trusts, it can happen that only 95 per cent is invested, and the other 5 per cent will disappear, counted as commission. In that case, we say we want all 100 per cent invested. With a life assurance company, if say we are investing for inheritance tax reasons, most companies will automatically pay a commission as part of the arrangement. When that happens, we offset that against the fees we are charging the client. So it can happen, if someone has a big enough life assurance policy, that the commission will be bigger than our fees.

'I make all this clear to our clients because the thing that does worry me, which they mostly don't realise, is that if they stick to one bank, or one insurance company, they will be offered only that company's products. That means internally, sizeable costs can be made out of their money. I've had one horror story of a big winner who was contacted by a very well known insurance company – a public winner, who was tracked down because his name was in the papers. This salesman got in before our panel met, and sold him lots of policies. His commission was many many times the size of our fees, and the financial planning was all wrong. Some of them are not looking at the whole market, or the client's real desires.'

Philip gives all his winners a secret code, which remains on their files, so other members of his staff never know the real names. 'Only I know the key to each code.' Some winners become very concerned, he says, about people knowing their private affairs, whether private or public winners. 'One big winner went for a few days' break to watch a Test Match. While he was there, he ran out of cash. Next morning he went to the nearest bank and, to his surprise, he was met by the bank manager on the steps, surrounded by photographers. He was then taken inside and given champagne. He was concerned how anyone knew he was going into the bank, and asked the bank manager how he had found out. The manager stared in amazement. It turned out to be opening day of a new branch, and my client just happened to be the first customer!'

None of his winners would he describe as middle class, but then top accountants do have their own ways of judging such categories. 'I have had one doctor, but he wasn't earning any great amount, and a government employee earning even less. The rest were basically working class. Interestingly enough, they all had bank accounts before they came to me, including those who were unemployed. Out of them all, I haven't so far had one I would call very financially sophisticated.'

Few of his winners have given much to charity yet. 'Some people might eventually, so they say, but I don't encourage it in the early days of a big win. If things go wrong, or you change your mind, you might get some money back from your family, but not if you give it to charity. I'm always surprised by how large people's families can be. It's sometimes like *Dallas*. People come out of the woodwork as soon as someone has won a lot of money.

'But they have usually given to members of their family. The most generous winner I've had is one who has given away £1 million out of his £3 million. One-third, that's a high proportion. Actually, this particular person gave away even more. He was one of my £11 million winners and, legally, might have been able to keep it all, but he honoured informal promises he had made in the past. So strictly speaking he gave away £8 million at once, then he gave away another million, leaving himself with only £2 million. He came to see me recently, wanting to know if it was OK for him to buy himself a £50,000 Mercedes. I put my arm round him and gave him a hug. I suppose I become friendly with them because they know I am neither jealous of them, nor am I trying to take money off them. I am here to help them, at any time.'

The other day he got a call from one winner in Casablanca who was unable to pay his hotel bill because there was some problem.

'It was his gold credit card, which I recommend for its worldwide use, but there can be a problem before the first payment has been made, when you are just starting to use it. He had millions at home, of course, in his bank, so I had to track down his bank manager, who was out at dinner. I got him to sort it out with various phone calls and faxes.'

In his experience, the majority of his winners are much happier since their win. 'Only two, or at the most three, out of my twenty have been unhappier than they were before. It's always to do with family squabbles. They've been a feuding family anyway, but the Lottery win has brought things to a head. I have one winner who's now sitting at home on his own, because his daughter has left him. He says the Lottery has spoiled his life. But that is most unusual.'

None of his twenty has gone on a wild spending spree. 'I can't think of any of them, no matter how big their win, who has bought a new house for more than £300,000. In the context of their win, they buy modestly.' So no one has done a Lee Ryan? He smiled. 'Not even Lee Ryan has done a Lee Ryan, not in the Viv Nicholson, football-pools-winner sense. I estimate he's spent only £2½ million out of his £6 million, according to newspaper reports. That's not quite spend-spend-spend ...'

He clearly loves dealing with his Lottery-winners, and with Camelot, and gets upset only when he sees them being criticised. 'Camelot has been fantastically efficient, from my personal experience. It's the British habit of knocking firms and people when they have been successful.'

Philip himself does the Lottery every week, spending the vast sum of £2. 'One winner did tell me his secret, how he had chosen his winning line. He did it by drawing pictures on the lottery coupon – the one with all the numbers on – imagining, say, the shape of a cufflink or a tree, then picking numbers around that shape. I did it with my son in a supermarket, making him stand still while I did the outline of his face. I won nothing. Now I just pick the numbers randomly.

'I know what I'd do if I won. I'd immediately buy a villa in the south of France and hope to arrange a consultancy with Binder Hamlyn. I'd still look after my Lottery-winners, but from the south of France. That would save me traipsing all over the country. Once a year I'd send each of them the air fare to Nice, pick them up, and spend a few days reviewing their investment fund. Oh, I wouldn't mind them staying with me. I like to think most of them are my friends. During the rest of the year I'd sit in my south of France villa and write a novel.'

What about? 'A lottery-winner, of course!'

## RUTH, HASTINGS

Now we come to the big ones, Mark Gardiner and Paul Maddison, the glaziers who won £22.5 million in June 1995. Over a year later, it was still the biggest jackpot so far, enough to make any accountant's eyes go glazed. Whatever happened to the likely lads?

The damning predictions by various of Mark's former wives and or mistresses, and his real or adopted mother, that it would all end in tears, with Mark totally ruining what remained of his life by dissipation, continued to be repeated in the press during that year, although he gave no interviews.

He had apparently remained in Hastings, so several papers said, and from time to time he was doorstepped and little stories were written about him, usually still referring to him as the 'Lottery Rat'. Not just the tabloids, either. The *Daily Telegraph*, on 11 November 1995, repeated the old descriptions of him as a 'love cheat'. They had tried to talk to him, but all they got was a refusal from his solicitor whom they quoted as saying, 'I should think he'll tell you to bugger off.'

Paul Maddison, meanwhile, managed to keep well out of the papers. It was said he had left Hastings, and no one knew his new address. He and his wife Ruth had always appeared to be the maturer, more sensible and solid couple at the time of the win, and less likely to do anything extreme or extravagant.

I remembered that Ruth, the teacher, had said she was not giving up her work whatever happened, so when the new term began in September, I wrote to her at her old address. The phone number had been changed, and whoever was living there was now ex-directory, so I half feared she might have moved. But she wrote back, giving me the new number. So I went down to see her on a Sunday, her day off.

She was wearing white leggings, and a green T-shirt with the name of her primary school emblazoned on the front. She looked lean and athletic, more like a PE mistress than a deputy head. She was not only back at school but about to start work on her MA at the University of Sussex, an in-service degree, while still teaching. She was feeling a bit nervous about all the work it would entail, apart of course from school duties. There would be a seminar one evening a week, regular essays and then dissertations. She was planning to specialise in two particular areas – Special Needs and Reading Skills. The course would last two years, at a cost to her of £1,000 a year.

She had never done her BEd back in her training college years, leaving with only a teacher's certificate. For a long time she had realised that, to get further promotion, she needed a degree. 'It's the only way I'll ever be a head. That was always my aim. The plan was to spend three years as a deputy head, get a degree, then apply for headships. During the last three months, of course, I've started to ask myself – do I really want to be a head, do I need all that stress? I don't need to earn the money any more, so why bother?

'The strange thing is, since the win, I have worked even harder, if anything. I do about fifty hours a week. I leave at seven each morning, as my school is twenty-seven miles away, and I never get back till after seven in the evening. Now I've got the MA course as well, and a horrendous reading list. I must admit that last Monday morning, driving to work for a new week, I did think to myself, I must be mad! I never did work for money. That was never the motivation. Of course I moaned I wasn't being paid enough, as most teachers do, but that wasn't the reason for working. I happen to enjoy it.

'I denied in the old days that I was ever under stress, refusing to admit it. "Stress, me? I'm not stressed. What do you mean?" I would say that, all stressed out, of course. One thing about having the money, which I hope is already having an effect, is that when I feel stress coming on I'm better able to step back and be calmer, get things in proportion.

'It's hard to explain why I still want to do it, and put up with any stress. Perhaps it's the example of my mother. She brought me up on her own, a one-parent family on a council estate, as my father had long left. She made a go of life and was never a spender, always a saver. She never put money first, but she was always independent. I have a friend, another deputy head, who keeps saying to me I must be certifiable. Imagine coming back to work after what has happened to me!'

Ruth has kept a diary recording the main events of every day since the win in June. 'I do it before bed each night, always have done. It's not just events, but my concerns and worries. Since June, some have been positive. Some not so positive . . .'

She went straight back to school on the Wednesday after the win, as she said she would, wanting life to be normal. She checked with her head first, and the chairman of the governors, that by doing so, she would not create more problems or pressures for the school. 'The first thing I did was to go round every class, one by one, and told them the same thing – I am here, back at school, because I want to be here, because I enjoy school. I then asked if they had any questions. They wanted to know how I was going to spend the money. I pointed out it was my husband's money, not mine, but I asked if they had any suggestions. "You could go to Australia, miss," said one. "You could put a roof on the school pool." The object was to show them I was still the same person, and nothing was going to change.'

But things had changed. All that day the press were hanging around the school, trying to photograph her. 'A *Sun* reporter did get into the school office, while I was actually there putting something into a filing cabinet, but I kept my head down and he didn't recognise me. All the press were told the same thing – I would be giving no interviews, talking to no one. I was impressed by the fact that they didn't try to talk to any of the children, or try to enter the school until the children had gone home. But the pressure was pretty unbearable. I had to leave by a back door and go in someone else's car. I didn't go back to school on the Thursday and Friday, waiting for it all to die down.

'The day we came back from Camelot on the Tuesday, Paul and I arrived home late at night and within an hour our house was staked out. There were two reporters sitting in a car outside, with binoculars. Paul got more upset than I did. In the middle of the night, he said we had to leave. He wouldn't let me put the light on, so we were crawling around the bedroom in the dark, on our hands and knees, just so we wouldn't be seen through the window. We packed our bags, made a dash for the car, and went to stay with friends.' Eventually, after a couple of weeks, press attention tailed off as other winners were pursued instead. Ruth and Paul then started discussing what to do with the rest of their lives.

Paul had decided almost at once that he was giving up work and going to Scotland. He also wanted to buy himself some nice cars and have a luxury holiday. He went off to Scotland to stay with his sister near Perth while he looked for a suitable country house for him and Ruth. They had lived near Perth in the first two years of their marriage, from 1988–90 (both had decided they wanted to go off to a new area and try new careers). In Perth, Ruth took a sequence of odd jobs in offices or shops. Paul's new business was in car valeting, but it did not work out. So they had returned to Hastings, and eventually Paul joined Mark in the glass business.

'I didn't realise how badly their firm was doing,' said Ruth. 'Until the time of the win, I never knew they had such big debts. But I knew at least our house was safe because, when we bought it, Paul had put it in my name, just in case. When Paul started thinking about houses in Scotland, he asked me to give up the school, and this house, and go with him. I had that career break for two years, and had now got back into teaching. I didn't want to move again, so I said No.

'I've decided I want to stay put, for the next two years anyway, while I do my MA course. I can't manage any more upheavals till I've finished that. Then I might buy another house, locally, and give this away. We've paid off the mortgage, that was one of the first things we did. At one time I was thinking of it becoming a refuge for battered wives, but I think the neighbours might raise objections. My plan now is to give it to an Aids charity. It is in my name, after all.'

Paul stayed most of the summer in Scotland, making only fleeting visits south. He also went on a luxury holiday to Mauritius with his sister and her husband, but Ruth did not go. 'It coincided with the beginning of the school term and I had too much to do.'

But surely in the school holidays you had some free time? 'Not much. I did spend some time in Scotland with Paul, staying in very posh places which I thought a waste of money, but Paul loved it. I managed a few days away with a couple of girlfriends for my fortieth birthday, which I'd planned back in the spring. We went to Chester. Oh, and I had two days on my own in Cambridge. That was wonderful. I did brass rubbing and went to see *As You Like It*. I just pleased myself, did all the things I wanted to do. Then, when I came back, I redecorated my bedroom, I mean our bedroom.'

Meanwhile, Paul had found his dream house near Perth. He then had to supervise builders and workmen, gardeners and decorators and organise all the improvements and additions he wanted. 'He has been very occupied, and quite happy I think. He eats out at expensive places every night and buys designer clothes. That's something I can't bear to do. I still buy the same kinds of clothes. He keeps asking me to join him.

'One of the things he's suggested is that I could go to a university up there, such as Stirling, and do my MA, which is true, I suppose. But I don't want to. It's not just the MA course – I am committed to my school. The head and myself have a vision for it, things we want to achieve in the next two years. I want to carry on with these plans, so that means I can't take time out, or move away.'

Ruth has given a handsome sum to the school for their library fund, though she was worried at first that the head, who is a strong Methodist, or the governors might reject the gift on the grounds that they didn't want to accept any money which came from gambling. 'It was all OK in the end. The head is against gambling personally, but realises that schools do gain from things like raffles. It's been great being able to help the school.'

But is it just the school and her MA course which are stopping her from joining her husband in Scotland? She paused for a while, and thought. 'The thing is, he doesn't really understand me and my values. I don't know what will happen. I honestly don't. We speak every day on the phone and are still good friends. It's just that he can't understand what I'm doing, why I want to stay here and still teach. And I can't understand what he's doing. He is enjoying his new house and all his gadgets but, to me, he has no purpose in his life. Our tastes are, well, just so different.'

Paul, apparently, has bought three luxury cars, each with

personalised number plates, which Ruth thinks is funny, considering he says he is so concerned about anonymity and security. 'On the phone yesterday he was moaning that one of the cars is playing up. Then he's got some problem with his new pond, which is so big it's really a lake . . .'

Ruth still has the same car she bought earlier in the year, a Volvo, and sees no reason to give it up. It still works, even though it is slow and sluggish. 'I suppose I would like a car with a better image, a more sporty image. I went with a girlfriend who was buying a very nice Toyota. I could easily afford one, or several, but I just couldn't. I don't need another car. It's needs I think about, not desires. That's another way Paul and I are so different.'

It then emerged, because she had said she could buy several cars, that Paul has settled a large sum upon her, for her personal use, to spend how she likes. She has met Camelot's bank adviser (not the panel) and made a few basic decisions. 'I don't think Paul has done anything about that yet. I suppose he has so much money that he feels no need to invest. He'll never spend it all. At one time he did think he might, which is ridiculous. I've put my money in National Savings and in a unit trust. I've also put a large amount in a capital investment bond, quite a risky one. I now buy the *Telegraph* to see how it's doing. It's gone up and down since I bought it. I see all the money as long-term savings and security, not for an income to live on.'

She earns £24,000 a year as deputy head and has always managed to live on that – even managing to save her own £1,000 for the first year of the MA course. Among the many begging letters were some from teachers – after a piece about her appeared in the *Times Educational Supplement* – asking her for money for their course, the one she is doing. 'The cheek! I saved my own £1,000 so why can't they?' None of the begging letters was answered. 'Some were heartbreaking, but how can one differentiate between one begging letter and another?'

Her own personal self-indulgences so far have been fairly modest. The biggest outlay has been £1,500 on a Hewlett Packard computer, with Windows 95, so she can work at home on school projects. She has turned the lobby under the stairs into a little office for herself. 'I was saving for a computer anyway, but wouldn't have spent as much. I suppose the single wildest thing I've done was when I was on holiday with my friends in Chester. We happened to walk into an art gallery one day and I fell in love with some paintings. I asked about the artist, and he turned out to live nearby, so we went to see him, and I bought one of his paintings. The price wasn't too enormous.' She took me to see it on her dining-room wall, and I guessed £1,000 or even £3,000 if he was a local name. 'It was £400 but I've never done that sort of thing in my life before! I suppose having money has given me more confidence. I think to myself, I'm a millionaire now, I can do that, go there. Even though I don't do it. Talking to the investment people at Drummond's [part of the Royal Bank of Scotland] was an interesting experience. I quickly realised that they needed me more than I needed them. That gave me confidence. Before the win, I would have been completely intimidated by such people in such a situation, thinking I know nothing, therefore I am inadequate. Now I know that I might know nothing, but I can soon find out. Therefore there is no need to feel inadequate or intimidated. It was the same in the art gallery in Chester. Without money, I would not have had the confidence to ask to see the artist and would have been intimidated.

'But I don't think people have changed towards me, not really. With my close friends, the ones who know me well, we're just the same. With professional people who know me only as a teacher, that's the same, though I do get irritated when they make jokes about my money, saying, Why do you bother coming to school? Apart from that, I'm anonymous. Strangers don't know about me. I don't actually know many of the neighbours. I did go with Paul to Bexhill, where he used to work, and that was embarrassing. So many people came up to us because they recognised Paul. But I suppose even that will have stopped by now. People soon forget.'

What about the singing? With your own money, you can now lash out and have proper lessons? 'I did mention that at the press conference, half as a joke, and I thought someone might offer me lessons, but they haven't. I would like to be able to sing. I have to sing in assembly each morning, so it would help to be able to do it properly.'

She had no children by her previous marriage, unlike Paul, and no one from her past has reappeared in her life to haunt or pester her. 'The day I left my first husband, his new partner moved in. I've heard nothing from him since, though pre-sumably he must have seen or heard about our news in the papers.'

Ruth has kept her own cuttings book, the pages neatly arranged, and has only nice memories of the press conference day – and no regrets about going public. 'We couldn't have kept it secret, anyway, so it was best to get it over with, all in one day. But I don't want any more publicity, thank you very much.'

Does she regret the money itself, and the effects on her life? 'The first effects were very strange, for all four of us, even Mark, during the first twenty-four hours or so. He's the so-called ebullient one, always on his mobile phone, but he felt just as strange as we all did. Unhappy, even. The initial feelings were not all positive.'

I mentioned that Alasdair, the original Winners' Adviser, had likened the shock of winning to the shock of bereavement. 'I can see that. It was very like when my own mother suddenly died, and I wasn't there. Winning all that money was a similar shock. The rug is suddenly pulled away from under your feet. You think it's not really happening, find yourself thinking to yourself, "What's happening?" as if you are not there. You are simply looking in. You can't sleep, you can't eat, you feel unhappy when you shouldn't be. You don't or can't do all those things you planned to do. It's as if someone has torn up your life into pieces, like little bits of paper, then thrown them in the air. Even now I don't feel settled. The jigsaw has not been put together. The pieces are still in the air. As for the money, I think it was far too much. It's silly money. Who needs all that? I think there should be a cap on the jackpot with a maximum prize of £1 million – if, of course there has to be a Lottery. Personally I think it's all a waste of time. I can't believe it when I see all those people queueing up for a ticket on a Saturday when they must know their chances are so very slim. I gather Mark still does it, but Paul doesn't.'

I asked about Mark and Brenda, but she said she had little contact with them, and didn't want to make any comments about them. 'We didn't have much beforehand. I've always been working such long hours. He was Paul's business partner, that's all. I admit I was always a bit ambivalent about him and his personal life, but from what I've heard, I have to admit I am impressed by what he has done since.'

She said she would leave me to track him down myself to find out what had happened to him. 'I've seen Brenda, and I know she was upset at one time. She was chased by the press more than I was. She hated going out feeling she should dress up and look smart, even going to the shops, just in case she was followed. She said to me something interesting. "We're just ordinary people, but now other people expect us not to be ordinary." I think in a way she felt a bit of a second-class citizen. It was Mark who won the money, not her. So it has been good of Paul to give me money in my own right, to allow me my independence.'

I asked about her immediate future, how she saw things going over the next couple of years. 'My desire at the moment is to have a structure that stays the same, something constant in my life. The world divides into reflective and reactive people. I'm reflective. I need time to adjust, to internalise events before I decide to change anything. Paul is reactive. He needs to act first and then make adjustments later. You see, we are different types. That's one of the problems.

'I can't guess the future. I know our relationship sounds strange, but it suits me. We have honestly not discussed what might happen. I enjoy living on my own. I don't feel guilt any more. When Paul was here, I always felt guilty coming home so late at night, exhausted, feeling I should be making him a meal. I don't feel that now. I suppose there is a lack of understanding on both sides. I think he resented my working so hard, but I never resented it when he was working hard, when he was on call in the middle of the night. That didn't worry me; that was his job. I feel happy, looking after myself. I suppose I am selfish. That's it. And it's probably unfair on Paul.'

How about the longer term? Say seven years ahead? 'If forced to think seven years ahead, well, I don't think Paul will still be in Scotland. That phase will pass. He is a searcher, always wanting other things, different things, the grass is always greener. In seven years, I don't know. He might be living in Greece, perhaps, the owner of a little bar, just as a hobby, which he wanders down to every day. No, I won't be with him. Perhaps he'll be with another woman, I don't know – someone half his age, maybe, but not blonde. Paul prefers brunettes. Will he be happy? I don't think he will ever be really satisfied with life.

'Paul will search and never find, because he's not sure what he's looking for, what his values are. I am more spiritual. I am very conscious of the need for spiritual strengths. That's one of the reasons I am planning to go on a retreat this Christmas. I am more aware than I was before that there is something in this life apart from money and success. I don't think Paul realises this yet. As for me in seven years, well, I expect I'll still be living in this area, but not in this house. Out in the countryside somewhere. I'll still be in education, perhaps doing a PhD. Who knows? Or I might be doing voluntary work in some school.

'It's been harder for Paul than me. I like being on my own; he doesn't. He is a creature of routine. But it was his decision to go to Scotland, not mine. I told him from the beginning I wouldn't go with him. On the Sunday night of the win, when we first heard and neither of us could sleep, I told him straight – I'm not going back to Scotland. I hadn't been happy there. But the discussion was all very amicable. It still is. But both of us are alike in one sense – once we've decided something, that's it. We won't be swayed. He has said to me, "I'll give it all up if you'll come and live with me." I'm not sure what that means. Does it mean he'll give all the money away? I'm not sure. But I'm not going.

'The Lottery win has been very disrupting. If it hadn't been for the Lottery, I'm sure Paul and I would still be here, living together, so that has been one disruptive aspect. No, I don't wish it hadn't happened. All I wish is that it had not been such a big win. On the positive side, I do now feel I *can* do anything, go anywhere I want to in life, even if I never do.'

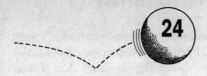

## 24

## PAUL, EX-HASTINGS

It took a while to fix up a meeting with Paul Maddison. He was hard to contact in Scotland, where he was very busy with his house. But he was polite enough whenever I got him on his mobile, even calling me Mr Davies, which has not happened for years, unless of course he thought I was a glazing customer from the old days.

Several times we made arrangements and then he changed them, saying he wasn't sure of his movements. He clearly didn't want to be bothered – by Camelot, by me, by anyone, but most of all by the press, whom he suspected were chasing him. All very understandable. He was also, I assumed, not very keen on talking to me about his domestic arrangements, knowing that I had seen Ruth and must know roughly what had happened to their marriage.

But two weeks before Christmas he agreed to see me in Hastings, on the same day I had arranged to visit Ruth's primary school. As the author of several children's books, Ruth had asked me to give a talk to the pupils. What a mistake. Not because of the school or the pupils, but the December weather. There was ice and fog and snow, and I got stuck at East Croydon station, arriving at her school almost an hour late, to discover that there were no kids. The heating had packed up and all the children had been sent straight home, except for five whose parents could not be contacted.

Not to worry, said Ruth, ever organised, ever efficient. She now appeared a much bossier deputy head than I had imagined when I'd sat with her at home in her weekend leisure wear. She said I could give my talk, and a little quiz I had prepared, to the staff instead. So it came to pass, one very cold December morning, that I sat in the staffroom of Denton County Primary School, Newhaven, Sussex, and gave a talk to sixteen members of the staff, plus five pupils. (The teachers were hopeless in the quiz, but the pupils were excellent.)

It was interesting to see if there was any staffroom banter with Ruth about the Lottery win, but there was none. Only one person made a remark in passing, saying that Ruth could now easily afford £5 for some whip-round. A harmless enough remark, but observing it happening, I could understand why so many winners find these fairly harmless remarks annoying. The person making them doesn't seem to realise how frequently and boringly they get made.

Paul had arranged to meet me for lunch afterwards, which was of course a big attraction about going down. But with the school being partly closed, Ruth suggested that Paul could take the whole staff out to lunch as an end-of-term treat. So all sixteen teachers, plus Paul and me, went off for lunch at a local roadside inn, very nice, lots of trimmings.

'Thanks very much, Paul,' each teacher said as they left, leaving him to pay the bill. 'Very good of you. Cheers. Ta. Very nice, Paul. Thanks . . .'

'I hate all that,' said Paul, when we were left alone and all the teachers, including Ruth, had gone back to school.

'You mean people thanking you?'

'Yeah, I hate people being grateful.'

'But surely you wouldn't like them to say nothing?'

'That would be ignorant. It's just one after the other, trailing out in a line, saying Thank you, Thank you, Thank you. It's embarrassing. I don't like it.'

I hadn't seen him in the flesh since meeting him in the winners' suite at Camelot HQ six months previously. He didn't look as tall, but perhaps it was because he now appeared a bit plumper. 'I'm not actually fatter, but I have been. In the first two months after the win, I put on one and a half stone. It was with eating two meals a day, big lunches and big dinners, eating just for social reasons as much as anything, but now I've got most of it off again. I had all my trousers let out when I put on weight. Now they're all too big for me.'

One of Paul's first decisions, first realisations, the moment he won the Lottery, was that he could leave the firm – and leave Mark. I had assumed, on first meeting them, that they were bosom pals, best friends as well as workmates. 'I put up £6,000 to buy my way into the firm, so I was then stuck. I was responsible with Mark for everything. It took me a year to realise I'd made a mistake. The last four years were not happy, shall we say. I saw him through two marriages and a lot of social drinking, with the firm doing badly. I had to do a lot of night-time call-outs when he couldn't make them. As things got worse, I couldn't get out of it. We just had to plod on. Luckily I'd put our house in Ruth's name before I joined the firm, so if we had gone bust, we would not have lost that.'

Paul had had financial and marital problems in the past, but none of them had been revealed by the tabloids. Fortunately for him, the papers had concentrated on Mark's past, which had given them more than enough material. His own story, for various reasons, would have been harder to unravel, unless he or someone else had co-operated. 'They never found my mother, for example,' he said. 'This was because some years ago she went to work for a woman and was given a basement flat, rent free, though she had to pay the bills. The phone was in the woman's name, and my mother never changed it. Even today, you wouldn't be able to track her down.'

So what is she doing? 'Oh, she's still in the same flat. I gave her a good sum of money, months ago, to buy herself her own place, but she hasn't spent a penny. She's left it lying in the bank. She's happy with her own life and her own friends. Her big excitement is bingo.'

Do her friends know that her son is worth £11 million? 'Some of them do, but she has good friends. And good friends don't talk to the press.'

Then there was the matter of his first wife, whom no one was able to find for the simple reason that she died at the age of thirty-three of cancer of the throat. 'No, she never smoked.' By this wife, Paul had two daughters, now late teenagers. He had in fact left his first wife some time before she died, to live with another woman whom he subsequently married. 'She left me for someone else, but when we got divorced, I had a long struggle over the money, with her claiming £10,000 from me which I hadn't got, but I had to pay most of it.'

So Ruth was his third marriage, the same number as Mark's – which never came out at the time. 'They never found my second wife, either, or my daughters, though one was hassled by a reporter. I think some boyfriend must have told the press. The younger daughter was at school at the time of the win and some kids at her school did say to her, "Is it your dad, the Lottery Rat?" They got me mixed up with Mark. But, luckily, nothing got in the papers about them.'

Paul's second decision, having told Mark he was leaving the firm for good, was to head for Scotland. 'Ruth always knew it was my ambition to return to Scotland one day, when I retired. I love the people and I love the countryside. Even though I'm a southerner, I don't like most of the south. I knew Ruth loved her job and her school, but I honestly thought, because of the money side of things, she would come with me. Well, I hoped she would.'

So Paul went off to Scotland on his own, staying with his

sister and brother-in-law. He says he was disappointed that Ruth wouldn't come on their holiday to Mauritius.

After his holiday, Paul started house-hunting in Scotland, but tried to remain as private as possible, not telling people who he was, avoiding all attempts by the press to track him down. 'It was a very hot summer, as you know, and when I went into estate agents in shorts and T-shirt and flipflops, asking to look at £300,000 houses, they didn't take me seriously. When I first went into a BMW showroom and asked to look at the new 740, one salesman was very off-hand and said to me, "I'm busy." Luckily, another salesman came over and helped me.'

Weren't you tempted to drop just a little hint about your wealth? 'Never. It never came into my head. I'm not a boaster. I have never said to anyone that I want this because I've won the Lottery. The nearest I came to letting it out was sitting in a pub in Scotland one day, not long after I'd won, and two women at the next table were discussing the Lottery, and talking about me and Mark. They were wondering where we were now, and how we were spending our money, and one of them said, "Well, he won't be in a place like this." I had to laugh. Just to myself, of course.'

Paul went on to buy not one but two BMWs. 'When I went back to order, I made sure I got the salesman who had been polite, so that he would get the commission.' He bought a BMW 740, price £44,000, and a BMW 328i convertible at £33,000. He then went on to buy a Range-Rover for £47,000. Any discounts, buying all those cars for cash? 'No, not really. There's a waiting-list for them. All I got was a few extras thrown in.'

The previous day, Paul had driven down to Hastings in his Range-Rover, a ten-hour drive, in bad weather, so I sympathised. 'No, I loved it. Cars have always been my passion. When I was sixteen, my ambition was to have a BMW.'

But why two, plus the Range-Rover? You live on your own and can only drive one car at a time. 'Well, the 740 is my luxury car, top of the range. My best one, you might say. The convertible is my summer car. The Range-Rover is the winter car, good for long and hard journeys. I love them all. I have been thinking about the new BMW that's out soon, as seen in the James Bond film, but I would have nowhere to put it. I have to leave the Range-Rover out as it is, 'cos the garage holds only two cars.'

Each of his cars does indeed have a personalised number plate, in sequence, each of them ending in PTM (his full name is Paul Thomas Maddison). 'I would have liked PM, but I think the Prime Minister wants that!' And Paul McCartney, I added. Plus Paul Merton, Paul Merson, Pete Murray, Patrick Moore, Peter May, plus all the Macs – in fact you could easily re-sell any PM registration. It was the name Paul Maddison which appeared on the real Lottery cheque, as opposed to the reproduction one that appeared in the press conference. The rule is that it has to be paid out to one person. 'That was Mark's idea, to put it in my name in case any of his ex-wives caused trouble.'

The number plates didn't cost much, he says, around £300

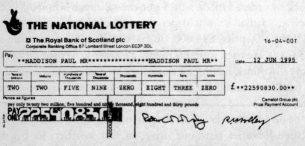

each. The expensive plates are those which make words or
people's names. All the same, if he was keeping a low profile,
wasn't he rather drawing attention to himself? 'It was just a bit
of fun,' he said. 'Though I was reading in a motoring mag the
other day that people who have their initials on their cars are
rather sad.'

Paul eventually bought his house, a reproduction shooting
lodge costing £350,000, on which he has spent a bit of money,
making it look as old and tasteful and as distinguished as
possible. He has used an interior designer for the décor and
furnishings. He has put in a large pond, a games room,
electronic gates and surveillance cameras. Most of his time
these last six months has been spent working on it. He got out
a drawing to let me admire the situation. 'There's not a bad
angle to it.'

Several people around Perth now know who he is, but he
can live with that. 'I think, when I was buying the house,
someone must have realised. It's not too hard to check my
name. It's even in the *Guinness Book of Records*. You have to
look under "Gambling", for the biggest win so far in Britain.
But it's only what you might say among the higher class of
local business that it's got out. Mrs Gloag, that amazing
woman who runs Stagecoach, she's a local woman. She knows
about it because I've been to her house and met her. I don't
lie, if asked directly. I just don't tell people. Since the news
leaked out in the business community, I've had two offers to
buy night-clubs, but I'm not interested.'

Has the local press found out? 'I've had one call. I didn't
deny it, but asked them not to print it, saying one day I'll give
them an interview. They haven't printed anything, so that's
good. But the *Daily Mirror* did find out, and I have a suspicion
about who tipped them off. A few weeks ago, this car drives
straight into my drive. I was testing the security gates at the
time. This bloke gets out and says he's from the *Mirror*. I

chucked him out, didn't I, saying I wasn't giving no interviews. He went out shouting "Where's your swimming pool then?" I haven't got one, actually. Too cold up here.'

He has never been to a Camelot panel. He says they haven't approached him about one (which Camelot denies), nor has anyone from Camelot contacted him for research or follow-up purposes. He has of course been very hard to contact. 'Oh, they could have got me; they know how to. But I wouldn't go to their panel now anyway, or talk to their advisers. I'm quite happy with what I've done.'

Put simply – he's done nothing. Which has been very lucky for the Royal Bank of Scotland. Six months later he still had around £10 million deposited with them. 'My philosophy is that if I do nothing at all, I'm still earning £10,000 a week, every week. I'm happy just to sit back and enjoy it and not have any worries. Yes, I'll have a large tax bill to pay, probably about a quarter of a million, but my bloke from the Royal Bank is looking after that as well. He's been brilliant. I can ring him up at any time. He explained to me about inheritance tax, which I'd never heard of. Oh, you know, if you live seven years there's nothing to pay, but you can get round it by having an insurance policy to cover it or you can have it written in that the estate will pay capital gains on any gifts. He explained all that to me in layman's language. He was very good.'

But why haven't you got Tessas or National Savings Certificates or Bonds or the other ways in which you pay little or no tax? 'I can't be bothered. Ruth has done all that, invested it properly, but it's not for me. I know that putting all your eggs in one basket is probably not a very good idea, but I'm not worried. I prefer just to deal with one person and know where I am.'

But are you aware how much the Royal Bank of Scotland must be gaining from you, in various ways? 'Listen, whatever you do with your money, someone will be making money out of you. I know that – and it doesn't worry me. I'm happy with what I've done.'

He has been generous to various members of his family (but not his previous wife) and set up a trust for his two daughters when they reach the age of thirty. 'They have been brilliant, no problems with them. Well, one rang me the other day and asked for more money, and I said No. I want them to make lives for themselves. One does want to be a PE teacher. I'm not so sure about the other one.' He has also given odd gifts to friends, such as £15,000 to one whose house was in danger of being repossessed. 'He didn't come to me asking for money. I just heard about his problems and offered the money. He refused at first, then agreed it as an interest-free loan, so I put it in his bank. Now I've told him it's a gift, and he's finally accepted that. It gives me great satisfaction to do that sort of thing for my friends, the ones I know would have remained friends, whatever happened.'

He has given nothing to charity, apart from buying odd items at charity auctions. His biggest gift has been to Ruth, a settlement of £1 million. 'No, it's not a settlement – don't use that word. It's just a present for her so she has some money in her own name. If she wanted more money and came to me for another million, say, then I would give it to her, but she won't. She's not that type. She's not interested in money. I admire her for that. If we were ever to split up, Ruth would never come to me for half my money. I have no fears about that, but a lot of them would. I know that type.'

He has seen Mark only twice since the win, and has no plans for future meetings. 'We haven't got a lot in common. We've got different outlooks. I know he's upset that I didn't go to his wedding, but we were getting ready for my forty-sixth birthday party and I couldn't get away. From what I hear, he's spending a lot, much more than me. I hope he doesn't end up skint.'

If he came to you in ten years for a loan, would you help him? 'No.'

Paul says he is very happy at the moment thanks to his house, and has never been bored or fed up since the win. He has made lots of new friends, more than he had in Hastings. He's bought a season ticket for St Johnstone, his local football club, and takes parties of friends to their executive suites. He has been too busy to think about taking a job, but he might, one day. 'I would go gaga if I had absolutely nothing to do. But I won't go back to glass, that's for sure. I wouldn't take a pub or a bar either. Perhaps a hotel, a nice little one. Or I might do charity work. We'll see.'

Most of the time his money is still just figures on a bit of paper, and he hardly thinks about it. 'I went up to London to see the bank not long ago, and I was moaning about the train being crowded. The bank man said, Why didn't you go first class? I'd completely forgotten that I could now afford it. I have spent a bit of money on better clothes. I now go to Austin Reed's, but I'm still waiting for their January sales to get bargains. Leaving tips is a problem. If you're out in company and leave £10, they think, Uh, tight devil! Leave £50 and they think, Uh, flash devil!'

Do you feel guilty, ashamed in any way, and wonder why it happened to you? 'No. Why should I be guilty? I've worked hard ever since I left school and became an apprentice glazier, and I've never been unemployed. What I feel is lucky, not guilty. Lucky to be able to enjoy what's happened to me.'

He now keeps an eye on too much enjoyment, having cut down on lunches out, and tries to do more walking. He still smokes, but only five mild cigars a day, Café Crème, the same brand and the same amount he always smoked. 'I never smoke in my cars; never have done.' His cars are a great pleasure. As he drove me to the station after lunch in his Range-Rover, he demonstrated one of his extras – wing mirrors that automatically dip when you go into reverse, so that you can see exactly what's behind. Jolly useful.

'My house is wonderful. I love being able to buy nice things like Burmese mahogany, which I'm using at the moment, or the best china, getting Royal Doulton instead of, say, Denby ware.' But who is going to enjoy it with you, if you are living and eating alone? 'I'm not always alone. My sister and brother-in-law will be coming for Christmas, and my mother. I've left the interior designer to get a tree and decorate it while I'm away, so it's ready when I get back.'

Is Ruth coming for Christmas? 'No, she says she's going into a retreat, but she's promised to come in the New Year, so she says.' That is of course the only thing spoiling his complete happiness – the absence of Ruth, full-time, in his life.

'The thing about money is that it gives you freedom of choice, but it doesn't give you absolutely everything you want. I am much happier now than before the win. I wasn't unhappy then. OK, I had worries with the business, such as £20,000 tax demands for VAT, but I was happy enough because I've always liked life. Before the win, I'd give it seven out ten. Today, I'm not completely happy, because of Ruth living in Hastings, but I'd give it nine out of ten. If we end up in Scotland together, then I'd give it eleven out of ten.'

Is that really likely? He paused for a while, looking a bit sorrowful. 'Friends keep asking if we've split up, but I say, No, we haven't. I hope we haven't. I still love her. Very much so. In the last six months, I've been to a few night-clubs in Scotland, because that's the only place to have a late-night drink, but I haven't gone looking for women, to chat up birds, as some might be thinking. I have been loyal. When I split up from my last wife I used to go to pubs, looking for company, because I was depressed and fed up and lonely, which is how I met Ruth, in a pub. But it's not like that now. Ruth and I are still together, as far as I'm concerned. We've made no decisions.'

If you know her career is so important to her, why don't you go back and live with her in Hastings? 'I suppose you could say we are both being a bit selfish, wanting to do our own things, but I look at it this way – if I was living with her in Hastings, I'd never see her anyway. With her job and this MA, she's working till ten at night. I'd never see her at all during the week. If I thought it was just my new house what was splitting us up, I would sell it tomorrow. But the house isn't the problem. It's her job. Yes, I know she loves it. I would never ask her to give it up. I would never say to her, "You can't do that." But that's the way it is. I see no reason to go back, as we'd be living almost separate lives anyway, if I was down there.

'At the moment, I'm just playing everything by ear. I try to get down once a month or so. I haven't always managed that as I've had to supervise the builders. You have to be there or they'll do the wrong thing. If I ever wanted to get down quickly, I could fly down in an hour, then it's only a two-hour drive. The crunch will come when she finishes her MA. That's when I hope she'll come and join me in Scotland.'

But why should she join you rather than you join her? 'I could come back to Hastings, but I wouldn't sell my house. I'd always want to keep it. She's told me that herself – that I'd regret giving up Scotland. The problem is not my house but what she wants to do about the future, once the MA is over. I think the next thing might be that she'll want to be a head teacher. I dunno. She is 100 per cent determined when she wants to do something. She's very stubborn. We'll have to see.'

Can you predict seven years ahead, guess what you'll be doing, what she'll be doing? 'I can't predict six months ahead! We'll have to see. I've also got to work my own things out.

When I'm properly on top of the house, and done everything I want to do, then it depends how lonely I get, how much time hangs when I'm really on my own with nothing to do. You never know. Perhaps that time won't come. I'm going to take up golf soon. Someone's going to get me in at Gleneagles. Then I'm going to do some fishing. I also want to go to the Boat Show. I used to be very interested in boats, as well as cars.'

You can have fun in a car, on your own, but there's not much fun messing about in a boat, all on your own. 'Yes, I know that. So I wouldn't have a boat on my own. You have to share those sorts of things.'

Say he and Ruth did split up, but only if, would he contemplate getting married again, for what would be the fourth time? 'That is a worry because of what has now happened to me.' How? 'My money. I don't think about the money, myself. When I wake up each morning I think of the jobs I have to do. I don't think, Oh yeah, I've got ten million in the bank. But some people will think about it. Some people will think, Let's have two years with him, then take him for all I can get. How will I ever know if they married me for love? You don't even have to get married these days to have that problem. Live with someone, in the same house, for two years, or even two months, and they can have a claim on you. So, if I ever did decide to marry again, I'd have a special clause in the marriage agreement, like they do in Hollywood. I am frightened of that happening. My second wife took me to the cleaners when I was poor. What might happen, now that I'm rich . . .'

Two months later, Paul and Ruth's marriage appeared finally to end after a rather traumatic few weeks for both of them. In January, the *News of the World* carried a story implying that Ruth was having an affair with Andrew, her headmaster, alleging he had spent two nights at her house. They quoted Ruth as saying it was platonic – he was having temporary marriage problems and she was just helping him.

This was enough for Paul in turn to talk to the *Sun*, stating that he had suspected as much for as long as a year, how she was always working late at school, always going on about the head. As far as he was concerned, the marriage was now over.

It had been clear that their marriage was in difficulties long before the Lottery win, and each had freely talked to me about that. The gift of £1 million, as soon as Paul had won, had suggested some sort of imminent finality to their relationship. Some weeks later, when the news was out, I asked Paul why he hadn't mentioned earlier what he'd suspected might be the real reason. 'Because I didn't want everyone to say the Lottery had split us up. I told no one, not even my friends. We didn't have the finances to walk away from each other, then when I won the Lottery, I hoped that might change things. I did always think she might join me in Scotland. They say money can't buy you love, and I found out that's true. It doesn't matter how much money you've got; if someone doesn't love you, you can't make them. I did ask her back in April, before the win, if she still loved me, and she said, No. That did rather shatter me . . .'

The end of his marriage spurred Paul into another buying spree and a whirl of expensive holidays. He went off to Florida, where he bought a large house next to a golf club. 'You should see the pool! Designer built with synchronised underwater lighting. I don't know how long I'll spend in Florida in future. Most winters, probably, depending on the visa situation, but I hope my family and friends will use the house as well.'

He came back to Perth for a week, then set off on a Far East tour for six weeks, with a woman companion called Evelyn. 'I'm the new woman in his life,' she told me. She is thirty-five and lives locally in Perth. He met her in a night-club. 'We only started going out five weeks ago,' said Paul. 'She said she didn't know for some time that I was worth £11 million, and insisted on paying her share when we went out on dates. It's a great relief the marriage is finally over. I've been unable to go out with anyone else because I didn't want any friends saying I was an old sod, leaving my wife on her own down south while I was out enjoying myself. Several have apologised, because they suspected that I must have been unfaithful.

'The good thing now is that I have a companion, to enjoy this house with me and go on luxury holidays. After the Far East, we're back for two weeks and then off to Dubai. I can never spend all the money I've got, so I might as well enjoy it.'

Meanwhile, Ruth had left home because of the press interest and for a while was unobtainable, but she eventually rang me.

'When I was approached by a *News of the World* reporter, my motives were to protect both Andrew's family and Paul from any unwanted publicity. I obviously failed miserably! The way the story broke made it appear that the marriage breakdown had been entirely due to the developing relationship between myself and Andrew. In fact Paul and I had grown apart and were having difficulties in our relationship a long time before Andrew and I became close. Yes, I was the one who committed adultery. Paul didn't, so in those simplistic terms I am the guilty party. Paul has come out as the goodie. He's done an excellent job by giving an exclusive to the *Sun*.

'I was seeing Andrew before the Lottery win, but those late nights were real. I was working very hard. Nevertheless, as time went by, our relationship developed. I realised Paul suspected. When he asked me if I loved him, which was in June, I don't believe he was shattered. He knew then. That's why, when he won the Lottery, the first thing he said was, That's it, I'm going off to Scotland, and he immediately settled the money on me. He didn't want the full story to come out because it would have got mixed up with the Lottery win, and neither did I, because of Andrew's wife and family.'

Did the money, her money, in any way hasten the split? 'Not really. It would have come to a head about the same time whatever happened. The Lottery delayed it, but we were delaying it anyway. We wanted to wait till Andrew's children were a bit older before it all came out. I suppose what might have happened was that I would have left Paul and we would have moved into a cheap rented place together, living on my salary, with Andrew's salary going to his wife and children. Now, thanks to the Lottery, we can contemplate buying a lovely house together. At the moment we are in a rented place, but we do have our eye on a very nice Grade II listed farmhouse.'

How did it all come out? 'I don't know. I can only presume some local rang the *News of the World* when they saw Andrew. The papers had gone up and down our streets at the time of the Lottery, so perhaps contacts had been made.'

They are still teaching, and Ruth still plans to finish her MA, but she is now not so sure she wants to be a head teacher. 'You never know. I might decide to run a tea-shop on an old railway line. But I cannot tell you how happy I am. At last I have found someone I want to share the rest of my life with.'

The Lottery clearly did not cause the marriage break-up of the Maddisons, but perhaps it will eventually help each partner find real happiness in the future.

# 25

# MARK, HASTINGS

So many workmen, so much machinery, yet such a relatively modest house. Modern, detached, in a quiet cul-de-sac, semi-rural setting just outside Hastings, architecturally fairly ordinary with a sloping garden at the back. It was the slope which had annoyed Mark Gardiner when he moved in. He wanted the slope removed, at once, and the back garden levelled. The next job was to have the existing rather jerry-built back addition removed, and a brand-new, much more spacious and luxurious, back addition built which would incorporate a heated indoor swimming pool, sauna, and a sun lounge where they will have their morning coffee, lounging the while, looking down towards Hastings and the sea. What could be nicer?

Mark could easily have bought a much grander house much further out, with a lot of land and all the requisite luxuries already in place without the need for so much building work. Rural Sussex has many choice properties, as seen in *Country Life*, but Mark wanted to stay near his roots, near his past and near his future. The house seemed a bargain at £105,000, even if he will probably spend twice as much on it, and have workmen living with him for another four months.

I counted twenty workmen of various sorts and persuasions, from tilers doing the front porch to bricklayers building retaining walls at the bottom of the garden. Outside the front garden were vans and lorries queueing up, plus a dumper and a tractor, dumping and tractoring. Such activity, such scurrying. It reminded me of a toytown building-site. Trumpton, perhaps.

I'd arrived at ten in the morning as arranged, and weaved my way through the workmen, stepping over the holes, avoiding the machinery, only to find that Mark wasn't at home. The front door was open, so I walked in and saw Brenda on the phone, looking remarkably slim. Last seen, in the winners' suite at Camelot, she was pregnant. In the distance I could see an even more attractive and much younger blonde floating around in bare feet and a pale, loose-fitting cashmere cardigan.

Mark wasn't in, said Brenda, rather suspiciously. She clearly didn't recognise me, or know anything about my appointment. Mark was due home, she said, but then they were going somewhere. She rang him on his mobile. The message came back: Could I go for a walk for two hours and have something to eat? I'd got a taxi from Hastings station, so all I could do was wander off on foot. Brenda suggested going to Tesco's, and pointed vaguely along an empty road.

So sorry, said Mark when I arrived back. He was all apologies and explanations. He'd expected me at one o'clock, not ten. He'd just been to hospital with Brenda and their new baby. No, no problems. The baby, Kate, was born two months premature, weighing only 3lb 12 ounces. She had to have regular check-ups, but she was fine, just fine.

Brenda, now much friendlier, wheeled the baby in, and I admired her, followed by the young blonde. She turned out to be Karen, Brenda's seventeen-year-old daughter from a previous relationship. I didn't know about her, though why should I have done? 'We all have our pasts,' said Brenda. The daughter was on holiday from college, where she studies hairdressing and beauty.

Mark and Brenda are now married, a modest affair but a happy one, with all his nearest and oldest friends, apart from one. The day was captured exclusively by the *Daily Mirror*, to whom Mark had given exclusive access, for a handsome fee. Not for himself. It had all gone to local charities in Hastings, such as the life boat and a maternity hospital. He'd worked out that the tabloids would be bound to find out, probably gatecrash it and ruin it for everyone, so he might as well sell it to one only.

'But I won't do that again. Yeah, you'd have thought I'd had enough the first time, with the things they printed, but this time, being my wedding, I thought they'd be on my side. But what did they do? They just printed photos down the side of the column of my first three wives. I never expected that, did I? So that's it. No more interviews or photos, with nobody.'

Mark took me on a tour of the building site, followed by his dog, an English setter called Muska. I could understand his desire to be in this area and this sort of house, but wondered why he, Brenda and the new baby hadn't moved into a hotel or rented property for four months until all the mess was over. 'Ah, but I want to be here while they're doing it,' said Mark. 'They'll have problems which need to be settled. By being here, I can give a decision straight away. Anyway, the noise doesn't bother me.'

Do they know, er, who you are, joint holder of the nation's biggest Lottery prize so far? 'Of course they know who I am,' he said. 'I went to school with some of them.'

He pointed out where the pool would be, and above it the breakfast lounge. He was going to get a lot in, for a relatively small site. Yet it will still not be what one might call an exclusive, secluded residence. Neighbours will still see over the fence and into their lives.

'People say to me all the time, ever since the win, why ain't I in Barbados, living in the sun full time? That's what they'd do, no question. But this is my home, where all my friends are. I'm only thirty-three; I've got a lot of life yet. There's things I want to prove, things I want to do. After all the awful things that were said, people might now see the other side of me.'

While those awful and dreadful things were still being said about him back in flaming June, Mark and Brenda had taken themselves off immediately to a secret destination, determined to get some privacy, hoping to have a taste of the luxury life to come.

'Jack [their Camelot Winners' Adviser] said he would help us, so we left it to him. He passed the request on to a contact of his in the tourist business and he booked us a seven-day holiday in Tenerife. We had to go from Stansted, which seemed a bit funny, I mean for a luxury holiday, but we thought, Good thinking, Jack. The press will all be watching for us at Heathrow and Gatwick. We hadn't been told the place or the hotel we were booked into, but that also seemed smart. If we didn't know, how could anyone else find out? The flight turned out to be an el cheapo package tour. Everyone on the plane was sitting reading the *Sun* or the *Mirror*, looking at our photographs. We sank into our seats, too scared to go to the toilet. The in-flight entertainment was Jasper Carrot, making jokes about Lottery-winners!

'When we got to Tenerife, we went outside the airport and saw a bloke holding up the name Gardner. Spelled wrong, but that didn't worry us. He said something about expecting three people. I thought Jack had been really clever – throwing the press off the scent completely. Then three girls rushed over, one of them called Gardner. It took ages to find the hotel we had been booked into. It was a nightmare, bleeding horrible. Well, let's say Mark the glazier might have liked it, with not a penny to his name, but when you're worth £11 million, and hoping for a bit of luxury, well it was diabolical. We were knackered by then, as it was the middle of the night by the time we checked in. At two in the morning, I rang my solicitor and said, Quick, get me out of here!'

Camelot's solicitor? You can't have had your own, from your previous life as an impecunious glazier, can you? 'Course I did. I had several legal problems, and of course marital things. Always had a solicitor. He's a friend of mine, Ian. Leave it to me, he said. He had a contact in Thomson's he could trust. At nine in the morning we were moved to this amazing complex, dead private, with security fences, a luxury village in its own grounds. They weren't told our story, just that I was a very wealthy client of Ian's. We were left completely alone, and had a brilliant holiday. No, we didn't come back on the package flight. Ian sent out a private jet, just for us. So in the end it was all brilliant. Wasn't it, Brenda?'

Mark tells a good story, complete with voices, and Brenda had obviously heard it several times before, but she smiled and nodded while bending over to inspect the baby in her cot. 'I remember one funny thing Brenda said,' he continued. 'When we were in the luxury village and had heard our own jet was coming to take us home, Brenda said, "That's it, then." "What you talking about?" I said to her. "That's it," she said. "We'll be left with nothing."' Mark laughed aloud. Brenda made a face.

While on holiday, sitting in the sun, Mark made one important decision about his future. He would keep the firm, Croft Glass Ltd, going, whatever happened. 'I knew from the beginning Paul wasn't interested any more. On day one, when Jack was driving us to Camelot for the press conference, he stopped the car in a lay-by, waiting for the security people at Camelot to get the gates and the passes ready, so we would go straight in. Me and Paul went for a stroll on our own, and Paul said to me then, "I don't want to continue the business." He offered me a million, to clear off the debts, then he wanted out of it and have no more connection. We had often talked in the past about the money going three ways if we ever won the Lottery. A third to each of us, and a third to the company. We'd always bought the Lottery tickets out of the firm's cash, when we had it. So that was our plan. If, say, we'd won £150,000, it would have suited us fine, getting £50,000 each. Enough for us, and to solve the company's problems. We never thought for one moment of winning £22.59 million.'

'Fifty thousand would have suited me fine,' said Brenda, a bit wistfully, I thought, but Mark was in full flow, explaining his deal with Paul.

'In the end I didn't take a million off Paul. What we done was take the odd money – the £0.59 million – and hand that over to Croft Glass. That paid off all the back taxes and debts, and all the bills to come. So everyone was paid, everything was squeaky clean. Paul was out of it for ever. Technically we closed down that firm, to keep the records straight, drew a line under it. I have started again – but with the same staff and stuff. I rang the staff from Tenerife, as I knew they all thought I would be packing it in as well. I said their jobs were secure, and they had to keep everything going. Get in new orders, and I'd check the prices when I returned. I bought forty T-shirts in Tenerife, as presents for when I got back. Nothing really expensive, but they loved them.'

Croft Glass had a staff of four at the time of the win, who were replacing broken windows, installing new windows and double glazing. Now they employ sixteen. Mark has bought and expanded their old premises in Beaconsfield Road, Hastings, and started a sister company in Eastbourne which manufactures windows. 'We danced to other people's tunes in the past. Now people dance to our tunes. Business is booming and we're doing very well. If we had gone to the bank manager last year and asked for a £50,000 loan, saying that would be enough to quadruple business in six months, we would have been laughed at. But that's what's happened. We are about the biggest clients of Southern Sound, the local commercial radio. Our adverts are on all day long, twenty times for 45 seconds each, seven days a week. The cost is £33,000 for two months, but well worth it. The orders are flooding in and yet we haven't put up our prices at all from last year. Do you want to hear the tapes? I have the final say on them. The latest ones are like *Star Trek*. You must hear them.'

I declined his offer, saying they might wake the baby. Brenda nodded. 'They're good,' she said, 'but I think they'll be driving listeners mad very soon.'

Mark has no wish to expand further. The firm is now the size he can handle. 'I don't want to go multi-national. This will do me. The firm is totally financially secure, 'cos of all the money that's been pumped into it. It won't have to ponce off me, ever again. It will run itself, if I want it to.' He goes in every day, but not usually for a full day. 'I don't tell them what time I'm arriving,' he admitted, 'just to keep them on their toes.'

After the odd change from the £22,590,830 went into Croft Glass, that left him personally with £11 million to spend. Some of it has gone on buying three cars – a Ford Maverick for going out with the family, a Ford Escort for Brenda and a Toyota Celica soft-top. 'That's my toy.' Not quite such luxury cars as Paul, but Mark has spent almost as much on his cars as on buying his house. 'Well, you might not think £105,000 is much to spend on a house, but to me this is Buckingham Palace. Five bedrooms, a TV in every one, what more can you want? But I've also given a lot away.'

He estimates that so far he has given away almost £1 million to friends, either in cash or property, and also quite a lot to charities. 'I gave only to those people who stuck by me and Brenda – not the ones who bad-mouthed us in the papers.

They got nothing.' (A warning there to all friends of future winners, should the newspapers ever ring for a quote.) 'I told them they can tell people I've given them money, or not. It's up to them. I won't, because I didn't do it for publicity, but if they find it hard to explain their new-found wealth to their own friends, then they can tell them.'

No presents have been given to any of his relations – and not a penny to those ex-wives, supposed girlfriends or his real or adopted mother, who came forward to accuse him of dastardly deeds. 'Apart from my last wife, as I was still married to her at the time. I was obliged to make a proper settlement for her. In a way, I've created a mini-boom in Hastings. All the money I've given away, to people or charities, or into the firm, has been local. I like to think of it all trickling down, helping others. I've been given a new start in life, and I want others to have a bit of the same. If you can't spread a little happiness when this sort of thing happens to you, then you must be truly sad. I don't want some Gardiner Memorial erected in Hastings for helping the town. I just like to know it's been spread around.'

He has been very kind to his work friends, endlessly treating them. He regularly hires coaches and takes up to ten of them for the day to London, to have a slap-up meal and the best seats and hospitality at the best football grounds. His own team, the one he's always followed, is Queen's Park Rangers. In a week's time he was going with his mates to see QPR play at Spurs, and had tickets booked in the west stand and the VIP suite, not a cheap outing. I arranged to meet him there, or at least wave from the cheaper seats.

'There used to be six of us that met regularly in this pub, and all of us did the Lottery. Not in a syndicate, just individually. But we all used to say that if one of us ever won anything, we'd treat the others. What we were thinking of was winning a few thousand, in which case we'd buy the rest a meal. If it was millions, then that meant a slap-up holiday.'

And are you sticking to this promise made in the pub, many moons ago? 'I certainly am. In January I'm taking them all – with wives and girlfriends, which comes to fourteen people – on Concorde to Barbados. We're booked into the best hotel, Sandy Lane, for seven days. I've paid the basic bill in advance, £92,000. There'll be extras for drink and that, which I'll pay as well.' Brenda and her daughter Karen will be going, too. They can't wait.

I said that by chance my wife and I would be there at the same time, but at Cobblers Cove, a different hotel. 'What's Barbados like?' Brenda asked. I said, Lovely, but Sandy Lane was a bit, well, up-market and glitzy. Mark laughed. That sort of thing wouldn't worry him now.

'Do you think I'll get a tan in a week?' asked Karen.

When Mark has finally stopped spending, he will then think of some safe long-term investments for his money. At the moment it is still lying in the bank.

'After Barbados I'll go up to London and see Drummond's, listen to what they advise. I don't want anything high risk. And I'll still want some with easy access in case of emergencies. No, not just for me and Brenda, but in case any of my friends need help. If their house burns down and they're not properly insured or they lose their job, I'd wanna help. Even if I keep on giving it away and get down to my last million, it won't worry me. I'll have enough to live on and get food each week from Tesco's. If not, I'll go back to fitting windows. But that won't happen.'

Was this all somehow an act of exorcism, helping the community, helping his friends, in order to make up for, well, the rather selfish life of the past, the 'Lottery Rat' antics the tabloids so graphically described? He sighed. 'Most of that was rubbish. I didn't know half those people who came forward and said I was a rat. There was a stripper who got her photograph in one of the papers, saying I'd had an affair with her. I'd never met her in my life, honest. Complete cobblers! They all said I'd had a daughter by one of my old girlfriends, and printed it as a fact. But she's not mine. I've offered to pay for DNA evidence to prove she's not mine, but she's always refused. People just came out of the woodwork and said anything without me having the right of reply. If Winnie the Pooh had turned up and said she'd had honey with me, some paper would have printed that!'

So why didn't you sue? You can afford it. 'I intended to. It really did upset me, all that stuff. I suppose what hurt most was my mother, the one who brought me up. You'd have thought she might have said something in my defence. That's what mothers are for, aren't they? You come home with a bleeding head, which you've got by accident in some disco, but you don't expect your mother of all people to think you've gone and murdered someone, do you? Mothers are meant to take your side, through thick and thin. Not one person did that. So I decided we would sue. We went up to London, me and my solicitor, and we saw counsel in some Inn. Gray's Inn, I think. I'd sent him all my stuff, my evidence, told him the truth about things like this stripper. He comes in and says, First the good news. He personally thought I had a very strong case, and would win. Then he says, Now the bad news. It will take two years before the case would come to the High Court, by which time it will all have been forgotten and your life will have settled down. It'll mean you and Brenda will have to appear in court – and your mother, and ex-wives, and the stripper and the rest – and the press will love it. That's just what they want – the same story all over again. He'd said he'd go out all guns blazing if I did decide to sue, but it was up to me. So I thought about it. And I decided, No, it wasn't worth it. My real friends know I'm a good bloke at heart. That's what matters.'

But some of the basic facts, such as three failed marriages, are surely correct, and at the age of only thirty-three, that might suggest a certain, let's say instability? Mark gave a slow, rather sheeplike grin. 'Oh, he has lived, has our Mark.' said Brenda. 'For a young man, you have done a lot in a short life. You have lived life to the full. Yes, I think you could say that.'

Very slowly, Mark went through his life story, starting with being adopted – though being careful not to blame being adopted for some of his more erratic behaviour later on. 'But I do think I was *told* I was adopted too early, when I was only seven or eight, when I couldn't quite take it in. From then on, I remember whenever I'd done something good, like, say, doing well in the Sea Cadets and swimming in their Sussex team, I would think, Well, I'm not a bad lad, really. So why was I given away? I passed for the Royal Navy, which I thought was good, and I did quite well, in sport and classwork, but I decided to leave after a short time, which my parents didn't like. They wanted me to stay. I didn't like having to clean the barracks. I didn't like being told what to do. Never have done.

'My mum said I couldn't just loll about at home; I'd have to get a job and pay for my keep, so I went off to the careers office to look for something. I fancied being a plumber. There were no vacancies, so I became a trainee glazier instead. And that's what I've always done. I liked sticking in glass. Each day is different. You might go to a shop, a school, then a house. I know the image of double-glazing salesmen is pretty dodgy, like second-hand car salesmen, but that was only part of the job. It was mainly fitting glass.

'I began Croft Glass Ltd. It's my firm. Paul only joined me later, when he came back from Scotland. I started it ten years ago, the same time as I got Muska, my dog. They're both my babies and I want to look after them like babies, protect them and help them grow up and be adults. I used to sit up at nights worrying about Croft Glass, how would I pay the VAT man, pay the bills. We did go through some very bad patches. Now

I've got the means to make it thrive. Not to show off and prove other people wrong, but for my sake, because it belongs to me. I'm too young to retire and just mess around playing golf or fishing. I might do that eventually but, for now, I need an activity, an interest in life, and it's Croft Glass. I am a very active person, let's put it that way.'

Hence all those wives? He sighed, smiled, then took off his spectacles. Brenda and Karen, both still in the room, listened quietly, but tried to look the other way, as if occupied with the baby, while Mark went through his marital history. 'My first wife was a childhood sweetheart. I went out with her for six years before we got married. Part of the reason for getting married was that I'd got this very nice flat, which I'd gutted and done up. It seemed the sort of thing to do, get married and live in it. I'd got some money from an insurance claim after I'd cut my arm very badly. An industrial injury. That's how I bought the flat. She expected me to play the husband thing, but that's not me. I was out six nights a week playing darts, wasn't I? I was a very good player, though I say it myself. Up to county standards. Sometimes I was playing seven nights a week. I would have to go off to Brighton, say, to play in county matches and be back late, if at all. Naturally, someone else started paying her attention as I was neglecting her, I admit that. So that was it. We were too young, really. But I'm now on good terms with her.

'Wife number two was an estate agent. She always liked my flat. I'd bought it for £16,000, spent a bit on it, and it was worth £55,000 at the height of the property boom. She wanted to turn me into something I'm not, get me away from my old friends, the sort who stays at home with slippers and pipe, or goes off visiting stately homes. That's not me. Yeah, I was still playing darts at the pub, almost every night, and she didn't like it.

'Third wife, well, she was a bet – and I wish I'd never won

it. I was at a club with two friends, right, and they were trying to pull birds. I was just drinking and talking, that was all, but one of them said, "I bet you can't pull that bird over there!" I did. Then she sort of moved in, doing the washing and cooking for me. At the time I was living on take-aways and caffs. It was the time when my own family had cut me off, so I didn't have anyone. That marriage didn't last very long before I found out what a mistake I'd made. So that's all there is to it, really.'

There was a bit of silence while they cooed over the baby, then I asked Brenda if it had worried her, when she met Mark, and found out that he'd already been married three times. 'No,' she said. 'We all have our past. That didn't concern me. I knew he was a decent bloke, despite what some people might have said. People have read those things about him in the papers and believed them, even when they weren't true.'

Has he changed at all since the Lottery win? 'Oh no,' she laughed. 'He's still a nut-case! Still got too much energy.' Mark laughed at this rather back-handed compliment.

I asked Brenda if she felt she herself had changed. 'No, and I never will. I am what I am. If I had to marry Prince Charles, I'd still be the same and not take on airs and graces. I know what it's like having to survive. All these luxuries might well go overnight, so then I'd have to survive again, wouldn't I? I'd have to go back to work, and I wouldn't want people to think I'd changed, and had put on airs and graces. Technically, I haven't left work yet. I'm on maternity leave. After our Tenerife holiday, I went back to work at the old folks home. I like looking after old people. You have a good laugh. I have some good friends. I treat the old people like real people. If some old lady's in a wheelchair and asks me to get something, I say, Get it yourself! Just having a bit of fun, of course. They love it.'

Will she go back to work when the baby is a bit older? 'I

might,' she said, looking at Mark. 'I wouldn't mind if she did some work,' he said. 'Within reason.' If she does, her work will be only part-time in future, as they plan to have three really good holidays a year from now on. 'After Barbados, I fancy Hawaii,' said Mark. 'Then perhaps Canada.'

They can't see themselves moving house again, or to another area. This is it. 'What would be the point? If we went to the back of beyond in Cornwall, the postman or someone would soon find out, and be telling everyone I was a Lottery-winner. Most people in Hastings know, because really Hastings is just a village. I'll have to put up with that for a while longer. I don't think I've changed, but people's attitudes to me have changed. Not my close friends, but strangers. If I go into a pub, someone will always say, "Hello Mark," greet me like a long-lost brother, and I think, Who the bleeding hell are you? Or the opposite happens. Someone comes and says, "You rich bastard!" He's hoping for a fight, but of course I can't do anything. I'd lose either way. I'd either get beaten up, or, if I flattened him, then it's headlines in the papers – "Lottery Rat Beat Me Up". So I just have to say nothing and leave.'

That of course will always be a problem, staying in the same area and being a sociable, extrovert sort of person. He will be picked out, and perhaps picked upon, for many years to come. Mark shrugs. That's the price, a minor price, he has to pay. But, on the whole, he thinks it's worth it.

Brenda, however, often wishes it had not happened. 'All it caused was trouble. I'd be pleased if he'd spent it all, then we might be left alone at last. The press hounded us; wouldn't leave us alone. I don't see what right the press and the public have. We just want to get on with our lives, but they wouldn't let us. The stress and pressure was terrible. I'm sure that's why I had the baby three months early. It just got too much. At the moment, though, it's not too bad. We're not being hounded as much.

'I was happy before, living with Mark, both working, managing to pay our bills. I'm just as happy today, when we're not being pestered. It's the biggest thing that's ever happened in Hastings – apart from 1066. That's one of the problems. Until something bigger happens, I suppose we'll still get pestered. You just have to put up with it and try not to let them get you down. If one door closes, another one opens.'

Mark offered to drive me to the station, which was kind, and gave me a Croft Glass T-shirt, also kind. Brenda had had a lot to put up with, he said. She has been pestered by her friends and relations for money, but of course it's not her money. Anyway, they made a rule only to help those who in the past had helped them when they had nothing. 'I've no regrets. It's not just my pleasure in the money, but seeing my friends get pleasure. When one of the blokes at work says he's bought a new car or is going on his first holiday for years, I feel really pleased. The only bad thing about the whole business was that the press got my, what's the word, something heel – Achilles heel – that's it. But I survived that. Cheers! See you in Barbados . . .'

# 26

## MICHAEL HAYES, LAWYER

Mark and Paul did not take advantage of Camelot's panel, neither the accountant nor the lawyer, but instead used the services of the professional who first meets all the big winners, a gentleman from Drummond's, the Royal Bank of Scotland's discreet banking arm, who hands over the cheque – so discreet they don't want to be identified or quoted. There is of course a bit of keen competition between the bankers and the accountancy firms as they jostle to give advice or take care of any spare millions the winners might have.

The lawyers don't have such a fruitful time. They don't handle the money, and they don't get as much follow-up business as the financial experts, but every panel does have a lawyer, and his or her advice can be very useful, not only with wills, the obvious necessity, but if and when people start crawling out of the corners of a winner's past life.

Michael Hayes is one of the London lawyers Camelot provides for the jackpot-winners. He is fifty-two, grammar school and Oxford, a solicitor all his working life, married with three children and lives in Wimbledon. He looks suitably legal, with his pinstriped suit and impeccable accent, but is in fact un-pompous and approachable. The day I went to his office he had just been out and bought the new Beatles album.

He is a partner in one of the City's oldest and most

respectable firms, Macfarlanes, founded in 1875. It has 170 lawyers, with offices in Brussels and Tokyo. They do the usual City work, takeovers and businesses going public, but they also have a number of private clients, individuals wealthy in their own right who want personal advice about wills, trusts and inheritance tax. This is the area in which Michael Hayes specialises. 'Camelot decided there should be some outside advice offered, so a few months before the Lottery began, we were approached. Camelot, of course, doesn't pay us for attending the panel, nor do the winners, so some of my partners thought it could be a waste of time, but I felt it would be interesting – and might lead to a little bit of business, if not very much.'

Michael serves on the panel for London and the south-east, which means he frequently has to go to Reigate, Camelot's regional office, which he now finds a bit tiresome. The London office, off Trafalgar Square, is much handier for him. After a year of seeing winners, he has also become a bit blasé about giving advice to anyone who has won less than £500,000. He tries to deal with £1 million plus winners. So far, in the first year of operation, he has met thirty winners.

'I never know their full names when we first meet, just their first names, but I know in advance the basic details – age, job if any, family, marriages, children, debts – which the Winners' Advisers have got from them. I can understand it when you say many of them come out of the panel meeting with their heads reeling. It can be a bit complicated, but I think we are managing to simplify it. In the early months, when we were finding our way, both the lawyer and the accountant would sometimes pack too much into the spiel, sometimes rather showing off their knowledge. Now I always start by asking them what their concerns are, what's worrying them, what they want to find out. It is now less of a lecture, more of a conversation. But, all the same, it is complicated. A lot of the people I have seen, how shall I put it, are not very sophisticated.'

Almost every winner he has met has not made a will, so that's the first thing they discuss, especially when it is pointed out what might happen to their new-found wealth should they suddenly drop dead without one. 'For example, if you have just won £10 million, your spouse gets the moveables, £125,000 and a life interest in half the balance. The children get the other half – in trust for them at eighteen if they are still minors. You might of course not want your spouse to get all that money, nor your children, especially if they are still at a vulnerable stage in their life. Few people like the idea of their children getting their hands on their money when they are still prey to fast women or fast cars.' Simple legal steps can be taken so that it all goes to one's spouse, at the same time setting up a trust which will keep money at arms length from the children until they are eighteen or twenty-five, or whatever age you want them to inherit.

Then there is the problem of inheritance tax – a subject which Paul Maddison had said he'd never heard of. At present only the first £200,000 is tax free. So someone who has won £10 million will find that £9,800,000 is subject to 40 per cent tax should they drop dead, which means almost £4 million going straight to the government. Gifts, free of inheritance tax, are allowed, as long as you live seven years after giving them.

'All these notions are totally foreign to most of the winners. They are from families who have lived and died without any money or assets, and therefore never had to bother about wills or trusts or probate or inheritance tax. When I'm dealing with people who have inherited wealth, or earned it over a long period, they know about trusts and tax. Most middle-class families understand wills and can remember who got auntie's fur coat or uncle's gold watch. They have heard of probate.

But, to most winners, you are speaking a foreign language. Having said that, Lottery-winners can be just as shrewd as the third-generation wealthy, just as sensible, or not, as the case may be.'

One of the first questions he is asked, once the will is out of the way, is whether an ex-wife or ex-husband can get her or his hands on any of the money. The simple answer is No, not if the divorce was long since finalised and there was a 'clean break' clause, though future maintenance payments might have to be increased. If no divorce has taken place, as in Mark's case, then yes, there could be problems.

One of the first things Michael asks is, Who won? Who paid the money, bought the ticket, whose name is on the cheque? Even with a syndicate, the cheque is paid out in one person's name. He has to get it straight, and know the background, because there could be complications afterwards. 'Let's say the wife won, as she bought the ticket. She then puts the money into a bank account in the joint names of herself and her husband. But then the marriage collapses – the wife runs off with the milkman and demands all her winnings. The husband might argue that she had given him half the money as she had put it in their joint account, to which the wife would reply that it had never been her intention to give him half of her winnings. She had only put the cash in the joint account for convenience as she was in a hurry. Previous case history has often taken the wife's side in such rows. It is harder for a husband to prove that his wife gave him the money than the other way round. If the husband had won and put the cheque in his name into a joint account, and proceeded to run off with a barmaid, the courts would be more likely to find that he had made a gift of half of his winnings to his wife.'

He naturally doesn't go into all these possibilities, but just gets it clear about who technically won, for future reference. 'On the whole I have found most people remarkably sensible, even those who have led somewhat complicated lives. There must be a few Viv Nicholsons out there who have gone spend-spend-spend, but not the ones I have seen. And they don't seem to have been conned either, by unscrupulous advisers telling them to invest their millions in Afghanistan futures.'

Most of his winners have been private ones – because the majority of them are – and all have been roughly from the same background. 'Out of the thirty, there is only one winner who was in socio-economic class AB, plus one other family whose children were obviously clever and would probably end up in the professional classes.'

None of his winners has been the remotest bit interested in making any donations to charity, which surprises him. 'In my job as a City lawyer, I have dealt with many wealthy people who have suddenly made a lot more money, say from selling a family firm, or floating on the stock exchange, and it is absolutely normal for them to give away a proportion of their windfall to charity. It happens all the time, despite any image you might have of such people. They set up a trust, put a few million into it, and slowly give it all away to worthy causes. Yet out of my thirty millionaire Lottery-winners, not one has even considered giving anything to charity.'

I said that was my experience as well, although Camelot points out that a number do, especially among the 25 per cent of jackpot-winners who decline to use the panel. His comparison, however, with City wealth wasn't quite fair. They know about things like trusts, which do have certain tax advantages. 'Lottery-winners could still do the same – and gain by it. Say you have won £10 million. Your normal interest on all that will be £500,000 a year, out of which you will pay tax at 40 per cent, so let's say you pay £200,000 in tax. Now it is perfectly simple and legal to give that sum to charity, by the use of Gift Aid, and end up paying no tax. So the winner ends up with exactly the same amount, but has given £200,000 to charity. It can go directly into a trust, which he and his wife can invest and administer, and dish it out to causes they like. That's quite a pleasant thing to do, yet not one person has done this.'

Yes, well, it is a bit complicated, and needs a fairly sophisticated mind to appreciate all the advantages. Most winners believe charity begins at home. No one helped them when they were poor, so why should they now? 'I suppose it is basic greed, in a way. I have often in my time rattled a tin in the High Street for a charity, and it is a very depressing experience. The young always say they care, they want to help – but you'll find it's only little old ladies with not much money who will help total strangers.'

I asked about the proportion of winners who come back to him for further advice, and he seemed a bit cagey at first, estimating one in four. Later he looked up their records. 'Our success rate in 1995 was eleven out of thirty-one. I regard one out of three quite good and am satisfied with it.' It's not a large proportion, compared with some of the accountants.

Most of them, however, just want a will prepared, and even a big-shot City firm can't charge too much for that. A few also come back for help with trusts, especially those with complicated families. In one case, a winner with a handicapped child wanted special arrangements in the event of sudden death of the parents. Most of these one in three returnees came back only once, for a specific purpose. At the end of the first year, only three out of his thirty-one winners looked like being ongoing clients, who would bring their legal problems to Macfarlanes from now on. So, not a great return on the hours invested, but he has enjoyed it.

Michael doesn't buy Lottery tickets himself, but if he did, and won the jackpot, he would give some to charity, into a trust, which he already has, set up for charitable purposes. 'The rest I would invest in the stock exchange, in property, and also abroad, in things like dollars or Swiss francs. I would diversify a lot, which of course most winners don't do. But I wouldn't give up work, nor would I change my house. I am perfectly happy with both of them, thank you.'

## JOHN, DURHAM

John Heaton won on the same day as our window glaziers, with the same sort of shock when the news came through, the same sorts of feelings of excitement mixed with fear, but in rather different proportions. John Heaton, the Durham college kitchen porter, a vastly different character from either Mark or Paul, seemed to be overwhelmed by his fear. In fact it had been hard to detect any element of excitement. I often wondered, over the following months, if he had survived. His main reaction had been panic, mixed with acute embarrassment. What happens when those sorts of feelings wear off, if they ever do?

I had spoken to him a couple of times on the phone, keeping in touch, but got little out of him. He does tend to mumble and mutter. He was worried about Sheila, his landlady, so he said, as she was having problems with her eyes. I could understand his concern. Sheila, aged sixty-nine, was not just his southern-born, God-loving landlady, but his mentor and friend.

She opened the front door on my return visit. Still in the same house, still with the same lodgers – including the two Spaniards and John. She was in a very nice bright blue suit and looked her usual, bouncy, open-hearted, kindly self. Not quite the same, she said. She pointed to her left eye, where there were seven stitches still to come out. But she was fine. Oh yes, the eye operation had been a success.

John was sitting by the fireplace, in his usual place, smoking a cigarette. He put it out when I entered, leaning over a stool on which he had a clutter of books and tapes, notes and papers. He was obviously studying something, judging by his serious expression. I could see his furrowed brows bending over some serious-looking instructional material. Had John the college kitchen porter become a college cad himself? Headline writers everywhere would be pleased.

Carmen, one of the Spanish lodgers, appeared wearing her outdoor coat, and shook my hand and asked me how I was. Sheila bustled off to make me tea and biscuits, same as before. She'd remembered I'd liked the onion and sesame seeds sort from Marks, with Primula spread. She returned and sat at the dining table, spreading the biscuits, till she dropped one, showing that her eyes were not quite perfect. Her knife had slipped, and for a second she was about to utter some oath. 'Oh . . . sugar!' she exclaimed.

We all laughed, especially Carmen, so I asked her what the Spanish for sugar was. This took some explaining as I did not mean sugar, as sugar, but the comparable expletive. What children and well-brought-up people say in Spain is very similar, so Carmen explained. Instead of saying '*mierda*', meaning shit, they say a word which at first sound is much the same, '*miercoles*'. In Spanish this means Wednesday. So instead of sugar, polite people mutter Wednesday. Sheila clapped her hands in delight at this explanation. She does speak Spanish and once lived there for five years, but has never heard this before. John, I noticed, got out his biro and made a note.

Over the tea and biscuits, scrumptious as ever, I asked John to take me back and describe what happened after I saw him last. Did he go back to work, as he had vowed? He did, for the next five weeks, by which time the summer vacation had begun and, as usual, some of the kitchen staff were being put on part-time employment. This happens every year. In term time, the college is full and the work non-stop, but in the three months of the long vacation there can be gaps, depending on conference bookings.

'It didn't seem fair for me to stay on. I was offered five hours a day, and the chef wanted me to stay on, but it meant some of the other lads would be getting very little, and they could do with the extra hours. They all need it more than me now, like. I didn't want to think of some lad having to sign on the dole. So I said I'd leave, and someone else could have my five hours a day. I stayed on for another week, to help out, then I left.'

Did you want to leave? 'Yes and no. I liked the company and enjoyed the work, but I felt selfish keeping the job. Sort of selfish and guilty, about having all this money yet still working, if you know what I mean, like. I did miss it when I left. In fact, it drove me crazy and I got very depressed for a few weeks, but then we went away and that helped a bit. Just away. Nowhere special . . .'

His voice was tailing off, as if exhausted with talking so much, so Sheila took over. It was an invitation out of the blue, she said, from a cousin of hers in Somerset who was celebrating her sixtieth birthday. Sheila was invited, and asked John to go with her as her companion. So they both went, staying in a farmhouse for ten days. They both had a lovely time. 'I was fed up anyway, hanging around the house, waiting for my cataract operation,' said Sheila. 'I was told the waiting time would be a year, but I had to stand by every Thursday in case I could be fitted in, because that was the only day the surgeon did cataracts.'

After their holiday, they sat around at home, waiting. It meant that John was at least spared any fall-out from his Lottery win by not going out, not going to work, but his two brothers and his sister, he says, had to put up with various comments. Such as? 'Oh, you know, just little remarks. People would ask them all the time if I was still working. I'm sure no harm was meant, it was all a bit of a joke. They'd never had any hassle at work before, and now they were getting it, all because of me. So I just sat at home, watching the telly all day, not enjoying anything at all.'

Presumably at least his £628,947 was earning some good interest for him? What had he done with it all? Not a lot, is the simple answer. 'I wanted to treat my dad, give him some money or something, but he refused everything. I said, What about a bungalow? He could leave his council flat and have a place of his own. "Too late," he said. "If your mam had been alive, I might have done, but not now. I'm happy here." In the end,' John continued, 'all he agreed to have was a new television. So that's about the only thing I've bought so far, apart from a few clothes. And I have taken everyone from here out for a meal.'

'Oh, we had a lovely meal out,' said Sheila. The cost of the dinner for the four of them – Sheila, the two Spaniards, and himself – came to £50. Not exactly going mad.

He has helped his brothers and sister financially, but didn't want to go into details. He has given them money, bit by bit, as they need things, and will probably give some more in due course. The total given so far has been around £80,000.

'And I also gave £2,000 to charity.' This came about after a letter addressed to him arrived at Collingwood College, not to his home. No one knows his home address, so he hasn't been pestered by begging letters. Two letters in all arrived for him at work – the other was from someone trying to sell him a time-share. The charity he gave to is a medical one that helps child victims of Chernobyl. Sheila had heard of them, and approved of what they did, so John gave them a donation. He might give them more, as Sheila has since been to see them in operation, using the form of a covenant next time.

For the first month or so after his win, his cheque was left in the Royal Bank of Scotland. (Which, of course, the Royal Bank of Scotland was pleased to look after.) He did meet the insurance rep he'd made contact with beforehand, but decided against him. He also refused help from Camelot's panel. Eventually, after consultation with the Royal Bank of Scotland experts, he has put about half in an investment portfolio organised by the bank. The remainder has been left in the bank itself. Out of this has gone the £80,000 he gave his family, which would have bought his father a bungalow, had he agreed. He clearly finds it very embarrassing to talk about his money in any way, or even think about it.

His recent holiday in Spain with Sheila was planned long before John's win. She had been invited to borrow a friend's holiday flat in Malaga, for free, so all they needed was their air fare and spending money. John had been saving hard for some months, thanks to being in work. It wasn't the Lottery that altered their dates but the uncertainty over Sheila's eye operation, being forced to stand by, week after week, and just wait for the National Health Service to call her name. Then John had a sudden idea, the sort of idea money can make possible. Why didn't she go private, get it over at once – and he would pay? Sheila agreed. It turned out there was still a waiting list, around six months as opposed to a year, but they were at least given a firm date – 2 November. So, before the operation, they decided to fit in their long awaited Spanish holiday.

'Oh, it was wonderful,' said Sheila. 'The place was empty, even the beach, as the season was over, but the weather was delightful, so hot and beautiful.'

It was during this holiday that something happened which might, just might, change John's life. 'He kept on asking me about the prices,' said Sheila. 'So I had to keep translating the

Spanish numbers for him. Then in the evening, when we sat watching Spanish television, he wanted to know what was going on. In the end I said, "Come along, John, it's about time you started learning a few words."'

So during their holiday, John set himself the task of learning to count in Spanish, from 1 to 20, and the days of the week, both of which he managed. He came home so pleased with himself, delighted with Malaga and the flat they had borrowed, that it inspired him to think of returning to Spain, but next time better equipped. 'When you've learned Spanish, you're going to buy your own villa in Spain, aren't you, John?'

That sounds great, I said. What a good and positive way of spending some of your money. 'I don't know about that,' said John. He clearly felt embarrassed at having his business, and his dreams, revealed. 'I might buy a small apartment. It's on the cards ...'

It would still be marvellous, I said. Your brothers and sister and their children could use it; and Sheila, of course, any time she wanted. It would be a good investment as well, not just fun. But why not make it a villa, with a pool? An agent would look after it for you, rent it out when you weren't there. The income would pay for the running costs, the gardener and the maid, and you'd never have to worry. That's what we did for twenty years in Portugal, and what fun we got out of it, pleasing all the family, pleasing ourselves ... I was getting rather carried away. We can all be experts at spending other people's money.

John stared at me, looking worried. 'An agent? I wouldn't be able to talk to an agent.'

'But she'll be English. Spain's full of ex-pat Brits doing this sort of work. You can pick and choose a nice one.'

'Huh,' said John.

The idea of having a Spanish home had presumably come into his head at some time, as Sheila would never tell a lie. But, being a careful person, he was taking one step at a time, he explained. Step one was learning Spanish. That was what the pile of books were in front of him. He was well into his studies, as I could see; perhaps even obsessed. He was now studying every day, said Sheila. He had bought a BBC learning scheme called '*Suenos* – World Spanish'. He'd listened to the first tapes and tried the first lessons, but mainly he was skipping ahead to little stories in Spanish, and trying to translate them.

'It's more like transliterating,' said Sheila. 'He's not translating sentences and thoughts into normal English but trying to transcribe, word by word, what each word means. He writes down the English underneath by looking in the dictionary, which of course you can't do. He keeps asking me impossible questions, such as what does "*de*" mean. Oh goodness, I say, "*de*" can mean so many things, depending on the context.'

Sheila has tried to help him with pronunciation, but that has been hard as well. '*Seis*, meaning six, for example. I told him to pronounce it to rhyme with place, but I pronounce place differently from him. He has a north-east accent, and I don't.'

Wouldn't it be better to employ a one-to-one tutor, now he's got the money, to come to his home and give him private lessons? There must be lots around in a city like Durham. Or what about evening classes, Spanish for beginners? They must exist for people like him, coming to Spanish late, who want it for their next holiday. 'I want to try to teach myself a little first, just to help me, as a beginner, like.'

Sheila admitted that she found what John was trying to do very hard. 'I can speak Spanish, but I can't write it. I just picked it up when I was there.'

I said most English-speaking people found understanding a new language hard. Learning about verbs and nouns was like a new language in itself, as grammar is hardly taught today.

Conversational Spanish would be enough for him, which he could pick up by going to live there for a while.

'I might manage two or three months at a time,' said John. 'I'd like that. But I don't think I could leave here for good.'

In that case, why not buy a house in Durham as his base? Houses in a university town are excellent investments, as Ken Southwell has found out. (They both listened for a bit, while I talked about Ken, but my experience of Lottery-winners is that they don't really want to hear about other Lottery-winners. The only exception was about Steve and Helen. They all liked that story.) 'You mean buy my own house in Durham?' said John. 'Oh, no. I've never thought of that.'

People have suggested that he should take up some activity such as golf. The very notion makes him smile. He does like snooker, so wouldn't it be nice to buy a new house complete with a snooker room? 'Aye, that thought has gone through me head, but that's all.'

John paid for their flights to Spain and train to Somerset, and will pay for the eye operation when the bill comes in. They expect it to be around £1,500. But apart from that, his expenditure has been very modest. What about buying a car? It would of course be more convenient all round if one of them had a car, for shopping and holidays. 'I have thought about learning to drive,' said John, 'going on one of these intensive driving schools. That might be good.'

I had noticed, if only marginally, one slight difference in John, compared with the time of his win. He didn't look quite so hunched and defeated. He appeared healthier as well. The Spanish holiday, and his slight tan, might also have helped. I wondered if he felt more confident since his win. And, of course, Sheila herself. 'Oh, I've always been self-confident,' said Sheila. 'Not to say bouncy. John has never been confident, but I do think he's improved.' John looked uneasy at being discussed so personally, so I changed the subject and asked about his future. Had he considered finding a job of some sort? 'I'll have to get some work some time. I can't sit around all day. I'll do something, have some sort of business. I might do some painting. We'll see.'

By that he meant house painting, for which he did some training but never managed to get as a job. He could probably slip back easily into low-profile work like that. Unlike most Lottery-winners who came out, he has managed to retain his privacy locally and not become the sort of person who is pointed out in the streets or is contacted by the local media. Except for one instance.

Sheila bustled out of the room to fetch it, while John went back to his Spanish book. She returned with a copy of *Palatinate*, the Durham University student newspaper. (Which I was interested to see, as an ex-editor.) After the long vacation, a *Palatinate* hack had tracked John down and interviewed him. The story made the front page of their 4 October issue. 'Cleaning up pots of cash,' read the jokey headline. Did that upset him? 'Not really,' said John. 'They got most of it right, except they called Sheila Mrs Shearburn, not Miss Shearburn . . .'

John still plays the Lottery, putting on £3 a week as he did before. I found that strange, as his win doesn't seem to have brought him many pleasures. Think what a real panic he would be in if he won £20 million next time. 'I wouldn't want to win that much. I enter it as if I haven't won. I know that sounds silly, but I'm trying to feel like everyone else does, that's the reason.'

'He even bought a lottery ticket in Spain,' said Sheila, 'and he won 100 pesetas. Didn't you, John?'

I asked if he regretted, with hindsight, doing the photo-call, low key though it had been. 'I had nothing to hide, so I didn't worry about that. But if I did win again, I wouldn't want anyone to know. I hated all that posing for the photographers.'

His brief moment of local limelight has had no unpleasant repercussions, in that no one from his past has come forward to claim friendship or money. Not even his wife? 'I think she got married again and had children, but that's all I know.'

At the time he did seem very thrown by the win itself. Did he now regret winning? He thought about this and eventually said, 'No. I have managed to bring a bit of happiness to some people, so that's good. I can now do things, go places, if I ever want to.'

As for basic happiness, he thought he probably was marginally happier before his win. At that moment in his life he had been very happy, for him, having landed a job after being unemployed. He was also happy living at Sheila's. 'I suppose I'm getting less worried as time goes on. I try to put it out of my mind. But, well, I still can feel a bit down. But it is getting better all the time. I could be happier if I was doing a job or something, but at least I've got the Spanish to keep me occupied.'

With that, he went back to his books. A new occupation for him in life. Perhaps even a new future . . .

# 28

# RONALD AND DIANA,
# THE NORTH-EAST

Nine months after their win, Ronald and Diana were still in the same modest terrace house in a village not far from Newcastle, despite their £2.5 million. There was nothing to suggest from the house, or their external lives, that they had become millionaires. They had never come out – and still retained their privacy. Their life, to all intents, was going on just the same as before.

But Ronald did have one little secret. It was a mild, and relatively trivial, piece of self-indulgence, but a month previously he had, for him, gone a bit wild and out of character. However, he was going to great lengths to make sure none of his neighbours discovered it. Twice a week he leaves his terrace house, on foot, and walks two streets away to his brother-in-law's house. His brother-in-law has an old and battered lock-up garage beside his house which Ronald has rented. He lets himself in, puts on his helmet and protective clothing, and then, zoom-zoom, he is off round the remoter roads of rural Northumbria on his Honda 600, a brand-new motorbike which cost him £7,000.

He had seemed such a solid, serious chap, so I was a bit surprised to find he had been harbouring Toad of Toad Hall fantasies. Wasn't he worried some neighbour would spot him? 'No. Once I come out of that garage, on my bike, dressed in my leathers with my helmet on, no one knows it's me. I can't be recognised. I love getting out in the country and going fast, but I also like the secrecy bit. It gives me a bit of a giggle.'

I asked Diana, his wife, if she was worried about him starting motorbike-riding at his age, with three young children. 'Crikey, no. It's a very solid bike. I'd be more worried if he'd bought a racing car. I know he won't do anything dangerous. He's wanted a bike all his life, so why shouldn't he?'

They still have their old Escort parked outside, almost twenty years old, which is now officially his car. Ron had got Di another one – a Mazda, only one year old, in spanking condition with just 5,000 miles on the clock, for which he had paid £10,500. A bargain, he thought, which would have cost £16,000 new. He could, of course, have bought twenty such cars, or even two hundred, but this was more than ample for their needs. It would also not raise any suspicions. They have had the second car for several months now, and been able to explain it away successfully. But he didn't fancy getting into a complicated rationale for his motorbike. 'The car was admired by one or two neighbours the moment we got it, and I've told them all the same thing. They know my mother died last year, so I've said her house was sold for a bit more than we expected and my share went into the new car. That's been accepted by everybody.

'Nobody round here thinks for one moment we've won the Lottery. We know the neighbours, but we don't live in each other's kitchens or have them in for meals. Most of them are out working all day, the men and the women, so you hardly see them, anyway. So, yes, it's still a total secret.'

Apart, of course, from their brothers and sisters, and her parents, who have managed to bite their tongues when sometimes they were on the point of blurting it out. They have now been handsomely rewarded, each receiving a sum of around £40,000, making a total of £200,000 Ron and Di have so far given away. 'They all had their own houses already, on a mortgage, of course. Some have paid it off, some have just invested the money. With all of them, it's made them financially fairly secure, able to afford little treats and good holidays. I worried for a long time about the tax situation, not knowing anything about gift tax or inheritance tax. But now I've seen Camelot's lawyer and accountant, they've helped us sort that out. No tax will have to be paid as long as we live seven years.'

It took Ronald some time to get round to seeing Camelot's panel, wanting to take every stage as slowly as possible and make no hasty decisions. It also took him some time to take up the offer from the accountants Ernst & Young for their financial department to arrange a portfolio for him. 'The money has been a bit of a worry: knowing what to do with it, how to invest it. I did sit up for a few hours now and again, after Di had gone to bed, going through all the papers and stuff, wondering what to do. It's not a worry, as such, because we don't worship money, but it did nag at the back of my mind, wondering what to do. Should we make the money work for us, so it makes more money, or just safely invest it? In the end, we have put £2 million in simple, guaranteed, low-risk investments, which is earning us around £1,500 a week in interest. We'll have to pay higher-rate tax on that, at the end of the year. The rest is in the bank, with easy access, ready for when we buy the new house.'

They have been looking at a few just a few miles away, more out in the country, and hope to get a five-bedroom detached house, with a playroom and a snooker room for Ron, plus perhaps two acres, for around £200,000. 'This is not a very expensive area. You can get a lot for your money. We'll have to work out a suitable story for the new neighbours, if they ask us, but I don't think that will be a problem. I'm hoping we might get £50,000 for this house, now I've spent so much time and money on it. Old neighbours coming to see us in the new house might be a problem, so I'll have to think of something. Perhaps create a new job for myself? I'll just say I'm self-employed, often working away. Going to an estate agent was also a worry, knowing they'd want to know our situation, especially when I made it clear we would be paying cash. I'm not sure they can be trusted, but I've got two agents who are sending us information. I've said we've got our existing house to sell, some money from my mother's house, and I've been working away on an oil rig, earning big money these last few years. I couldn't say I was a brain surgeon, could I? I did actually think I might have to try the oil rigs when we were really hard up last year.'

Since the win, Ronald has been completely happy at home, working on the house, finishing all the improvements he always planned to do. He's been able to afford proper tools at last, especially carpentry tools, and hopes to have a good workshop in the next house. He'll probably also take up golf, as well as snooker. Di has taken up pottery at evening classes, and plans to have a kiln at the new house.

'We've always got on well together,' he said, 'and I have spent a long time at home over the years, since I was made redundant. I don't want to go out to work again. There's no reason to at all. I enjoy carpentry, so that'll be my main occupation. I might even start making furniture. By pottering around home, I'll have all the school holidays and half-terms free, so we can do things as a family. After we've moved to the new house and got settled, we're going to buy a property abroad, perhaps in France or Spain. It'll be good for the children's education.'

Their three children are still at the same village school – which Ron and Di have secretly helped, giving anonymous donations for books, computers and extra facilities. The children don't appear to know about their win, even the twins, now aged nine, who were present during the original excitements. 'They haven't mentioned it since. I don't know whether they've forgotten, or what. And we don't intend to tell them. We have made trusts for them, which they'll come into when they're twenty-five, so they'll get to know then. Until then, we'll try to live as normal a life as possible, but of course we'll have money for all school trips and extras, and for university education, if they want it. They'll go to the local comprehensive, the one they would have gone to anyway. Why should they be treated any different? We're no different, really.

'We got them better Christmas presents than usual, but not much more. Tara likes surprises. Anything wrapped up in a parcel surprises her and pleases her. Tom is a bit more "Can I have", but we haven't given in to that, and never have. Luke likes anything he is given. They are happy children. They were before, and we don't want them to change. We have never contemplated private schools. It's not in our character. I'd worry that they might out-grow us. All parents at private schools have got money, so they would be mixing only with those sorts of people, and get a different upbringing from the one we had. If they brought friends home with them, I'd feel on trial. They might be ashamed of us. I just want to be myself, doing silly things with them, playing silly games. I don't want to change – or them to change.'

There are people who believe private schools give children a better chance in life. Doesn't that concern you? 'It might give them a better chance of being a doctor or a lawyer, I suppose, but does that make them better people? I don't think so. Money has altered our lives, and will alter theirs. But I don't want us to change as people.'

Their lives have of course changed marginally. They are now a two-car family with a secret motorbike, and on their white leather couch I noticed a mobile phone on a charger. They have had one extravagant holiday, a trip to Euro-Disney in France, taking their three children plus relations, fifteen people in all. They went in the holidays, for just three days, so their schooling wasn't interrupted. The basic cost was £2,000, plus another £250 in spending money. 'It was funny going to pick up the £250 French money before we went away. We went into Barclays Bank, and when I was about to pay by cheque, the girl said, Oh, we can't take cheques for that amount. Then I showed her my gold cheque card. That soon changed things. I didn't say anything, but inside I do get a little buzz out of that sort of thing.'

All the same, he has never been tempted to come out and boast in any way about his new-found wealth. 'The nearest I've been to letting it out was when we were buying the new car, looking round the car showrooms. I'd parked our old Escort in what I thought was a good place, not blocking anyone, but this second-hand car salesman came out of his office and said in a loud voice, "You can't park it there." I automatically walked back to the car, to do what he wanted, but I was very annoyed. He was a right jobsworth. He didn't even look at me, or acknowledge my presence, just walked across the forecourt. I walked behind him and said very loudly, "Amazing how people can be wrong about appearances." Then I turned to the wife and the kids and said, "Let's go. They haven't got time here for the likes of us." For a split second I was about to add, "Even though I have got two million in the bank," but I just stopped myself. I thought, I am above this guy. I don't have to prove anything.

'Since then, it's never been an effort. I like the fact that people don't know. It's been a self-imposed challenge to keep it secret. The brothers and sisters still find it harder to keep it quiet. There are two friends I play snooker with, at the club, and if it ever comes out, they'll be very upset I didn't tell them.

I like them both, but I know they can't keep secrets. It will be hard facing them if they ever find out. But we have no regrets about keeping it secret. It has caused some pressure, but we've handled it. There was only one real moment of paranoia, and that was on the Tuesday when we came home, after going to Camelot for the validation and to get the cheque. As I got out of the car outside our house, I did find myself looking down the street, to check if there was anyone with a camera around or a strange car I didn't recognise. That's the only occasion I've felt that.'

If you'd been a single person, living alone, no children and no family, would you have done the same? 'Yeah, that might have been different. I might then have gone public. It must be hell having no one to talk with, to discuss it all, no wife or husband, brothers or sisters. You just need people close to you to know, otherwise you would explode. If you didn't have people, you might as well tell everyone and get it over with. But I have to say that, all this time, there has not been one moment when I've wanted to walk down the street and have people know about me, to know what's happened to us. Not for one second.'

Camelot has rung them once or twice to ask how they're getting on. 'Maggie asked if I was feeling any pressure, and I said, No – I'm revelling in it.'

They still do the Lottery and have put their normal stake up to £5 a week. 'Not out of greed, just the amusement, the entertainment value. I look upon it as giving some of the money back. If we won again – and I think actually I will – I'd give more to my family, but not tell them this time. What we've won is more than enough for us. I think winning £22 million is obscene. There shouldn't be a roll-over week. It should all be distributed to the other winners if no one has the jackpot.

'I feel we have handled it well, but we've been lucky

because there was no conflict in our lives, apart from being hard up. I feel sorry for those who win when their marriages are on the rocks, or if they have family and relationship problems. Becoming a millionaire can exaggerate your problems and make everything worse. I sometimes forget we have won, when I'm wandering round the house, or doing some job; then I smile and think about it. It's like I've taken a pill, and it's cured us of financial worries.'

It's also taken them a while to remember in shops that they now can buy what they like. That's happened very slowly. 'We buy more steak now than we did,' said Di. 'And we do a lot more shopping generally.'

'Yeah, I'll have to watch her,' said Ron. 'She could go mad.'

'Oh, I have done,' she said, standing up to show off a pair of new black linen trousers she was wearing. Which designer label? 'C & A. Cost me £20, the most I've ever spent. Until the win, all my trousers and skirts cost me £1 or 50p, bought from charity shops.'

'Look at this watch,' said Ron. 'I paid £50 for this. I still can't believe it. The most I've paid before is £5, but my old one packed up so I needed a new one. I picked this up in the shop without looking at the price.'

'My handbag,' said Di. 'This cost me £17. Wicked! I always got them at jumbles before. I now have three pairs of good shoes. I used only to have one.'

'What's happened is that the put-back days are over,' said Ron. 'You know, the days when you pick up something in the supermarket, look at it, then put it back because you can't afford it. We don't have to do that now. We also have meals out when we feel like it. Nothing fancy, just without thinking about it. On Sunday we were house-hunting, and we saw this hotel and went in for Sunday lunch. That's the first time in our married life we've had Sunday lunch in a hotel.' 'Well, it was really just a pub,' said Di, 'but it was very nice.'

Not much of an extravagance. At this rate, you are only ever going to be spending a fraction of the interest, never mind making holes in the capital. 'I do think of that, but it's not in our nature to splash out. We get enough of a buzz from little treats. Every week we buy something new, however small, or do something different, like having that meal out. Before we went to France we did go out to do a *big* shop, money no object, telling ourselves we would buy clothes without looking at the prices. We bought lots, and when we came home and started unpacking them, I remembered we were prepared to spend about £2,000. But when we added it up, we'd only spent £450. And £100 of that was a computer game for the children.'

Thinking back to their state of happiness before their win, Diana gave it only five out of ten. 'The day before, I was fairly low because I knew it was Ronald's birthday – on the day we won – and I was fed up 'cos I hadn't been able to buy him much.' Ronald, at the time, was not as unhappy. 'We were always happy as a family. My only worry was not being able to do things for the children, and thinking about their future, so I'd give it seven out of ten.'

Today, they both give it ten out of ten. 'It's got to be,' said Di. 'The biggest pleasure is not having to think about money,' said Ron. 'We have secured the future for our children and helped our respective families. In the old days we dreaded letters popping through the letterbox, knowing there would be more bills to pay. Now we don't have that. When friends and neighbours used to say to me, "How's it going?" I always said fine, and managed to put a smile on my face. Now I smile – and mean it. But of course they don't know why. And that's another pleasure in itself. And there is more to come.'

The new house, for example. Ronald that day had picked up the details of two houses they liked the look of, which they had decided to visit, even if people might ask him personal questions about himself and his situation. So far, they had been either reading estate agents' descriptions or driving past quickly and looking from the outside.

'I want to have my own garage now. Keep my own motorbike in it and not have to worry about being recognised when I'm riding it ...'

# 29

# BOB AND ANNE, ALLOA

On the face of it, their £3.79 million win had hardly changed the outward lives of Bob and Anne Westland, if you consider the signs of outward change to be a new and expensive house plus a clutch of flash cars. That is the most common common denominator among the big jackpot-winners who have gone public, in line with their new wealth and new self-image.

Some do it in weeks, most take a few months. But, within a year, almost all big winners have made some major and visible changes in their lives. The day I met Bob and Anne again, they were still in their old house in Alloa, living their same sort of lifestyle. But it did look as though their future might change. It was that very week, when I saw them again, that they had decided on something which might or might not go through, a decision which greatly surprised me.

No, they are not planning to move. They aim to stay in their own house. Mind you, it is a nice five-bedroom house, where they brought up their four sons, situated in a nice area of a nice wee town which they have known all their lives. Why move? They have even kept their own phone number, which is still in the telephone directory. That is unusual. Most winners, even public ones – in fact particularly public ones – are driven mad by long-lost relations, remote friends, fund-raisers and fun-hopers.

The Westlands happen to be calm, kind, sensible, reasonable people who neither jumped around nor got too excited when it all happened. They were happy and contented anyway, though Bob did lash out, not long after their win, and bought two seats for Glasgow Rangers, for himself and his son Robert. (An expensive treat. They had to buy two bonds at £1,900 each, which last thirty years and entitle you to buy two season tickets, costing them a further £300 each for the current season.) They also bought an answerphone and fax machine, which set them back £376. That was Mark's suggestion before he went back to Abu Dhabi, saying it would help to control the number of phone calls they were getting.

They then made three small gifts – £1,000 each to Bob's two regular assistants in his post office, and also to the woman who has cleaned their house for many years while they have both been out at work. At that time they had made no decisions about gifts to their four sons, Mark, David, Chris and Robert.

Anne went back to work, as planned, to her job as deputy head at the local primary school. 'The week after the win,' she said, 'it was by chance a reunion of my year at Moray House, where I trained thirty-five years ago. The woman who actually wrote to me, fixing up the event, didn't actually know what had happened, as she'd been abroad. There were sixteen old girls there, and of course all of them knew, except her, but were too polite to mention it, apart from one or two of them saying, "You won't be going on teaching *now*!" The woman who didn't know soon found out, and she was the only one who cross-examined me, wanting to hear all the details. I don't think the others were jealous or anything. They just didn't want to talk about it. They wanted to talk about the old times.'

They got lots of begging letters, being well known locally and still in the same house. 'We didn't answer any of them,' said Anne. 'You can never tell who is making it all up. Funnily enough, one of them sent a second letter saying we hadn't to bother sending him any money, as it had all worked out fine anyway. I can't remember now what his problem was.'

'We also had one fairly mad person on the phone,' said Bob, 'wanting £300,000, at once.'

They went to see Camelot's legal and financial panel, and listened to their advice. 'The first thing they said was, Have you made a will?' said Bob. 'We hadn't, in fact. They pointed out that if we both drop dead, then £1.7 million would go straight to the government. So we made a will, pretty quickly.'

'You can never know the whole story when people recommend investments,' said Anne. 'You don't know what cut they are on, or whether they are just recommending their own firms. When we borrowed money from the Scottish Amicable to buy the council house [an investment before their Lottery win], we were amazed that Robert earned himself £600, of our money, because he had fixed it up. The panel seemed to think we should invest everything, saying that £2 million for example would bring us in £80,000 a year, enough to live on. Then put the rest in a trust, perhaps. They don't seem to consider that, at our age, we might just want to spend the money, not invest.

'David had one daft idea, the week after we won. He'd cut out this advert from the paper about a big estate on the west coast of Scotland with thousands of acres. He said we should buy it – then he could spend his time shooting. Then Robert started talking about opening a pizza place. He can't even boil an egg. Pizza parlour – the very idea!'

Bob did eventually buy a new car, a BMW 520, not the Jaguar he was talking about. That, so far, has been the only visible change in their domestic setting, though they did finally get round to making gifts to their sons. In the early weeks they had been thinking of £250,000 each, a rather generous sum, though it would still have left themselves about £2.8 million. Gradually this went down and down. Anne became concerned that the boys' lives would be ruined if they were each suddenly given such a huge sum. 'We've had to work hard all our lives for what we've got. We want them to do the same.' So they then decided to help each of them in turn, whenever they thought of some reasonable project or object in life.

The first was Chris, the lorry-driver, who was employed by a firm which specialised in bulk whisky deliveries. He was offered the chance to buy his own lorry, second hand, for only £10,000, plus a trailer for another £25,000. Anne and Bob would have preferred to have bought him a new lorry rather than one which might go wrong, but it was what he wanted. The deal also came with some built-in work, which was an extra incentive. So they gave him the money, and he became a self-employed, self-owning, lorry-driver.

Having done that, they decided that it was only fair to advance the same amount, £35,000, to their other three sons when their needs were clear; a lot less than the quarter million each they were first thinking of. 'Well, when we go,' said Anne, 'they're going to get it all anyway, so it doesn't make a great deal of difference. I just don't want them having delusions of grandeur.' Six months later they upped the presents all round, giving each son in turn around £100,000, making a total of around £500,000 given to their family.

'Chris has done very well with his lorry business,' said Anne. 'Last week he made £1,700, which is a great deal, but then he has big expenses and he did do an awful lot of hours. I think he's now thinking of changing things a bit, either hiring his own driver or hiring out his lorry. But, basically, he's still doing it and doing well.'

As Christmas 1995 approached, Mark, the eldest son, was still teaching in Abu Dhabi, David was still managing Pet City in Edinburgh and Robert was still with the Scottish Amicable – but Bob and Anne had both left work.

Bob finally sold the post office in November and officially retired, aged fifty-eight, on 15 November 1995, the twelfth anniversary of joining the Post Office. By that time he had become a little bored with hearing the same sort of banter in his post office: 'Well, your post office won't run out of money, will it, Bob? You can always use your own!' His plan was to play golf and take a lot of holidays, including the inaugural cruise in January 1996 of the *Oriana*.

Anne had continued teaching until November, but when Bob sold the post office she too retired, for good, aged fifty-seven, giving her a fairly decent pension. Was there a farewell present, after all those years? 'There was, but it was a bit embarrassing. The staff room usually just give money on these occasions, but how can you give money to someone who is a millionaire? They had collected £400. Informally, I let it be known what I wanted, and they gave me a lovely Victorian pendant.'

In July, at the time of their win, they had vaguely thought of starting a little business together, but had almost immediately decided against it. 'It would all be too much of a tie,' so Anne had said. 'I'd prefer a peaceful retirement.' They'd also had the idea of buying a flat in Edinburgh, so that they could go for short cultural trips, and perhaps also buy a cottage in the south of France for their summer holidays. Neither of these plans had come to pass. 'Everyone is now leaving France, so we've read,' said Anne.

What they had now done, to their own surprise, as much as anyone else's, was make an offer for a local hotel that had suddenly come on the market. I was amazed. After all, they have had no experience of the hotel trade, or similar, and they don't actually need the income or even the capital growth. Their £3 million, still unspent or un-given away, would be enough to see them out, considering they are both now approaching the age of sixty. 'It's really her idea,' said Bob, passing the buck, but recovering and nodding. 'Aye, and I think it's a good idea as well.'

'When Robert originally cut out that advert for the west coast estate,' said Anne, 'it was just his fantasy, though we did think about it for a few weak minutes. What's happened now is that the Dunmar, a local hotel in Alloa which we know very well, has suddenly come on the market. We often went there in the past and always liked it, but it has become rather run down. We were just saying it was a shame that it couldn't be brought back to its former glories. Then two of the boys thought of this idea, and they got very keen, and, well, we put in a bid . . .'

They got out some photographs, to let me see, and it does look very handsome, sort of mock-baronial with Tudor overtones. Not too big, just nine bedrooms, but with nice gardens. It was built in 1906, about the same age and style as their own house. It was on the market for £320,000, but by offering cash, no strings attached, they have secured it for £270,000. 'We don't take it over officially till 10 January.' All being well, they reopen it in 1996, after some major rebuilding and refurbishing. They plan to add a new wing, with a sauna, gym and swimming pool, making it into a leisure club, with a function-room. In all, they expect it will cost them half a million. There is no reasonable function place in Alloa, so they say, and the nearest private health and leisure club in Stirling has a long waiting-list. So that is one attraction about doing up the Dunmar.

The most important element in the purchase, and in its future, is that David, their son who is the successful shop manager, will give up his job to manage the hotel. He will be helped by Robert, their younger son, the one who wanted to give up his job in the Scottish Amicable, which they wouldn't allow him to do until he had another job. 'David is already telling Robert that he must go on a course in hotel management before he's allowed to start work in our hotel,' said Anne. 'I can see some arguments between them, but I hope it will work. The conversion work is yet to begin, so we've a long way to go. We won't be involved in it from day to day. We'll just be supervisors.' They cancelled their *Oriana* trip, partly because of the hotel, and partly because they realised they didn't want to spend three months at sea.

Having bought and redeveloped the hotel, their remaining two and a half million will be invested in a portfolio which they mainly devised themselves. 'We did come out with our heads reeling, after the Camelot panel. I think Camelot should provide independent banking advisers and not be connected to just the one bank. We know from Robert's experience at the Scottish Amicable that they have to push their own products, and they are well rewarded. In fact we have put half a million into a Scottish Amicable bond, because we know Robert will get £28,000 just for securing our business.'

Anne no longer worries that she or Bob will suddenly die and not have spent or enjoyed the money. Those dreams ceased after three or four months. The fact that they have bought the hotel indicates her hopes for the future. But she still worries how in the long term their sons, and their grandchildren, will be affected by having money in the family.

They still find it hard personally to lash out and be extravagant on their own pleasures. They recently came to London for a short visit and I took them to the Groucho Club, which they took in their stride as if they went there every day. They had thought of staying at the Savoy while in London, so Bob rang to ask how much. 'I was told £350 for the night. I asked if that was for the two of us, but no, it was per person. I asked if it included breakfast, and they said No, breakfast would be extra. So I hung up.' But, Bob, wouldn't it have been fun to stay there one night and boast back in Alloa? He shook his head. 'Not at that price!' But you can afford it? He shook his head again. OK, then, you could have considered it a useful experience, now you are going into the hotel business? He still shook his head, but not quite as fiercely. Right then, as a hotel proprietor, I bet you could charge it as a business expense, calling it market research. He was more interested this time.

Without realising it, buying a hotel might be a smart move. If you run a business, even one which makes little money, there are certain tax and financial advantages. None of my winners had thought along these lines so far, nor their advisers. Bob and Anne listened, but said none of that had been in their mind. Their reasons for buying the hotel were twofold – to create a business for their sons to run, and to give themselves an amusement in their retirement.

I suggested that when it reopens, they change the name to the Camelot Hotel, which might get them some publicity. 'Oh, no, it's always been called the Dunmar, and it's well known locally. But we are going to change it slightly, into the Dunmar Country House Hotel.'

The hotel project could all end in tears, with either financial losses or family rows, but I wished them well. I do like to see Lottery-winners doing something positive with their money, which very few do. On the other hand, it might thrive and blossom and become part of an international chain. There is a precedent for such ventures beginning in Alloa. That was where the Forte family began in 1911 with the little Savoy Café after their arrival from Italy.

On their happiness scale before their win, Anne could think of no blemishes. They owned their own house and had four healthy sons, all grown up and in work. 'We had nothing really to worry about,' she said. 'I'd have to give it ten out of ten.' Ten? 'Well, that was because the week we won happened to be the school holidays, and I was always at my happiest then.' Bob was a bit less rapturous. 'We did have some debts, but none we couldn't manage, so I'll give it between eight and nine.' So what about today?

'The scale of happiness is different,' said Anne. 'Everything is different. In the past we never stayed in hotels, for example. Now we own one. We can go anywhere, do anything. I'd have to give today ten plus.' Bob was pleased that all their money worries were over for ever but was slightly less euphoric. 'I'll give between nine and ten.'

One of the things about winning several millions relatively late in life – in the case of Anne and Bob when they had already begun to think seriously of retirement – is the thought of what might have been. Would they not have preferred it much earlier?

Each of them fell silent. 'No, I wouldn't have liked the money any earlier,' said Bob at last. 'I enjoyed my working life. I would have missed all the experiences I had, the good experiences and the not so good.' Such as? 'Well, after I'd had the post office for a year, it wasn't doing so well, so I sub-let and went off to Saudi Arabia as a chemist, returning to my old job. I worked in the oil business, and I thought I would make some money and have a good time. I signed on for two years, but came back after six months. I couldn't stand the restrictions – the police, including the religious police. I couldn't stand being alone, living a bachelor life. At the time, it seemed a terrible mistake and I was very unhappy, but, looking back, I'm glad I did it. It was an interesting experience, which made me appreciate what I have here in Scotland. I'm not tempted now to rush off abroad, for example.'

'I would have liked the win to have come five or even ten years earlier,' said Anne. 'Although I loved teaching, and enjoyed it till I left, I would have liked the freedom and independence to go round the world when I was a bit younger, with Bob of course, enjoying ourselves. I still have a minor worry that I won't live till I'm old, say eighty or ninety, and won't get the full benefit of all the money we've won. But every day I am more hopeful we will live to use and enjoy it fully.'

I left by wishing them good luck with the hotel. 'Oh, I'm not too bothered,' said Anne. 'If it fails, we can just go and live in it ...'

---

Ref no: **290109**

# PRIZE CLAIM FORM

*Please read notes overleaf*

THE NATIONAL LOTTERY®

### 1. CLAIMANT'S PERSONAL DETAILS – BLOCK LETTERS PLEASE

Full name: ........................................  Date of birth: ........................................

Address: ........................................  Tel nos: (day): ........................................

........................................  (evening): ........................................

Town: ..................... Postcode: .....................

### 2. CLAIMANT'S DECLARATION/AGREEMENT

I declare:

* that the above information is true and complete
* that I am aged 16 or over
* that, subject to this claim being accepted under the rules of the National Lottery game to which this claim relates, I am legally entitled to the prize claimed and I agree to indemnify Camelot Group Plc against any costs, losses, damages and expenses it may suffer as a result of any misrepresentation.
* I agree to Camelot Group Plc or its representative contacting me with a view to publicising my win.          YES/NO (delete as appropriate)

Claimant's signature: ........................................  Witness signature: ........................................

Witness full name: ........................................  Witness address: ........................................

Date: ........................................

*Complete Section 3 only where someone else is collecting the prize on your behalf. Section 3 should not be completed for postal claims except where the claimant is deceased or under a legal disability.*

### 3. PERMISSION FOR SOMEONE ELSE TO CLAIM

I AUTHORISE the person named below to collect my prize, by cheque payable to myself, on my behalf.

Representative's full name: ........................................  Claimant's signature: ........................................

Address: ........................................  Witness signature: ........................................

Town: ..................... Postcode: .....................  Witness full name: ........................................

Relationship with Claimant, if any: .....................  Witness address: ........................................

Why this person is claiming on your behalf: .....................

........................................  Date: ........................................

**REPRESENTATIVE'S DECLARATION**

I DECLARE that I am 16 years or over.

Representative's signature: ........................................  Witness full name: ........................................

Witness signature: ........................................  Witness address: ........................................

Date: ........................................

*The personal representative(s) of a deceased minor should enter the deceased's details in Section 1, enclose Letters of Administration or Grant of Probate, write personal representative(s) name(s), address(es) in Section 3 and complete Section 4.*

### 4. POSTAL CLAIMS

For postal claims, see information overleaf.

**FOR ADMINISTRATION USE ONLY**

**Game Information:**

Name of game: ........................................  Control number: ........................................

Draw date: ........................................  Ticket number: ........................................

Ticket is in good order:  Y/N  **Means of identification:**

Validation completed by: .....................  Driving licence no: ........................................

Claim authorised by: ........................................  Credit/Bank card no: ........................................

Amount of prize claim £: .....................  Other (specify): ........................................

Cheque no: ........................................

Date: ........................................  Cheque received by: ........................................

# THE PRESTON SYNDICATE

Six months later, and life goes on much the same inside Walne's chemist shop in Preston, Lancashire. Four out of the five people in the syndicate which won a total of £2.2 million are still working there.

Three of the female assistants are continuing with their two and a half days a week for £55, although each of them is now worth £446,952 – or more, if they have been wise with their investments. Andrew is still the pharmacist in charge, manager of the shop. Outside their working lives, there have been changes. All four female assistants have left their council houses and bought their own homes. Andrew is still in his house, but he is hopeful soon for changes in his domestic life, as well as in his working life.

A new assistant has taken the place of the one who has left. She is called Maria, a smiling, glowing, motherly woman. Was she envious, that she had not been part of the winning syndicate? 'I don't begrudge them one penny,' she said. 'I just feel lucky to have got the job. I know Hilary, and I know Andrew because he was very kind to my father. I live on the estate, you see, so I've always known it was a happy shop. I'm just thrilled to be working here.'

The assistant who has gone is June, aged fifty-five, the quietest, longest serving of the assistants, the one who was

worrying about her pharmacy course. That wasn't the reason
for giving up. It was simply that the house she has bought, a
bungalow costing £80,000, is on the edge of another town
some twenty-five miles away. It would have meant a long
journey to work each day, and she still can't drive. 'Before we
moved, it was only a ten-minute walk to work. Yes, I never
finished my course, which is a shame. I do miss the shop and
the girls.' She still sounded rather overwhelmed by what had
happened to her, unable to say whether she felt happier or
unhappier since her win. 'I haven't really come down to earth
yet. It's still very strange. I can't tell you how I feel. It's too
early.' She wouldn't say how much she has given to friends and
family: 'That's personal.' In fact she clearly did not want to
talk about the subject at all, so we'll move on.

The other three women, however, all of whom have stayed
in the Preston area, were more than happy to talk about their
experiences, their thoughts and reactions, since winning. All
seemed ebullient and pleased with what has happened to
them, with only one or two minor reservations.

Linda, thirty-eight, married to Dave, the car salesman,
with two teenage children, has bought the most expensive
house – a converted barn in a rural setting which cost
£150,000. 'It was more than we intended, but we were driving
past and just fell in love with it. It's got a garage and a driveway
and a big garden, with a bit more behind we might buy later
on.' They have also bought two cars, a Williams Renault Clio
that cost £15,000, a rather special car (but then her husband
is a Grand Prix fan), and a Vauxhall Astra estate which Linda
uses for her half-hour drive to work. 'I don't intend to give the
job up, for the moment. I enjoy it. They're all good company.'

She took advantage of the Camelot panel, and went to see
their lawyer and accountant in Liverpool, along with Hilary.
'They were very nice, but they didn't tell me much I didn't
know, so we've just used our own advisers.' Having bought the

house and the two cars, and given about £20,000 to their parents and children, Linda was left with roughly £200,000, which she has invested in the Bradford and Bingley. 'I wanted long-term growth, with no risks. No, it wasn't much of a worry. Now we've just forgotten about it, and get on with life. I still look at prices in the shops. I still don't buy things I think are expensive.'

She has given nothing to charity. 'Alas, I know it sounds greedy, but in the situation we were in, and all the girls were in, money was very tight. I've wanted to help my family, because charity does begin at home. Before the win, living in our council house, I did worry that if anything happened to me or my husband, the children would be left with nothing.' She was slightly concerned, at the time of the win, that her son David might be carried away and think life was going to be easy from now on. 'He's been fine. They've both been very good and sensible. They've now got a car each, but it's up to them to tax and insure and pay the running costs. It's their problem, not ours. So far, they're doing well. I'm very pleased with them.'

Her husband David, however, has lost his job, through moving so far away. He's now looking for something part-time, locally. 'I like to think we haven't changed at all,' said Linda, 'it's just other people's attitudes to us which have changed. All the girls agree on that. Oh, you know, people will make little remarks they would never have made before. In the shop, I might be getting out several cough medicines and I'll say this one is more expensive, and they'll say, "Not to you it's not." I know it's a little joke, but it does annoy me. Things that were expensive are still expensive, as far as I'm concerned. It is nice having the other girls at work to discuss these things with. You can be easy with them, whereas with some people you have to watch what you say about money and things, in case they think you're showing off. You don't want to offend people. With the girls, they all understand.' She says she was happy enough before the win, and gave it eight out of ten. Her happiness score is now ten out of ten. 'It's been so nice helping the family.'

Sarah, the youngest of the four women, and the one who actually bought the ticket that week, has moved to a modern detached four-bedroom house, with garage, which cost £112,000. Her partner John, an out-of-work welder, is still out of work, still suffering from a bad back. 'Moving house hasn't helped his back.' They didn't have a car before the win, and now they have a Peugeot that she uses for work. 'People are surprised I'm still working, and tell me I must be mad, but I enjoy it. I can't see myself packing it in, not yet, anyway.'

She has so far given a total of £4,000 to members of her family, and invested the rest in a building society. 'I didn't go and see the panel. I couldn't get away that day, but it's all been taken care of. The National & Provincial building society has been very good. They helped me invest it. I've got no worries.'

She has had a holiday in Lanzarote with her partner and two children, the first one they have ever had. 'The last holiday I had myself, like, was when I was little, with my parents to Bournemouth.'

Christopher, her elder boy, is ten, about to go to secondary school, but she has no thoughts of paying for his education, even though she could. 'He will go to the same school with everyone else. Why shouldn't he? If it's in him to do well, he will, wherever he goes.' She was happy enough before the win, despite the financial worries. 'It's very nice not having them any more, but really I'm just as happy as I was. So I'll say eight out of ten, before and after.'

Hilary, perhaps the most ebullient of the staff even before the win, has clearly had a great time in the last six months. She threw a house-warming party for her fellow winners and their families. (Plus me, but I couldn't make it.) She has got her dream house, and had a wonderful holiday in Benidorm. 'The house is brilliant! Four beds, massive size, with a granny flat attached for my mother. We have our own land, which is massive as well. I saw it in the Halifax and it was billed as "House of the Week", so I had to see it. Far more than I intended to pay, but I loved it at first sight. They wanted £139,000, but I got them down to £135,000. Probably got more off if I'd waited, but I'd just fallen in love with it. I seem to have spent a lot of time getting deals, since the win. It's brilliant being able to pay cash. We bought a new car, but it was an old model, superseded by a new one, so they were keen to get rid of it. A Vauxhall, Envoy or something, which we got for £7,000. It should really have been £9,000. At Christmas we were able to buy what we liked, paying cash. It's the first year I've not had a catalogue. In fact, that was one of the first things I paid off.'

Her husband Ricky, a lorry-driver, is not working at present, but will eventually look for something. 'He can't hang around doing nothing, but at the moment it's not worth his while from a tax point of view. They charged him emergency tax, for his last job, which was enormous, so he's better off not working.'

Having bought the house, helped her mother with the granny flat and given £1,000 each to her two children, she was then left with £260,000 to invest. 'I soon left the Royal Bank of Scotland. I thought they were rubbish. The Yorkshire Bank has looked after us brilliantly. They've done everything.'

But doesn't that mean all your money is in their products? 'Oh, no. We've got it in GA, the Prudential, Tessas, PEPs, the lot. They looked for the best deal for me, I'm sure of it. They only charge us, what is it, I've forgotten now – hold on, I'll look it up – just 1 per cent. That seems fair to me. We get a monthly income of £1,000, with no tax to pay on that. I think there isn't. I hope there isn't! Anyway, it's all been brilliant.'

Today, she would give her state of happiness nine out of ten, as opposed to seven out of ten before the win. The only minor blemish has been certain people making certain remarks. 'I've had some aggravation. I was told by someone that we weren't wanted in the club any more – the club we've always gone to, where we were on the night of the win – because we've got too much money. That was terrible. So we hardly go any more, which is a shame. It's the only sad thing that's happened to us. Some people will make these snide remarks. I know it's just jealousy, but it's very annoying. I went to one Christmas party, with people I've had Christmas parties with many times in the past, and there was a different atmosphere between us and them. They wouldn't have a drink with us, which I thought was pathetic. Maybe it's me being too touchy, but I don't think so. We don't change – it's people's attitudes to you that change.

'It happens in the shop. Oh, you know, people say you can now afford things, you'll be paying for the Christmas street party. I think it was those sorts of remarks which got June down, and partly why she left. We did think at one stage it was making her ill, all these silly snide remarks. I find it just annoying, not worrying. They can't get me down. Either I just switch off or answer them back. There was one woman who said to me it was disgusting that we still have our Lottery syndicate, hoping to win more. "Next time I want a million," I told her. "I won't settle for half a million next time." I was just saying it to wind her up. That's why it's great coming to work, with the other girls and Andrew. We're all in the same boat. It makes you feel safe.'

Andrew, the pharmacist, was making up a prescription, counting out the tablets, or at least letting a counting machine count out the tablets. 'It's a little marvel, this machine. I never worked with one till I came to this shop. It doesn't matter the size or shape or weight of the pills, it counts to the exact number you want. It's all done with a beam of light. Amazing.'

Maria, the new assistant, appeared in the back dispensary to tell him that a woman wanted the strongest possible pain-killer. 'Is she on anything?' 'Voltarol,' said Maria. He then went to the front counter and talked at length to the woman. When Andrew returned, a rep had appeared, and needed to talk to him. Then some supplies arrived which had to be checked, followed by a glazier. That weekend, the front window had been kicked in. Nothing stolen. Just young kids doing a spot of amateur vandalism.

Andrew had on his serious face, as ever, looking solemn and concerned, coping with all these queries and problems. Hadn't he contemplated packing it all in since the win, just for a moment? 'No,' he said. 'The thought has never crossed my mind. I don't feel any different about my work than I did before. I get a bit stressed, now and again, but that's part of the job. Reps do say to me all the time, "You still here? I'd be off like a shot if I had your money." For a start, the money's not really enough to retire on, not at my age. Secondly, I still enjoy it. Thirdly, I'd be bored out of my mind, sitting at home doing nothing.'

But he is hoping that the owner of the shop will very soon decide to sell it to him. They had discussed it before the win, with the idea that Andrew would be ready to buy it some time around the year 2000. Now he is ready, mentally as well as financially. If, in the next few months, nothing is agreed, he will look elsewhere, but still in the Preston area. 'This shop suits me. I know the estate and the customers, and the situation is ideal for me. So I hope we can agree on a price.

'Since the win, business has been even better than it was. In the beginning I think a lot of people came into the shop just to gape at us, but we've ended up with a lot of new regular customers. Perhaps people think this is a Lucky Pharmacy.'

Almost all of Andrew's money has been invested. One largish sum is in a special account, earning 8 per cent with the National & Provincial. That's the one he'll use when the time comes to buy a business. He has also invested in Tessas, PEPs and his pension, and paid off his mortgage. 'That was a weight off my shoulders. The rest is invested long term for ten years, by which time we should have a family and have plenty of money to give them a good start in life with their education.'

He didn't go to the panel either, not being able to find a locum to cover for him on the day, and made his own financial decisions. He and his wife Lynn have given away a total of £44,000, to parents and relations. At first, he gave them £1,000 each, then £10,000 as a surprise Christmas present. Nothing so far to charity. 'It's funny. I did always say I would give something to an arthritis charity if ever I had any money. I saw my grandmother in agony with it when I was young. It's a sort of illness which isn't glamorous, down the list when it comes to charities. I might give them some one day.'

Andrew and Lynn are still in the same house – the semi they bought for £60,000 – which means that most of his women assistants are now in houses twice as expensive as his. 'I couldn't face moving. The house is too big for us as it is, with just the two of us. I can never find time in the summer to cut the grass or do all the jobs.' He would like to add a garage, but Lynn has refused. 'It would mean giving up a bit of our little garden, and she's against that. A garage would be handy, as we've each bought a brand-new car.'

Andrew, hadn't you just bought yourselves a brand-new car each at the time of your win? 'Yes,' he said, looking embarrassed. 'I am a bit of a car freak. I read all the car mags. I remember last year reading in some car mag about Ken Southwell, the first Lottery-winner. It showed a photo of him with his Porsche and his Range-Rover. I remember thinking at the time, you lucky bastard!' So, what have you got now? 'Well, I've got a Saab 9000, which cost £23,000, and Lynn has a Mazda MX5, which cost £19,000. Hers is the flashy one!' While yours is, well, a bit staid? He blushed. 'When we have a family, if we have a family, that will be – er, the family car.' They have finally decided the time is about ripe, so they will have to see what happens. After starting a family, and going on perhaps to have two or three, the ultimate plan is still the same – for Lynn to join him in his own chemist shop complete with clinic. She can run it part-time at first, if she wants.

Personally, he doesn't think he has changed since the win, but he has noticed Lynn is now more likely to lash out on some extravagance, rather than he. 'I was always the fritterer, not able to save any money, while Lynn has always been a brilliant saver. She still is, but she surprised me by buying personalised number plates for her car – N10 LYN. That cost her £1,500! Amazing. I never thought she'd spend that amount. I wouldn't be able to do that.'

How about when you have your own chemist shop, maybe a string of chemist shops right across Lancashire, wouldn't it be nice to have a car which said P ILL S, if you can get such a thing? 'P reg will be out soon, so that's not a bad idea!' If and when he does buy his present shop, he won't put his own name up in lights. He'll simply call it Larches Pharmacy after the estate. And he does hope, one day, that he might have a small chain of chemist shops.

'What the money has done is save me ten years. I plan to begin this year, 1996, aged twenty-eight, to start my own business, not at thirty-eight, which is what I would probably have done.' All the same, he doesn't think his state of happiness is much different from what it was. 'It's only the financial worries that have gone. Everything in life is the same. People do treat you a little bit different, shout out at you in the street, things like, "Have you spent the money yet?" That gets a bit boring.

'I have been rung up a few times by the local paper, asking for my comments on various things as if I was somebody.' Such as? 'Oh, when Asda was dropping the retail price maintenance on various medical goods, they wanted my opinion. Then when the first anniversary of the National Lottery was coming up, they wanted my views on Camelot's profits. I said I'd need to know more details. They have to make a profit, to run any company, so I couldn't see anything wrong with that. I don't enjoy that sort of thing, being asked for my comments. It's not me. I'm glad we went public, rather than hiding behind a bush, but I'd rather not be pointed out and known.

'But I have enjoyed the experience. It's been very interesting. What has been nice is having the girls bouncing things off each other, exchanging experiences. Hilary for example got fed up early on with the Royal Bank of Scotland. Something had gone wrong, and she was threatening to take all her money out, so they offered her a higher rate. Next day she rushed into work and told all of us, so we all asked for higher rates. That was funny. In the end we all took our money out of that bank, anyway. Only having one person, your partner, to discuss your Lottery win with, must be a bit limiting. We've gained by having each other. That's been a plus about being in a syndicate.'

# RICHARD BRANSON

There was a great deal of national rejoicing as we got near November 1995 and the first year of the National Lottery. Well, there certainly was at Camelot HQ, where they were making plans for an anniversary party to celebrate their brilliantly successful first year. The government were equally delighted. The new Heritage Secretary, Mrs Bottomley, patted Camelot on the back, and her good self, and the government, for creating and distributing billions to good causes and assorted worthy enterprises. Peter Davis, Oflot's Director General, was equally pleased that the company he had chosen had done so well. The media were tooling up to mark the anniversary, in newspaper articles and TV programmes, looking for ways to get at Camelot (as is our national tradition with any successful enterprise), but having to admit, taking any factual benchmarks, using any statistical analysis, that it had been a very satisfactory first year for our National Lottery, far exceeding any expectations of incomes and distributions. There were also 102 new millionaires who had been created by 14 October, all feeling pretty pleased with themselves.

However, there was some slight gnashing of teeth and furrowing of brows from one person who could see little reason to celebrate Camelot's first year – Richard Branson. In

November I met up with him in Majorca, at a hotel he owns as a minor part of his Virgin empire, which stretches all round the world, employing 10,000 people in fifteen different countries. Their products and services include the Virgin airline, Virgin Cola, Virgin Megastores and MGM Cinemas. Quite enough, one might think, to keep him happy and contented. But that is not always the case with apparently successful people whom we all admire or envy from afar. Paul McCartney will always be annoyed that he doesn't own all the rights to his song, 'Yesterday'. No doubt my Lottery million-aires will find things to annoy them.

A year later, Richard Branson was still clearly bugged by his failure to secure the National Lottery licence. I had seen him only recently on a TV programme, being asked by Esther Rantzen what he would most like to be remembered for, and being astounded that he chose the National Lottery, some-thing he has had nothing whatsoever to do with. So far. But he is determined to have an effect on its future. 'Peter Davis of Oflot made a ghastly mistake,' he told me. 'We would have contributed far more to charities and the government's good causes than Camelot has done during this year.'

What? How could this possibly be? Even speaking hypo-thetically, it seemed a wild exaggeration. I had with me a copy of Oflot's annual report for 1994–5, in which the Director General repeated his explanation for choosing Camelot – that they were going to retain the least amount. Therefore the Branson consortium was going to retain more, and the government's good causes would receive less. So, under the rules, Peter Davis had no alternative but to turn down your consortium? 'If those were the rules, then the rules stink. He should have taken into account that we were going to give all our own profits to charities. But he is as conservative as they come, and showed no imagination.'

What precisely were the figures in your bid? For example,

what proportion of the total income were you going to take for yourself, out of which you were going to pay your running costs and then give away profits to your own designated charities? This figure has never been published. Mr Branson said he couldn't remember. Ten per cent? He shook his head. 'Not as much as that. In fact it was only a fraction of a percentage above Camelot's. You'll have to ask John Jackson. He organised our bid.'

John Jackson is now chief executive of Sketchley. I later asked him to dig out the figures, which he eventually did. 'Our basic submission,' he said, 'was that 12 per cent should go in tax, 50 per cent on prizes, 28.1 per cent to good causes and 5 per cent to retailers, which left our Foundation's take at 4.9 per cent.'

That would have made it less than Camelot's? 'Well, over the full range of possibilities, our take was possibly just over 5 per cent.'

All the same, according to those figures, you can see one reason why Richard Branson has been so upset. Their take would appear to be much the same as Camelot's. Ah, but behind these basic figures lie some other figures. All bidders had to explain where their 'take' would go. Camelot was going to spend roughly 4 per cent on running costs and take only 1 per cent as their profit. Branson's bid gave a figure of 3.4 per cent for running costs, leaving a profit of 1.5 per cent. So if you are looking at the basic end profit for the firm running the Lottery, then Camelot was going to end up with far less than Branson's?

'But we were going to give all our 1.5 per cent to charity,' said Mr Jackson. 'There would be no corporation tax to pay either, as it was going to charity. I think this should have been taken into account. Our bid would have provided far more for all charities than Camelot's. I would like to see the full details of all the bids published, which they haven't been so far, so that everyone can see exactly what the figures were. What we have is Peter Davis saying Camelot's bid was the lowest, which we still maintain is not strictly fair.'

So why did he not give the licence to your Foundation? 'I assume we fell down on the fifteen scenarios which he created. It is true that in the worst possible scenario, with the Lottery not doing very well, we would have been penalised. We did not have a capital base, unlike Camelot, with their five shareholders putting up substantial sums. All our money was borrowed equity. If things went wrong, we could have been in financial trouble, which would have been overcome by Richard agreeing to put up a £40 million guarantee. But if you look at lotteries round the world, his worst-case scenario is impossible. They have all been successful. I have to agree that Camelot probably did come out cheaper over his fifteen tests, but our belief is still that our basic bid was the best and lowest. The full facts should be published.'

Back to Richard Branson. I am a great fan of his and like to think I am a friend, and I know his bid for the lottery was eminently sincere and worthy, but it seems to me that Oflot did have a reasonable objection – that his bid took a higher profit than Camelot's and that his research was not adequate. Given the rules, what else could they have done? Or does he himself think there were deeper, more mysterious, reasons why his bid failed?

'I suspect that in this instance my high public profile worked against me. It did look as if it was "Richard Branson's Lottery", which of course was not the case. I was only part of the initial consortium, and would have stepped back once it started. I also think that the Tories find it hard to cope with entrepreneurs like me. In theory, you would think Tories would approve of all entrepreneurs, but they don't. They feel much more comfortable with big business, the corporate bodies, the PLCs – the sort which so often take ex-Tory ministers as directors. They don't like people like me. I'm a loose cannon. They think, "Is he one of us?" I have no interest in party politics, never have done, and have always sent all political parties packing when they have asked for donations. That might help to explain why I failed with the National Lottery and also with Channel 5.'

Although not involved in politics, he has had talks with Labour Party officials, so he says, about the future of the National Lottery. 'I have been told that in the next Labour Party manifesto they will promise to ensure the Lottery will be run by a non-profit-making company in the future.'

Yes, but that can't happen until Camelot's present licence finishes in 2001. 'We'll see about that. The Labour Party is also planning to bring in a windfall tax, which will hit the profits of companies like Camelot. What they might then do is to say to Camelot, OK, we'll let you have three years without paying a windfall tax, but then you must give up your licence. So, if that happened, the licence could become available earlier than people expect.'

And would you then reapply? 'My object is not to run it, but to have it run as a non-profit-making concern, as it is in almost every other country in the world. It is obscene that Camelot is making profits of £1 million a week, from something that is so easy to run. Oh, yes, it is easy to run. GTECH might be a good supplier of systems, though I have some worries about their affairs in the USA, but we would have had IBM to do our systems. They would have done it just as well.

'Six years ago, when I saw Douglas Hurd about it, we could easily have started then and have given billions and billions to charities by now. But they were so blinkered. The thing is, you can't lose if you have the licence. You can only make a fortune. Everyone knows that. We had raised backing through J.P. Morgan of £300 million for our bid – no problem, because everyone knew that whoever won would make a fortune, which is what has happened. Some people talked about Camelot not making any profits for the first three years, which turned out to be rubbish. They did it in six months. I want to see a lottery which is not just run on greed – greed by the punters hoping to win, and greed by the operators. I still believe that if it was known that no commercial profits were being made, more people would enter, as we pointed out in our submission. I estimate if we had won, then a billion pounds more would have gone by now to the government's good causes, as well as to our own.'

Looking back, don't you wish now you had put in a different submission? You lost by creating your own way of contributing to good causes, separate from the government's. 'In retrospect, we made a mistake, but we thought Oflot would understand what we were doing, use some imagination, and we would get the licence. The point of us giving our profits to certain charities was to compensate them for the losses we knew they would suffer when the National Lottery began. The medical charities, for example, who had their own scratch cards, were bound to lose money, and that's what has happened.'

On the actual running of the lottery, he says that the system would have been much the same if he had won, with an on-line draw and scratch cards, but they might have capped the top prize, making it around £2 million at most. 'Under Camelot, where there have been around fifty multi-millionaires created, we would have aimed for 200 single millionaires.'

But he has nothing personal against Camelot as such; his displeasure is with the government and Oflot. 'If it was in my gift now, I might still leave the same people to run it. I would probably keep Tim Holley as chief executive and David Rigg. Nothing wrong with them or the other Camelot executives.

But I would get rid of the five shareholders who own Camelot. They should not be raking in all the profits. The British people should be getting the profits. If the government had had any sense, when they established Oflot and appointed Peter Davis, his job should have been to control the National Lottery directly, not hand it all over to a private, commercial company. We spent £1 million on our bid and many months of work, and I'm sure the others spent much the same. All of it wasted. Except that, because of us, the government is getting more than it might have done. Once it was known our bid was going to be non-profit-making, the others trimmed their bids. Oh, I'm sure we all found out what the others were doing.

'The government should not have gone to the private sector at all. They should have put up the initial money, and then taken all the profits. They would also have made sure that all the provision of services and systems was done openly. Camelot has naturally used the services of the companies who own it. That's another reason why I think the Lottery has been discredited, apart from their vast profits.'

According to studies of lotteries in other parts of the world, they might in theory be run by civil servants, but in practice, the suppliers behind the scenes have a great deal of control, and make a great deal of profit. And if government, or even quasi-government agencies, do keep strict control, it is always assumed they can never be as efficient, flexible or as enterprising as a commercial profit-making concern.

'I don't believe that. People like Tim Holley and David Rigg and everyone else would still have incentives, with bonuses based on results. They would earn just as much, if they did well. I also believe there is extra satisfaction for people who work for a non-profit-making organisation, which makes them work even better. I know I sound like a bad loser, and a pain in the bum, but I don't intend to give up until it is run as a non-profit-making concern. There are not many times in one's life when something as big as this comes up, so it has to be seen to be done decently.'

# 32

## ALAN AND LINDA, MARGATE

Alan Baker, the bookmaker, and Linda Hill, the Butlin's chambermaid, the last in my year of jackpot-winners, returned from their London excitements to their council flat in Margate. It's on the ground floor, small and neat, with pink fitted carpet, modern furniture, newly decorated, all done by Alan. They were having their evening meal – a large sirloin steak each, with mushrooms and coleslaw, eating it on trays on their laps, sitting in front of the electric fire. With them was Caroline, Linda's youngest daughter by her previous husband, just visiting. She lives round the corner with her father. She is seventeen, pretty and blonde, open and sunny natured, and heavily pregnant. Her baby was due in ten days. Like her mother, she smoked cigarettes. Alan was smoking a slender cigar. They were still bubbly and excited, radiating happiness and good nature, constantly touching and petting each other. Linda had bare feet and legs, a very short mini-skirt and a tight top.

'She's the star,' said Alan, giving her a cuddle. 'Show him the make-over photographs.' The *Sun* had had Linda professionally made-up and coiffured, and dressed in a slinky frock, for 'before' and 'after' photos, though they had not yet been used.

Both local and national TV and newspapers had continued

to be fascinated by Linda's being a Butlin's chambermaid, and by her good nature in agreeing to pose with bucket and mop. 'Two rang me again today. Dunno how they got our number, as we're ex-directory. They're supposed to ring Butlin's or Camelot, not me. But that's the end. I'm fed up with being pestered all the time. I've had enough. I'm not doing no more.'

Most of the first week of the win had been spent in London, staying at the Charing Cross Hotel for the press conference and then TV interviews. The second week they decided to get well away and have a holiday. 'My boss at Butlin's promised to find us a nice quiet place where we wouldn't be recognised,' said Linda, 'so he booked us into the Grand Hotel in Bayswater.'

'Crafty sod,' said Alan. 'It's a Butlin's hotel. You can imagine the possible publicity: "They could have stayed at the Savoy, the Dorchester or the Ritz – but they chose Butlin's!" But it was a free week. All we had to pay for was our telephone calls.'

'I enjoyed it,' said Linda.

'No, it was a bit crummy, compared with the Charing Cross,' said Alan. 'You had to queue up for breakfast. But I enjoyed it as well. I couldn't find it at first. Do you know, there's no sign in London saying "Bayswater"? At least, I couldn't find it. We went there from the BBC after the lottery show. We drove round for about an hour, till in the end I put the car in a car park in Kensington and got a taxi to the Grand. I was in a hired car, as I'd given my old car away to a friend. The car cost £40 a day to hire, and we never drove it all week, and the parking for the week came to £139. It was an expensive free week!'

They booked in as Mr and Mrs Smith, which led to nods and smirks from the late-night receptionist. Then, as they got their keys, they were recognised by six girls who by chance had all been in the audience at the Lottery show. 'They screamed when they saw us,' said Linda. 'They were all Geordie girls, lovely girls. In London that week they'd seen Sylvester Stallone, Robson and Jerome, the singers – and now us. And they said meeting us was the most exciting thing of all!'

'They were bloody drunk,' said Alan, tucking into his steak.

During their London week they went sightseeing on an open-top bus, had a medieval banquet near the Tower of London and did a lot of shopping. They spent £1,300 between them on clothes at Selfridges, then Linda spent another £150 on herself at Top Shop.

'What did you get, Mum?' Caroline asked. Linda brought her clothes out on hangers for Caroline to inspect. A mini-skirted real suede suit was much admired. They also went to Hatton Garden, where Alan bought Linda a £700 diamond ring, out of his bank account into which half of the money had gone, while Linda bought Alan a gold ring for £190 from her half of the money.

'We had a brilliant week,' said Linda. 'We were treated ever so well. In every shop, they were wonderful. People kept on telling us we were a lovely couple, so down to earth. Really, lots of people said that. Even in Boots, people were so nice.'

Because people knew you had won the Lottery and were spending a lot of money? 'No, we didn't tell them.'

Because you were radiating happiness, then? 'It probably did show,' said Alan, 'but we have always been affectionate. Linda often sits on my knee when we're out. In fact yesterday, at a friend's house, this friend said we could go up to his bedroom, if we wanted to ...' Loud shrieks of mock-horror laughter from both Linda and Caroline.

After their holiday, Linda went back to work, as she had said she would. The first day, the press were waiting for her, organised by a delighted Butlin's PR, and she posed for snaps. So that made an easy day.

Since then she has been back to her normal chambermaiding. 'Some of the guests do recognise me. "Are you the woman who ..." they start saying. I say "Yes," and they all say, "You must be crazy" and I say, "That's me."' Her colleagues, she said, have all been lovely, with no signs of bitchiness. 'If anyone's jealous, I haven't noticed it. I'd ignore it, anyway.' She intends to carry on working indefinitely, as she enjoys it so much, but will take unpaid holidays when necessary, such as for the birth of Caroline's baby and their exotic holiday in the New Year, still at that time to be decided.

Alan hopes Linda will not stay at work for ever. 'But it's up to her. She's got a mind of her own. I would like her to give it up and enjoy herself more.'

'Oh, I can't give up till after Christmas. Christmas is our busiest time of the year. I don't need the money, but I can't sit at home all the time like Lady Muck.'

Alan, who had given up his job as a manager of a Tote betting shop as soon as he won the Lottery, had found himself missing work more than he had expected. After a month of idleness, he applied to start work again – this time self-employed as a bookie at the local dog track in Ramsgate. 'I got a great reception from all the other bookies. There was a nice piece about me in the *Racing Post*, did you see it? I'm running a book three nights a week with a clerk and an assistant. Gambling is my big interest in life. In London, I went to the Casino and lost £80 on blackjack.'

On his first day back, running his own book, he lost £3,000 on the night's work. Well, he can afford it now, and he did make it up later. It was gambling, he says, which helped to cause the failure of his marriage, though it did last twenty-six years. 'I didn't keep her short, but I used to come home pretty late sometimes. After an evening as a bookie, I'd often go to the Casino till two or four in the morning. She hated gambling, all aspects of it, though she knew I was a bookie when she married me. I was nineteen at the time. She divorced me when I was on the verge of bankruptcy. I'd hit a bad time, had the Customs and Excise after me, lost my job, and was doing part-time taxi-driving. I'd always lived beyond my income. I suppose it's an easy-money profession, in the sense that it comes in cash, easily when it's doing well, and then goes out again. I thought nothing of taking my wife and children out for Sunday lunch and spending £70 or £80. Back in the 1980s, this was. We got divorced, and I lived on my own for a year, then she took me back for three or four years. What happened was that my post was still being delivered to the old address, so I'd pop in from time to time to pick it up, stay for a cup of tea, then a meal, and eventually I moved back in again. That lasted till one night I decided to leave. I was living alone again when I met Linda. She's the only relationship with a woman I've had, apart from my wife. But we're still good friends and I'm close to all my children.'

Alan's three children are now grown up. His oldest, Steven, aged thirty, went to City University in London and works in a Tote betting shop as his dad did. Anne-Marie, twenty-four, is at Cambridge. 'She's not just clever, she's a lovely girl. She loves racing and has been to lots of race courses with me.' Gary, his other son, did not go to university and is currently unemployed. 'He's more like me.'

Linda's personal life has been more complicated, as her brother had hinted on the day of the Lottery press conference. Her first marriage lasted just six months. 'He went off with someone else, taking our daughter, and leaving me pregnant.' The second child was also a daughter, now twenty-five. She says she doesn't know the age of her first daughter, or where she lives. 'I then met someone and had a child by him – a son, now aged twenty-three. But no, I didn't marry him. You must be joking!' But she did marry her next partner, in 1973, and had two daughters by him, the youngest of whom is Caroline. 'I liked him enough, but when I tried to cuddle him, he'd say I was too hot. Eventually I said I can always go elsewhere for a cuddle, and in the end I did. I got myself a new boyfriend.' That relationship lasted seven years, though they lived in separate places, staying together mainly at weekends. 'It was a grave mistake. I'd felt much securer with my previous husband. It took me a long time to get up the courage to leave him, but I did in the end.' Her second husband, whom she had always liked, then had a stroke, and she moved back to nurse him. He is now disabled, but they are good friends.

As all the Winners' Advisers observed, such complicated family relationships are quite normal these days. What of course it means to winners is that when they come to giving out gifts, not everyone related by blood or marriage is bound to be a winner. Alan and Linda had taken some time to decide which relations would get money and which would not. It didn't seem to have caused undue aggravation, though Alan had talked Linda into giving the second daughter of her first marriage some money, which had not been her original intention.

Alan and Linda had that day agreed to purchase their new house, a fairly quick decision as Lottery-winners go. 'It was in the local paper, that we were looking for a bungalow, and one cheeky woman sent us three identical letters, trying to sell us hers. But we'd seen this one by then, and loved it at first sight.' It's a detached bungalow, with a fish-pond, a fountain and some mature trees, just half a mile away from their council flat. Linda wanted to stay in the same area, so that it would be handy to get to her work at Butlin's. 'That did rather restrict our choice,' said Alan. 'I suppose we would have looked further away, but for Butlin's; perhaps as far as Broadstairs. But I'm delighted by it. I like staying in the same area.' The bungalow was on the market at £99,500. Alan offered £92,000 for cash, but the owner wouldn't budge. 'It had previously been reduced from £115,000, so I could understand why he was sticking out for £99,500. When I put my offer up to £97,000, they said split the difference, so we agreed on £98,250. It was done very quickly.'

That same day, after they had confirmed the house purchase, Alan went out and bought a new car, a Ford Mondeo. That was the model he'd hired for the London visit and liked it very much. He got £1,000 off for cash, as anyone would these days, and paid £14,000.

The gifts to the various members of their family, when they eventually settled on them, were generous. Linda gave her stepfather and mother £20,000, her brothers and sisters £10,000 each, four of her children £5,000 each, and her grandchildren £1,000 each. One of the minor problems, said Alan, in giving such gifts to people in Linda's family is that most of them are on social security. 'If you have capital of more than £3,000, it affects your dole money and other things, so it's had to be done carefully, step by step.'

Alan, in his turn, gave £20,000 to each of his three children and £10,000 to his ex-wife, even though he did once leave her. 'I did think hard about how much to give and I think that will be enough for them to have a cushion in life. Not enough for them to go mad and go out and spend it, but enough to put down on a house or whatever.'

Linda, in all, gave away around £100,000 to her chosen relations while Alan gave £70,000 to his family, a total of £170,000 out of their joint £1.89 million. They have so far given nothing to charity. 'Except I did sponsor a dog race for £50, which went to the Retired Greyhounds Trust,' said Alan. 'I think your family comes first,' said Linda, 'before any other buggers.'

In January 1996, after Caroline gave birth to a son, Liam

(Linda's first grandson), they didn't go to Florida, which was their first intention, or to Las Vegas, Alan's choice. He had been interested in seeing Las Vegas gambling in action, especially their small-stake poker games, but Linda talked him out of it. Instead they flew to Puerto Rico, then joined a Caribbean cruise. It was Linda's first trip abroad, and they both loved it.

On their return in February 1996, safely settled in their new bungalow, they still appeared as happy and delighted with life, and each other, as they had at the time of their win. 'We were happy beforehand, but financially we were scratching,' said Alan. 'Now we are even happier, as we have no money problems to worry about.'

Any plans to get married? 'What would be the point?' said Alan. 'We know we love each other, and that's what matters. It wouldn't make us any happier.'

'If we had young children,' said Linda, 'that might be different. But I won't be having any, not at forty-eight, especially now I've had my hysterectomy.'

They have no regrets about coming out and going public, although Linda did get fed up very quickly after the first week, and soon stopped giving interviews. But they would do the same again, as they enjoyed their week of fame. They still spend £7 a week on the Lottery, using the same numbers, just for the amusement. 'We're ordinary people, still with the same friends and ordinary interests.' Linda eventually reduced her hours as a chambermaid, but says she is not interested in taking up anything new. 'I couldn't face the responsibility of running a shop or a café. And I don't have any hobbies.'

As with all Lottery winners, their winnings trickled down through their families, and small gifts gave as much unexpected pleasure and excitement as the big one did. One of Alan's family who benefited was his student daughter Anne-Marie. On the actual day of her father's win in October 1995, she heard another bit of good news – she had been awarded a PhD at Cambridge. Her first degree was in Natural Sciences, specialising in medical genetics. Her PhD thesis was on genetic resistance to infectious diseases, with special reference to leprosy. 'Half an hour after I'd heard I'd got my PhD, I rang my mum in Margate and told her. She was delighted, of course, and said she had some good news as well – my father had won the Lottery! I thought it was brilliant. Really terrific.'

The £20,000 gift from her father has helped her to visit the USA, and the rest will go towards a deposit on a flat. It also helped to clear her mind about her future career. She had originally assumed she would stay in academic research or lecturing, once she'd got her PhD. 'But in the end the research got me down. I found it very frustrating. So I'm now hoping to go into scientific publishing instead.'

She herself has always spent £1 a week on the Lottery, but only managed a £10 win so far. 'Oh, I'm all for the Lottery. It gives everyone a bit of hope and unites the nation every Saturday night. It's something to talk about instead of the weather. Only good comes out of the Lottery. All my Cambridge friends were thrilled when they heard my father's news. I got six proposals of marriage!'

# 33

## THE END OF THE YEAR

To celebrate its first year, Camelot gave a party on 18 November 1995 at Syon House, Brentford, south-west of London. A smart address, as it is a historic and imposing stately home set in a large park beside the Thames, crammed with masterpieces and fine furniture, but a sad address as well. The 11th Duke of Northumberland, Harry Percy, whose London home it was, had recently died, aged only forty-two. I'd lunched with him just a few months earlier, a boyish if rather bloated-looking man, friendly and affable. He appeared to be one of the nation's richest and most eligible bachelors, said to be worth £200 million, but underneath there was a mass of worries and phobias, mysterious illnesses and depressions.

As I arrived for the party, I fell to wondering about any possible symbolism. Syon, the seat of one-time kingmakers. Camelot, the seat of a legendary king. Camelot, today's company, like the late duke, appeared to be rich and desirable, with an income of £275 million from the National Lottery, yet underneath, behind the scenes, would we in years to come find mysterious illnesses and depressions? A boyish firm, which could end up bloated? Perhaps even suffer a sudden collapse, if Richard Branson's predictions come true and a Labour government do not renew their licence? Unhappy and cynical

# CAMELOT

### THE DIRECTORS OF
### CAMELOT GROUP plc
REQUEST THE PLEASURE OF THE COMPANY OF

*Hunter Davies*
*and Guest*

AT SYON HOUSE, MIDDLESEX

ON SATURDAY 18TH NOVEMBER 1995

*Invitation to the first anniversary party, November 1995*

thoughts, which I immediately banished from my mind. This was going to be a happy evening, after a happy year.

There were 650 guests assembled – Camelot directors and senior staff, suppliers and retailers, charities and beneficiaries, representatives from the House of Commons and the media. Peter Davis of Oflot was there, looking healthy after his Australian trip. I spotted Esther Rantzen. No, not there representing the media, but as a charity worker. It was a black-tie event that began in the fairly formal stately rooms of Syon House, where we sipped champagne, but the dinner itself, and the entertainment, took place in a sequence of huge marquees adjoining the house. The heating bill, for a cold November evening, must have been equally huge.

A chosen handful of jackpot-winners were there and, to my delight, I spotted several of 'mine'. I rushed up to say Hello to Bob and Anne Westland from Alloa, with Bob resplendent in his best kilt. We discussed the latest on their hotel plans. Then I saw Audrey and Andy from Hartlepool, equally smart in their evening wear. Andy said his heart had missed a beat when he arrived to see a photographer waiting outside the main gates of Syon. 'Oh no, here we go again,' he thought. I assured him he was worrying unduly. I didn't think a London photographer, standing in the dark on a pavement, would recognise Andy from Hartlepool out of 650 guests. I compli-mented Audrey on her hair. It was a last-minute panic, she said, getting it done. They had left Teesside Airport only at four that afternoon. At one stage she had offered to pay Andy's sister, who is a hairdresser, to fly with them to London just to do her hair, but she'd managed to get it done before she left. Shades of Elizabeth Taylor.

Then I talked to Ken Southwell from York, whose hair was still as long, like a seventies footballer, and his girlfriend Julie. They had some big news. She would not be his girlfriend for much longer. They had decided to get married on 1 June

*The party (left to right): Andy Voss, Anthea Turner, Bob Westland and Ken Southwell*

1996. Any significance in the day? 'Dunno,' said Ken. 'She chose it.' On their marriage, said Julie, she would probably give up her job and think about starting a family.

Six other winners were invited to the party, whom I hadn't met before. They included the Bensons from Hull (who won £20 million and got burgled while they were in London), the Duffs from London, Michael Williams from Wales, Sharon Younger from Sunderland and a syndicate from London who worked for Credit Suisse. They were invited, so I was told, as a thank-you, because they had all been helpful to Camelot.

Tim Holley, the chief executive, gave a short introductory speech, followed by Sir George Russell, the new chairman of Camelot. (He took over during the year from Sir Ron Dearing, who retired.) He urged all Camelot staff and associates present not to be ashamed of their huge success, not to be hurt when the company was attacked for doing so well.

He had had thirty-five years of start-up companies and this was the biggest and best start-up he had ever known.

He then announced that Camelot was going to give £50 for every person present to certain good causes. He paused, but fortunately nobody started clapping, the way they do on the *Lottery Live* whenever money is mentioned. I worked out this would come to £32,500, a generous, if not enormous, amount, compared with their reported £50 million profit on the year. But then whenever a wealthy person or company gives money away it is always easy to say it is never enough.

After the speeches, and before the dinner, we were shown a short video film on a giant screen, extolling the delights and achievements of Camelot during the last year, starting with a shot of Bob Westland going about his post office duties. It was a very simplistic little film, more suitable for ten-year-olds than an audience who already knew all about the wonderful achievements of Camelot. But the dinner was very good, and the wine and conversations flowed well. I was seated at a table with a Camelot lawyer, a Camelot director, the London boss of GTECH, a charity organiser and the editor of the *News of the World*. The evening was enjoyable and low-key, rather than flash or showy, a subtle contrast to some of Camelot's more noisy and attention-seeking advertising and promotional campaigns. There were no star names in the cabaret, which consisted of groups who had received Lottery funding, such as Zippo's Academy of Circus Arts and the Adzido Pan African Dance Ensemble.

Three weeks later, on 11 December, any self-satisfied feelings Camelot might have been allowing themselves were badly shaken by a BBC TV programme. Not quite as dramatic or with as high viewing figures as their earlier Princess of Wales programme, but it contained some rather controversial material and allegations, particularly about the activities of GTECH in the USA. Richard Branson appeared in the programme, repeating some of the things he had said to me, but he also alleged that it was GTECH who had tried to offer him a deal. (This resulted in GTECH denying it, and in turn Branson saying he would take legal action.) Branson also alleged he had told Peter Davis about this – which Mr Davis denied. What then happened, in the next few days, appeared almost like a witch-hunt against Peter Davis. It was revealed that he had accepted the use of a private jet supplied by GTECH, when making inspections of US lotteries before the launch of our National Lottery, but after Camelot had got the licence. Mr Davis confirmed it, but said he had not gained personally from these trips, defending himself by saying it had simply helped him to do his official work more easily and cheaply, and he'd done it openly and after consultation. The front pages of all the national newspapers confidently predicted that Mr Davis would lose his job. Several editorials suggested that as Regulator of the Lottery he had been seen to be too close to Camelot, so he could not possibly remain in charge. There was some surprise when, on 19 December, Mrs Bottomley, the Heritage Secretary, announced she was standing by Mr Davis. She had no doubts about his integrity, but indicated he had been 'unwise' to have used the free flights.

So the first full year of the Lottery had ended with another avalanche of newsprint. On average, there had been 1,300 stories about the Lottery every month in the national newspapers. (The highest month had 2,300 stories, the lowest, 900.) The tabloids had been mainly obsessed by the winners. The broadsheets were keener on reports by various economists and think-tanks, most of them warning that elements of the economy were becoming damaged or lop-sided as a result of the Lottery's success. Vernon's pools had sacked 500 staff during the year. It was predicted that 2,400 out of Britain's 9,300 betting shops would soon have to close. Some charities announced that they expected to lose millions – though in the event overall charity-giving turned out to be much the same as the previous year. Several bishops and moral guardians complained we had become a nation of gamblers.

There was a lot of attention given to the monies being handed out to the government's good causes, with most of the distributing bodies and many of the recipients being attacked. It was frequently argued that it was the poor (i.e. the ordinary Lottery punter) who was subsidising the rich (i.e. wealthy opera patrons). The most frequently mentioned recipients were the Royal Opera House, £55 million; Tate Gallery, £50 million; Sadlers Wells, £30 million; Royal Court Theatre, £15 million; Churchill Papers Archive Trust, £13 million. The vast majority of the year's 2,300 awards were under £100,000, given out to little local bodies and receiving only local publicity. There were numerous suggestions for spending the Millennium Fund Money but, by the end of 1995, nothing as imaginative as the British Museum or Westminster Bridge seemed likely to be created. It did begin to seem that there was more money around than good causes to give it to – at least good causes as originally designated by the government. Judging by the suggestions and criticism and admissions, inside and outside Parliament, it looked obvious that the next government of whatever complexion, would redefine good causes and perhaps even the rules governing the size of jackpot prizes. Most new organisations, after their first year, do need and expect certain adjustments to be made.

The total income of the National Lottery in its first year was £4.4 billion. (One Camelot official had at one time predicted £1.4 billion.) This was greater than the national income of Costa Rica, Ethiopia or Paraguay, reported the *Sunday Times*, comparisons hard to take in as most Britons were not aware of their national incomes. It was easier to appreciate when compared with such famous household name firms as Boots, Guinness and Cadbury Schweppes. Camelot, in one year, starting from scratch, had reached the same turnover as each of these firms, most of whom had been going for about a century. As a cash-cropper, their turnover arriving every week in ready money, it is hard to think of many firms of their size in the world taking in more money.

The monies available for the good causes had turned out to be over £1.2 billion. (The Heritage Department's predictions, in July 1994, had been £375 million – Camelot's, £500 million.) No wonder there was such a fuss about where all this money was going, and should go, in the future. The government had also done well, making itself £530 million in Lottery duty, but surprisingly little was made of this. During the year, 90 per cent of the population had played the Lottery at some time. Over 30 million people were playing every week, or around 65 per cent of the population above the age of sixteen.

Virginia Bottomley pronounced the Lottery 'a stunning national institution'. We were late, as a country, to start a national lottery, she said, but we had shown the rest of the world how to do it. 'We have delivered the most efficiently run national lottery in Europe. Nobody runs a lottery for as little. Nobody returns as much money to good causes.' She revealed that she herself took part every week as part of a family syndicate. 'We have played every week since the first draw. One year on, I still haven't won a penny. This apparently makes me a "statistical anomaly"!'

Camelot's directors made lots of pennies in the year, and were naturally attacked for doing so well. The much-quoted profits of £1 million per week after tax was based on the published figures which, for some accountancy reason, referred only to the twenty-four weeks up to 16 September 1995 and were given as £23.6 million. Camelot made much of the fact that it was taking only 1 per cent in profits from the Lottery's annual income.

It was reported, but not confirmed, that Tim Holley's

earnings for the year, including his performance bonus, were £331,000 and that David Rigg earned £200,000. Mr Rigg was doing around twenty radio and press interviews a day, making it clear, among other things, that Camelot's profits were simply a decent reward for having invested £115 million in capital expenditure to set up the Lottery, and another £82.7 million in running costs.

'Back in May 1994,' said Mr Rigg, 'what I predicted over the seven years was that total sales would reach £32 billion – with £5.5 billion in the peak year – and that £9 billion in all would be going to good causes. There were many people who said this was impossible. I still think these estimates will be very much on line. What's happened is that we have reached the peak much earlier than expected. It always amuses me when people say we could not have failed. I am also amused, rather than angry, by suggestions that a group of civil servants would run it better than Camelot.' As for the salaries of Camelot directors, he maintained that they were being paid much as they were beforehand, when they were employed by Camelot's parent companies. 'We are earning a lot less than the directors of the privatised industries. Bonuses have to be earned out of post-tax profits, and only if certain targets are reached.'

There were 26,300 retail outlets selling Lottery tickets, of which 7,700 sold scratch cards only. Over 90 per cent of the population were living within a couple of miles of a lottery outlet. Camelot's computer system was bigger than the four High Street banks put together, and was capable of handling 400,000 tickets per minute.

By the end of the year the actual winners, even the big jackpot-winners, were not quite dominating the newspapers as they had done in the beginning. The *Lottery Live* show on BBC 1, which had started with about 18 million viewers, was down to an average of 11 million. (Richard Branson in 1994 had predicted 35 million for a TV lottery show.) The delightful and talented Anthea Turner, the nation's favourite little sister, had decided to leave the show.

Architects, engineers, designers and consultants were looking forward to a bumper year as Lottery money began to fund multi-million pound projects. Car salesmen and estate agents in some regions had already done very well – at least those with jackpot-winners living locally.

The National Lottery had entered the national consciousness, but we were beginning to take it as part of the landscape, part of our life, as though it had been there for decades. The 1996 editions of *Chambers Dictionary*, and the Oxford and Collins dictionaries, signalled its final acceptance by including several new definitions, such as 'scratch card', 'roll-over', 'Oflot' and 'instants', which had entered the language thanks to the Lottery. The Lottery had already entered fiction as a plot for a TV play and at least one novel. An exciting-sounding story for children about a lottery win was due out in March 1996. So much, so many, such a lot, all in such a short time.

It was the winners who fascinated me when I began this book, rather than the possible effects. The full story of the birth and rise of our National Lottery, and its political, social, moral and economic implications, has yet to be written. And it is the winners who still fascinate me. I asked those questions about their happiness for my own amusement, to see how they would reply, and also to test a generally held view that most winners are unhappy, that it all ends in tears and family squabbles. This of course is a comforting view, to compensate for our not winning. 'The bigger the win, the unhappier people become,' so an American psychologist was quoted as saying in a BBC2 TV documentary about the effects of the Lottery. Most people like to hear this, to console themselves when they lose. From my experiences, and Camelot's own research, it is completely untrue.

The ten big wins that I followed in this book contained twenty-four individuals – seven winners with partners, one single person, one shared between two couples, plus one syndicate of five people – all of whom in effect became Lottery-winners. I asked them all the same sets of questions (see Appendix C3 and D4).

Out of the twenty-four, only one thought he was less happy after the win than before. (That was John Heaton of Durham, a rather unusual case.) Four thought they were just as happy, before and after. One wasn't sure. But eighteen of them maintained that they were definitely happier. Even the only couple who had experienced marital differences (Paul and Ruth Maddison) still felt that, on the whole, they were happier than before. My follow-up interviews were done between six months and a year after the wins, so things might change again in the years ahead. Post-win euphoria is bound to fade as time moves on.

But I would venture to suggest, with no proof, not even amateur research, that among those who have inherited wealth, which is somehow deemed in Britain to be eminently more respectable and admirable, or even among the self-made wealthy, there are just as many, if not more, unhappy people as there are among our Lottery millionaires. While the happiness quotient was high, far higher than folk legend would have us believe, there was a significant proportion who had reservations about having gone public. Among those who did, half had found the media pressure, real or imagined, a far greater strain than they had expected to. My two private, anonymous winners have remained private and anonymous (at the time of writing) and not only have they had no regrets, they enjoyed an extra pleasure in keeping it all secret. Would I come out, if I won? Yes, but my wife would never forgive me.

Eight out of my ten winners, or groups of winners, originally went public, which is the reverse of the national trend (only 20 per cent now go public). It was surprising that I got any anonymous ones at all, given their desire to stay private and that there was nothing at all in it for them. (I persuaded them by saying they will now have a record for themselves and their children of what happened to them.) In the end, though, most of the so-called public winners, who originally came out, went private, in the sense that they changed houses, changed lives, desperate to avoid further publicity.

Like the Winners' Advisers, I was constantly brought up short by my own preconceptions, being too quick to categorise by outward appearances. I also found some lives remarkably complicated, confirming all the divorce statistics, but it was equally remarkable and reassuring that there are so many happy partnerships, loving relationships, people trying to bring up their children as well as they can and lead decent, ordinary lives. It has been endlessly fascinating to step through the front doors of a random sample of the population, able to ask them direct questions about their marriages and their money, two areas hard to venture into, and expect honest answers. I like to think I got some insight into real life, real problems, in the 1990s, even before we got on to the topic of their sudden millionaire status.

All year, coming back with stories and titbits of Lottery-winners, there were two main reactions. 'You must have found some very unhappy people.' That was number one. 'Personally, I am deeply against the National Lottery.' That was the second reaction. (Which shows the sort of social circles I move in.) A *Guardian* editorial during the year said that the Lottery 'has replaced the circus as the people's opium'. Forget the circus, which seems several decades out of date, the implication was that the great unwashed, having no sense or discernment, have been conned, taken in, doped and duped, and have lost all their individuality. We must therefore pity the poor saps who get pleasure out of the Lottery.

An even more elitist article appeared in the *Daily Telegraph*, written by Alasdair Palmer, the home affairs editor of the *Spectator*. This took a high moral stance against the winners, not just the half-witted players. 'An element of struggle is essential to a sense of purpose and a sense of worth. Enormous wealth deprives people of both. No wonder so many hugely wealthy people are deeply miserable.' The writer particularly had a go at Mark Gardiner, presumably basing his opinions on the more lurid of the tabloid accounts, but not very accurately, as of course Mark's win was shared. 'The God that put £22 million in Mark Gardiner's pockets certainly had a malicious sense of humour. But events may prove that he also has a sense of justice. Though it is hard to think of anyone less entitled to receive such a windfall, the effects of Mark Gardiner's Lottery win on his own life may turn out to be exactly what he deserves.'

This moral superiority, of those who condemn Lottery-winners and players, is widely held among the professional educated classes. I have had endless discussions with people who maintain the poor are being tricked into spending their meagre money. One reply is to point out that the average weekly outlay is in fact a relatively modest £2.40. They then say: Ah, but the poor suckers are being tricked into stupid expectations because the odds are stacked against them. True, the chance of winning the jackpot, one in 14 million, is laughably unreal. But the chance of harmless, cheap amusement and family fun is real. And it seems to me well worth £2.40 a week, compared with cigarettes and alcohol, each more expensive and containing nasty side-effects. (I am talking here, by the way, about the Saturday on-line Lottery. I can think of no defence for scratch cards, which I believe might be addictive. It is interesting to note that their popularity has decreased.)

Far from deadening the spirit, dampening and demeaning individuals, as an opiate might, the enormous popularity of the weekly National Lottery is based on the fact that, for seven days, people are engaged in shared fantasies and daydreams. You hear it discussed everywhere, what each person would do if they won, most of them saying, 'You won't see me for dust.' Each Saturday evening there is a communal involvement. Families, of all sorts, all classes, do wait for the results, either on television or elsewhere, and then swap thoughts about what happened, or what nearly happened. Families talk to each other, which we have been told hardly happens these days, not since we started sitting in our isolated corner of the electric village. The Lottery is reactive. People are involved, not passive. They don't expect to win – yet they look forward to next Saturday, to not winning again, knowing they can enjoy and share their daydreams with the rest of the nation for another week. And I haven't mentioned the good causes as even a passing justification – which they are – though I think most people don't actively think about them when they buy a Lottery ticket, whatever Mr Branson might believe.

I was fascinated, personally, as I said in the Introduction, to observe the effects of sudden wealth on people's lives and people's personalities. When I made a sudden sum of money, I did nothing with it for seven years, concerned about the tax situation, not knowing how much I would end up with. But having it did change my work patterns and my attitudes. I immediately turned freelance, taking only six-month assignments at most, ready to give up the minute I didn't like what I was doing or the boss I was doing it for. Ah, such freedom. With books, it enabled me not to do the same book twice, moving on each time to a quite different area, regardless of what a publisher might think. (They like you to stick to your last – in both senses of the word.) We lived abroad for a year, and I am surprised that none of my winners has wanted to do that. It helped us get such fancy notions out of our system when we were still young. After five weeks we were waking up thinking, 'Oh God, not another perfect day.' I am still as careful as ever, still count the pennies, still shout at the family to put the lights out.

Perhaps the strangest thing of all is that I have worked even harder these last thirty years, and I have moaned just as much. When a book is going badly, or people are not helping (which did happen with this book), you have nobody to blame but yourself. You have chosen to do this book, this work. Wage-slaves have the pleasure of blaming the boss, blaming the system, blaming their poverty, which can be marginally reassuring. It has been interesting to discuss and compare these experiences with the Lottery-winners, and also watch them agonise over their PEPs and Tessas, new feelings, new topics they find hard to share or discuss with their pre-Lottery friends.

I was slightly surprised that few of them, so far, have used their money positively. This could lead to boredom, if not depression, in the future. Whatever you might think of Mark Gardiner, his desire to use his money by putting it back into his firm is commendable. Ken Southwell might not have a structured job, but he is determined to make his money work for him. I was surprised by the Westlands' buying that hotel, but that is certainly a positive use of their money. Andrew Hall, the Preston chemist, seems likely to go far, but who can tell what will happen to Paul Maddison.

Where will they all be in seven years? There will doubtless be more changes before their new lives are finally established, before they have settled into their new personalities. That is a project for the future. In seven years I hope to return to their lives, and find out what really happened afterwards.

# APPENDICES

# APPENDIX A: FIRST YEAR FACTS AND FIGURES

## Appendix A1: Results of first 52 National Lottery Draws, 19 November 94–11 November 95

| DRAW NO. | DRAW DATE | DRAW NUMBERS | | | | | | B | MATCH 6 £ | NO. | MATCH 5+ £ | NO. | MATCH 5 £ | NO. | MATCH 4 £ | NO. | MATCH 3 – £10 NUMBER |
|---|---|---|---|---|---|---|---|---|---|---|---|---|---|---|---|---|---|
| 1 | 19/11/94 | 03 | 05 | 14 | 22 | 30 | 44 | 10 | 839,254 | 7 | 46,349 | 39 | 528 | 2,139 | 32 | 76,731 | 1,073,695 |
| 2 | 26/11/94 | 06 | 12 | 15 | 16 | 31 | 44 | 37 | 1,760,966 | 4 | 216,734 | 10 | 2,087 | 649 | 74 | 40,070 | 802,871 |
| 3 | 03/12/94 | 11 | 17 | 21 | 29 | 30 | 40 | 31 | 0 | 0 | 265,637 | 8 | 1,916 | 693 | 66 | 43,792 | 843,672 |
| 4 | 10/12/94 | 26 | 35 | 38 | 43 | 47 | 49 | 28 | 17,880,003 | 1 | 337,644 | 10 | 4,461 | 473 | 164 | 28,244 | 657,025 |
| 5 | 17/12/94 | 03 | 05 | 09 | 13 | 14 | 38 | 30 | 3,403,310 | 2 | 149,596 | 14 | 1,575 | 831 | 47 | 60,325 | 1,151,351 |
| 6 | 24/12/94 | 02 | 03 | 27 | 29 | 39 | 44 | 06 | 7,789,557 | 1 | 342,398 | 7 | 4,104 | 365 | 93 | 35,321 | 987,567 |
| 7 | 31/12/94 | 09 | 17 | 32 | 36 | 42 | 44 | 16 | 6,554,085 | 1 | 336,106 | 6 | 987 | 1,277 | 34 | 80,231 | 1,137,786 |
| 8 | 07/01/95 | 02 | 05 | 21 | 22 | 25 | 32 | 46 | 0 | 0 | 368,000 | 7 | 2,678 | 601 | 76 | 46,339 | 978,819 |
| 9 | 14/01/95 | 07 | 17 | 23 | 32 | 38 | 42 | 48 | 122,510 | 133 | 7,872 | 246 | 181 | 6,660 | 16 | 165,738 | 1,932,744 |
| 10 | 21/01/95 | 06 | 16 | 20 | 30 | 31 | 47 | 04 | 1,373,571 | 7 | 134,475 | 22 | 2,137 | 865 | 80 | 50,393 | 903,050 |
| 11 | 28/01/95 | 04 | 16 | 25 | 26 | 31 | 43 | 21 | 2,293,628 | 4 | 176,432 | 16 | 1,353 | 1,304 | 66 | 58,223 | 993,762 |
| 12 | 04/02/95 | 01 | 07 | 37 | 38 | 42 | 46 | 20 | 10,350,387 | 1 | 796,183 | 4 | 4,087 | 487 | 159 | 27,456 | 807,216 |
| 13 | 11/02/95 | 15 | 18 | 29 | 35 | 38 | 48 | 05 | 9,015,108 | 1 | 53,343 | 52 | 1,596 | 1,086 | 64 | 59,496 | 1,043,806 |

| DRAW NO. | DRAW DATE | DRAW NUMBERS | | | | | | B | MATCH 6 £ | MATCH 6 NO. | MATCH 5+ £ | MATCH 5+ NO. | MATCH 5 £ | MATCH 5 NO. | MATCH 4 £ | MATCH 4 NO. | MATCH 3 – £10 NUMBER |
|---|---|---|---|---|---|---|---|---|---|---|---|---|---|---|---|---|---|
| 14 | 18/02/95 | 16 | 19 | 21 | 29 | 36 | 45 | 43 | 987,022 | 9 | 170,830 | 16 | 1,429 | 1,195 | 62 | 59,750 | 1,036,040 |
| 15 | 25/02/95 | 05 | 08 | 10 | 18 | 31 | 33 | 28 | 7,056,280 | 1 | 48,248 | 45 | 1,195 | 1,135 | 40 | 74,241 | 1,401,587 |
| 16 | 04/03/95 | 11 | 12 | 17 | 26 | 36 | 42 | 13 | 8,807,149 | 1 | 387,127 | 7 | 2,001 | 846 | 72 | 51,172 | 1,064,943 |
| 17 | 11/03/95 | 02 | 13 | 22 | 27 | 29 | 46 | 36 | 6,527,880 | 2 | 60,573 | 46 | 1,242 | 1,402 | 47 | 80,473 | 1,304,496 |
| 18 | 18/03/95 | 09 | 18 | 19 | 24 | 31 | 41 | 21 | 3,987,786 | 2 | 98,160 | 25 | 1,267 | 1,210 | 47 | 71,061 | 1,277,813 |
| 19 | 25/03/95 | 04 | 17 | 41 | 42 | 44 | 49 | 24 | 0 | 0 | 390,858 | 8 | 7,786 | 251 | 142 | 30,079 | 845,951 |
| 20 | 01/04/95 | 22 | 25 | 30 | 32 | 41 | 43 | 29 | 11,135,715 | 2 | 338,715 | 11 | 3,627 | 642 | 101 | 50,717 | 1,103,456 |
| 21 | 08/04/95 | 14 | 17 | 22 | 24 | 42 | 47 | 34 | 2,691,547 | 3 | 67,148 | 37 | 2,043 | 760 | 54 | 62,896 | 1,316,087 |
| 22 | 15/04/95 | 01 | 04 | 06 | 23 | 26 | 49 | 08 | 2,442,406 | 4 | 111,334 | 27 | 2,174 | 864 | 83 | 49,354 | 1,007,003 |
| 23 | 22/04/95 | 08 | 18 | 20 | 33 | 36 | 38 | 46 | 0 | 0 | 154,828 | 17 | 1,711 | 961 | 56 | 64,270 | 1,203,869 |
| 24 | 29/04/95 | 09 | 15 | 22 | 31 | 34 | 48 | 23 | 1,355,975 | 14 | 97,243 | 33 | 782 | 2,563 | 52 | 83,324 | 1,341,437 |
| 25 | 06/05/95 | 05 | 14 | 17 | 35 | 43 | 48 | 22 | 3,097,415 | 3 | 32,490 | 88 | 1,706 | 1,047 | 71 | 55,022 | 1,035,673 |
| 26 | 13/05/95 | 07 | 16 | 25 | 26 | 28 | 41 | 19 | 2,842,118 | 3 | 93,696 | 28 | 1,669 | 982 | 58 | 62,065 | 1,189,896 |
| 27 | 20/05/95 | 15 | 16 | 17 | 28 | 32 | 46 | 22 | 0 | 0 | 416,143 | 7 | 3,205 | 568 | 91 | 43,642 | 982,790 |

| DRAW NO. | DRAW DATE | DRAW NUMBERS | | | | | | | B | MATCH 6 £ | MATCH 6 NO. | MATCH 5+ £ | MATCH 5+ NO. | MATCH 5 £ | MATCH 5 NO. | MATCH 4 £ | MATCH 4 NO. | MATCH 3 – £10 NUMBER |
|---|---|---|---|---|---|---|---|---|---|---|---|---|---|---|---|---|---|---|
| 28 | 27/05/95 | 12 | 13 | 25 | 37 | 44 | 45 | | 09 | 6,624,951 | 3 | 133,430 | 24 | 2,271 | 881 | 66 | 66,499 | 1,363,268 |
| 29 | 03/06/95 | 01 | 21 | 29 | 31 | 32 | 40 | | 27 | 0 | 0 | 288,849 | 11 | 3,841 | 517 | 107 | 40,623 | 931,366 |
| 30 | 10/06/95 | 12 | 15 | 26 | 44 | 46 | 49 | | 14 | 22,590,830 | 1 | 628,947 | 6 | 4,408 | 535 | 139 | 37,157 | 890,537 |
| 31 | 17/06/95 | 27 | 30 | 33 | 38 | 40 | 48 | | 02 | 1,481,262 | 7 | 398,801 | 8 | 2,655 | 751 | 97 | 45,108 | 976,283 |
| 32 | 24/06/95 | 05 | 15 | 21 | 42 | 43 | 45 | | 20 | 9,896,801 | 1 | 435,024 | 7 | 3,362 | 566 | 89 | 46,912 | 999,505 |
| 33 | 01/07/95 | 05 | 07 | 08 | 25 | 44 | 48 | | 03 | 0 | 0 | 247,545 | 11 | 2,400 | 709 | 70 | 53,187 | 1,172,809 |
| 34 | 08/07/95 | 01 | 03 | 11 | 14 | 20 | 40 | | 45 | 20,088,838 | 1 | 216,136 | 16 | 2,232 | 968 | 78 | 60,492 | 1,142,270 |
| 35 | 15/07/95 | 01 | 04 | 20 | 31 | 41 | 43 | | 38 | 2,803,919 | 4 | 492,996 | 7 | 3,907 | 552 | 135 | 35,123 | 795,456 |
| 36 | 22/07/95 | 02 | 03 | 21 | 22 | 23 | 40 | | 24 | 2,501,994 | 4 | 513,229 | 6 | 2,629 | 732 | 106 | 39,705 | 952,001 |
| 37 | 29/07/95 | 28 | 34 | 41 | 45 | 46 | 49 | | 11 | 3,791,092 | 3 | 583,244 | 6 | 3,871 | 565 | 150 | 32,007 | 684,405 |
| 38 | 05/08/95 | 01 | 08 | 25 | 30 | 35 | 45 | | 15 | 5,128,025 | 2 | 50,090 | 63 | 2,626 | 751 | 88 | 49,225 | 880,947 |
| 39 | 12/08/95 | 11 | 25 | 28 | 33 | 34 | 47 | | 48 | 0 | 0 | 50,885 | 6 | 556 | 3,432 | 97 | 42,929 | 950,309 |
| 40 | 19/08/95 | 05 | 08 | 23 | 24 | 28 | 48 | | 19 | 3,822,330 | 5 | 94,239 | 30 | 1,523 | 1,160 | 47 | 82,044 | 1,588,909 |
| 41 | 26/08/95 | 16 | 18 | 21 | 27 | 38 | 41 | | 26 | 2,234,759 | 4 | 275,047 | 10 | 1,444 | 1,190 | 57 | 65,700 | 1,243,473 |

| DRAW NO. | DRAW DATE | DRAW NUMBERS | | | | | | | B | MATCH 6 £ | MATCH 6 NO. | MATCH 5+ £ | MATCH 5+ NO. | MATCH 5 £ | MATCH 5 NO. | MATCH 4 £ | MATCH 4 NO. | MATCH 3 - £10 NUMBER |
|---|---|---|---|---|---|---|---|---|---|---|---|---|---|---|---|---|---|---|
| 42 | 02/09/95 | 01 | 15 | 22 | 28 | 40 | 49 | | 44 | 1,420,508 | 7 | 235,350 | 13 | 1,559 | 1,226 | 75 | 55,631 | 1,015,058 |
| 43 | 09/09/95 | 02 | 12 | 20 | 22 | 41 | 45 | | 47 | | 0 | 744,791 | 4 | 1,841 | 1,011 | 68 | 59,830 | 1,045,213 |
| 44 | 16/09/95 | 02 | 10 | 14 | 25 | 37 | 41 | | 05 | 2,681,192 | 8 | 88,309 | 41 | 1,722 | 1,314 | 79 | 62,929 | 1,186,903 |
| 45 | 23/09/95 | 05 | 10 | 19 | 24 | 34 | 46 | | 28 | 963,820 | 10 | 102,262 | 29 | 1,654 | 1,120 | 67 | 60,622 | 1,126,075 |
| 46 | 30/09/95 | 10 | 11 | 29 | 32 | 33 | 40 | | 16 | 9,981,262 | 1 | 146,245 | 21 | 2,722 | 705 | 86 | 48,644 | 1,041,765 |
| 47 | 07/10/95 | 10 | 22 | 28 | 30 | 36 | 37 | | 45 | 3,089,417 | 3 | 259,251 | 11 | 2,636 | 676 | 70 | 55,827 | 1,170,017 |
| 48 | 14/10/95 | 04 | 05 | 09 | 25 | 30 | 47 | | 17 | 1,891,543 | 5 | 90,939 | 32 | 1,876 | 969 | 70 | 56,689 | 1,143,504 |
| 49 | 21/10/95 | 02 | 06 | 17 | 19 | 21 | 47 | | 05 | 2,991,262 | 3 | 83,671 | 33 | 1,388 | 1,243 | 56 | 67,572 | 1,233,455 |
| 50 | 28/10/95 | 07 | 16 | 27 | 33 | 35 | 44 | | 05 | 1,594,352 | 5 | 42,290 | 58 | 796 | 1,924 | 37 | 88,896 | 1,434,454 |
| 51 | 04/11/95 | 06 | 14 | 18 | 27 | 44 | 48 | | 01 | 2,798,623 | 3 | 73,809 | 35 | 975 | 1,655 | 43 | 81,956 | 1,335,232 |
| 52 | 11/11/95 | 07 | 10 | 23 | 28 | 30 | 48 | | 03 | 1,700,159 | 5 | 72,656 | 36 | 1,239 | 1,319 | 50 | 70,921 | 1,326,080 |

Notes:
- The biggest jackpot was 10 June – £22,590,830 (only one ticket had the correct numbers, but it was shared by two people).
- The biggest single jackpot winner was £17,880,003 – the Asian from Blackburn.
- The smallest jackpot was 14 January – £122,510 (because 133 people had the same numbers).
- The average jackpot-winning ticket received £5 million.
- The average jackpot-winner, as opposed to jackpot-winning ticket, is hard to estimate, because many were shared or held by syndicates, but received approximately £800,000.
- Each week there were around one million winning tickets.
- Altogether, 200 million winners shared £2.15 billion.

## *Appendix A2:* Income and distribution

*Lottery share-out:*

Prizes, 50%
Good causes, 28%
Government duty, 12%
Retailers, 5%
Camelot, 5%

| *Sales:* | *million* | *Outlay:* | *million* |
|---|---|---|---|
| National Lottery game | £3,300 | Prizes: | |
| Instants | £1,100 | National Lottery game | £1,530 |
| | | Instants | £620 |
| Total income | £4,400 | Total | £2,150 |
| | | Good causes | £1,220 |
| | | Government duty | £530 |
| | | Retailers | £225 |
| | | Camelot | £275 |

Estimated sales over the seven years of the Camelot licence from 1994 to 2001, £32 billion, out of which £9 billion will go to good causes.

## *Appendix A3:* Profile of regular players as percentage of population over 16

*Gender:* 70% of men play, 66% of women

*Age:* 16–24, 53%
25–34, 75%
35–54, 74%
55+ 66%

*Social class:*

| | |
|---|---|
| AB (professional, managerial) – | 58% |
| C1 (non-manual white collar) – | 65% |
| C2 (skilled manual) – | 78% |
| DE (semi and unskilled) – | 68% |

*Geographical:*

| *Sales per capita in each region* | | *Jackpot-winners in each region* | |
|---|---|---|---|
| Scotland | £1.26 | Scotland | 22 |
| N. Ireland | £1.13 | N. Ireland | 9 |
| NE | £1.37 | NE | 11 |
| NW | £1.31 | NW | 27 |
| Yorkshire | £1.33 | Yorkshire | 36 |
| Wales | £1.30 | Wales | 13 |
| SW | £1.21 | SW | 18 |
| Midlands | £1.31 | Midlands | 53 |
| London | £1.55 | London | 50 |
| SE | £1.25 | SE | 28 |

## *Appendix A4:* Camelot

*Camelot's profit:*
In the 24 weeks up to 16 September 1995 it was £23.6 million, or £1 million per week (equal to 1% of total Lottery income).

*Camelot's costs:*
In the first year, £115 million capital expenditure plus £82.7 million running costs.

*Camelot consists of five shareholders:* Cadbury Schweppes, Racal, De la Rue, GTECH (each of whom has $22\frac{1}{2}$%), plus ICL (10%).

National Lottery line on Merseyside (Tel. 0645 100000) handles some 28,000 player enquiries per week.

Tickets can be bought in retailers for 8 weeks ahead.

Subscription services available for 26 weeks or 52 weeks (Tel. 0645 125000).

There are 26,300 retail outlets (of which 7,720 sell Instants only).

Over 90% of the population live or work within two miles of a lottery outlet.

Average weekly Lottery sales (on-line game) per retailer, £4,000.

Camelot employs 600 people, based mainly in their HQ at Watford or on Merseyside. There are also ten regional headquarters – Belfast, Birmingham, Cardiff, Central London, Exeter, Glasgow, Leeds, Liverpool, Reigate and Sunderland.

## *Appendix A5:* Good causes

The five bodies chosen by the government to distribute Lottery money to good causes, with the amounts awarded in the first year up to 22 December 1995:

| | | |
|---|---|---|
| Arts Council – | £232.7 million, | 669 awards |
| Sports Council – | £152.7 million, | 1,089 awards |
| National Heritage Fund – | £99.4 million, | 171 awards |
| Millennium Commission – | £336.3 million, | 303 awards |
| National Charities Board – | £159 million, | 2,460 awards |
| | | |
| Total awards made in first year – | | 4,692 |
| Total distributed – | | £980.2 million |

Eleven distributing bodies decide on the specific amounts to be awarded and to whom. Where to apply for Lottery funding:

**THE ARTS**

The Arts Council of England,
14 Great Peter Street,
London SW1P 3NQ
Tel: 0171 312 0123

The Arts Council of Wales,
Museum Place,
Cardiff CF1 3NX
Tel: 01222 388288

The Scottish Arts Council,
12 Manor Place,
Edinburgh EH3 7DD
Tel: 0131 226 6051

The Arts Council of Northern Ireland,
185 Stranmillis Road,
Belfast BT9 5DU
Tel: 01232 667000

**HERITAGE**

The National Heritage Memorial Fund,
20 King Street,
London SW1Y 6QY
Tel: 0171 930 0963

**CHARITIES**

The National Lottery Charities Board
St Vincent's House,
30 Orange Street,
London WC2H 2HH
Tel: 0171 747 5300

**MILLENNIUM PROJECTS**

The Millennium Commission,
2 Little Smith Street,
London SW1P 3DH
Tel: 0171 340 2001

**SPORT**

The Sports Council,
16 Upper Woburn Place,
London WC1H 0QP
Tel: 0345 649649

The Sports Council for Wales,
Sophia Gardens,
Cardiff CF1 9SW
Tel: 01222 397571

The Scottish Sports Council,
Caledonia House,
South Gyle,
Edinburgh EH12 9DQ
Tel: 0131 339 9000

Sports Council for Northern Ireland,
House of Sport,
Upper Malone Road,
Belfast BT9 5LA
Tel: 01232 382222

## *Appendix A6:* **Further National Lottery facts and figures**

- 30 million people play every week, or 65% of the population over 16.
- Over 37 million, or 90% of the population over 16, played at some time.
- 15% of players are in a group or syndicate.
- Average spent, £2.40 per week.
- Odds on winning, 1:14 million for the jackpot, 1:54 any prize.
- 50% of tickets are bought on a Saturday.
- It is the largest lottery in the world in terms of total income and players.
- It is one of the most efficient lotteries in terms of giving highest returns to good causes and the government.
- Average weekly jackpot pool, around £9 million.
- Average sales for a non-roll-over week, £65 million.
- Number of roll-overs in first year, 9.
- On average, sales in a roll-over week increase by 15–20%.

- Unclaimed prizes at the end of the first year, £22 million.
- Largest single unclaimed prize, £259,251.
- After six months, unclaimed prizes are added to good causes.
- Total unclaimed prize money handed over in first year, £16 million.

*INSTANTS*
- Average weekly sale, £25 million.
- Prizes normally range from £2 to £50,000.
- Prize pay-out, 55% of sales.
- Total of £50,000 prize-winners, 200.
- Chances of winning any prize, 1:5.
- Around 5 million winning tickets sold per week.
- Total winners in first year, 180 million.
- Total won, £557 million.
- 50% of the population over 16 have played.
- Average spent, £2 per week.
- Instants players buy throughout the week.

*Note:* Most of the facts and figures were supplied by Camelot's research department, plus an NOP survey commissioned by the *Sunday Times* Magazine, 12 November 1995.

# APPENDIX B: CAMELOT'S SURVEY OF WINNERS

At the end of the first year, Camelot contacted by phone some of their major winners – jackpot and match 5+ bonus – and asked them a series of questions for their own in-house research purposes. These are the major conclusions.

- 99% of all major winners are happy with their win.
- On average, nearly a fifth of all major winners do not feel that their life has changed at all as a result of their win.
- 91% of major winners said that their win had not changed them as a person.
- All major winners did think that their outlook on life had changed for the better, with most feeling that they had a more relaxed attitude and felt good through helping others.
- The best three things about winning were:
  – Financial security for life
  – Ability to help family and friends
  – Ability to fulfil lifetime dreams/ambitions
- On average, 94% of major winners said that their family/friends had adjusted to their win.
- Over half of major winners are still working after their win.
- On average, major winners have invested 51% of their total win.
- On average, major winners have spent 14% of their total win.
- On average, major winners have left 21% of their winnings in the bank.
- On average, major winners have given away 14% of their win.
- On average, major winners will give away 5% of their win to charity.
- Almost half of all major winners have bought themselves a house.
- On average, 11% of major winners have bought a new house for someone else.
- Non-publicity winners are more likely to buy a new house for others.
- On average, 68% of major winners have bought a new car.
- On average, 51% of major winners have gone on holiday.
- Publicity winners are more likely to go on holiday after their win than private winners.
- On average, 27% of major winners have carried out improvements to their homes since the win.
- 99% of major winners have spent some of their winnings on paying off debts.
- 5% of major winners have spent money on business ventures.
- On average, 47% of major winners have spent money on clothes.
- 85% of jackpot-winners had taken up the option of the Camelot Advisory Panel.
- 49% of Match 5+ bonus had taken up the option of the Camelot Advisory Panel.
- The main reason for not taking up the option of the panel was that the winner already had an adviser.
- Approximately 84% of major public winners were glad that they took publicity.
- On average, 90% of major winners are still playing the Lottery.

# APPENDIX C: SURVEY OF MY WINNERS – BEFORE THEIR WIN

While interviewing the people who benefited by the ten major wins I described in the book, which consisted of 24 individuals, I asked each of them questions about themselves; basic facts about their life and situation before and after their win. I also asked them to estimate their state of happiness before and after the win, and if they had any second thoughts on going public or staying private. I have numbered them 1–10, the order in which they appear in the book, apart from the syndicate, which I have made number 10.

## Appendix C1: Basic facts at the time of their win

| | Name | Town | Age | Job | Partner/Spouse | Children | House | Car | Last holiday |
|---|---|---|---|---|---|---|---|---|---|
| 1 | Ken Southwell | York | 34 | Communications engineer | Julie, 31, insurance administrator | (1 by previous relationship) | Vic. terrace, £50,000 | Firm's transit van | Italy, skiing |
| 2 | Audrey Jenkins | Hartlepool | 28 | None | Andy Voss, 28, unemployed taxi-driver | Carl, 9, Claire, 5 | Council house | B reg. Vauxhall Cavalier | Butlins, Skegness |
| 3 | Barry | East London | 37 | Disabled, ex-security guard | Wife, Chris, 37 | Glen, 5, Karen, 2 | Terrace, £65,000 | E reg. Montego | Caravan, Great Yarmouth |
| 4 | Steve | Lancashire | 27 | Farm labourer | Wife, Helen, 28, care assistant | Lee-zette, 9, Glen, 4, Darren, 2 | Council house | 22-year-old Dormobile | None for two years |
| 5A | Mark Gardiner | Hastings | 33 | Glazier | Brenda, 39, care assistant | (1 by previous relationship) | Rented flat | Firm's Escort | Isle of Wight |
| 5B | Paul Maddison | Hastings | 45 | Glazier | Wife, Ruth, 40, deputy head teacher | (2 by previous relationship) | Modern semi. | V reg. Cavalier | Greece |
| 6 | John Heaton | Durham | 44 | Kitchen porter | None | None | Room in guest house | None | None, except day trip to Blackpool |

| | Name | Town | Age | Job | Partner/Spouse | Children | House | Car | Last holiday |
|---|---|---|---|---|---|---|---|---|---|
| 7 | Ronald | NE | 36 | Unemployed ex-shop manager | Wife, Diana, 36 | Tom & Tara, 8, Luke, 5 | Terrace, £45,000 | E reg. Escort | In-laws |
| 8 | Bob Westland | Alloa | 57 | Sub-postmaster | Wife, Anne, 56, deputy head teacher | Mark, 32, Dave, 29, Chris, 24, Robert, 22 | 1900s semi., £100,000 | J reg. Cavalier | Turkey |
| 9 | Alan Baker | Margate | 54 | Tote manager | Linda, 47, Butlin's chambermaid | (3 by previous marriage) | Council flat | D reg. Hyundai Stella | None |
| 10A | Andrew Hall | Preston | 27 | Chemist | Wife, Lynn, nurse | None | Modern semi., £60,000 | New Fiat Punto New Nissan Micra | Honeymoon, Venezuela |
| 10B | Hilary Williams | Preston | 39 | Chemist's assistant | Husband, Ricky, lorry driver | Jennifer, 18, David, 10 | Council house | None | Tunisia |
| 10C | June Cross | Preston | 54 | Chemist's assistant | Husband, William, traffic warden | Annette, 32, Maria, 27 | Council house | V reg. Cavalier | Scotland |
| 10D | Linda Ford | Preston | 38 | Chemist's assistant | Husband, David, car salesman | Lisa, 18, David, 16 | Council house | A reg. Carlton | Wales, three years ago |
| 10E | Sarah Bradley | Preston | 28 | Chemist's assistant | John, unemployed welder | Chris, 10 | Council house | None | None |

## *Appendix C2:* Lottery history

| Names | Lottery outlay per week | Numbers chosen | Previous wins | Win date | Amount |
|---|---|---|---|---|---|
| 1 – Ken Southwell | £3 | Birthdays | None | 19 Nov., 94 | £839,254 |
| 2 – Audrey and Andy | £1 | Birthdays | 1 × £10 | 18 March, 95 | £3,986,786 |
| 3 – Barry | £5 | Random | 1 × £10 | 29 April, 95 | £1,355,975 |
| 4 – Steve | £5 | Birthdays | None | 13 May, 95 | £2,842,118 |
| 5 – Mark and Paul | £30–£50 | Random | 3 × £10 | 10 June, 95 | £22,590,830 (between two) |
| 6 – John Heaton | £3 | Random | 1 × £10 | 10 June, 95 | £628,947 |
| 7 – Ronald | £2 | Own system | None | 22 July, 95 | £2,501,944 |
| 8 – Bob and Anne | £10 | Random | 12 × £10 | 29 July, 95 | £3,791,102 |
| 9 – Alan and Linda | £7 | Birthdays | 1 × £91 (4 nos) | 14 Oct., 95 | £1,891,543 |
| 10 – the Preston Syndicate | £6, between five | Random | 2 × £10 | 26 Aug., 95 | £2,234,759 (£446,952 each) |

## *Appendix C3*

*Happiness at the time of the win – points out of 10*

1 – Ken: 'I wasn't very happy with my job – 8'
   Julie: 'From a personal point of view, I was very happy – 10'

2 – Audrey: 'We'd had a few rows, but they were over – 7'
   Andy: 'We were happy enough, but we had money problems – 7'

3 – Barry: 'I'd had to retire through MS, and was worried about the future of my family, but I'm not really an unhappy person – 5'
   Chris: 'We lived like Mr and Mrs Average. We could survive – 5'

4 – Steve: 'We've always been happy together. The family matters more to me than money – 9'
   Helen: 'My best moment in life was marrying Steve. Nothing can compare with that – 9'

5 – Mark: 'I was happy enough, though there were work problems – 8'
   Brenda: 'We were happy together, both working to pay the bills – 9'
   Paul: 'I had worries with the business, such as £20,000 tax demands, but I was happy enough – 7'
   Ruth: 'I was very happy, because I'd just heard I'd got on the MA course – 8'

6 – John: 'I was happy with my job, which I'd just got, and living here in Sheila's guest house – 7'

7 – Ron: 'We were always happy and content as a family. My only worry was not being able to do things for the children – 7'
   Di: 'The day of the win was Ron's birthday and I was feeling low, not being able to buy him anything – 5'

8 – Bob: 'I was working hard to keep the kids in style, but they were all working and healthy and we were happy – 8½'
   Anne: 'It was the school holidays, so I was very happy – 10'

9 – Alan: 'We were a happy couple, in love with each other, but financially we were scratching – 8'
   Linda: 'We were very happy together, and that's what matters – 8'

10 – Andrew: 'I loved my job and was happy in my marriage – 8'
   Hilary: 'Happy enough, apart from money problems – 7'
   June: 'We were ordinary people, like everyone else – 7'
   Linda: 'I worried about not owning a house, and what would happen to the children – 8'
   Sarah: 'I had plenty of worries, but I was happy enough – 8'

## *Appendix C4*

*Reasons for deciding to go public or stay private*

1 – Ken: 'The *Sun* and *Mirror* were shouting through the letter-box, so we couldn't really avoid it.'

2 – Audrey: 'Pressures from the press, at the door all the time. It felt like being in prison, so it seemed best to get it over with.'

3 – Barry: 'Camelot said it was a good story, me having MS and that, so the press would pick it up anyway.'
   Chris: 'I didn't want it to come out.'

4 – Steve: 'It's your relations that can cause you misery, so we decided to tell no one. We also wanted to protect the children.'

5 – Mark: 'We couldn't really avoid it, could we . . .'
   Paul: 'No option – we were outed. But we couldn't have kept it secret anyway, because of the size of the win.'

6 – John: 'If you don't go public, you get hassled, so I read in a newspaper. You can't hide it, I was told. Someone will find out.'

7 – Ron: 'We decided to stay private because we did not want the lives of our children to be affected, or the neighbours to know.'

8 – Bob: 'The *Daily Record* turned up and said they knew, so we couldn't keep it quiet, not with four children. Anyway, we didn't want to have to stay indoors, worrying it might come out.'

9 – Alan: 'We wanted to spread our happiness. And we had no young children to worry about.'

10 – Andrew: 'The press had already found out.'
   Hilary: 'It came out at the club, when the call came through.'
   June: 'We couldn't stop it.'

# APPENDIX D
## SURVEY OF MY WINNERS – AFTER THEIR WIN

### *Appendix D1:* Changes in their domestic lives between six months and one year after their win

|  | House | Job | Car | Last Holiday |
|---|---|---|---|---|
| 1 | Det. village house, £165,000 (plus three others) | None, apart from looking after own properties | 1 Range-Rover 2 Suzuki Vitara 3 Porsche | Ski, twice |
| 2 | Det. modern, £90,000 | None | 1 Vauxhall Omega 2 Peugeot 306 | 1, Florida (Disneyworld) 2, Spain |
| 3 | Det. modern, £280,000 | None | 1 Vauxhall Cavalier 2 Escort Ghia | 1, Menorca 2, Florida (Disneyworld) |
| 4 | Georgian manor, 60 acres, £400,000 | None | 1 Espace 2 Old van 3 Old Jaguar | None yet |
| 5A | Mod. det., £105,000 | Same – but firm expanded | 1 Ford Mustang 2 Ford Estate 3 Toyota Celica | 1, Spain 2, Barbados |
| 5B | Det. lodge, Scotland, £350,000 | None | 1 BMW 740 2 BMW 328i 3 Range-Rover | 1, Mauritius 2, Florida 3, Far East 4, Dubai |
| 6 | Same; still in guest house | None | None | 1, Somerset 2, Spain |
| 7 | Same house | None | 1 Mazda 2 Motorbike | Paris (Euro-Disney) |
| 8 | Same house | None | BMW | Ski, Austria |
| 9 | Bungalow, £98,250 | A – Bookie L – Chambermaid | Ford Mondeo | Caribbean cruise |
| 10A | Same | Same | 1 Saab 9000 2 Mazda MX 5 | Cyprus |
| 10B | Semi., £135,000 | Same | Vauxhall | Benidorm |
| 10C | Bungalow, £80,000 | None | Same | None |
| 10D | Det., £150,000 | Same | 1 Williams Renault Clio 2 Astra estate | None |
| 10E | Det., £150,000 | Same | Peugeot | Lanzarote |

## *Appendix D2:* Lottery monies after their win

|     | Lottery outlay, per week | Wins | Gifts to family and friends | Gifts to charity |
| --- | --- | --- | --- | --- |
| 1 | £5 | 4 × £10, £70 + £90 | None | None |
| 2 | None | None | £800,000 | None |
| 3 | £5 | 4 × £10, £30 | £310,000 | None |
| 4 | £5 | None | None | None |
| 5A | None | None | £1 million | 'Quite a lot' |
| 5B | None | None | £1½ million | None |
| 6 | £3 | None | £80,000 | £2,000 |
| 7 | £5 | None | £200,000 | None |
| 8 | £25 | £40, £70, 4 × £10 | £500,000 | None |
| 9 | £7 | 2 × £10 | £170,000 | None |
| 10A | £7 between six | None | £44,000 | None |
| 10B | £7 between six | None | £50,000 | None |
| 10C | £7 between six | None | Personal | None |
| 10D | £7 between six | None | £20,000 | None |
| 10E | £7 between six | None | £4,000 | None |

Notes:
'Gifts to family and friends' means voluntary gifts. Mark Gardiner's does not include payment to his ex-wife, but Paul Maddison's includes money to his wife. As a proportion of the total win, the most generous benefactor has been Barry, who has given away approximately 24%. Other givers range between 1% and 15% of their win, apart from Audrey, who gave away 20%. Two have given nothing. Charity: only two have given, John Heaton and Mark Gardiner, but most of the others say they will in due course.

## *Appendix D3*

*After the win: second thoughts on going public or staying private*

1 – Ken: 'I have no regrets. I enjoyed my moments of fame and would recommend it to any other winner with the right temperament.'

Julie: 'It made no difference to me. I kept out of the publicity, but Kenny loved it ...'

2 – Audrey: 'We regret going public. The press didn't leave us alone and we haven't gained anything.'

3 – Barry: 'I regret it. People still come up and congratulate me, but I want to forget it and move on. It was selfish of me. I should have thought about the children. In future people might come up to them and say, "Your dad got his money by luck."'
Chris: 'I didn't want publicity, and I was right.'

4 – Steve: 'We have no regrets about staying private. It hasn't been a burden at all. I've enjoyed keeping it secret.'

5 – Mark: 'I wish it hadn't come out because of all the diabolical things written about me, but my real friends know the truth.'
Brenda: 'I wish it hadn't come out, but we couldn't avoid it.'
Paul: 'I was pleased to get it over with. I wasn't hassled too much as I ran away to Scotland.'
Ruth: 'It upset my school life for some weeks, so I wish it hadn't happened, but the press conference was an experience.'

6 – John: 'I had nothing to hide, so I didn't regret it, but I wouldn't do it again. I hated posing for photographs.'

7 – Ron: 'No regrets about staying private. Not for one moment have I wanted to walk down the street and have people know about me.'
Di: 'It was hard at first, keeping it secret, but now it's OK.'

8 – Bob: 'No regrets at all. Everyone has been very kind to us. They like to meet a real winner and know it does happen.'

9 – Alan: 'No regrets. I've enjoyed it, but Linda got most publicity.'
Linda: 'After a week, I'd had enough. I got fed up being pestered.'

10 – Andrew: 'Camelot were right. It was best to come out, get it over.'
Hilary: 'Never again. It caused a lot of aggravation with people being snide. I know it's jealousy, but it's been very annoying.'
June: 'I don't know. I'm not sure. I can't think about it.'
Linda: 'No regrets. I liked going on TV. But I wouldn't do it again.'
Sarah: 'I would have preferred to have remained private, but we would have been hounded otherwise, so it was a good idea.'

*Comments*:
The two private winners had no regrets whatever about staying private, but about half the public winners did have some, mainly about being hounded, with the press attention going on longer than expected.

## *Appendix D4*

*Happiness after the win – points out of 10 for how they feel now*

1 – Ken: 'I am very happy, so I'll give it my best mark. You can't have 10 out of 10, there's no such state, so – 9'
   Julie: 'I was very happy, and am now the same, so – 10'

2 – Audrey: 'We're happier than we were, because our rows were about money, but I'm getting a bit bored, as I've not enough to do – 8'
   Andy: 'I've got my golf, and things to do, so, yes, I'm happy – 8½'

3 – Barry: 'I'm a lot happier, not just for myself, though I feel at the moment my MS is in remission. There is less strain, which has helped it. I'm happy to have helped our parents, brothers and sisters. My own children will not have to have menial jobs – 8'
   Chris: 'Oh everything is a lot better – 9'

4 – Steve & Helen: 'We were happy anyway, but I suppose I'll have to say we are both even happier now, so – 10 each'

5 – Mark: 'I had problems with lies in the press, but I've enjoyed helping so many people, putting money back into the town – 10'
   Brenda: 'I often wished it hadn't happened, when we were being hounded, but at present I feel much better, so I'll say – 10'
   Paul: 'I wasn't very happy at first, because my wife stayed in Hastings doing her MA. But it all ended happily. I love my new house, my cars, everything, so I'll say – 10'
   Ruth: 'It has been disruptive, but I now have my independence, I can go anywhere, do anything, so that's good. I'll say – 9'

6 – John: 'I get less worried as time goes by, and I try to put it all at the back of my mind, but sometimes I feel down and go into a bit of panic. So – 6'

7 – Ron: 'I have secured the future for my children and helped our families – 10'
   Di: 'It's got to be 10, hasn't it?'

8 – Bob: 'We were not hard up before, though we had a few debts. Now we have none. So, for general happiness, I'd say – 9'
   Anne: 'Today, the scale of happiness is so different. We can stay in hotels, go anywhere. I was perfectly happy before, so I'll have to say it's now – 10'

9 – Alan & Linda: 'We were happy together anyway, but now we

have no problems of any sort – so 10 each'

10 – Andrew: 'Same, really, except our financial problems are gone – 8'

Hilary: 'It's all wonderful, except for a few snide people – 9'
June: 'I haven't really come down to earth yet, so I can't say'
Linda: 'The best thing has been helping the family – 10'
Sarah: 'Just the same, really, but it's nice not having worries – 8'

*Comments*:
Happiness: All very subjective, of course, but it was they who were contrasting their own lives before and after the win. Only 1 person out of the 24 felt he was less happy (John Heaton – at the time of his win, he had just got a job). One didn't know (June, the chemist's assistant, but I suspect she might be less happy), while 4 felt they had stayed much the same. That leaves 18 out of 24 who felt positively happier. The biggest increase was Ron and Di (up 3 and 5 points), Barry and Chris (up 3 and 4), Paul and Ruth (up 3 and 1, but there were special circumstances there).

So, does it prove that money *can* buy you happiness?

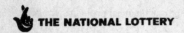 **THE NATIONAL LOTTERY**

MADDISON PAUL MR

**Congratulations on being a National Lottery winner!!**

Remember that every time you play the National Lottery you are helping
a good cause. Approximately one quarter of the price of a ticket is
split equally between five good causes:

- The Sports Councils
- The Arts Council
- The National Lottery Charities Board
- The Millennium Commission (for projects that will celebrate
  the advent of the year 2000)
  The National Heritage Memorial Fund.

Best of luck for the future and please play The National Lottery again.

Winnings from the Lottery are not chargeable gains for the purposes of
UK Capital Gains Tax, and will not normally be assessed to UK Income Tax.

```
Prize amount: 22,590,830.00
         Date: 12 JUN 1995
Cheque number: 014763
```

 **THE NATIONAL LOTTERY**

**The Royal Bank of Scotland plc**
Corporate Banking Office 67 Lombard Street London EC3P 3DL

16-04-001

Pay

\*\*MADDISON PAUL MR\*\*\*\*\*\*\*\*\*\*\*\*\*\*\*\*MADDISON PAUL MR\*\*    Date 12 JUN 1995

| Tens of Millions | Millions | Hundreds of Thousands | Tens of Thousands | Thousands | Hundreds | Tens | Units | |
|---|---|---|---|---|---|---|---|---|
| TWO | TWO | FIVE | NINE | ZERO | EIGHT | THREE | ZERO | £\*\*22590830.00\*\* |

Pence as figures

pay only twenty two million, five hundred and ninety thousand, eight hundred and thirty pounds

Camelot Group plc
Prize Payment Account

PAY ONLY

⑈014763⑈ 16⑈0400⑈ 20070449⑈

*Paul Maddison's letter and cheque – the biggest single
Lottery-winning cheque so far*

Warner Books now offers an exciting range of quality titles by both established and new authors. All of the books in this series are available from:

Little, Brown and Company (UK),
P.O. Box 11,
Falmouth,
Cornwall TR10 9EN.

Fax No: 01326 317444.
Telephone No: 01326 372400
E-mail: books@barni.avel.co.uk

Payments can be made as follows: cheque, postal order (payable to Little, Brown and Company) or by credit cards, Visa/Access. Do not send cash or currency. UK customers and B.F.P.O. please allow £1.00 for postage and packing for the first book, plus 50p for the second book, plus 30p for each additional book up to a maximum charge of £3.00 (7 books plus).

Overseas customers including Ireland, please allow £2.00 for the first book plus £1.00 for the second book, plus 50p for each additional book.

NAME (Block Letters) ........................................................

....................................................................................

ADDRESS .........................................................................

....................................................................................

....................................................................................

☐ I enclose my remittance for ...........................................

☐ I wish to pay by Access/Visa Card

Number ⬚⬚⬚⬚⬚⬚⬚⬚⬚⬚⬚⬚⬚⬚⬚⬚

Card Expiry Date ⬚⬚⬚⬚